VOLUME 605

MAY 2006

THE ANNALS

of The American Academy of Political
and Social Science

ROBERT W. PEARSON, *Executive Editor*

Democracy, Crime, and Justice

Special Editors of this Volume

SUSANNE KARSTEDT
Keele University
GARY LaFREE
University of Maryland

SAGE Publications Ⓢ Thousand Oaks · London · New Delhi

Origin and Purpose. The Academy was organized December 14, 1889, to promote the progress of political and social science, especially through publications and meetings. The Academy does not take sides in controverted questions, but seeks to gather and present reliable information to assist the public in forming an intelligent and accurate judgment.

Meetings. The Academy occasionally holds a meeting in the spring extending over two days.

Publications. THE ANNALS of The American Academy of Political and Social Science is the bimonthly publication of the Academy. Each issue contains articles on some prominent social or political problem, written at the invitation of the editors. Also, monographs are published from time to time, numbers of which are distributed to pertinent professional organizations. These volumes constitute important reference works on the topics with which they deal, and they are extensively cited by authorities throughout the United States and abroad. The papers presented at the meetings of the Academy are included in THE ANNALS.

Membership. Each member of the Academy receives THE ANNALS and may attend the meetings of the Academy. Membership is open only to individuals. Annual dues: $84.00 for the regular paperbound edition (clothbound, $121.00). Members may also purchase single issues of THE ANNALS for $17.00 each (clothbound, $26.00). Student memberships are available for $53.00.

Subscriptions. THE ANNALS of The American Academy of Political and Social Science (ISSN 0002-7162) (J295) is published six times annually—in January, March, May, July, September, and November—by Sage Publications, 2455 Teller Road, Thousand Oaks, CA 91320. Telephone: (800) 818-SAGE (7243) and (805) 499-9774; Fax/Order line: (805) 499-0871; e-mail: journals@sagepub.com. Copyright © 2006 by The American Academy of Political and Social Science. Institutions may subscribe to THE ANNALS at the annual rate: $577.00 (clothbound, $652.00). Single issues of THE ANNALS may be obtained by individuals who are not members of the Academy for $34.00 each (clothbound, $47.00). Single issues of THE ANNALS have proven to be excellent supplementary texts for classroom use. Direct inquiries regarding adoptions to THE ANNALS c/o Sage Publications (address below). Periodicals postage paid at Thousand Oaks, California, and at additional mailing offices.

All correspondence concerning membership in the Academy, dues renewals, inquiries about membership status, and/or purchase of single issues of THE ANNALS should be sent to THE ANNALS c/o Sage Publications, 2455 Teller Road, Thousand Oaks, CA 91320.Telephone: (800) 818-SAGE (7243) and (805) 499-9774; Fax/Order line: (805) 499-0871; e-mail: journals@sagepub.com. *Please note that orders under $30 must be prepaid.* Sage affiliates in London and India will assist institutional subscribers abroad with regard to orders, claims, and inquiries for both subscriptions and single issues.

Printed on acid-free paper

THE ANNALS

© 2006 by The American Academy of Political and Social Science

Editorial Office: 3814 Walnut Street, Fels Institute for Government, University of Pennsylvania, Philadelphia, PA 19104-6197.
For information about membership* (individuals only) and subscriptions (institutions), address:
Sage Publications
2455 Teller Road
Thousand Oaks, CA 91320
For Sage Publications: Joseph Riser and Esmeralda Hernandez

From India and South Asia, write to:
SAGE PUBLICATIONS INDIA Pvt Ltd
B-42 Panchsheel Enclave, P.O. Box 4109
New Delhi 110 017
INDIA

From Europe, the Middle East, and Africa, write to:
SAGE PUBLICATIONS LTD
1 Oliver's Yard, 55 City Road
London EC1Y 1SP
UNITED KINGDOM

*Please note that members of the Academy receive THE ANNALS with their membership.
International Standard Serial Number ISSN 0002-7162
International Standard Book Number 1-4129-4466-X (Vol. 605, 2006 paper)
International Standard Book Number ISBN 1-4129-4465-1 (Vol. 605, 2006 cloth)
Manufactured in the United States of America. First printing, May 2006.

The articles appearing in *The Annals* are abstracted or indexed in Academic Abstracts, Academic Search, America: History and Life, Asia Pacific Database, Book Review Index,CABAbstracts Database, Central Asia: Abstracts &Index, Communication Abstracts, Corporate ResourceNET, Criminal Justice Abstracts, Current Citations Express, Current Contents: Social & Behavioral Sciences, Documentation in Public Administration, e-JEL, EconLit, Expanded Academic Index, Guide to Social Science & Religion in Periodical Literature, Health Business FullTEXT, HealthSTAR FullTEXT, Historical Abstracts, International Bibliography of the Social Sciences, International Political Science Abstracts, ISI Basic Social Sciences Index, Journal of Economic Literature on CD, LEXIS-NEXIS, MasterFILE FullTEXT, Middle East: Abstracts&Index, North Africa: Abstracts&Index, PAIS International, Periodical Abstracts, Political Science Abstracts, Psychological Abstracts, PsycINFO, Sage Public Administration Abstracts, Social Science Source, Social Sciences Citation Index, Social Sciences Index Full Text, Social Services Abstracts, SocialWork Abstracts, Sociological Abstracts, Southeast Asia: Abstracts& Index, Standard Periodical Directory (SPD), TOPICsearch, Wilson OmniFileV, and Wilson Social Sciences Index/Abstracts, and are available on microfilm from ProQuest, Ann Arbor, Michigan.

Information about membership rates, institutional subscriptions, and back issue prices may be found on the facing page.

Advertising. Current rates and specifications may be obtained by writing to The Annals Advertising and Promotion Manager at the Thousand Oaks office (address above).

Claims. Claims for undelivered copies must be made no later than six months following month of publication. The publisher will supply missing copies when losses have been sustained in transit and when the reserve stock will permit.

Change of Address. Six weeks' advance notice must be given when notifying of change of address to ensure proper identification. Please specify name of journal. POSTMASTER: Send address changes to The Annals of The American Academy of Political and Social Science, c/o Sage Publications, 2455 Teller Road, Thousand Oaks, CA 91320.

THE ANNALS

OF THE AMERICAN ACADEMY OF POLITICAL AND SOCIAL SCIENCE

Volume 605   May 2006

IN THIS ISSUE:

Democracy, Crime, and Justice

Special Editors: SUSANNE KARSTEDT
GARY LaFREE

Section Three:
Democracy and the Governance of Security:
Safe Societies and Strong Democracy

Section Four:
Justice for All: Democracy and Criminal Justice

Quick Read Synopsis

Democracy, Crime, and Justice

By
SUSANNE KARSTEDT
and
GARY LaFREE

The connection between democracy and criminal justice is so fundamental as to be self-evident: the rule of law guarantees due process, and the observation of human rights is an integral part of the emergence and institutionalization of democracy. Indeed, most measures of the strength of democracy include an index of criminal justice and due process guarantees. By contrast, the connection between democracy and crime is less obvious and has only recently begun to attract the attention of scholars from different disciplines, notably political scientists. However, the focus of political science has been less on crime than on violence more generally. Thus, recent political science perspectives on violence and democracy range from the assumption that "violence is anathema to the spirit and substance (of democracy)" (Keane 2004, 1) to accusations that "violent democracy" (Ross 2004) is the typical connection. Mann's (2005) empirically based analysis of "murderous ethnic cleansing" as the "dark side of democracy" can be seen as occupying the middle ground between these

Susanne Karstedt has a chair of criminology and is director of the Centre for Criminological Research in the Research Institute for Law, Politics and Justice at Keele University, United Kingdom. She also teaches at the International Institute of the Sociology of Law in Onati, Spain. Her main research interests include (1) cross-national and cross-cultural research on violence and corruption; (2) cross-national research on moral economies and middle-class crime; (3) emotions, crime, and justice; and (4) public opinion on transitional justice.

Gary LaFree is director of the National Center for the Study of Terrorism and Responses to Terrorism (START) at the University of Maryland as well as a professor in the Department of Criminology and Criminal Justice and a founding member of the Democracy Collaborative. Much of his recent research has dealt with national and international macro-level crime trends. For the past few years, he has been working on a variety of projects related to the development and analysis of a large new global terrorism database. He will serve from 2005 to 2006 as president of the American Society of Criminology.

DOI: 10.1177/0002716206288230

two positions. Similarly, the study of state crimes and corruption in the context of democracy are more in line with the disciplinary agenda of political science than criminology and have played a marginal role in criminological research.

By contrast, this volume documents the increasing interest in connections between democracy, crime, and justice among criminologists. To a large extent, the individual chapters reflect the challenges for criminology that arose from the extension of democracy around the globe during recent decades. In broadening its geographical scope, democracy faced new challenges in confronting crime and maintaining principles of criminal justice. Meanings attached to the term *democracy* became more vague and fluctuating, and many taken-for-granted assumptions of democratic theory, reflecting conditions in the highly industrialized world, were submitted to critical examination, including the connections between democracy, crime, and justice. As Loader points out in this volume, the so-called third wave of democracy (see Huntington 1993) also brought home an important message to countries in which democracy appears to be securely in place: when, Loader asks, "did one last hear a U.S., British, or Italian police officer proclaim that his or her job is to contribute to 'democratic political development'?" (p. 203)—a responsibility often assumed in recent years for police in societies transitioning to democracy.

Criminologists have the advantage of firmly established traditions in their field that link democracy systematically to both crime and justice.

The study of democracy, crime, and justice is presently confronted with great variation between cases; different democratization trajectories; and widely differing outcomes from "illiberal," "deficient," and "disjunctive" to "mature" democracies. Criminologists are engaged in democratic dialogue on crime and justice in their countries and contribute to the development of democracy through their concerns with crime and criminal justice. Analyses of the democratic process in relation to criminal justice in mature democracies like the United States or the United Kingdom, and case studies of failed states and transitions to democracy, all deepen our understanding of the role of crime and criminal justice for the future of democracy. However, democracy also needs to be studied at the cross-national comparative level, a unit of analysis that has never been a special strength of criminology. Criminology research is still focused primarily on the local level, and in most countries, criminology's noncomparative nature is encouraged by the local emphasis of government funding agencies.[1] The contributors to this volume attempt to advance the study of democracy, crime, and justice across the whole spectrum of research from large and small cross-national samples to regional comparisons and case studies from a wide range of countries and different types of democracy.

Criminologists have the advantage of firmly established traditions in their field that link democracy systematically to both crime and justice. Ever since Edwin Sutherland (1947, 1) offered his famous definition of criminology as "the study of the making of laws, the breaking of laws, and reactions to the breaking of laws," the field has been divided into those concerned with either reactions to crime ("the making of laws," "reactions to the breaking of laws") or criminal etiology ("the breaking of laws"). At its most elemental, a concern with reactions to crime is a concern with justice; likewise, at its most elemental, a concern with etiology is a concern with social order. We would therefore argue that the two main branches of criminology are those focused on either criminal justice or social order. Both have clear connections to democracy.

With increasing frequency, issues of criminal justice have entered the discourse on emerging democracies from East and Central Europe to Latin America and Sub-Saharan Africa. In all of these regions, policy makers have come to rely on criminal justice officials to actively promote the rule of law, human rights, and what Bayley (2001, 13) termed "democratic political development." As countries move away from autocratic forms of government, police and criminal justice officials are often seen as the cornerstones for the development of strong democracies. The behavior of the police and other criminal justice agents, both in mature and transitional democracies, is clearly critical to public perceptions of democracy.

But democracy is just as closely linked to crime and the maintenance of social order as it is to criminal justice. The third wave of democratization has been accompanied in many cases by an abrupt and extraordinary rise in crime. Criminal violence, white-collar and organized crime, and corruption in the successor states of the former Soviet Union have threatened the fragile market economies and democratic institutions of these fledgling democracies. In addition, collective violence, including ethnic cleansing, dramatically increased during the 1990s in the successor states of the former Yugoslavia and the Soviet Union and was an integral part of the transition from communism to democracy (Mann 2005).

Rapid crime increases are not limited to transitional democracies. By the 1960s, the long-term decline of violent crime rates in many of the established Western democracies had stalled. In fact, in recent decades several Western democracies have experienced abrupt and serious increases in street crime rates. As crime rates have increased in the Western democracies and as public feelings of insecurity have surged (in some cases only weakly related to actual crime rates), there has been growing populist pressure to increase the punitiveness of criminal justice sentences and to restrict the protection of civil liberties in the fight against crime (Garland 2001; Roberts et al. 2003).

The main purpose of this volume is to begin to fill what we see as a research gap located at the intersection of democracy, crime, and justice. We call on researchers to address the urgent questions that fall at this intersection: Under what circumstances does the process of democratization initiate a wave of violent crime or collective violence? Do established democracies produce more violent crime as they mature, or are there built-in dynamics of democracies—their institutional order, values of individualism, rights or autonomy, the legitimacy of their institutions—that may enable democracies to contain and restrict violence? What impact do rising crime rates—from criminal violence to white-collar crime and corruption—have on newly established as well as secure democracies? Under what circumstances does crime endanger the transition to democracy? If we are inclined to assign a leading role to the delivery of criminal justice in the process of democratization, what conclusions are to be drawn about the relationship between crime, security, and justice? How do taken-for-granted assumptions about criminal justice institutions in mature democracies sustain or inhibit the flourishing of democratic values and institutions?

We believe that questions such as these define the emerging contours of a new field of inquiry that brings together criminology, political science, and the other social and behavioral sciences and forges new interdisciplinary links between these fields. For many, the emergence of this area of study coincides with a deepening skepticism toward democracy, its values, and its institutions. Mann's (2005) argument about ethnic cleansing represents this pessimistic view of democracy. This skepticism encompasses a broad range of voices, from those who attribute the increase of crime and in particular violent crime to Western values of individualism, to those who decry the negative impact of market economies largely associated with contemporary democracies, and to those who equate the process of democratization with a profound loss of law and order and security. It should be clear that the contributors to this volume do not agree that this dark view of the future of democracy is a foregone conclusion. While our contributors are themselves very critical of democracy and democratization, they all share a profound conviction that it is possible to democratize without sacrificing security from criminal victimization and the protection of individual civil liberties and justice.

Democracy, Democratization, and Crime

Crime and social control have direct connections to the strength and stability of democracies. High levels of crime raise feelings of personal insecurity and undermine levels of trust in a society, which in turn undercut the legitimacy of democratic institutions (LaFree 1998). Crime also exacerbates existing social cleavages in a society, which may threaten the stability of democratic regimes. Crime thrives on high rates of economic inequality, and inequality undermines democracy. Rising crime rates drive a wedge between economic, racial, ethnic, and religious groups. Driven by fear, those with more resources are able to abandon high-crime areas. Increasingly, the wealthy in high-crime societies live in a highly protected environment, moving from gated communities in walled suburbs with private security systems, traveling in automobiles with burglar alarms and other safety devices, to work in offices with private security and elaborate crime-prevention features.

These developments not only magnify problems for high-crime areas but also cause a growing rift between the well off and everyone else. Similar barriers increasingly separate high- and low-crime nations. And to the extent that economic inequality overlaps with racial, ethnic, and religious cleavages, problems are even more severe. These divisions make it difficult to develop and sustain strong democratic institutions. And finally, rising crime rates can directly undercut economic growth and development, which again threatens the stability of democratic institutions. Witness the incredible flight of capital out of U.S. central cities following the rapid crime increases that began in the 1960s and, more generally, the obstacles to economic development created by the persistent high violent crime rates in parts of Latin America, Eastern Europe, and Africa.

Not only does crime discourage direct investment, but high crime rates and violence also increase the resources needed for crime control and prevention. Many have noted that in recent years large states like California have actually been spending more on prisons than on higher education. And again, these processes are especially devastating for fledgling democracies like the newly emerging democratic nations of Latin America and Africa and the transitional nations of Eastern Europe.

In the first section of this volume, we include four articles that explore the relationship between democracy, democratization, and crime. Because of the substantial variation across countries in legal definitions of crime, researchers have increasingly relied on homicide as a gold standard for cross-national comparative research. Accordingly, three of the articles in this section rely mostly on homicide data in their analysis. The articles by LaFree and Tseloni and by Karstedt both include analyses of cross-national homicide rates. The article by Pridemore and Kim analyzes a unique homicide database that provides homicide trends for Russian regions (roughly equivalent to states) from 1991 to 2000. The final article in this section looks at connections between the strength of democracy and international rates of software piracy. LaFree and Tseloni argue that three major theoretical perspectives in criminology (civilization, conflict, and modernization) all make predictions about long-term connections between democratization trends and violent crime rates. The civilization perspective predicts that violent crime rates will decline along with the civilizing effects of democratization, the conflict perspective predicts that violent crime rates will increase along with the brutalizing effects of the market economies that so far have universally accompanied democratization, and the modernization perspective predicts that violent crime rates will initially increase with the transition to democracy but then decline as democracies mature. The authors analyze data for forty-four countries from 1950 to 2000 and find the most support for a modernization perspective: violent crime rates were highest for transitional democracies. However, the authors also find that as predicted by the conflict perspective, during the second half of the twentieth century homicide rates have been gradually increasing for full democracies.

As with the LaFree and Tseloni article, the article by Karstedt also explores the seemingly paradoxical relationship between democracy and crime. As Karstedt notes, the democracy ideal represents a process that is by definition nonviolent. But in contrast to this ideal, the rise of democratization during the second half of the twentieth century has been accompanied by one of the most violent periods in all of human history. Karstedt explores the ways in which democratic institutions and values can both inhibit and encourage violence and identifies comparative advantages and disadvantages for democracies in contrast to autocracies. Based on data from twenty-six countries, Karstedt argues that the core democratic values of individualism and egalitarianism both reduce levels of violence. She shows that high individualism and egalitarianism are associated with democracies but also that these values are associated with low crime rates within democracies.

The theoretical starting point for the Pridemore and Kim article is Emile Durkheim's argument that acute political crises produce increased homicide rates because such crises pose a threat to sentiments about the collective. To test this hypothesis, the authors take advantage of the natural experiment that was created by the collapse of the Soviet Union—a collapse that can reasonably be expected to have produced political crises. Based on data from seventy-eight Russian regions, the authors estimate the association between political change and change in homicide rates. Their results show that regions exhibiting less support for the Communist Party in 2000 (and thus greater change in political ideals because the Party had previously exercised complete control) were regions that also experienced greater increases in homicide rates. Thus, while democratization may be a positive development relative to the Communist juggernaut of the past, it appears that the swift political change in Russia is partially responsible for the higher rates of criminal violence there following the collapse of the Soviet Union.

Piquero and Piquero study the relationship between democratic strength and a very different form of crime in their cross-national comparative study of software piracy theft. The authors examine how democratization relates to rates of software piracy from eighty-two countries between the years 1995 and 2000. They use an innovative new method called trajectory analysis to identify groups that vary in their rates of software piracy. The main focus of the article is on how distinct groups of countries (based on software piracy rates and trends) vary according to national measures of democratic strength. The authors find substantial support for their hypothesis that more democratic countries and countries with strong political and civil liberties have lower software piracy rates.

Building Democratic Societies:
The Role of Criminal Justice

The rule of law is a cornerstone of the institutional regime of democratic societies. All actions of citizens, the state, and government are equally subject to legal scrutiny, independent of position, status, and power. The criminal justice system figures as a powerful institutional symbol of the state's monopoly of the use of violence against its own citizens, and its restrictions are emblematic of the firm establishment of the rule of law in democracies. That autocratic regimes often are characterized as "police states" emphasizes the crucial role of criminal justice in liberal democracies (Bayley 1985). When autocratic regimes become police states, criminal justice degenerates to being an instrument for the exertion of governmental power over the citizenry, and relationships between government and citizens are dominated by threats of prosecution and punishment. Most important, government and criminal justice in autocratic societies become indistinguishable in the use of unrestricted power and the violent use of force when pursuing their goal of total control over the citizenry.

[I]n the manifold transitions toward democracy in the second half of the twentieth century, democratic transition within criminal justice has often and considerably lagged behind the democratization of other political institutions.

Although citizens rarely have direct contact with criminal justice agents, criminal justice is a highly sensitive and crucial point of entry and access where citizens are most likely to experience government in their daily lives. Thus, encounters with criminal justice are a crucial part of the *lived experience* of democracy. Tyler (2003) and others (MacCoun 2005; Sherman 2003) have demonstrated the crucial role of such encounters for compliance with the law and how criminal justice procedures and the behavior of criminal justice officials can instill trust in government among citizens. Widespread perceptions of unfair treatment by criminal justice institutions and its officials are at the root of legal cynicism (Sampson and Bartusch 1998) and general distrust in government among ethnic minority groups are also capable of sparking civil unrest and strife (Wortley, Hagan, and MacMillan 1997; LaFree 1998). Given the importance of criminal justice even in mature and stable democracies as demonstrated by this body of research, the need and urgency of building democratic criminal justice institutions during the transition to democracy can hardly be overrated. If anything, a thorough democratization of criminal justice and the firm establishment of the rule of law should convince citizens of the advantages of a new democratic regime and educate them on the values and habits of democratic society.

In a similar vein, historical perspectives on the evolution of democracy emphasize that reform of criminal justice institutions needs to be given priority in the transition from the rule of power to the rule of law. Historically, the development of the rule of law preceded the democratization of societies, and it can be argued that this was the first and most decisive step in the secular movement toward democracy. Accordingly, the democratization of criminal justice is deemed decisive for "democratic political development" (Bayley 2001, 13). However, in the manifold transitions toward democracy in the second half of the twentieth century, democratic transition *within* criminal justice has often and considerably lagged behind the democratization of other political institutions. This *democratic lag* of criminal justice in countries transitioning to democracy has produced what Caldeira and Holston (1999) termed "disjunctive democracies," where criminal justice agencies operate according to the rules of former autocratic regimes, with massive human rights abuses, failure to observe the rights of defendants, and severe deficiencies concerning the accountability of criminal justice officials, in particular for the use of force and violence. Such a disjunction between criminal justice and other institutions in transitional democracies has been observed in a number of Latin American states (Huggins, Haritos-Fatouros, and Zimbardo 2002; see also Rodrigues's article in this volume), as well as for Central and Eastern European postcommunist societies (Pridemore 2005; Los 2003).

The fact that a number of disjunctive democracies have nonetheless developed into comparatively stable political democracies, though perhaps not yet into fully effective liberal democracies, challenges two common notions: first, that transitions toward democracy are doomed to failure if not based on a swift and thorough democratization of criminal justice; and second, that criminal justice institutions, in particular the police, are indispensable in actively promoting the rule of law and democratic political development in general during the transition phase (Bayley 2001). There can be no doubt that from a long-term perspective criminal justice is essential in achieving democratic objectives, but in the short run and at the start of transitional processes, the formal institutional framework of democracy has an often underrated role in the provision of the contextual framework in which the first steps toward the rule of law and the democratization of criminal justice can actually take place. Transitions to democracy greatly differ in terms of their starting points and the trajectories they follow. The downfall of Latin American autocratic regimes differ from the multicolored "velvet" revolutions that ousted the communist regimes of Eastern and Central Europe, and both transitions differ from those in failed or weak states such as East Timor, Bosnia, and Kosovo or in Africa (Oakley, Dziedzic, and Goldberg 2002). In each of these cases, the challenges to criminal justice come in varying shapes and, accordingly, in varying degrees of urgency and priority.

However, three challenges for criminal justice seem to be common to all recent transitions to democracy. First, criminal justice institutions are deeply compromised by the autocratic regimes in which they originate, with accusations ranging from torture and mass killings to endemic corruption. Distrust in criminal justice institutions may be so deeply rooted in the population that implementing the formal institutions that guarantee the rule of law and enforcing these among criminal justice officials may be an enormous task. Second, transitions to democracy are typically accompanied by crime waves. In particular, violent crime is seen as indicative of the profound changes that turned these societies and the life of their citizenry upside down, and feelings of insecurity increase (Los 2003). Citizens find that new democratic regimes fail in the provision of routine safety, and they in turn may look back to (and reelect) the autocratic regimes of law and order from the past. Finally, the first task assigned to criminal justice and deemed as decisive in advancing the rule of law and legal liberalism is the prosecution of the crimes of the past regime and its representatives. The highly contentious issue of transitional justice, if it can be done and how it should be done, burdens the fledgling institutions of criminal justice in transitional democracies and may endanger their fragile consensus.

The three contributions in this section each engage these criminal justice problems and in different ways address the question of how the institutions of criminal justice can foster the values and practices of democracy. They provide lessons for widely differing contexts of democratization (Bosnia and Croatia, Kosovo, and South Africa), for the role of international law and international institutions in this process, and finally for the importance of the local and wider institutional context of democracy. Hagan and Kutnjak Ivković analyze the local impact of international institutions of transitional justice in the former Yugoslavia, namely, Croatia, Bosnia, and Kosovo. If the International Criminal Tribunal for the Former Yugoslavia (ICTY) is to contribute to the goals of democratization and the rule of law through prosecuting war criminals and bringing them to justice, confidence in its judicial independence is essential. It is exactly the presence of defended and defeated parties along the lines of ethnic divisions that make such confidence precarious. Support for the ICTY is generally based on confidence in its fairness and independence, but contours of local support and evidence of localized cultural norms continue to emerge. "Serbs in Belgrade are distinctive in insisting that war criminals be tried in their places of origin, while Serbs in Sarajevo and Vukovar agree with other groups in these settings that war criminals be tried in the settings where their crimes occurred" (p. 149). Despite the ethnically embedded support, there is a surprising level of agreement across the ethnic divide that war crime offenders should be tried in local courts. Legal justice is ultimately local justice, and international institutions need to be sensitive to localized democratic norms if they want to foster democracy. International legal assistance is vital in starting the process, but Hagan and Kutnjak Ivković conclude that the "tempo and terms of a return to local legal institutions" (p. 146) is the real challenge to be managed.

Wilson's contribution provides lessons on how to confront and manage this challenge from the reconstruction of Kosovo's criminal justice systems. His study covers the period of "nation-building" in Kosovo from 1999 to 2005 and the role of international assistance in building local democracy and criminal justice institutions. The United Nations and Western governments were directly involved with massive assistance in providing both security and justice for the Kosovars. In the context of deeply engrained ethnic conflicts and after an ethnic war, building localized criminal justice institutions and legal culture in Kosovo was predominantly directed toward meeting primary security challenges and dealing with lawless violence. This included guaranteeing safety for returning refugees, reconstructing and training an indigenous police force, as well as establishing courts and recruiting a judiciary. Each of these efforts had to be guided by the principle of proportionate representation of the different ethnicities, which was achieved for the police force but remains problematic for the judiciary. Wilson concludes that Kosovo has been comparatively successful in these efforts, and the lessons and insights this case of democratization provides might turn out as particularly useful for our understanding of how criminal justice contributes to nation-building and democratic political development.

In mature and transitional democracies alike, citizens . . . are sometimes willing to sacrifice civil liberties, human rights, and rights of defendants for increased security.

Marks and Fleming focus on the decisive role of the police force in building democracy through criminal justice. Based on an intensive study of the South African police union, Marks and Fleming address a major issue haunting disjunctive democracies: how do members of the police force adopt democratic values and practices in their work of ensuring security for citizens? They argue that if police are expected to behave democratically in encounters with citizens, "it is important for police themselves to experience democratic engagement within the organizations in which they work" (p. 179), and thus turn attention toward a rather neglected, however potentially promising, route to foster such engagement. If police employees gain experience in the active promotion of labor and social rights, the authors argue, they will be more willing to foster democratic values and practices in their own police work. This would not only improve police working conditions but also help curb police corruption and the use of unwarranted violence by officers, who are responsible for hundreds of deaths each year in both transitional and full democracies. Thus, they take up anew the promising yet ambiguous role of unions in the process of democratization. On one hand, ever since Michels's (1911/1959) seminal work, unions have been shown to be suspicious of authoritarian tendencies. On the other hand, unions emerged as powerful players in the process of democratization in Central and Eastern Europe in recent years, and contemporary perspectives in particular stress this potential. Presently, such democratic engagement among the police is constrained by national and international regulatory frameworks, in particular International Labor Organization (ILO) conventions permitting restrictions of the right to unionize in the interests of national security or public order. If police unions are to contribute positively to democratic political development during the transition to democracy, the authors conclude, international support of police unions is needed.

Democracy and the Governance of Security: Safe Societies and Strong Democracies

On January 6, 1941, U.S. President Franklin D. Roosevelt proclaimed the "Four Freedoms": Freedom of Speech and Religion, Freedom from Want, and Freedom from Fear (cf. Neumann 1957, 270). In the context of an imminent war against two autocratic powers—Germany and Japan—the proclamation of freedom from fear meant that citizens in democratic societies did not need to live in fear of their governments, nor in fear of each other. They were neither governed by state terror, nor by a police state and the constant threat of prosecution, and their anxieties were neither exploited nor directed against an imagined enemy. Freedom from fear set democratic states apart from authoritarian states that terrorized their citizens, and it was democracies, not authoritarian states, that provided security to their citizens (Neumann 1957; see also Waldmann 2002).

Six decades later, citizens in Western democracies are again haunted by fear. But now they do not fear their governments, but crime and terrorism. Their fears range from being assaulted on their way to work, or having their homes burgled, to fears of a terrorist attack, and they turn to their governments for protection from violence and crime (Garland 2001). In mature and transitional democracies alike, citizens demand harsher sentences for offenders and fewer controls over police power. They are sometimes willing to sacrifice civil liberties, human rights, and rights of defendants for increased security. Feeling unprotected by the state, they purchase security devices, retreat into gated communities, or organize communities to fend off criminal attacks (Hope and Trickett 2003). In fact, "anxious citizens make bad democrats," as Loader notes (p. 216). Among the predictors of intolerance, perceived threat from all who are defined as "others" is an extremely potent and completely exogenous variable (Gibson 1992). In a similar vein, psychological insecurity and individual dogmatism, in sum the characteristics of the "authoritarian personality," are linked to intolerance (Sullivan and Transue 1999). Core democratic values are endangered by fear, and democracies are particularly vulnerable if they are unable to curb the insecurity of their citizens.

Governments in turn have responded to these demands from the electorate by providing new strategies of policing, ranging from zero tolerance to community policing and partnerships, including citizens and local government. These crime-prevention strategies have been part of the transition from a *democratic welfare contract* toward a *democratic security contract* in the democracies of Western Europe and Australasia. Since the 1980s, the welfare contract, which had dominated democratic policies during the post–World War II era, has been replaced by government policies promising to provide safety and protection from crime as a primordial collective good, a task that mainly rests on investment in the state's authority (Hope and Karstedt 2003). The new crime-prevention strategies can be seen in many ways as more intrusive into and less distant from civil society and as less restrictive with regard to the power of criminal justice institutions. However, protective activities by citizens or the engagement of citizens in the provision of security are not by definition dangerous to democracy, and some might even be seen as genuinely democratic grassroots efforts. Do safe societies still make strong democracies, as we may conclude from Roosevelt's proclamation, or is the governance of safety and the power invested in criminal justice institutions threatening to democracies?

The first two contributions in this section by Loader and Innes can be read as a debate on this question. Both contributions treat as a case study the new strategies of policing being developed and deployed in the United Kingdom. Loader's starting point is the argument that democratic communities need to provide a sense of universal recognition and belonging to their citizens, regardless of their culture, religion, or ethnicity. Policing practices play an important part in reinforcing the sense of security that flows from a feeling of confident membership in a democratic community. "Democratic police" have to pursue their crime control and "social ordering tasks" in ways that contribute to this sense of recognition and belonging and, therefore, acknowledge the legitimate claims to security from all social groups. Loader argues that "ambient" police strategies—such as community, broken windows, and problem-oriented policing—"rest . . . on a *shallow* but *wide* understanding of the police-security relation" that makes . . . "security institutions a *pervasive* feature of everyday life" (p. 204). He contrasts this with an account of the policing-security nexus that is *deep* as it is fundamental to people's sense of security, but *narrow* as police institutions should be minimal agencies of last resort. Security needs to be an "*axiomatic*—rather than [a] pervasive—ingredient" (p. 204) of the lived social relations of democratic communities. A deep and narrow strategy of policing is decisive in meeting the challenge of relations between police and disadvantaged groups, and addressing the pattern of "over-suspicion and underprotection" (p. 212) that has long characterized the distribution of security benefits and burdens among advantaged and less advantaged groups.

Nowhere are these strains more evident than in relations between police and the Muslim communities of Western Europe in the wake of the terrorist attacks of 9/11 in the United States and 7/7 in London. Innes's contribution addresses the sensitive question of police relations with the Muslim population of the United Kingdom. His analysis is informed by interviews with police officers involved in intelligence and counterterrorism strategies. He clearly opts—in contrast to

Loader—for a broad understanding of the police security relationship in the context of the highly uncertain threats and security risks posed by terrorism. As terrorism amplifies a wider "ambient insecurity" emanating from everyday experiences of crime and disorder, democracies find themselves under increasing pressure to provide security to their citizenry. Terrorist attacks can also feed into social divisions based on ethnicity and faith, and consequently the response to terrorism in democracies encompasses a range of potential harms, not the least of which is the vulnerability of democratic institutions themselves. Overt and direct engagement with Muslim communities and their leaders, Innes argues, is not only more democratic but also strategic: by restricting covert intrusions into predominantly Muslim communities, police can reduce growing feelings of alienation and thus support for the terrorists' cause. Such engagement also can help to attenuate conflicts arising in the wake of terrorist attacks, between those groups who feel endangered and those who are blamed, reducing the likelihood of hate crimes and other forms of violence. Democratic policing in the face of terrorist threats is locally based and takes the form of neighborhood policing with intensive and pervasive ties between local police and small communities. Innes argues that such grassroots policing can provide the intelligence "feed" from the community and back to the community that offers the best chance of preventing future violence.

Criminal justice institutions in disjunctive democracies . . . fail in establishing democratic authority that is based on the provision of basic security to their citizens, who in turn seek remedies in less democratic policies and practices.

As Rodrigues shows, the nexus between security and democracy as discussed by Loader and Innes for a well-established democracy in the Northern Hemisphere has decisively different contours in the "disjunctive democracy" of Brazil. The high level of "lawless violence" in Brazil, both in general and within the institutions of criminal justice, indicates a "clear abdication of democratic authority" (Mendez 1999, 19). Citizens are not provided with basic levels of security, and far from feeling "freedom from fear," many fear violence by others as well as the police. Lacking basic security, citizens engage in violent vigilante practices and turn to organized crime in their search for protection, while the police are accused of both negligence and abuse of citizens. Rodrigues explores how the typical characteristics of disjunctive democracy affect citizens' fear of crime and perceptions of victimization risks for various crimes. Her analysis is based on a survey of the population of the metropolitan area of Belo Horizonte, the third largest city of Brazil. Her findings speak to highly complex relationships between perceptions of risk and safety and democratic institutions. Those who endorse democracy feel safer, which—given the cross-sectional nature of the data—also supports the conclusion that a certain level of safety is a precondition for the development of democracy. However, Rodrigues's analysis shows that preference for authoritarian forms of government and distrust in the police *decrease* perceptions of risk. This result demonstrates the disjunctive nature of democracy in Brazil. Such feelings of insecurity generate support for get-tough policies against crime, including the use of violence and illegal or discriminatory practices by the police, and for nondemocratic policies and practices more generally. Criminal justice institutions in disjunctive democracies seem to be caught in a vicious cycle of lawless violence and crime. They fail in establishing democratic authority that is based on the provision of basic security to their citizens, who in turn seek remedies in less democratic policies and practices. In widening the geographical scope of democratic policing, Rodrigues's contribution points to a number of unexamined assumptions in democratic policing, which mainly reflect the context of well-established democracies. Freedom from fear, it seems, is as essential for democracies today as it was sixty years ago.

Justice for All: Democracy and Criminal Justice

It is a truism that the character of a society's reaction to crime can undercut basic civil liberties and shake the foundations of democratic institutions. This was clearly a concern that animated the founders of the American republic in the third quarter of the eighteenth century and remains just as much of a concern today as the U.S. Congress debates the reach of the Patriot Act. Concern about democratically imposed criminal justice penalties and civil liberties are evident in the U.S. Constitution's references to cruel and unusual punishment (Eighth Amendment); the right to trial by jury, counsel, and to confront accusers (Sixth Amendment); freedom from multiple prosecutions and the right not to testify against oneself (Fifth Amendment); and the right to be free from unreasonable searches and seizures (Fourth Amendment). The ongoing tension between democratic institutions and civil liberties was clear in the influential observations about American democracy in the 1830s made by Alexis de Tocqueville (1835/1956, 119), who expressed serious apprehension about the potential "tyranny of the majority." In fact, said de Tocqueville, majority rule is especially dangerous in the United States because its legal system bestows all power in the hands of those supported by majority vote. He concluded that "the main evil of the present democratic institutions of the United States does not arise, as is often asserted in Europe, from their weakness, but from their irresistible strength" (p. 115).

The three chapters in this section all deal with the connections between democracy and criminal justice. However, Zimring and Johnson as well as Uggen, Manza, and Thompson focus mainly on criminal processing in the United States, while Sung instead develops a cross-national comparative analysis. Zimring and Johnson develop the provocative argument that draconian criminal sentencing laws in the United States, epitomized by the three strikes law in California, are a product of an unrestrained populist democracy that has become especially strong in the past couple of decades. Uggen, Manza, and Thompson examine how state laws that provide for the permanent political disenfranchisement of ex-felons are now blocking millions of Americans from full democratic participation. And finally, Sung provides evidence that the fundamental nature of criminal justice systems change from a crime control to a due process orientation as countries transition from autocratic to democratic forms of government.

Using examples mostly from the United States and other mature democracies, Zimring and Johnson explore the different ways that punishment policy is produced in democratic societies. They argue that hostile attitudes toward criminals were not the major cause of the explosive increase in punishments in the United States after 1970 because such hostility toward criminals has been a constant theme in the United States throughout its history and is also endemic to other mature democracies. They argue instead that growth in the salience of crime as a citizen concern and increasing public distrust of government competence and legitimacy were two of a number of changes that transformed ever-present hostile attitudes into a dynamic force in American politics. With the increasingly populist nature of democracy in the United States, many of the traditional safeguards against extremely punitive public attitudes toward offenders have eroded, resulting in historically unprecedented levels of criminal sentencing. The authors make a strong case for the conclusion that punitive sentencing regimes are not necessarily limited to authoritarian regimes but, under the right circumstances, may also be adopted by mature democracies.

While Zimring and Johnson concentrate on how the traditional institutional firewall between populist democracy and sentencing in the United States has eroded in recent years, Uggen, Manza, and Thompson explore one of the major consequences of this policy shift and its implications for democracy in America. Researchers have repeatedly demonstrated that convicted felons face both legal and informal barriers to becoming productive citizens at work, responsible citizens in family life, and active citizens in their communities. But as criminal punishment dramatically increased in the United States after 1970, collateral sanctions such as voting restrictions have taken on increasing significance. Uggen and his colleagues place such restrictions in comparative context and consider their effects on civil liberties, democratic institutions, and civic life more generally. Based on demographic life tables, the authors estimate that approximately 4 million former prisoners and 11.7 million former felons now live and work in the United States on any given day. The authors describe historical changes in these prisoner groups, their effects on social institutions, and the extent to which they constitute a caste, class, or status group within American society. Uggen and his colleagues conclude by arguing for reintegrative criminal justice practices that offer hope for strengthening democratic institutions while preserving, or even enhancing, public safety.

While the Zimring and Johnson and Uggen, Manza, and Thompson articles concentrate on threats to justice in the United States, in the final article in this volume, Sung instead considers whether the democratization process itself produces a criminal justice system that is more oriented toward justice than punishment. Sung hypothesizes in this chapter that as nations move from authoritarian to democratic forms of organization, their criminal justice systems transition from a crime control to a due process orientation. He reasons that in authoritarian countries, where the consent of the governed is systematically ignored, criminal justice systems are more often devoted to the maintenance of social order and emphasize policing of their citizens for the effective suppression of crime. In this setting, a disproportionately large law enforcement apparatus and high rates of apprehension, prosecution, conviction, and incarceration are necessary. By contrast, in democracies, where political power is at least in part under popular control, justice is sought as the defense of civil liberties through the promotion of the due process of law. Thus, Sung predicts that criminal justice systems in liberal democracies will make a heavier investment in the judiciary and will be characterized by lower rates of apprehension, prosecution, conviction, and incarceration. He finds considerable support for these general hypotheses based on an analysis of comparative cross-national data from 1997 to 2002 collected by the United Nations.

We would like to conclude this introduction by expressing our gratitude to all those who in various ways supported this special issue. Lawrence Sherman, then president of the American Academy of Political and Social Science, first suggested the topic for this special issue. The editors of the *Annals*, Robert Pearson and Julie Odland, provided invaluable help from the first outline to the final editing. Nothing could have better demonstrated the growing interest in this area than the overwhelming response from the scientific community that the editors received when we announced the call for papers. We could accommodate only a small proportion of the papers we received, even though a great many were relevant and interesting. Of course, many regions, countries, cases, and in particular problems are not represented in this volume, and our readers will certainly detect important gaps. In fact, we sincerely hope that the gaps in this volume will encourage others to pursue additional related studies in the future. Equally enthusiastic was the global response to the call for thematic sessions on democracy, crime, and justice for the XIV World Congress of Criminology in Philadelphia in 2005, which resulted in contributions from all over the world, some of which are included in this volume. Response was also enthusiastic to the call for papers for the American Society of Criminology's meeting in Los Angeles in 2006, whose theme is "Democracy, Crime, and Justice." Finally, we wish to thank our authors for their contributions, which we hope will encourage criminologists to work toward strengthening democratic institutions and justice around the world.

Note

1. For example, consider the relatively trivial amount of research money made available for cross-national comparative research by the U.S. National Institute of Justice or the British Home Office.

References

Bayley, David H. 1985. *Patterns of policing: A comparative international analysis.* New Brunswick, NJ: Rutgers University Press.
———. 2001. *Democratizing the police abroad: What to do and how to do it.* Washington, DC: National Institute of Justice.
Caldeira, Teresa P. R., and James Holston. 1999. Democracy and violence in Brazil. *Comparative Studies in Society and History* 41 (4): 691-729.
Garland, David. 2001. *The culture of control: Crime and social order in contemporary society.* Oxford: Oxford University Press.
Gibson, James L. 1992. The political consequences of intolerance: Cultural conformity and political freedom. *British Journal of Political Science* 19:562-570.
Hope, Tim, and Susanne Karstedt. 2003. Towards a new social crime prevention. In *Crime prevention. New approaches,* ed. H. Kury and J. Obergfell-Fuchs. Mainzer Schriften zur Situation von Kriminalitaetsopfern, Mainz, Germany: Weisser Ring.
Hope, Tim, and Alan Trickett. 2003. Angst essen Seele auf . . . But it keeps away the burglar. Private security, Neithburhood Watch and the social reaction to crime. In *Soziologie der Kriminalitaet* (special volume of the Koelner Zeitschrift fuer Soziologie und Sozialpsychologie 43), ed. D. Oberwittler and S. Karstedt. Wiesbaden, Germany: VS Verlag.
Huggins, Martha, Mika Haritos-Fatouros, and Philip G. Zimbardo. 2002. *Violence workers: Police torturers and murderers reconstruct Brazilian atrocities.* Berkeley: University of California Press.
Huntington, Samuel P. 1993. *The third wave: Democratization in the late twentieth century.* Norman: University of Oklahoma Press.
Keane, John. 2004. *Violence and democracy.* Cambridge: Cambridge University Press.
LaFree, Gary. 1998. *Losing legitimacy: Street crime and the decline of social institutions in America.* Boulder, CO: Westview.
Los, Maria. 2003. Post-communist fear of crime and the commercialization of security. *Theoretical Criminology* 6:165-88.
MacCoun, Robert J. 2005. Voice, control and belonging: The double-edged sword of procedural fairness. *Annual Review of Law and Social Science* 1:171-202.
Mann, Michael. 2005. *The dark side of democracy. Explaining ethnic cleansing.* Cambridge: Cambridge University Press.
Mendez, Juan E. 1999. Problems of lawless violence: Introduction. In *The (un)rule of law and the underprivileged in Latin America,* ed. J. E. Mendez, G. O'Donnell, and P. S. Pinheiro. South Bend, IN: University of Notre Dame Press.
Michels, Robert. 1911/1959. *Political parties. A sociological study of the oligarchical tendencies of modern democracy.* Translated by E. and E. Paul. New York. Dover (Originally published as *Zur Soziologie des Parteiwesens in der modernen Demokratie. Untersuchungen ueber die oligarschichen Tendenzen des Gruppenlebens,* Leipzig, Germany, 1911)
Neumann, Franz. 1957. Anxiety and politics. In *The democratic and authoritarian state: Essays in political and legal theory,* ed. H. Marcuse. New York: Free Press.
Oakley, Robert B., Michael Dziedzic, and Eliot M. Goldberg, eds. 2002. *Policing the new world disorder: Peace operations and public security.* Honolulu, HI: University Press of the Pacific.
Pridemore, William A., ed. 2005. *Ruling Russia: Law, crime, and justice in a changing society.* Lanham, MD: Rowman & Littlefield.
Roberts, Julian V., Loretta J. Stalans, David Indermaur, and Mike Hough. 2003. *Penal populism and public opinion. Lessons from five countries.* Oxford: Oxford University Press.

Ross, Daniel. 2004. *Violent democracy*. Cambridge: Cambridge University Press

Sampson, Robert, and Dawn Bartusch. 1998. Legal cynicism and (subcultural?) tolerance of deviance: The neighborhood context of racial differences. *Law & Society Review* 32:777-804.

Sherman, Lawrence. 2003. Reason for emotion: Reinventing justice with theories, innovations and research. The American Society of Criminology 2002 Presidential Address. *Criminology* 41:1-38.

Sullivan, John L., and James E. Transue. 1999. The psychological underpinnings of democracy: A selective review of research on political tolerance, interpersonal trust and social capital. *Annual Review of Psychology* 50:625-50.

Sutherland, Edwin. 1947. *Principles of criminology*. 4th ed. Philadelphia: J.B. Lippincott.

Tocqueville, Alexis de. 1835/1956. *Democracy in America*. Edited by Richard D. Heffner. New York: Mentor Books.

Tyler, Tom R. 2003. Procedural justice, legitimacy, and the effective rule of law. In *Crime and justice: A review of research*, vol. 30, ed. M. Tonry. Chicago: University of Chicago Press.

Waldmann, Peter. 2002. *Der anomische Staat. Über Recht, öffentliche Sicherheit und Alltag in Lateinamerika*. Opladen, Germany: Leske + Budrich.

Wortley, Scot, John Hagan, and Ross MacMillan. 1997. Just des(s)erts? The racial polarization of perceptions of criminal injustice. *Law & Society Review* 31:637-76.

SECTION ONE:

Democracy, Democratization, and Crime

Democracy and Crime: A Multilevel Analysis of Homicide Trends in Forty-Four Countries, 1950-2000

By
GARY LaFREE
and
ANDROMACHI
TSELONI

Despite simultaneous increases in democratization and violent crime rates in many countries during the second half of the twentieth century, the authors could find no prior studies that have directly examined possible connections between these two processes. The civilization perspective predicts that violent crime rates will decline along with the civilizing effects of democratization, the conflict perspective predicts that violent crime rates will increase along with the brutalizing effects of the market economies that so far have universally accompanied democratization, and the modernization perspective predicts that violent crime rates will initially increase with the transition to democracy but then decline as democracies mature. Our analysis of data from forty-four countries from 1950 to 2000 shows the most support for a modernization perspective: violent crime rates are highest for transitional democracies. However, as predicted by the conflict perspective, we also find that during the second half of the twentieth century homicide rates gradually increased for full democracies.

Keywords: democracy; violent crime; modernization; conflict; transitional democracies; homicide; civilization perspective

Two of the most important trends in the second half of the twentieth century are rarely discussed in the same sentence: the dramatic rise in the proportion of the world's countries that are democracies and the steady increase in global violent crime rates. The "third wave" of democratization (Huntington 1993) that got under way in the early 1970s has produced

NOTE: We would like to thank the World Health Organization for supplying the homicide victimization data, Nancy Morris and Rachelle Giguere for help with data collection, and Suzanne Karstedt and Susan Fahey for detailed comments. Earlier versions of this article were presented at the European Society of Criminology meetings (2nd Toledo, Spain, August 2002 and 4th Amsterdam, the Netherlands, August 2004) and the World Congress of Criminology meeting (Rio de Janeiro, Brazil, August 2003). The helpful insights of members of the audience of these presentations are gratefully acknowledged.

DOI: 10.1177/0002716206287169

an unprecedented number of new democratic countries. This rapid political transformation began in Southern Europe in the 1970s, spread to Latin America and parts of Asia in the 1980s, and then moved on to parts of Sub-Saharan Africa, Eastern Europe, and the Soviet Union in the late 1980s and early 1990s (Potter et al. 1997). While more countries than ever before have attained democracy in the sense of constitutionalism and multiparty electoral competition, an even larger number have adopted at least a partial framework for democratic governance. Annual surveys by Freedom House (2002) show that in 1975, less than one-third of the world's countries had partially democratic regimes (including competitive elections and formal guarantees of political and civil rights); by 1995, nearly three-quarters did.

[W]e could find no study to date that has systematically examined whether the wave of democratization in the last half of the twentieth century can help explain the global rise in violent crime rates.

But during the same period, substantial evidence shows that global rates of violent crime have also surged. In a recent cross-national study of homicide victimization rates in thirty-four countries, LaFree and Drass (2002) found that on average, homicide rates doubled during the last four decades of the twentieth century. Similarly, Fukuyama (1999, 4) claimed that there was a "great disruption"

Gary LaFree is director of the National Center for the Study of Terrorism and Responses to Terrorism (START) at the University of Maryland as well as a professor in the Department of Criminology and Criminal Justice and a founding member of the Democracy Collaborative. Much of his recent research has dealt with national and international macro-level crime trends. For the past few years, he has been working on a variety of projects related to the development and analysis of a large new global terrorism database. He will serve from 2005 to 2006 as president of the American Society of Criminology.

Andromachi Tseloni received her Ph.D. in econometrics and social statistics from the University of Manchester in the United Kingdom. She has taught undergraduate and postgraduate courses at the Universities of Manchester and Hull in the United Kingdom, the University of Maryland in the United States, and the Universities of the Aegean and Macedonia in Greece. Her research interests include multilevel and generalized mixed linear modeling. Results of her work have been presented at international conferences and published in criminology and statistical journals, edited books, and conference proceedings.

among Western industrialized countries beginning in the 1960s that created large increases in violent crime and social disorder among most industrialized countries of the world. More pointedly, at least some evidence indicates that rapid increases in violent crime have been especially pronounced in precisely those regions of the world in which democracy has recently taken hold, including Latin America (Fajnzylber, Lederman, and Loayza 1998; Diamond 1999; Mendez, O'Donnell, and Pinheiro 1999), Eastern Europe, the "breakaway" republics of the former Soviet Union (Hraba et al. 1998; Barak 2000; Backman 1998; Savelsberg 1995), and Sub-Saharan Africa (Reza, Mercy, and Krug 2000; Daniel, Southall, and Lutchman 2005).

Despite the apparent correlation between the spread of democracy and levels of violent crime, we could find no study to date that has systematically examined whether the wave of democratization in the last half of the twentieth century can help explain the global rise in violent crime rates. The absence of research on connections between democracy and crime is surprising because several of the leading theoretical perspectives on cross-national crime are closely related to the rapid rise of market-based democratic societies. Thus, Elias's civilization perspective (1939/1978) is consistent with the prediction that the spread of Western-styled democratic regimes will transform systems of social control and greatly reduce violent crime rates, conflict theorists (Chambliss 1976; Bohm 1982) argue that the income inequality and poverty generated by market-based democratic countries will result in an explosive growth of crime, and Durkheim's modernization perspective (1947, 1950) predicts increases in crime as societies undergo the kind of rapid transformation that is the hallmark of democratization. In this article, we build on these competing perspectives to develop four hypotheses about the effect of democratization on violent crime rates. We then test these hypotheses with an econometric analysis (random effects multilevel repeated measures modelling) of annual time series data for forty-four countries from 1950 to 2000.

Theory and Previous Evidence

The civilization perspective

While the argument that the growing strength of market economies will reduce interpersonal violence because such economies increasingly depend on the self-control and rationality of their citizens can be traced directly to Weber (1956/1978), Elias (1939/1978) is probably best known for making the argument with specific regard to violent crime trends. And although Elias's civilization perspective does not directly reference the role of democratization in reducing crime, his arguments are nevertheless centered on a set of West European countries that eventually became strong democracies (especially England, France, and Germany). Elias predicted long-term declines in rates of violent crime among these countries through two related processes. First, as modern states develop, they increasingly claim a monopoly on the legitimate use of violence. Thus, common crimes involving family members and close acquaintances that in earlier periods were routinely avenged by relatives and friends of the perceived wronged party are increasingly regarded as public matters and the subject of formal penal law. Second, Elias argued that along with urbanization and the growing division of labor, citizens of West European nations were embedded in increasingly complex social configurations such that advancing individual self-interest less often required the use of violence. Instead, more sophisticated action strategies were required, which result in higher levels of self control and declining violent crime rates.

To support his arguments about the declining levels of interpersonal violence in Western nations, Elias (1939/1978) relied mostly on qualitative evidence of the growth of civilized behavior through such indicators as advice in etiquette books and changes in children's literature. But more recently, historical analysis of long-term crime trends has been generally supportive of the conclusion that rates of personal violent crime among industrialized Western countries declined from the early Middle Ages until the second half of the twentieth century (Gurr 1981; Osterberg 1996; Spierenburg 1996). In the most comprehensive study to date, Eisner (2001) examined homicide rates from the thirteenth through the twentieth centuries for England, the Netherlands, Belgium, the Scandinavian countries, Germany, Switzerland, and Italy. For each analysis, he found evidence for substantial declines in homicide rates from the early Middle Ages until the mid-twentieth century.

However, Elias's (1939/1978) predictions seem to be contradicted by crime trends following World War II. In their study of crime trends in four cities for 150 years, Gurr, Grabosky, and Hula (1977, 169) concluded that "some common social and political dynamics created public order over the course of a century in western societies, then went crazily unsprung in a single generation." More recently, LaFree and Drass (2002) showed substantial increases in homicide rates for a sample of thirty-four mostly industrialized countries from 1958 to 1998. Likewise, Eisner's (2001) analysis of seven West European democratic countries and regions all show an increase in homicide rates beginning after 1950. Thus, while evidence indicates that violent crime rates among Western-styled democracies declined during much of the seven centuries leading into the twentieth century, violent crime rates increased in most Western democracies after World War II. However, for our purposes, such conclusions must be tempered by the fact that no study to date has specifically examined connections between levels of democratization and violent crime rates for a large sample of countries.

The conflict perspective

As with the civilization perspective, proponents of the conflict perspective (Taylor, Walton, and Young 1973; Chambliss 1976; Bohm 1982) claim that the evolving economic structure of Western nations is a critical determinant of their violent crime rates. Rather than arguing that a growing reliance on market economies reduces violent crime by increasing rationality, mutual trust, and self-control, however, conflict theorists argue that the capitalist market economies that have been closely associated with the rise of modern democracies have raised violent crime rates by increasing economic inequality, unemployment, and social misery both within and between countries. Within countries, the dominance of market economies fosters a growing gap between the rich and the poor, which raises violent crime rates by encouraging greed, selfishness, and diffuse aggression (Bonger 1916; Quinney 1977). Between countries, this gap is reproduced at the international level as the world economy increasingly separates an elite group of highly industrialized Western democracies from a much larger group of poor, economically dependent countries (for a review, see LaFree 2005).

As Neuman and Berger (1988) have pointed out, these conflict arguments can be readily combined with similar predictions from world system theorists (Wallerstein 1979; Hopkins and Wallerstein 1981; Chirot and Hall 1982), who conceptualize the world as divided between "core" countries that prosper by extracting raw materials and exploiting low-cost labor from "peripheral countries." As the economic gap between the industrial "haves" and the developing "have-nots" widens, poverty, slums, and unemployment become more commonplace among the latter. The growing expansion of global markets creates a fluctuating surplus population of unemployed and underemployed workers (Spitzer 1975; Applebaum 1978). The global system also constrains urban development in peripheral countries, which suffer increasingly from a shortage of decent housing, an absence of basic social services, and a lack of living wages, all of which drive crime rates up. Thus, to the extent that all contemporary full democracies are also strong market economies, the conflict perspective predicts that democratization should increase violent crime rates.

The same research on post–World War II violent crime trends that seems to challenge the civilization perspective (Fukuyama 1999; LaFree and Drass 2002) can be seen as supporting the conflict perspective. A growing number of regional studies are consistent with the idea that democratization has been associated with rapidly increasing violent crime rates. This connection is especially common in studies of the newly emerging democratic countries of Eastern Europe since the disintegration of the Soviet Union (Karstedt 2003; Hraba et al. 1998; Barak 2000; Backman 1998). Thus, in a recent study of crime trends in Poland, Bulgaria, Romania, and Slovakia, Cebulak (1996, 77) concluded that there have been "unprecedented and dramatic increases in crime." Similarly, Stamatel, Arato, and Dunn (1998, 243) warned that democratization and economic liberalization in the Central Eastern European countries (Poland, Bulgaria, Romania, Slovakia, and Hungary) are leading to an "Americanization" that is producing rapid crime increases. As with the civilization argument, however, these studies do not directly measure levels of democratization, and the regional studies concentrate mostly on very recent crime trends and, hence, do not rule out the possibility that crime rates were equally high during earlier periods.

Many researchers and social observers have also noted that the growing crime problems of Latin American countries appear to have coincided with democratization in this region (Fajnzylber, Lederman, and Loayza 1998; Diamond 1999; Mendez, O'Donnell, and Pinheiro 1999; Savelsberg 1995). Thus, Fajnzylber, Lederman, and Loayza (1998) used United Nations survey data to conclude that after a period of relative stability during the 1980s, homicide rates in Latin American countries rose sharply in the 1990s. This conclusion is echoed in a report by the Mexican Health Foundation (1999) that showed that several Mexican states experienced major crime increases following the economic crisis of the mid-1990s. Similar warnings are being sounded with increasing frequency in the fledgling democracy of South Africa (Daniel, Southall, and Lutchman 2005). But again, while informative, these studies have thus far not explicitly measured levels of democratization and have most often relied on case studies or cross-sectional analysis.

The modernization perspective

A modernization perspective on crime (Clinard and Abbott 1973; Shelley 1981; Neumann and Berger 1988) can be traced directly to Durkheim's (1947) assessment of the transition from traditional to modern society. According to this view, crime results when modern values and norms come into contact with and disrupt older, established systems of role allocation. The emergence of new roles not yet fully institutionalized and integrated into society make normative guidelines ambiguous and weaken traditional support mechanisms. These basic processes have been linked to rising crime rates and other forms of deviance through a range of distinct yet closely related concepts, including anomie (Merton 1938; Messner and Rosenfeld 1997), social disorganization (Davies 1962; Smelser 1962), breakdown (Tilly, Tilly, and Tilly 1975; Useem 1985), tension (Lodhi and Tilly 1973), and strain (Cloward and Ohlin 1960; Agnew 1992).

Nearly all the cross-national comparative tests of the modernization perspective to date have relied on cross-sectional multivariate analysis in which measures of development (most often, GNP or GDP) are included in statistical models that predict homicide rates (for reviews, see Neapolitan 1997; LaFree 1999). In general, empirical support for a connection between economic development and homicide rates from these studies has been weak. In fact, contrary to the modernization perspective, most of these tests have found that measures of economic development either have no effect (Bennett 1991; Messner 1989) or a negative effect (Messner and Rosenfeld 1997; Neapolitan 1996) on crime rates, leading Neumann and Berger (1988, 300) to question the "continued dominance" of the perspective.

As LaFree and Drass (2002, 774) noted, however, it may be the case that prior studies have not offered the most appropriate test of the modernization perspective. The idea of modernization is inherently longitudinal: as countries transition from traditional to modern, they experience a series of changes that weaken their social control mechanisms and make their normative guidelines ambiguous. Most of the research that has tested modernization views of crime to date has been based on cross-sectional designs that measure both crime rates and modernization measures at one point in time. By contrast, in their longitudinal study of homicide rates in thirty-four nations from 1956 to 1998, LaFree and Drass found considerable support for a modernization perspective: 70 percent of industrializing countries in the study had experienced homicide "booms" (defined as rates that increase rapidly and exhibit a positive sustained change in direction) during this period compared to fewer than 21 percent of industrialized countries (see also LaFree 2005).

Unlike predictions from either civilization or conflict perspectives, the modernization perspective predicts that the effects of democratization on crime should correspond only to the transitional phase of democratization. Thus, crime rates should increase as autocratic countries begin experimenting with democracy but should again diminish once a fully democratic regime has emerged.

While we could identify no prior research that has explicitly examined the possibility that countries transitioning to democracy will experience elevated levels of violent crime but that these levels will diminish once a full democracy is established, there is some support for such a relationship between democracy and other types of crime and deviance. Thus, in an analysis of cross-national data for the period 1980 to 1983, Montinola and Jackman (2002) examined the relationship between measures of democracy (from Bollen 1993) and perceived national levels of corruption and found that the highest corruption levels were in transitional democracies rather than either fully democratic or autocratic countries. Similarly, in a recent study of cross-national connections between measures of democracy (from Freedom House) and perceived levels of organized crime, Sung (2004) found that levels of organized crime were highest among those democratic countries in transition from full autocracy to full democracy.

We summarize expected relationships between democratization and violent crime from four competing hypotheses in Figure 1. The null hypothesis is that there is no connection between democratization and violent crime. A civilization perspective is consistent with the prediction that violent crime rates will decline as autocratic regimes give way to democratic ones. A conflict perspective predicts that the market economies associated with democratic countries will increase rates of violent crime as they move away from autocracy and toward democracy. Finally, a modernization perspective suggests that violent crime rates will be curvilinear with the highest rates in countries that are transitioning between autocracy and democracy.

Data and Method

Homicide rates

Important variation across countries in legal definitions has increasingly lead researchers (Savolainen 2000; Pratt and Godsey 2003; LaFree and Drass 2002) to rely on homicide data in cross-national comparative research. Scholars now agree substantially (Kalish 1988; Neapolitan 1997; Messner and Rosenfeld 1997) that among the major cross-national homicide data sources, those collected by the World Health Organization (WHO) are the most valid and reliable. The WHO homicide data are based on cause of death reports submitted by participating countries.

We collected annual time-series data from WHO on homicide victimization rates per one hundred thousand residents for forty-four countries for varying years between 1950 and 2000. The length of the series and the countries included were determined by data availability. We did not extrapolate values to the beginning or the end of individual series and excluded countries that had missing data for more than three consecutive years. Rates for Israel are reported only for the Jewish population. We substituted an average rate for one year for Israel that included deaths from the Six-Day War (1967). Several political changes affected the geographical boundaries of the countries included. Our analysis of Czechoslovakia is based on

FIGURE 1
EXPECTED RELATIONSHIP BETWEEN DEMOCRACY AND VIOLENT CRIME
FROM FOUR PERSPECTIVES

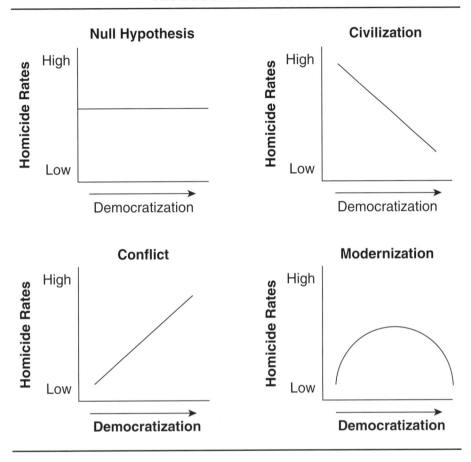

the Czech Republic after the political breakup of 1992. Data for Germany refer to the Federal Republic of Germany until 1990 and the unified Germany afterward. Similarly, French statistics include Algeria until 1962.

Table 1 shows the sample of countries and years included in this study together with the mean, standard deviation, and minimum and maximum values of homicide rates for each country. There is considerable variability in the total number of years of data that are available for each country, ranging from a maximum of fifty-one years to a minimum of eight years (Estonia). Altogether we assembled 1,827 country-year data points for the analysis, and thirty-seven countries (84.1 percent) had at least forty-four years of data.

Perhaps the most striking feature of Table 1 is the tremendous variation in average homicide rates represented by the countries in our study. Mean homicide

TABLE 1
DESCRIPTIVE STATISTICS FOR HOMICIDE RATES

| Country | Total Years | Years | | Homicide Rate | | | |
		First	Last	Mean	SD	Min	Max
Australia	50	1950	1999	1.70	0.26	1.04	2.39
Austria	51	1950	2000	1.23	0.23	0.84	1.77
Belgium	43	1954	1996	1.19	0.46	0.57	2.15
Bulgaria	41	1960	2000	2.95	0.99	0.80	5.07
Canada	49	1950	1998	1.80	0.52	0.99	2.70
Chile	44	1954	1999	3.32	1.23	1.75	6.60
Colombia	28	1951	1994	37.36	22.15	14.45	89.50
Costa Rica	46	1955	2000	4.28	1.15	2.39	8.35
Czechoslovakia	48	1953	2000	1.35	0.32	0.88	2.27
Denmark	49	1950	1998	0.89	0.32	0.39	1.45
Dominican Republic	25	1956	1985	5.05	1.64	2.08	9.38
El Salvador	24	1950	1993	33.86	6.63	24.31	51.53
Estonia	8	1991	1998	20.11	5.44	10.79	28.22
Finland	51	1950	2000	2.81	0.43	1.82	3.63
France	44	1950	1999	0.95	0.16	0.70	1.32
Germany	50	1950	1999	1.12	0.13	0.86	1.39
Greece	43	1956	1998	1.06	0.43	0.51	2.74
Hungary	45	1955	2000	2.54	0.70	1.56	4.09
Iceland	48	1950	1997	0.79	0.76	0.00	3.31
Ireland	50	1950	1999	0.60	0.32	0.18	2.00
Israel	40	1954	1998	1.27	0.60	0.12	2.43
Italy	50	1950	1999	1.49	0.45	0.81	2.84
Japan	50	1950	1999	1.28	0.55	0.55	2.37
Luxemburg	33	1967	2000	1.36	0.72	0.25	2.91
Mauritius	33	1968	2000	2.05	1.05	0.61	6.10
Mexico	39	1958	2000	18.88	4.97	9.78	32.28
Netherlands	50	1950	1999	0.74	0.34	0.21	1.36
New Zealand	50	1950	1999	1.28	0.54	0.00	2.40
Norway	50	1950	1999	0.78	0.34	0.26	1.56
Panama	34	1954	1987	4.14	1.63	1.73	7.24
Paraguay	18	1969	1987	11.71	3.56	6.54	16.60
Philippines	20	1957	1981	6.20	5.59	0.38	17.40
Poland	41	1955	2000	1.55	0.65	0.83	2.94
Portugal	48	1950	2000	1.29	0.29	0.73	1.88
Singapore	42	1959	2000	1.76	0.53	0.57	3.02
Spain	49	1950	1999	0.62	0.34	0.06	1.18
Sweden	50	1950	1999	1.01	0.28	0.56	1.50
Switzerland	50	1950	1999	1.04	0.38	0.54	2.84
Thailand	33	1955	1994	15.39	5.73	6.71	28.77
Trinidad and Tobago	30	1962	1994	6.09	2.30	2.10	11.43
United Kingdom	51	1950	2000	0.84	0.25	0.51	1.52

(continued)

TABLE 1 (continued)

| Country | Total Years | Years | | Homicide Rate | | | |
		First	Last	Mean	SD	Min	Max
United States	50	1950	1999	7.51	2.12	4.50	10.55
Uruguay	32	1955	1990	3.81	1.00	1.99	5.68
Venezuela	47	1950	2000	9.75	3.62	5.02	26.35
All countries	51	1950	2000	3.91	7.40	0.00	89.50

rates range from a high of 37.36 per 100,000 (Colombia) to a low of 0.60 per 100,000 (Ireland). All eight countries with average homicide rates that are less than 1 per 100,000 are West European: Denmark, England/Wales, France, Iceland, Ireland, the Netherlands, Norway, and Spain. Another eighteen countries (40.9 percent) have homicide rates between 1 and 2 per 100,000 over the time period examined. This group includes the rest of the West European countries (with the exception of Finland), all five of the Western Pacific countries, three of the five countries from Eastern Europe, Canada, and Israel. Four countries have mean homicide rates between 2 and 3 per 100,000: Bulgaria, Finland, Hungary, and Mauritius. Twelve of the fifteen countries with homicide rates greater than 3 per 100,000 are in the Western hemisphere. These include all eleven Latin American/Caribbean countries of the sample, as well as the United States, Estonia, the Philippines, and Thailand. Because of the highly skewed distribution of homicide rates, we use the natural log of homicide rates in the subsequent analysis.[1]

Democracy scale

Our democracy scale is a composite score created by Gurr and his associates (Gurr 1974; Gurr, Jaggers, and Moore 1990; Jaggers and Gurr 1995; Marshall and Jaggers 2003).[2] Gurr et al. developed additive 11-point (0-10) scales for annual rates of both democracy and autocracy for all countries of the world back to 1800. The democracy measure is derived from evaluations of four characteristics of national governments: (1) the competitiveness of political participation, (2) the openness of executive recruitment, (3) the competitiveness of executive recruitment, and (4) constraints on the chief executive. Countries get 3 points on the democracy scale for fully competitive political systems (those that have regular national competition between secular political groups and a voluntary transfer of power among competing groups), 2 points for transitional systems (between fully competitive and factional), 1 point for factional systems (polities with parochial or ethnic-based political factions), and 0 points for suppressed (some organized political competition occurs outside government) or repressed (no significant oppositional activity is permitted) systems.

Countries are assigned 1 point if in principle the entire politically active population has an opportunity to attain the executive position through a regularized process. Countries are assigned 2 points if their chief executives are chosen through competitive elections matching two or more parties or candidates, 1 point if there are dual executives and one is chosen by competitive election while the other is chosen by hereditary succession, and 0 points otherwise. And finally, countries receive 4 points if accountability groups (usually legislatures) have authority equal to or greater than the chief executive, 3 points as an intermediate category, 2 points if the executive has more effective authority than any accountability group but is nevertheless subject to substantial constraints, 1 point as an intermediate category, and 0 points if there are moderate to no regular limitations on the chief executive.

Cross-national theories of crime are generally vague when it comes to specific predictions about change over time.

For the most part, the autocracy measure is based on values on the opposite side of the scales that make up the democracy scale. Thus, the autocracy scale awards 8 total points for countries with suppressed (2 points) or restricted (1 point) competitiveness of political participation; closed recruitment of executives (1 point); chief executives determined by hereditary succession or designation (2 points); and slight to moderate (1 point), intermediate (2 points), or no constraints (3 points) on the chief executive. The final 2 points on the autocracy scale are based on evaluations of the extent to which countries have binding rules on when, whether, and how political preferences are expressed. Countries in which competitive groups, issues, and types of conventional participation are regularly excluded from the political process receive 2 points, and countries that oscillate between parties that favor their own group members in central allocations and restrict competing group members receive 1 point. Our democracy scale is obtained by subtracting each country's annual autocracy measure from its democracy measure. This produces a 21-point scale (−10 to +10).

Cross-national theories of crime are generally vague when it comes to specific predictions about change over time. Thus, the modernization perspective predicts rapid increases in crime as countries transition to modern society but does not tell us exactly how long this process should take. Similarly, the conflict perspective predicts rapidly rising crime rates in poor nations as the gap between wealthy core nations and industrializing peripheral nations widens but, again, offers no specific time table for these developments. Because our data are longitudinal, we are able to examine whether crime trends are related to the length of time a country has been classified as either a transitional or full democracy. In general, the civilization perspective suggests that homicide rates should decline over time for full democracies, while a conflict perspective predicts the reverse. The modernization perspective predicts

TABLE 2
DESCRIPTIVE STATISTICS FOR DEMOCRACY SCALE

	Percentage	Mean	SD	Min/Max
Democracy Scale[a]				
Autocratic (base, including Foreign Occupation)	21.7			
Transitional	19.7			
Fully Democratic	58.8			
Democracy Duration since 1950[a]		19.19	14.19	0/51

a. Gurr et al. data, www.cidcm.umd.edu.

TABLE 3
DESCRIPTIVE STATISTICS FOR CONTROL VARIABLES

	Percentage	Mean	SD	Min/Max
Log {GDP per capita (mean per country)}[a]		8.39	0.63	6.60/9.52
Gini coefficient (mean per country)[b]		35.56	8.03	22.25/55.28
Prosperity (country level)[c]		0.00	7.85	−18.61/12.54
Percentage population fifteen to twenty-four years old[d]		0.16	0.03	0.11/0.24
East Europe	10.0			
Latin America/Caribbean	20.1			
United States	2.7			

a. OECD, www.oecd.org.
b. Gini Coefficents (multiplied by 100) from Deninger and Squire (1999); Professor Tryggvi Thor Herbertsson provided Gini coefficients for Iceland.
c. Composite variable calculated as {0.926[log(GDP per capita) − Gini]} at centered values.
d. World Health Organization (2001).

short-term increases in crime for transitional democracies, but in the longer term, increases should end and declines begin—although the modernization perspective does not tell us how long these developments might take. To test these possibilities, we include an annual democracy duration measure based on the number of years each country has experienced either full democracy or transitional democracy since 1950.

We provide descriptive statistics on the democracy scale and the democracy duration measure in Table 2 and the control variables in Table 3. To test our hypotheses we collapse the democracy scale into three categories that distinguish autocratic (−10 to 0), transitional (1 to 9), and fully democratic (10) regimes. Because our sample includes nearly all of the highly industrialized Western democracies, it is unsurprising that fully democratic regimes were by far the most common outcome in the data, accounting for nearly three-fifths of the total country-year data points.

FIGURE 2
AVERAGE HOMICIDE VICTIMIZATION RATES, 1955-1998

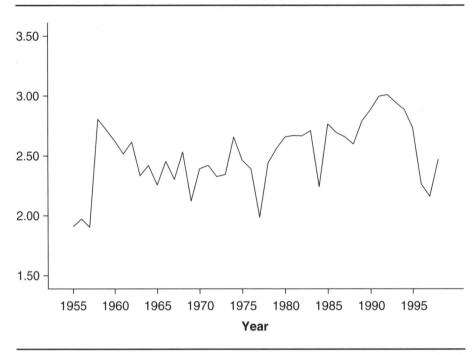

Table 2 also shows great variability on the democracy duration measure, with some countries changing their level of democratic governments immediately after 1950 (e.g., Bulgaria, El Salvador) and some not changing their democratic level for the fifty-one years spanned by the data (e.g., Austria, United States).

[I]n support of the modernization perspective, a shift from an autocratic to a transitional democratic regime produces a significant increase in homicide rates.

Figure 2 shows average homicide rates from 1955 to 1998 for the countries in our analysis. Although the increases are not large, Figure 2 does show a slow

FIGURE 3
MEAN DEMOCRACY SCORES, 1955-1998

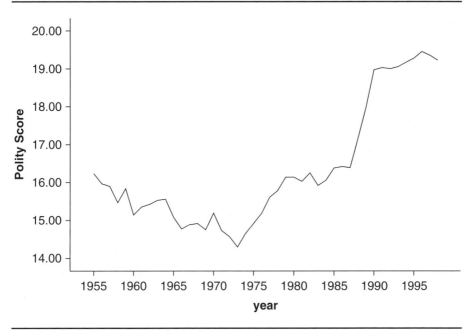

upward trend in homicide rates over the period spanned by the data. From the lowest point in the series (1.91) in 1955, rates increase to a high point in 1992 of 3.01—an increase of 57.6 percent. However, rates declined somewhat afterwards, dropping by 20.3 percent to 2.47 in 1998.

Figure 3 shows the mean democratization scores for all 51 countries for the same time period as shown in Figure 2. According to Figure 3, mean democratization levels declined somewhat from 1955 before reaching a series low point of 13.50 in 1973. Mean democracy scores then increased substantially, reaching a series high point of 19.34 in 1996—an increase of 43.2 percent. Taken together, these results suggest that mean democratization levels increased substantially and mean homicide rates more modestly for the countries included in the figures through much of the postwar period.

Control variables

Prior quantitative research on cross-national crime rates (for reviews, see Neapolitan 1997; LaFree 1999) has most often included three types of measures: economic development, economic inequality, and population structure. As shown in Table 3, we attempted to include each of these measures in our analysis. Gross national product (GNP) or gross domestic product (GDP) have been the most commonly used economic development measures in past research (Bennett 1991;

Fiala and LaFree 1988; Hansmann and Quigley 1982). We used the log of GDP per capita in our analysis. A positive association between economic inequality (usually measured by the Gini coefficient) and homicide rates is probably the most consistent finding in the cross-national homicide literature (Messner and Rosenfeld 1997; Neapolitan 1996; LaFree 1999). Our Gini measure of income inequality is from Deninger and Squire (1999).[3] However, because GDP and the Gini index were highly correlated in our data ($r = -.85$), we were unable to include both measures in our models and instead created a *prosperity* index, based on a factor analysis of the mean value of the logged GDP and Gini coefficients per country over the period under investigation.

Based on the widespread assumption that young people commit a disproportionate amount of violent crime, most prior studies of cross-national homicide (Messner 1989; Bennett 1991; Ortega et al. 1992) have included a measure of the proportion of young people in each country. Accordingly, we include the percentage of population aged fifteen to twenty-four years old from the United Nations WHO.

To control for substantial differences in homicide rates in the countries under investigation, we include three regional dummy variables in the analysis to distinguish East European and Latin American/Caribbean countries and, because it consistently has higher homicide rates than other highly industrialized countries, the United States.[4] To facilitate interpretation of the results in the discussion below, we centered the control variables on their mean value.

Method

We used a hierarchical linear model approach (Raudenbush 1995; Goldstein 1995)[5] with the software package MLwiN (Goldstein et al. 1998) to do the analysis. The units of analysis of our multilevel models are at two levels: (1) *time*, the total number of years of annual data for a country up to a maximum of fifty-one; and (2) *country*, the total number of countries in the sample. The democracy duration dummy variables and the proportion of young persons in our analysis operate at level 1 (i.e., time) and the three regional dummy variables and our measure of prosperity operate at level 2 (i.e., country level). We include a more detailed technical description of our methods in the appendix.

Results

According to the hypotheses developed above, a civilization perspective predicts that violent crime rates will be lowest in full democracies, a conflict perspective predicts that the capitalist economies associated with full democracies will produce the highest violent crime rates, and a modernization perspective suggests that violent crime rates will be curvilinear with the highest rates in countries that are transitioning between autocracy and democracy. The results of our test of these three hypotheses are presented in Table 4.

We can interpret Table 4 as showing the effects of our democracy measure on cross-national homicide rates, controlling for each country's demographic profile,

TABLE 4
ESTIMATED MULTILEVEL EFFECTS OF DEMOCRACY SCALE ON NATIONAL
HOMICIDE RATES (LOGGED), 1950-2000

	Baseline Model	Final Model
Time (centered)	0.0075°°°	0.0015
Democracy		
(base: autocratic regime)		
Transitional democratic		0.4343°°°
Fully democratic		0.0610
Wald test ($df = 2$)		17.3135
Interactions with years		
of democracy since 1950		
Transitional Democratic × Years		0.0089°
Fully Democratic × Years		0.0093°°°
Wald test ($df = 2$)		11.7929
Controls		
Percentage of population fifteen		3.1266°°°
to twenty-four years old		
Prosperity		−0.0447°°
Wald test ($df = 2$)		25.7742
East Europe		1.3951°°°
Latin America/Caribbean		1.0345°°°
United States		1.8118°°°
Wald test ($df = 3$)		49.7794
Joint Wald test for all	6.8203 (1)	151.0956 (10)
estimated parameters (df)		
Intercept	0.7879°°°	−0.0075

Note: Models are based on 1,827 observations. Estimates of random variances-covariances between countries and years are available on request.
°.05 ≤ p-value < .10. °°.01 ≤ p-value < .05. °°°p < .005.

prosperity, regional homicide outlier, and democracy duration. To allow comparisons, in the second column of Table 4 we present a baseline model where the natural logarithm of homicide rates is a simple linear function of time.[6] The estimated average homicide rate over the forty-four countries of our sample in 1975 is 2.20[7] with a between-countries standard deviation of 1.12,[8] when only time is allowed to affect homicide rates. Thus, in 1975, homicide rates varied between a low of 0.24 and a high of 19.75 for 95 percent of the countries in our sample.[9] It might be worth noting that 87 percent of the variation of homicide rates is due to country rather than over-time differences. Homicide rates increased very slowly, on average by less than 1 percent by year (exp[0.007]). Thus, the estimated average homicide rate increased from 2.20 in 1975 to 2.21 (2.20 × 1.007) in 1976, to 2.23 in 1977, and so on. This result is consistent with Figure 2, which shows low exponential growth of average homicide rates for most of the second half of the twentieth century.

In the third column of Table 4 we present the results for our full model.[10] We include Wald tests (which follow χ^2 theoretical distributions; see Greene 1997) with their appropriate degrees of freedom for each set of covariates (i.e., the democracy measure, youth population proportion and country's prosperity, regional outliers, and any interactions with democracy duration). Wald tests measure the statistical significance of sets of covariates rather than individual effects and can only be compared to other sets of covariates that include the same number of coefficients and degrees of freedom. For example, Wald tests in Table 4 show that the percentage of young in the population and prosperity are jointly more important (25.77) in explaining variability of homicide rates than the democracy measures (17.31), and the democracy measures are jointly more important than the democracy stability measures (11.79). Overall, Table 4 shows that the Wald test for each set of covariates is highly statistically significant.

[O]ur results support the conclusion that homicide rates increase significantly over time for full democratic regimes, but not transitional regimes.

Table 4 shows that compared to autocratic regimes, homicide rates in transitional democratic regimes were significantly higher (we estimate this increase to be on average 54.4 percent [calculated as $\exp(0.434) - 1$]). Thus, in support of the modernization perspective, a shift from an autocratic to a transitional democratic regime produces a significant increase in homicide rates. By contrast, our fully democratic regime measure did not have a significant mean effect on homicide rates. In other words, there is no consistent cross-national connection between homicide rates and democratization for the fully democratic countries.

Table 4 also shows interaction effects between each democracy category and the duration of the respective regime. Homicide rates for the fully democratic and transitional regimes both increase over time (.0089 for transitional, .0093 for fully democratic); however, the effect reaches statistical significance at the conventional level ($p < .05$) only for the fully democratic regimes. We note in passing that the effect for transitional democratic regimes is statistically significant at the $p < .10$ level. Thus, our results support the conclusion that homicide rates increase significantly over time for full democratic regimes, but not transitional regimes. According to Table 4, the mean effect of time (.0015) is not individually significant.

All the control variables in Table 4 are statistically significant with effects in the expected direction. Thus, countries with a higher proportion of their population between the ages of fifteen and twenty-four have significantly higher homicide rates, while countries with greater economic prosperity (based on the scale derived from the Gini Index and GDP per capita) have lower homicide rates. The three regional variables show especially high homicide rates for Eastern European and Latin American/Caribbean countries and for the United States.[11] The intercept implies that in 1975 the average homicide rate for a hypothetical country (apart from the United States, Eastern Europe, or Latin America/Caribbean) of average percentage of population fifteen to twenty-four years old and average prosperity under autocracy is effectively zero. If this fictitious country came from Eastern Europe or Latin America/Caribbean, it would have had average homicide rates of 4.007 and 2.793, respectively (calculated as exp[1.3951 − 0.0075] and exp[1.0345 − 0.0075], respectively; see Table 4]. The East European effect is strongly influenced by the high homicide rates for Estonia.[12]

Discussion and Conclusions

We argued above that a civilization perspective is consistent with the prediction that violent crime rates will decline as autocratic regimes give way to democratic ones. Contrary to this argument, we did not find that homicide rates were significantly lower in full democracies than in autocracies. We argued above that a conflict perspective is consistent with the argument that the market economies associated with democratic countries will increase rates of violent crime as they move away from autocracy and toward democracy. Contrary to this argument, we did not find that full democracies had on average higher homicide rates than autocracies. Finally, we argued above that a modernization perspective suggests that violent crime rates will be curvilinear with the highest rates in countries that are transitioning between autocracy and democracy. Consistent with the modernization perspective, our results show that countries moving from autocratic to transitional democracies experienced a significant increase in homicide rates. By contrast, homicide rates of full democracies were not on average significantly different from countries with autocratic governments. In light of this last finding, future research should attempt to determine the country characteristics that are associated with decreasing violence and investigate how these characteristics may be sustained during democratization.

Our finding that the longer a country remains democratic, the higher its homicide rates challenges the usual way that modernization is expected to explain crime rates over time. Once a country achieves modernization as epitomized by a fully democratic political system, modernization theory does not predict that its violent crime rates should continue to increase. In fact, this outcome is more in keeping with conflict explanations that see increasing violent crime rates as an inevitable outgrowth of the market economies thus far universally associated with full democracies. So, our direct test of the democracy scale best supports a modernization interpretation, while our more indirect test of stability of homicide rates for full and transitional democracies over time (that is, the tests for interaction with years of fully democratic and transitional democratic regimes) is supportive of a conflict perspective.

While common theoretical perspectives on crime have generally been longitudinal, most prior research has been based on cross-sectional data. Moreover, most studies of cross-national violent crime have been limited to a handful of highly industrialized countries. In this study we were able to assemble a database larger than any other published source of which we are aware. Although our data include a disproportionate number of highly industrialized countries, we were able to also include an unusually large number of industrializing countries in the analysis.

[It is possible] that it is not modernization that is driving crime, but social disorganization, and that the extent to which highly modernized countries have low levels of social disorganization varies.

While we have relied on the most complete cross-national homicide data that are currently available, our analysis is nevertheless based on a nonrandom sample that seriously underrepresents less than fully democratic countries. For the year 2000, our data include democracy rankings for 161 countries; 34 of these (21.1 percent) are rated as full democracies. Our analysis includes 29 of these 34 countries (85.3 percent). By contrast, of the 127 countries rated as less than full democracies in the year 2000, our data set includes only 15 (11.8 percent). It is of course possible that if we had data on all countries in the world, our conclusions about the connection between transitional democracies and homicide rates would change.

Although most criminological tests of modernization theory to date have simply examined the cross-sectional impact of level of economic development on crime rates, the theoretical basis of Durkheim's (1947, 1950) arguments about modernization and crime are more broadly rooted in the concept of social disorganization. Compared with industrialized societies, industrializing societies are more likely to experience rapid crime increases because the transition from traditional to modern society is associated with a breakdown of the normative order characterized by growing social disorganization. This raises the possibility that it is not modernization that is driving crime, but social disorganization, and that the extent to which highly modernized countries have low levels of social disorganization varies. Thus, fully democratic societies may enjoy many characteristics associated with low crime rates. But at the same time, they may well also develop characteristics associated with rising crime rates. Our research suggests that whatever these criminogenic characteristics are, they generally increase over time. Conversely, it may also be the case that some countries that score relatively low on democracy indicators may nevertheless have low levels of social disorganization.

Longitudinal tests of civilization, modernization, and conflict perspectives have been rare in cross-national comparative criminology. This research provides little support for the civilization prediction that crime rates should gradually decline with the "civilizing" spread of democracy—at least not since 1950. As predicted by the conflict perspective, we do find that violent crime rates of full democracies have increased during the period spanned by our data. However, contrary to the conflict perspective, we do not find that fully democratic countries have on average higher homicide rates than other countries. Instead, and as predicted by the modernization perspective, countries that are transitioning between autocracy and full democracy have the greatest increases in homicide rates.

During the third wave of democratization, policy makers in many countries have been concerned about rapid increases in violent crime rates. We hear these reports in particular from the emerging democracies of Eastern Europe and the former Soviet Union, the fledgling democracies of Latin America, and the emerging democracies in Africa and Asia. Our results suggest that this concern about crime in transitional societies is not merely alarmist overreaction. But the results also suggest that if transitional democracies can continue to move toward full democracy, their crime rates may eventually begin to decline. But finally, our results also show that attaining full democracy does not solve national crime problems permanently. At least for the second half of the twentieth century, the full democracies in this study experienced slow but steady increases in violent crime rates.

Appendix
Technical Description of Methods Used

Our data are organized according to what Snijders and Bosker (1999, 166) described as "unbalanced repeated measures" and can be appropriately analyzed using a hierarchical linear model approach (Raudenbush 1995; Goldstein 1995). The main advantage of the multilevel approach (as opposed, for instance, to panel data analysis) is that it is more efficient at dealing with unbalanced or incomplete data structures (Snijders and Bosker 1999). In addition to estimating fixed effects of time and/or country-specific explanatory variables on the dependent variable (as in conventional regression analysis), this method allows also for the estimation of within and between units of analysis variability of the predicted values. As noted in the text, the units of analysis of our multilevel models are at two levels: (1) *time*, denoted by $t = 1, 2, \ldots, T_i$, where T_i is the total number of years of annual data for a country up to a maximum of 51; and (2) *country*, denoted by $i = 1, 2, \ldots, 44$, where 44 is the total number of countries in the sample. Random variance of the intercept at a higher level of aggregation, region (classified as Northwest Europe, Southwest Europe, East Europe, North America, Latin America/the Caribbean, Asia, Oceania, Israel, and Mauritius), was statistically insignificant according to a Wald test (which is χ^2 distributed) with one degree of freedom (results available on request).

In the following empirical models, the natural logarithm of homicide rates, $\ln(h_{ti})$, is a function of time, $F_i(t)$; a set of s explanatory country-level variables, denoted by x_{qi}; l year-level variables denoted by x_{qti}; and level 1 residuals (e_{ti}), which are assumed to have a joint normal distribution $N(0, \Sigma)$. In the estimated models below, the variance of level 1 residuals (i.e., e_{ti}) is a quadratic function of time, where $\text{var}[e_{0ti} + e_{1ti}(t - t_0)] = \sigma^2_{e0} - 2\sigma_{e01}(t - t_0) + \sigma^2_{e1}(t - t_0)^2$ (Goldstein et al. 1998). We centered time here around the sample mean, $t_0 = 1975$.

The expected natural logarithm of the homicide rates is given by $\ln(\hat{h}_{ti}) = X_{ti}b + \Sigma^{q=p}_{q=0} u_{qi} z_{qti} + \Sigma^{q=Q}_{q=p+1} u_{qi} z_{qi}$ $t = 1, \ldots, T_i$, $i = 1, \ldots, 44$, where $q = 0, 1, \ldots, Q$, with $Q + 1$ being the total number of random coefficients in the model including the intercept and time; X_{ti} is a row vector of $K (K \geq Q)$ covariates for the tith country-year combination, including the intercept, time, and possible interactions; b is a vector of K estimated coefficients or fixed effects on $\ln(\hat{h}_{ti})$; $z_{0ti} = 1$, $z_{1ti} = (t_{ti} - t_0)$, $z_{qti} = x_{qti}$, for $q = 2, \ldots, p$ (with $p \leq l$) are the time-country measured characteristics with random effects for the tith country-year combination; $z_{qi} = x_{qj}$, for $q = p + 1, p + 2, \ldots, Q$ refers to the $Q - p \leq s$ country-specific covariates with random effects for the ith country; and $(u_{qi}) \sim N(0, \Omega_u)$ is the random departure from the ith country (Goldstein 1995).

Notes

1. Skewness of the distribution of ln(homicide rate) is considerably lower (0.34) than that of the original distribution of homicide rates (5.21). Similarly, taking the natural logarithms of the raw homicide rates decreased kurtosis from 39.75 to 3.03. Thus, the distribution of the transformed series, that is, ln(homicide rate), approximates the Gaussian.

2. The Gurr et al. (Gurr 1974; Gurr, Jaggers, and Moore 1990; Jaggers and Gurr 1995; Marshall and Jaggers 2003) democracy scale has been criticized for capturing only procedural aspects of democracy and failing to measure consensual democratic procedures and aspects of consolidated democracy (Bollen and Paxton 2000; Kruzman, Werum, and Bukhart 2002; Munch and Verkuilen 2002). We therefore experimented with several other democracy measures before choosing this scale, including measures developed by Freedom House (2002) and Bollen (1993). However, these other scales are highly correlated with the Gurr et al. scale, which also produced the largest and most diverse sample of countries for analysis.

3. Professor Tryggvi Thor Herbertsson kindly provided Gini coefficients for Iceland.

4. We also included three dummy variables to account for major historic changes in the collection of the homicide data series. First, until 1963, homicide statistics for France included Algeria. Second, after 1991, our data for West Germany are for unified Germany. And finally, after 1992, our data for Czechoslovakia are from only the Czech Republic. However, since none of these measures had a significant effect on the results (available on request), they have been excluded from the present models.

5. The main advantage of the multilevel approach (as opposed, for instance, to panel data analysis) is that it is more efficient at dealing with unbalanced or incomplete data structures (Snijders and Bosker 1999).

6. A quadratic term of time, that is, $(t - t_0)^2$, was also fitted but showed no statistically significant fixed or random effects.

7. This is calculated as $\exp(0.7879)$ from Table 4.

8. The total standard deviation (over countries and years) of the estimated mean homicide rates in 1975 is 1.199 calculated as $\sqrt{(1.2535 + 0.1838)}$; results available on request.

9. The lower and upper boundaries of homicide rate confidence intervals are calculated as $\exp(0.7879 - 1.96 \times 1.12)$ and $\exp(0.7879 + 1.96 \cdot 1.12)$, respectively; results available on request.

10. Each estimated coefficient in Table 4, $b_k (k = 0, 1, \ldots, K)$, gives, in general, the change in the predicted dependent variable, $\ln(\hat{h}_{ti})$, due to a unit increase in the respective covariate. Most covariates in this study are binary or nominal; therefore, b_k reflects the change in the predicted dependent variable due to the respective characteristic as opposed to the reference characteristic or base. Because the dependent variable in this study is the natural logarithm of homicide rates, the exponent of each estimated coefficient,

that is, $\exp(b_k)$, gives the multiplicative effect on predicted homicide rates due to a unit increase of the respective covariate or due to assuming the respective characteristic rather than the reference one.

11. The regional dummy variables of East Europe and Latin America/Caribbean do not significantly affect the slope of the relationship between homicide rates and democracy. Interaction effects between each of these dummy variables and the democracy scale were fitted in a preliminary analysis and were essentially zero. Similarly, income inequality was not found to interact with the democracy scale in affecting homicide rates.

12. Indeed, the effect of Estonia on homicide growth rates was found to be 2.26 in an estimated model, which differed from the one presented here by including a dummy variable for this country rather than the entire region of East Europe.

References

Agnew, Robert. 1992. Foundation for a general strain theory of crime and delinquency. *Criminology* 30:47-87.

Applebaum, R. P. 1978. Marx's theory of the falling rate of profit. *American Sociological Review* 43:67-80.

Backman, Johan. 1998. *The inflation of crime in Russia: The social danger of the emerging markets.* Helsinki, Finland: National Research Institute of Legal Policy.

Barak, Gregg, ed. 2000. *Crime and crime control: A global view.* Westport, CT: Greenwood.

Bennett, Richard R. 1991. Development and crime: A cross-national time series analysis of competing models. *Sociological Quarterly* 32:343-63.

Bohm, R. M. 1982. Radical criminology: An explication. *Criminology* 19:565-89.

Bollen, Kenneth A. 1993. Liberal democracy: Validity and method factors in cross-national measures. *American Journal of Political Science* 37:1207-30.

Bollen, Kenneth A., and Pamela Paxton. 2000. Subjective measures of liberal democracy. *Comparative Political Studies* 33:58-86.

Bonger, Willem A. 1916. *Criminality and economic conditions.* Boston: Little, Brown.

Cebulak, Wojctech. 1996. Rising crime rates in Eastern Europe. *International Journal of Comparative and Applied Criminal Justice* 20:76-82.

Chambliss, William J. 1976. The state and criminal law. In *Whose law? What order?* ed. W. J. Chambliss and M. Mankoff. New York: Wiley.

Chirot, D., and T. D. Hall. 1982. World system theory. *Annual Review of Sociology* 8:81-106.

Clinard, M. B., and D. Abbott. 1973. *Crime in developing countries.* New York: Wiley.

Cloward, Richard A., and Lloyd E. Ohlin. 1960. *Delinquency and opportunity: A theory of delinquent gangs.* New York: Free Press.

Daniel, John, Roger Southall, and Jessica Lutchman, eds. 2005. *State of the nation: South Africa 2004-2005.* Capetown, South Africa: Human Sciences Research Council.

Davies, James C. 1962. Toward a theory of revolution. *American Sociological Review* 27:5-19.

Deninger, Klaus, and Lyn Squire. 1999. *Measuring inequality: A new database.* Washington, DC: The World Bank Group.

Diamond, Larry. 1999. *Developing democracy: Toward consolidation.* Baltimore: Johns Hopkins University Press.

Durkheim, Emile. 1947. *The division of labor in society.* Translated by George Simpson. New York: Free Press.

———. 1950. *Suicide: A study in sociology.* Translated by George Simpson. New York: Free Press.

Eisner, Manuel. 2001. Modernization, self-control, and lethal violence: The long-term dynamics of European homicide rates in theoretical perspective. *British Journal of Criminology* 41:618-38.

Elias, Norbert. 1939/1978. *The civilising process.* 2 vols. Translated by Edmund Jephcott. New York: Urizen Books.

Fajnzylber, Pablo, Daniel Lederman, and Norman Loayza. 1998. *Determinants of crime rates in Latin America and the world: An empirical assessment.* Viewpoint Series. Washington, DC: World Bank.

Fiala, Robert, and Gary LaFree. 1988. Cross-national determinants of child homicide. *American Sociological Review* 53:432-45.

Freedom House. 2002. *Freedom in the world: Annual rankings, 2001.* http://www.freedomhouse.org/.

Fukuyama, Francis. 1999. *The great disruption: Human nature and the reconstruction of social order.* New York: Free Press.

Goldstein, Harvey. 1995. *Multilevel statistical models.* 2nd ed. London: Arnold.

Goldstein, Harvey, Jon Rasbash, Ian Plewis, D. Draper, W. Browne, Min Yang, Geoffrey Woodhouse, and M. Healy. 1998. *A user's guide to MLwiN.* London: Institute of Education.

Greene, H. William. 1997. *Econometric analysis.* Upper Saddle River, NJ: Prentice Hall.

Gurr, Ted Robert. 1974. Persistence and change in political systems, 1800-1971. *American Political Science Review* 68:1482-1504.

———. 1981. Historical trends in violent crime: A critical review of the evidence. *Crime and Justice: An Annual Review of Research* 3:295-350.

Gurr, Ted Robert, Peter N. Grabosky, and Richard C. Hula. 1977. *The politics of crime and conflict: A comparative history of four cities.* Beverly Hills, CA: Sage.

Gurr, Ted Robert, Keith Jaggers, and Will Moore. 1990. The transformation of the Western state: The growth of democracy, autocracy, and state power since 1800. *Studies in Comparative International Development* 25:73-108.

Hansmann, H. B., and J. M. Quigley. 1982. Population heterogeneity and the sociogenesis of homicide. *Social Forces* 61:206-24.

Hopkins, T. K., and I. Wallerstein. 1981. Structural transformations of the world economy. In *Dynamics of world development,* ed. R. Rubinson. Beverly Hills, CA: Sage.

Hraba, Joseph, Wan-ning Bao, Frederick O. Lorentz, and Zdenka Pechacova. 1998. Perceived risk of crime in the Czech Republic. *Journal of Research in Crime and Delinquency* 35:225-43.

Huntington, Samuel P. 1993. *The third wave: Democratization in the late twentieth century.* Norman: University of Oklahoma Press.

Jaggers, Keith, and Ted Robert Gurr. 1995. Tracking democracy's third wave with the Polity data. *Journal of Peace Research* 32:469-82.

Kalish, Carol B. 1988. *International crime rates: Bureau of Justice Statistics special report.* Washington, DC: Government Printing Office.

Karstedt, Suzanne. 2003. Legacies of a culture of inequality: The Janus-face of crime in post-communist societies. *Crime, Law and Social Change* 40:295-320.

Kruzman, Charles, Regina Werum, and Ross E. Bukhart. 2002. Democracy's effects on economic growth: A pooled time-series analysis, 1951-1980. *Studies in Comparative International Development* 37:3-33.

LaFree, Gary. 1999. A summary and review of cross-national comparative studies of homicide. In *Homicide studies: A sourcebook of social research*, ed. D. Smith and M. A. Zahn. Thousand Oaks, CA: Sage.

———. 2005. Evidence for elite convergence in cross-national homicide victimization trends, 1956 to 2000. *Sociological Quarterly* 46:191-211.

LaFree, Gary, and Kriss A. Drass. 2002. Counting crime booms among nations: Evidence for homicide victimization rates, 1956 to 1998. *Criminology* 40:769-99.

Lodhi, Abdul Qaiyum, and Charles Tilly. 1973. Urbanization, crime and collective violence in nineteenth century France. *American Journal of Sociology* 79:296-318.

Marshall, Monty G., and Keith Jaggers. 2003. *Polity IV Project: Political Regime Characteristics and Transitions, 1800-1999. Dataset users manual.* College Park: University of Maryland, Center for International Development and Conflict Management.

Mendez, Juan E., Guillermo O'Donnell, and Paulo Sergio Pinheiro. 1999. *The (un)rule of law and the underprivileged in Latin America.* South Bend, IN: University of Notre Dame Press.

Merton, Robert K. 1938. Social structure and anomie. *American Sociological Review* 3:672-82.

Messner, Steven F. 1989. Economic discrimination and societal homicide rates: Further evidence of the cost of inequality. *American Sociological Review* 54:597-611.

Messner, Steven F., and Richard Rosenfeld. 1997. Political restraint of the market and levels of criminal homicide: A cross-national application of institutional-anomie theory. *Social Forces* 75:1393-1416.

Mexican Health Foundation. 1999. *Trends and empirical causes of violent crime in Mexico: Final report.* Mexico City: Mexican Health Foundation.

Montinola, Gabriella R., and Robert W. Jackman. 2002. Sources of corruption: A cross-country study. *British Journal of Political Science* 32:147-70.

Munch, Gerardo L., and Jay Verkuilen. 2002. Conceptualising and measuring democracy. *Comparative Political Studies* 35:5-35.

Neopolitan, Jerome L. 1996. Cross-national crime data: Some unaddressed problems. *Journal of Criminal Justice* 19:95-112.

——— 1997. *Cross-national crime: A research review and sourcebook*. Westport, CT: Greenwood.

Neuman, W. Lawrence, and Ronald J. Berger. 1988. Competing perspectives on cross-national crime: An evaluation of theory and evidence. *Sociological Quarterly* 29:281-313.

Ortega, Suzanne T., Jay Corzine, Cathleen Burnett, and Tracey Poyer. 1992. Modernization, age structure and regional context: A cross-national study of crime. *Sociological Spectrum* 12:257-77.

Osterberg, Eva. 1996. Criminality, social control, and the early modern state: Evidence and interpretations in Scandinavian historiography. In *The civilization of crime: Violence in town and country since the middle ages*, ed. E. A. Johnson and E. H. Monkkonen. Urbana: University of Illinois Press.

Potter, D., D. Goldblatt, M. Kiloh, and P. Lewis, eds. 1997. *Democratization*. Cambridge, UK: Polity.

Pratt, Travis C., and Timothy W. Godsey. 2003. Social support, inequality, and homicide: A cross-national test of an integrated model. *Criminology* 41:611-43.

Quinney, Richard. 1977. *Class, state and crime*. New York: McKay.

Raudenbush, Stephen W. 1995. Hierarchical linear models to study the effects of social context on development. In *The analysis of change*, ed. J. M. Gottman. Mahwah, NJ: Lawrence Erlbaum.

Reza, A., J. Q. Mercy, and E. Krug. 2000. A global concern: The impact of violence-related deaths throughout the world. Manuscript, Division of Violence Prevention, National Center for Injury Prevention and Control, Atlanta, GA.

Savelsberg, Joachim J. 1995. Crime, inequality, and justice in Eastern Europe: Anomie, domination, and revolutionary change. In *Crime and inequality*, ed. J. Hagan and R. Peterson. Stanford, CA: Stanford University Press.

Savolainen, Jukka. 2000. Inequality, welfare state, and homicide: Further support for the institutional anomie theory. *Criminology* 38:1021-42.

Shelley, Louise I. 1981. *Crime and modernization: The impact of industrialization and urbanization on crime*. Carbondale: Southern Illinois University Press.

Smelser, Neil. 1962. *Theory of collective behavior*. New York: Free Press.

Snijders, Tom A. B., and Roel J. Bosker. 1999. *Multilevel analysis: An introduction to basic and advanced multilevel modelling*. London: Sage.

Spierenburg, Pieter. 1996. Long-term trends in homicide: Theoretical reflections and Dutch evidence, fifteenth to twentieth centuries. In *The civilization of crime: Violence in town and country since the middle ages*, ed. E. A. Johnson and E. H. Monkkonen. Urbana: University of Illinois Press.

Spitzer, S. 1975. Toward a Marxian theory of deviance. *Social Problems* 22:638-51.

Stamatel, Janet P., Nora Arato, and Christopher S. Dunn. 1998 The Americanization of juvenile delinquency? A comparison of Hungary, Poland and the US. *Security Journal* 11:243-53.

Sung, Hung-En. 2004. Democracy and organized crime activities: Evidence from 59 countries. *Security Journal* 17:21-34.

Taylor, Ian, Paul Walton, and Jock Young. 1973. *The new criminology*. London: Routledge & Kegan Paul.

Tilly, Charles, Louise Tilly, and Richard Tilly. 1975. *The rebellious century, 1830-1930*. Cambridge, MA: Harvard University Press.

Useem, Bert. 1985. Disorganization and the New Mexico prison riot of 1980. *American Sociological Review* 50:677-88.

Wallerstein, Immanuel. 1979. *The capitalist world economy*. Cambridge: Cambridge University Press.

Weber, Max. 1956/1978. *Economy and society: An outline of interpretive sociology*. Edited by Guenther Roth and Claus Wittich. Berkeley: University of California Press.

World Health Organization. 2001. *World health statistics annual, 2000*. Geneva, Switzerland: World Health Organization.

Democracy, Values, and Violence: Paradoxes, Tensions, and Comparative Advantages of Liberal Inclusion

By
SUSANNE KARSTEDT

Democracies represent an institutional framework and a way of life that is, almost by definition, nonviolent. Contrasting with this ideal are two simultaneous global trends: an extension of democratic regimes and rising levels of violent crime. This article explores this seeming gap between democracy's ideal and reality. The author identifies *comparative advantages* and *disadvantages* for both democracy and autocracy in restraining violent crime. Comparative advantages of two core democratic values—individualism and egalitarianism—are examined with data from a sample of twenty-six countries. Results show that compared to collectivistic and authoritarian patterns, individualistic and egalitarian values reduce levels of violence. Societies with high levels of violent crime are concentrated among autocracies, which mostly have collectivistic and authoritarian values. In contrast, democratic societies are mostly characterized by individualistic and egalitarian values and have lower levels of violent crime. Democratic values have comparative advantages if they are fostered by democratic practices and institutions.

Keywords: democracy; autocracy; democratic values; violent crime; individualism/collectivism; egalitarianism/authoritarianism

Ideally conceived, democracies understand themselves as nonviolent. "Violence is anathema to its spirit and substance" (Keane 2004, 1); democracies are strongly committed to nonviolence, and almost by definition they represent an institutionalized framework and a way of life that ensures nonviolent means to share power between communities of people with widely differing values and beliefs. In democracies, institutions ensure that the use of violence

Susanne Karstedt has a chair of criminology and is director of the Centre for Criminological Research in the Research Institute for Law, Politics and Justice at Keele University, United Kingdom. She also teaches at the International Institute of the Sociology of Law in Onati, Spain. Her main research interests include (1) cross-national and cross-cultural research on violence and corruption; (2) cross-national research on moral economies and middle-class crime; (3) emotions, crime, and justice; and (4) public opinion on transitional justice.

DOI: 10.1177/0002716206288248

is controlled and those who use it are held accountable. Both democratic values and institutions were developed and conceived of as remedies against violent conflicts in the bloody religious wars and revolutions from the seventeenth to the nineteenth centuries, and they are based on the premise of the *containment* of violence (Tilly 1992, 2004).

This account of inherently nonviolent democracies, as it emerges from recent political theory and philosophy (Keane 2004), however, is not supported by empirical evidence for the second half of the twentieth century. True, the incredible amount of violence and unspeakable atrocities the world witnessed during the first half of the century occurred between and was perpetrated by authoritarian states like Germany, the Soviet Union, and Japan, which dominated Europe and other parts of the world. But in its second half, when the trend toward authoritarianism had been turned around at least in Western Europe and Japan, and finally started to turn around in the mid-1980s as a "third wave" of democracy took hold in Latin America and Eastern Europe, both democracy *and* violence were simultaneously on the rise. Three trends, which will be explored in more detail in the following section, contributed to the increase of violence in democracies during this period. First, interpersonal violence increased in the course of the process of democratization in the countries of Eastern Europe and Latin America, as well as in South Africa (LaFree and Tseloni 2006 [this volume]; Pridemore and Kim 2006 [this volume]; Karstedt forthcoming). Second, increasing levels of ethnic rebellion and violence, in particular in the form of ethnic cleansing, coincided with ostensible democratization in the southern and later in the northern hemisphere (Gurr 1993, 2000; Mann 2005). Thus, for the second half of the twentieth century since 1945, estimates for the victims of genocide and mass killings worldwide as distinguished from war deaths range from 9 to 20 million in more than forty episodes of genocide and mass killings (Valentino 2004: 255; Gurr 1993).[1] Finally, since the 1960s, violent crime in the established Western democracies considerably increased, and a number of these countries experienced "booms" of violent crime (Eisner 2001; LaFree and Drass 2002). Late modern democracies, it seemed, had lost their capacities to contain interpersonal violent crime (see Karstedt [2001a, 2005] for an overview).

These disquieting facts clearly challenge any ideal conception of democracy as inherently nonviolent and raise two related questions. First, are democracies actually criminogenic producers of criminal violence? Second, are the institutions of democracy and the normally peaceful habits of their citizenry extremely fragile so that democracies can quickly turn toward violence (see, e.g., Mann 2005, chap. 1)? Democracies emerge as Janus-faced in this context. On one hand, they

NOTE: Earlier versions of this article were presented at a conference of the Democracy Collaborative at the University of Maryland, 2002; the World Congress of Criminology, Rio de Janeiro, 2003; the GERN conference on History of Violence in Ferrara, 2003; and the National Europe Centre at the Australian National University, 2004. I would like to thank John Braithwaite, Boerge Bakken, Manuel Eisner, Willem de Haan, Gary LaFree, Steve Messner, Tom Tyler, and Peter Waldmann for their comments and ideas. I am particularly indebted to the Australian National University for a generous Visiting Fellowship, during which I drafted most of this article.

appear to carry with them the possibility of high levels of individual and collective violence in contrast to more autocratic "law and order" regimes, and also to generate a wide range of "anomic tendencies" responsible for violence. On the other hand, it seems equally possible that democracies have built-in mechanisms that help them to retain and return to lower levels of violence than autocratic states, even after periods of mounting violence.

What values, institutions, and practices of citizens contribute to this Janus-face nature of democracies, making them more peaceful at times but more violent at other times?

In this article, I address both these possibilities. Ultimately, I seek to identify those generic features of democratic societies or "mechanisms" (Elster 1989, chap. 1)[2] that are capable of sustaining relatively low levels of violence in democracies and those that increase violence. When contrasted with autocracies, what are the comparative advantages or disadvantages of democracies in containing violence? What values, institutions, and practices of citizens contribute to the Janus-face nature of democracies, making them more peaceful at times but more violent at other times? In this article, I conceptualize democracy as a project of "liberal inclusion" and contrast this with "repressive inclusion" as the defining feature of authoritarian states. This approach stresses the nonstate and noninstitutional features of both democracy and autocracy, that, is the social mechanisms, values, and practices in contrast to institutional and state characteristics.

Although collective violence is also closely related to these issues (see Mann 2005; Rummel 1997), in this analysis I focus only on individual and interpersonal criminal violence. In particular, I explore the relation between core values of democracy—individualism and egalitarianism—and individual violent crime with data from twenty-six countries. The exploration of values in democracies as contrasted with those in autocracies seems to be an important step in examining whether these provide democracies with a comparative advantage. Values are the foundation for democracy's practices and institutions, which in turn foster democratic values. Thus, Jaggers and Gurr (1995, 476) found that "strong democratic institutions produce strong democratic practices." Recent studies based on the World Values Survey demonstrated that democratic values increase the probability of the development of democratic practices and institutions, reach higher levels in established democracies, and develop concomitantly with the process of democratization (Welzel and Inglehart 2005; Inglehart and Welzel 2005; Welzel 2002).

Democracy, Democratization, and Violence: Three Trends and Perspectives

The three trends of rising violence as described above have fuelled a deepening skepticism as to the capacity of democracy to deliver on its own promise of nonviolence. Rising violence has affected countries in the transition toward democracy as well as mature and established democracies. What is the role of genuinely democratic practices and institutions in each of these trends?

[T]hree trends of rising violence . . .
have fuelled a deepening skepticism
as to the capacity of democracy
to deliver on its own promise
of nonviolence.

The recent shift toward democracy came with an abrupt and extraordinary rise of crime mainly in the postcommunist countries. In particular, violent crime has been seen as indicative of the profound changes that turned these societies and the life of their citizenry upside down and as a severe threat to the still fragile market economies and democratic institutions in these countries (Pridemore and Kim 2006; Pridemore 2005). Outside of Europe, South Africa was emblematic of how the shift toward democracy was accompanied by a wave of violent crime that made its cities among the most violent in the world (Steinberg 2001). Some of the causes that have been identified include high levels of social inequality not attenuated by democratic practices; rampant market individualism that makes the loss of collectivistic solidarity deeply felt (Pridemore and Kim 2006 [this volume]); shortcomings in the democratic institutions of criminal justice and the rule of law; and a lack of civil society and its social bonds, termed as "civilizational incompetence" by Sztompka (1993; see Karstedt [2003] for a overview). In sum, the shortcomings of transitional democracies and the incomplete process of democratization are seen as root causes for the accompanying wave of violent crime. In a similar vein, Caldeira and Holston (1999) attributed increasing violence and insecurity among the citizens of Latin America's transitional democracies to what they label as "disjunctive democracy." While electoral and political democracies are now established in many Latin American countries, lawless violence pervades their institutions and indicates a "clear abdication of democratic authority" (Mendez 1999, 19).

Common to these analyses is a *deficiency perspective* that violent crime is the result of a not yet fully established democracy and of particular deficiencies and maladjustments that arise during the process of democratization. Not the generic features of democracy, but the incomplete development of its institutions and practices are seen by these authors as the root causes of violent crime. The deficiency perspective has, however, a more troubling side to it. Here, the turbulences created during the transition, and in particular the rise of crime and violence, are attributed to what are deemed *genuine* deficiencies of democracy and, consequently, as disadvantages when compared with autocratic regimes: the liberties democracies provide, the inequality they produce, and the diversity of beliefs and patterns of behavior, for which they open up a new social space that lacks the tight social control of more authoritarian regimes (see also Rodrigues 2006 [this volume]).

Transitions toward *democracy [are]* . . .
transitions from *authoritarian
and autocratic states, and the waves
of crime and violence during
the transition period might be* . . .
a legacy of the autocratic past.

From the deficiency perspective, transitions *toward* democracy tend to be mainly defined by its final goal, namely, the establishment of democracy. However, transitions are also transitions *from* authoritarian and autocratic states, and the waves of crime and violence during the transition period might be equally seen as a legacy of the autocratic past. From the perspective of the starting point of the transition, the downfall of the autocratic state was preceded by increasing tensions, a loss of legitimacy of its institutions, and declining trust of its citizenry (Los 2003). The legacy of the autocratic state in the transition process is not only an immediate consequence of its downfall, but it implies deeper and built-in anomic tendencies that affect the transition process in the long run (Waldmann 2002, 2003; Mendez, O'Donnell, and Pinheiro 1999). Consequently, the deficiency perspective is misleading as it overrates the impact of democratization and underrates the effect of *de-autocratization*.

The *vulnerability perspective* contending that democracies, their institutions, and their practices are fragile and easily destroyed has mainly been developed in relation to ethnic violence. Collective violence in the form of ethnic cleansing and individual ethnic violence dramatically increased during the most recent waves of democratization (Gurr 1993, 2000; Mann 2005, 505). "Murderous ethnic cleansing has been moving around the world as it modernized and democratized," and it is the "dark side of democracy" claimed Michael Mann (2005, 4). He argued that democracies are in danger of sliding into ethnic violence through the perversion of either liberal or socialist ideals of democracy because these are geared toward ethnic homogenization and inclusion. According to Mann, democracies have built-in mechanisms that make them particularly vulnerable to violence and violent crime in multiethnic environments.

The recognition and encouragement of individual choice, autonomy, and diversity, and simultaneously the effort to integrate these into the inclusionary project of democracy, are . . . at the core of the potential links between democracy and violence.

Finally, the perspective developed in relation to the increase of violent crime in mature Western democracies combines two arguments. In these democracies, it appeared that specific democratic values and practices had become too dominant— the *surplus perspective*—and had spiraled out of control or were not properly balanced by institutional regimes—the *imbalance perspective*. Both a surplus of democracy as well as a lack of balance were held responsible for steeply rising levels of violence in mature democracies. In fact, established Western democracies in North America and Western Europe had suffered from an increase of violent crime and disorder since the mid-1960s (Gurr 1977). At this time, the secular decline of violent crimes—as indicated by the decrease of homicide rates—had come to a halt in these countries. It can be assumed that the 1950s marked a historical low level of homicide in Europe and the United States. The considerable increase affected large democracies like the United States as well as the small democracies of Western Europe like the Netherlands or the Scandinavian states (Eisner 2005). Among the causes likely responsible, individualism, individual autonomy, and the related values of self-expression figured prominently. Violence was an indicator of a deepening crisis of Western democracies, in which rampant market and consumer individualism had spiraled out of control, diminished individual self-control, and destroyed patterns of informal social control (see for an overview Karstedt [2001a]; Eisner [2001]). Thus, a surplus of core democratic values and the forces unleashed by democratic practices had set Western democracies on a path toward violent crime.

The increase of violence coincided with an ostensible decline of generalized trust in the population as well as a decline of trust in institutions in all Western democracies (Pharr, Putnam, and Dalton 2000). Part of this process was a loss of legitimacy of vital institutions of democracies like the education system, the system of social welfare, and the criminal justice system, which LaFree (1998) identified as decisive in the increase of violent street crime in the United States during the 1960s and early 1970s. Messner and Rosenfeld (1994) argued that imbalances within democratic society, mainly between markets and those institutions that restrain their forces and impact on society, are responsible for the wave of violent crime that began in the United States in the 1960s. In their analysis, they referred—like LaFree—to a number of institutions that if not part of the political system of democracy itself are nonetheless vital for supporting it, including education, civic participation, and welfare regimes that level out inequalities and support egalitarian values on which modern democracies are built.

Both the vulnerability perspective and the surplus-imbalance perspective point toward built-in mechanisms in democratic regimes that affect their capacities to contain and restrict interpersonal violence. They attribute this neither to deficiencies of democratic institutions and practices nor to the presence of nondemocratic practices. Instead, the very institutions, practices, or values of democracy are seen as encouraging violent crime, as are in particular specific *dynamics* of democracies that affect their capacities to restrict violent crime.

The Paradoxes of Democracy: The Project of Liberal Inclusion

Democracy is a multidimensional concept, ranging from definitions based exclusively on institutional frameworks (e.g., Przeworski et al. 2000; Held 2005) to complex and integrated measures that include political and civil rights, democratic practices, values, and finally a diverse set of institutional arrangements in society, including welfare, education, industrial relations, and the legal system (Jaggers and Gurr 1995; Inkeles 1993; Lauth, Pickel, and Welzel 2000; Welzel 2002; Inglehart and Welzel 2005; O'Donnell, Cullel, and Iazetta 2004). This reflects the range of and distinction between merely formal electoral democracy and genuinely "effective liberal democracy" (Inglehart and Welzel 2005, 149). "Civil society" is universally seen as a necessary condition for effective liberal democracies (as opposed to low-intensity democracy) as it counterbalances state and majority power by complex relationships between the citizenry, establishes the dominance of choice, and produces trust among citizens (Keane 2004, 43; Inglehart and Welzel 2005, 151).[3] Civil society in particular provides a decisive link between democratic institutions and values. Cross-national research confirms that formal democratic institutions, different dimensions of effective democracy, and democratic values are strongly linked (Jaggers and Gurr 1995, 446; Inglehart and Welzel 2005, 154).

I start from the notion that liberal democracy is a *project of inclusion* of a plurality of people, classes, values, and practices.[4] This implies that democratic societies are historically based on the exclusionary notion of the nation-state (see Held 2005) and that the project of liberal inclusion is defined by its boundaries. Democratic societies have to deal with the tensions that arise from inclusionary values and practices, on one hand, and on the other hand from recognition of plural interests, values, and differences of class and ethnicity. The recognition and encouragement of individual choice, autonomy, and diversity, and simultaneously the effort to integrate these into the inclusionary project of democracy are—I argue—at the core of the potential links between democracy and violence and are constitutive for democracy's comparative advantages and disadvantages in contrast to repressive inclusion of autocratic regimes.

The tensions between the inclusionary mechanisms and procedures that modern democracies established and the autonomy and rights that they granted to individuals, as well as the tolerance that necessarily had to come with it, were seen clearly by one of the first observers of modern democracy, Alexis de Tocqueville (1935-1840/2000). In his analyses of the first democracy of modern times (the United States), he pointed to the paradox and inconsistencies that arise out of the innate tension between inclusion and individual autonomy. Democracy simultaneously gives rise to individual independence and high levels of conformity: the rights of individuals are counterbalanced by strong forces toward conformity. Majority rules imply dominance and authority and rely on submission at the same time that they provoke resistance. Tolerance and individual rights carry with them the simultaneous possibilities of strong belief and profound rejection of belief, of norm compliance and violation of norms. Tocqueville observed that egalitarian values coexist with envy, status differences, and social inequality. Democracy offers its citizens wide opportunities for deviant, licentious, and dangerous behavior and simultaneously reduces their desire to do what democracy allows them to do by establishing common and shared values and procedures that ensure the exertion of individual rights.[5]

Toqueville was convinced that the flaws of democracy could be overcome by more democracy (Elster 1999; Holmes 1993) or countervailing forces in its institutional arrangements. Thus, contemporary scholars have confirmed the seminal role of two cornerstones of democracy, the rule of law and fair trials for the acceptance of moral norms and sentences in case of criminal violation (Tyler 1990, 2003; Tyler and Blader 2000).

The pattern of core values of democracy reflects the tensions of liberal inclusion. It is prevalent to varying degrees in modern, industrialized countries, but it is most developed in liberal democracies (Triandis and Trafimov 2001; see also Karstedt 2001a, 2005). Democracies stress values that assign more importance to individuals than to groups and place individual rights before those of groups. Values of self-expression and choice appear as driving forces behind processes of democratization (Inglehart and Welzel 2005). These *individualistic* values override exclusionary boundaries of groups and integrate individuals on their own merits and not as members of groups. Furthermore, and linked to individualism, democracies stress values of equality as an underpinning of social mobility and inclusion, that is, *egalitarian* values. Finally, citizens in democracies are more willing to accept differences in values and behavior and are more inclined to include those who differ from themselves (Hofstede 1984, 1997; Triandis and Trafimov 2001; for relations to violence, see Karstedt 2001a, 2005; for toleration of deviance, see Inglehart 1997; Welzel 2002; Inglehart and Welzel 2005).

As Tocqueville observed, this value pattern was decisive for democracy but came with specific built-in antinomies and tensions. He saw the mechanisms that were capable of counteracting the innate tensions of democratic societies in the associations that citizens were capable of and free to develop in their communities. The associational bonds that develop within civil society provide mechanisms of outreach and generalized cooperation that can counterbalance individualistic practices. Values of tolerance of different views and lifestyles (even inequality) balanced by mechanisms of interpersonal trust, and individual autonomy balanced by mechanisms of social control, participation, and membership in associations and groups combine into a pattern of values and practices that can attenuate the innate tensions of democracy. Citizens engage with each other in "benevolent disinterest" (Hirschman 1988, 139), and cohesion in democracies is based on weak ties, comparatively low levels of consensus, and "pragmatic dissent" (Mann 1970; see Muller and Seligson 1994). It is important to stress the universal and generalized character of these relationships in contrast to the strong, but particularistic, bonds that dominate families, groups, and tightly knit communities. Generalized trust is strongly related to individualistic and egalitarian value patterns, and consequently democracies reach higher levels of generalized trust (Karstedt 2001b). Trust relationships are produced through universal bonds and the inclusionary mechanisms of democracy, with democratic institutions as equally strong providers and enforcers of these bonds.[6] These vital social bonds are endangered by processes like social inequality and ethnic or religious divisions that fractionalize society.[7]

The Janus-Face of Democracy:
Liberal Inclusion and Violence

In which ways does the inclusionary project of democracy contain violence on one hand and promote violent conflict on the other hand? As far as democracies rely on and enhance a particular value pattern through their institutions—individualistic and egalitarian values, as well as higher levels of trust and tolerance—the level of violence should be in principle lower within democratic societies. But democracies carry with them the possibility of high levels of violent conflicts—individual and collective violence—when built-in tensions within democracies reach high levels. This will happen when individualistic values of autonomy, self-expression, and self-assertion are not balanced by inclusionary mechanisms and sufficient mechanisms of social control; when structural inequality is high and thus egalitarian values are violated; when parts of the population are denied fairness and justice (see Tyler and Blader 2000); and when exclusionary processes affect specific groups of the population.

Mechanisms containing violence

When turning to those mechanisms that can keep levels of violence low in democracies, Durkheim's (1897/1979, 1900/1957, 1900) concept of moral individualism and its inclusionary impact is seminal. Durkheim argued that as societies became more individualistic, they developed a morality of individualism that was based on universal bonds and solidarity and not on the narrow range of tight bonds and group-centered solidarity that characterized traditional societies: violence as well as brutal and harsh punishments should decrease. Both Messner (1982) and Karstedt (2001a) provided evidence for Durkheim's claim of decreasing violence. In contrast, the Tocquevillean perspective stresses those mechanisms in democratic society that are capable of restraining the disruptive consequences of individualism. These are the universal bonds that develop in the form of trust as well as the bonds that unite citizens in civic associations. Studies that analyze the impact of social capital—measured as generalized trust—on violence generally confirm Tocqueville's claim. In cross-national studies, Lederman, Loayza, and Menéndez (2002) found that violence increased significantly (although the impact was small) along with a weakening of social capital. Rosenfeld, Messner, and Baumer (2001) found in a study of U.S. counties a complex causal pattern that showed a direct and negative impact of generalized trust on homicide rates, while civic engagement and participation had only indirect negative effects and were dependent on the level of deprivation. Sampson, Raudenbush, and Earls's (1997) study on collective efficacy provided further evidence of the impact of social bonds within communities as well as their bonds with institutions. They showed that collective efficacy reduces the level of violence even under the dire economic conditions in inner-city neighborhoods in the United States.

Mechanisms promoting violence

Democracies have a potential for waves of violence, or even continuously high levels of violence, if the built-in tensions of the liberal inclusionary project reach temporarily or continuously high levels. Thus, the process of increasing individualization and the dominance of values of self-expression had set democracies on a trajectory of social change that had weakened those forces that restrained individual self-assertion and autonomy. Not emancipation from social constraints as in the Durkheimian model, but detachment from vital social bonds and a decline of social control characterized this process. Established democracies today seem to be overwhelmed by the forces of individualization that they had set free in the first place: market individualism, autonomy, and self-expression values (Klages 1984; Inglehart 1997). Hagan et al. (1998) found that unrestricted hierarchical self-interest was related to violent behavior of juveniles. Eisner's (1997, 2001) claim that unrestricted values of self-expression were responsible for the violent turn in European democracies since the 1960s has been indirectly corroborated by findings from the World Values Survey (Inglehart and Welzel 2005, 154) that the more democracies mature, the higher they score on values of self-expression.

Tensions between egalitarian values and economic and social inequality are another source of violent conflicts and crime. Social and economic inequality is a strong predictor of violence in all societies (Messner and Rosenfeld 1998). However, it might have a particularly detrimental impact in democracies with highly developed egalitarian values, especially where liberal inclusion is endangered by ethnic fractionalization and economic discrimination against ethnic groups (see Karstedt 2001a). If democracies do not "make good" on their promises, it might elicit violent reaction among those who feel themselves to be victims of discrimination. Further tensions within the institutional framework and value patterns in democracies arise if these patterns are characterized by imbalances between the economic sphere and other institutions. Messner and Rosenfeld (1994) argued that markets and the values and attitudes that come with them need institutional restraints through welfare regimes, and the process of commodification needs to be counterbalanced by values of the common good and civic attitudes, which are important inclusionary values and practices. If such restraints and counterbalances fail or are at low levels, "institutional anomie" generates high levels of violence. The growing body of research that is based on this theory has mainly confirmed its core assumptions, and the theory seems to be particularly useful in explaining transitions to democracy that come with a transition to a market society, as in Eastern and Central Europe (Messner 2004; Savolainen 2000).

Autocracy, Totalitarianism, and Violence: Repressive Inclusion

In contrast to liberal democracies, modern autocratic states are based on repressive inclusion. The fascist states in Europe during the first half of the twentieth century, the communist states, as well as populist regimes particularly in Latin America all were inclusionary projects as far as they—ideologically and politically—explicitly tried to integrate the lower classes, different ethnicities, and economic interests. Like democracies, modern autocratic regimes not only promoted egalitarian values, but their practices and institutional patterns were geared toward equality (see also Mann 2005). However, while in communist Europe social inequality was—at least according to official measures[8]—lower than in many democracies where market societies and economic discrimination of minorities produced higher levels of social inequality, Latin American autocracies were among the most unequal societies of the world. Furthermore, as Mann (2005, 4) noted, stable authoritarian regimes are more successful in balancing the demands of powerful groups, in particular ethnic groups. This applies to the fascist regimes in the first half of the twentieth century in Europe, to some of the authoritarian regimes in Latin America, and presumably to the former Soviet Union and to the communist regimes in Central and Eastern Europe.

In the communist states in Eastern and Central Europe, inclusion was achieved through wiping out differences between classes, religion, lifestyles, beliefs, and values by imposing an overarching ideological system, prohibiting all those organizations and associations in which these can flourish, and substituting these finally by a unified state-run economic and social system. This produced what Sztompka (1993) has termed the "civilizational incompetence" of these countries; it is defined by high levels of distrust in others and institutions, lack of legitimacy in particular of the justice system, and prominently the lack of mechanisms to deal with a diversity of interests and the ensuing overt tensions (Nowotny 2002). The Latin American states took a much more etatist approach to inclusion that intruded less into society but relied more on continuous violent repression (Waldmann 2002, 2003; Huggins, Haritos-Fatouros, and Zimbardo 2002; Mendez, O'Donnell, and Pinheiro 1999). In both instances of repressive inclusion,[9] we find a high level of anomie that undermines social and legal norms and general compliance with them. The use of repressive constraints and mechanisms of control in the achievement of order comes with a considerable erosion of social and legal norms beneath the surface of "law and order" (Waldmann 2002, 11).

Because the implementation of security and order is not based on the rule of law, measures are applied arbitrarily and in a nonpredictable way. Norms, rules, and regulations become invalid as guidelines for behavior and lose their regulatory and inclusionary power. The fact that the rule of law is substituted by the "rule of power" on all levels of the state bureaucracy (Karstedt 1999; Hagan and Radoeva 1998) increases the feelings of powerlessness in the population and decreases the legitimacy of and trust in the authorities. Authorities use power, not the law, to impose far-reaching programs of economic and social modernization, thus increasing not only powerlessness but general feelings of lawlessness.[10] "Legal cynicism," which has been identified by Sampson and Bartusch (1998) as a source of violence, consequently should be widespread in autocracies (see also Waldmann 2002). As Mendez (1999, 19) observed for Latin American societies, "lawless violence" is as much exerted by the authorities as it prevails among the population.

The specific types of inequality and the values attached to these in authoritarian regimes can be identified as a further source of anomic tensions. Repressive inclusion relies on inequality of participation and power, and stable authoritarian regimes tend to govern by "divide-and-rule" between social and ethnic groups (Mann 2005, 5). As such, they promote collectivistic values and, consequently, tensions and conflicts between groups that generate violence. Notwithstanding their egalitarian ideology and overt political practice, the communist regimes in Central and Eastern Europe installed a system of privileges for the ruling elites that trickled down to the lowest levels of the bureaucracy (see Los 1988, 1990; Karstedt 1999) and produced a high level of covert economic inequality in these countries (Karstedt 2003). Autocratic regimes with capitalist economies exploit labor, and in transitions to autocracies income is frequently redistributed from labor to capital with the consequence of increasing social inequality (Przeworski et al. 2000, 168).

However, autocratic regimes can muster forms of social control unavailable in democracies that might be particularly successful in containing these tensions. State-run organizations control young people and include most of the citizens in one form or another. In particular, the former communist states in Europe established pervasive systems of social control. Collectivistic values mainly attached to social welfare might reduce tensions between social groups (see also Pridemore and Kim 2006 [this volume]). The repressive forms of control exerted by autocratic regimes and the far-reaching controls in totalitarian ones produced a certain level of order, and these states often reported comparatively low rates of violent crime. Crime statistics from these countries, in particular with regard to violence, are notoriously unreliable (Pridemore and Kim 2006 [this volume]), with the violence committed by authorities especially likely to be underreported. Thus Pridemore (2003), using mortality data, found that Russian homicide victimization rates were as high as or higher than in the United States for at least the past several decades.

Democracies, Autocracies, and Violence: Comparative Advantages and Disadvantages

Comparative advantages and disadvantages

Democracies and autocracies have both *comparative advantages and disadvantages* in their capacities to contain violence. Table 1 contrasts these for democracies and autocracies according to their dominant value patterns, their practices, and their institutions. Strong comparative advantages for democracies are their dominant value patterns of individualism and egalitarianism; practices that generate trust and civic engagement; and welfare institutions, the rule of law, and procedural justice. Strong comparative advantages of autocracies include

TABLE 1
CONTAINING VIOLENCE: COMPARATIVE ADVANTAGES
AND DISADVANTAGES OF DEMOCRACIES AND AUTOCRACIES

	Comparative Advantages	Comparative Disadvantages
Democracy	Value patterns: high individualism; egalitarianism; tolerance Practices: generalized trust; pragmatic dissent; civic engagement and participation Institutions: rule of law; procedural justice; mobility through education; inclusion through welfare	Value patterns: expressive values and individual choice not balanced by self-control Practices: lack of social control Institutions: imbalance between market institutions and welfare institutions; imbalance between egalitarian values and structural inequality; imbalance between egalitarian values and discrimination against groups
Autocracy	Value patterns: egalitarianism; welfare solidarity Practices: pervasive social control; divide-and-rule between ethnic groups Institutions: inclusion through welfare; social control through corporatism	Value patterns: Collectivism; authoritarianism; nonegalitarian; lack of tolerance Practices: violent means of social control; "covert" inequality; arbitrary treatment of citizens; legal cynicism; lack of generalized trust; lack of civic engagement Institutions: rule of power; violence by state agencies

values of welfare solidarity, practices of pervasive social control, welfare institutions, and social control through corporatism. Democracies have strong comparative disadvantages if they cannot attenuate their built-in tensions, and imbalances ensue. These include expressive values that are not balanced by self-control, a lack of social control practices, and imbalances either between their institutions or between values and structure. Comparative disadvantages for autocracies arise from the dominant value pattern of authoritarianism on which they are based, the practices they typically impose, and the institutions through which they govern. Strong comparative disadvantages for autocracies are collectivistic, authoritarian, and nonegalitarian values; practices of arbitrary treatment of citizens and the resulting legal cynicism, lack of trust, and violent social control; and institutions that are based on the rule of power.

On balance, democratic societies foster values and practices that reduce levels of violence, but they may have less effective social control compared to authoritarian societies. Autocracies in contrast foster values and practices that encourage violence (not the least through violent means of social control). They discourage values like tolerance and those practices that in democracies support nonviolent ways of dealing with conflicts. Consequently, and in contrast to democracies, autocracies have to rely on a strong state apparatus and sweeping social controls (including violent repression) to keep violent crime at low levels. Democracies that accumulate comparative disadvantages in the form of high levels of tension and imbalance should generally have higher levels of violence than other democracies or autocracies. Authoritarian regimes might be more successful in keeping tensions under control, and accordingly have lower levels of violent crime.

Table 1 further suggests that transitions from autocracy to democracy combine the comparative disadvantages of both autocracy and democracy, which push violent crime to the high levels that typically accompany the transition phase. When the grip of the authoritarian regime loosens, the anomic tendencies produced during the preceding period of autocracy erupt in violent conflicts and a wave of violent crime. Democratic values and practices that are capable of constraining violent crime in more mature liberal democracies are not yet firmly established, and the transition produces high levels of tensions and institutional imbalance in the fledgling democracies.

Values as Comparative Advantages and Disadvantages: An Empirical Exploration

In the discussion above, I identified individualistic and egalitarian value patterns and ensuing practices as strong comparative advantages of democratic societies. As Triandis and Trafimov (2001, 271) concluded from comparative research on the prevalence of individualism and collectivism,

> Political systems are shaped in part by individualism and collectivism, and also pressure towards these cultural patterns. Highly concentrated, dictatorial, central planning systems lead to collectivism; decentralised, democratic or laissez-faire systems favor individualism. Conversely, collectivism increases the probability that a dictatorship will develop.

Similarly, individualism increases the probability that a democracy will develop (Inglehart and Welzel 2005). Eisner's (2001, 2003) analysis of the long-term trends of homicide in Europe illustrates this point. The secular decline of violent crime in European countries started long before modern liberal democracies were established, and mostly within then nondemocratic societies. In Western European countries, which were among the first on a route toward democracy, levels of violent crime decreased earlier than in the autocratic states of Central and Eastern Europe. West European countries score high on individualistic value patterns, and it can be assumed that the development of less group-centered and collectivistic patterns, egalitarian values, and increasing generalized trust all contributed to the decline of violence and simultaneously promoted democracy. Once established, democratic institutions fostered those values and practices that restrict violence. In contrast, the countries of Eastern and

Central Europe (most of which were autocracies during this period) had higher rates of homicides at the end of the nineteenth and throughout the first half of the twentieth century, and those that remained under communist regimes in the second half of the twentieth century retained higher mean levels of violent crime than most of the democracies of Western Europe throughout this period (Karstedt forthcoming). In the following part of this article, I explore the relationship between values and violence in democracies and autocracies, focusing on the contrast between individualistic/collectivistic and egalitarian/ nonegalitarian values.

Sample, data, and results

The data and sample used here were selected because they provide a direct and extremely reliable cross-cultural measurement of these values that is unique because cultural values are measured (1) within a comparable setting and (2) not by structural proxies. In an exemplary study, Hofstede (1980/1984, 1997; see the appendix for details and country values) analyzed individual attitudes of workers and management of IBM branches in thirty-nine countries. His study was conducted between 1968 and 1972 and included countries from Europe, North and Latin America, Asia, and the Pacific Region but none of the countries that were at that time under communist regimes. Ecological factor analyses produced four cultural dimensions, with Individualism/Collectivism and Power Distance as the most powerful ones. Individualism/Collectivism measures the detachment from traditional group and family bonds and, as such, the dimension of democratic values that stresses individual autonomy and achievement (meritocratic values). Power Distance defines the extent to which relationships of dominance, power, and subordination and hierarchical relationships between different social classes prevail or are replaced by more egalitarian orientations; as such, it represents the egalitarian component of democratic value patterns and practices. High values on the Individualism/Collectivism scale indicate strong individualism; high values on the Power Distance scale indicate authoritarian and nonegalitarian value patterns. When compared to data from the World Values Survey collected between 1990 and 1993 (Inglehart 1997), Hofstede's value dimensions can be regarded as fundamental, long-term, and stable dimensions for cross-cultural research. The relative positions of countries in the dimensional space of analogous values seem to have much in common in both studies (e.g., Inglehart 1997, 82, 93, 98, 335; Hofstede 1980, 312). This indicates a high stability of *relative* cultural differences despite the changes caused by the process of modernization during the two decades between 1970 and 1990 (see also Triandis and Trafimov 2001).

The sample is biased in that it includes most of the European democracies and only a small proportion of the autocracies of that time (excluding communist regimes and including Latin American and Asian countries). Furthermore, the time period between 1968 and 1972 is at the very beginning of rising rates of lethal violent crime in some Western democracies and, therefore, might favor democracies that had comparatively low levels of violent crime at that period.

Notwithstanding these drawbacks, the direct and structurally independent measurement of value patterns was deemed to provide a unique advantage for the comparative analysis of violent crime and its relation to values in democracies and autocracies. For the measurement of violent crime, two data sets of lethal violent crime were used. For the period from 1968 to 1972, murder rates (per one hundred thousand population) were compiled from the Comparative Crime Data File of Archer and Gartner (1984) and complemented from other sources (Karstedt 2001a, 2005) for twenty-six countries from Europe, North and Latin America, Asia, and the Pacific Region in the Hofstede sample. The second data set is based on World Health Organization (WHO) homicide victimization data (and rates per one hundred thousand population), which cover the period from 1960 to 2000 for these countries to corroborate these results with a longer period and a more reliable data set. For both periods, the mean of the respective rate was used. Murder rates, which were more consistently available for the earlier time period, represent those severe cases of homicide, which were legally classified as such, and thus a proportion of all homicides. Both measures are highly correlated for 1968 to 1972 for the countries available.

Democracies and nondemocratic societies were classified according to Przeworski et al. (2000). They classified countries mainly according to elections, party systems (more than one), and actual regime change based on elections, which resulted in two types of democracies—parliamentarism and presidentialism—and two types of autocracies—dictatorships and party bureaucracies, the latter identifying communist regimes. This measure represents therefore only the degree of electoral democracy and the bare institutional framework of democracy. For the period from 1950 to 1990, they classified each country according to periods of regimes (pp. 59-77). The following eighteen countries in the Hofstede sample were classified as democracies: Austria, Denmark, Finland, France, Great Britain, Ireland, Italy, Netherlands, Norway, Sweden, Canada, United States, India, Israel, Japan, Colombia, Australia, and New Zealand. Portugal, Spain, South Africa, Pakistan, Philippines, Singapore, Thailand, and Peru were classified as autocracies.

To control for structural inequality, two indicators were used, income inequality (Gini Index of household income; Jain 1975) and an index of economic discrimination, a combined measure of the proportion of the (mostly ethnic minority) population that is excluded and confined to the lowest economic positions, and the intensity of such exclusion (Taylor and Jodice 1983).

My analysis proceeds in two steps. First, I present results for the relationship between violent crime and the democratic values of individualism and egalitarianism. Figures 1 through 4 show that lethal violent crime between 1968 and 1972 and for the longer period between 1960 and 2000 is related to the value patterns of collectivism/individualism and egalitarianism (power distance). Both democratic values reduce violence. This conclusion is further corroborated when countries scoring low on both value dimensions are compared with countries with high scores. When divided at the median, countries with high individualism and high egalitarianism have significantly lower rates of lethal violence. However, the increase of violence that affected all countries since the 1960s is clearly visible. Between 1968 and 1972, the mean rate of lethal violence in individualistic and

FIGURE 1
INDIVIDUALISM/COLLECTIVISM
AND LETHAL VIOLENT CRIME, 1968-1972

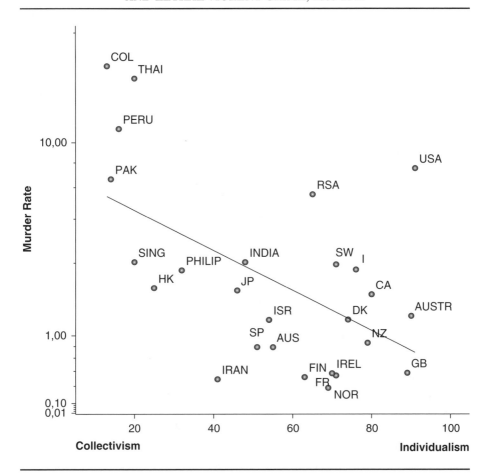

egalitarian countries was 0.85 and for collectivistic and nonegalitarian countries 4.8. This increased for the extended time period from 1960 to 2000 to 1.6 and 8.1, which indicates that it roughly doubled during the rest of the century, while the relative distance between the two types remained largely the same.[11] Democratic values could retain lower levels of violence, but they did not act as a bulwark against those forces that drove violence up. Multivariate analyses for the period between 1968 and 1972 that controlled for GNP, social inequality (Gini Index), and economic discrimination showed that individualism reduced lethal violence independently of both controls. However, egalitarian values had no significant impact independent of the structural inequality measures (see Karstedt 2001a, 2005). Among the core values of democracy, individualism is clearly the value dimension that keeps violence at low levels.

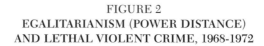

FIGURE 2
EGALITARIANISM (POWER DISTANCE)
AND LETHAL VIOLENT CRIME, 1968-1972

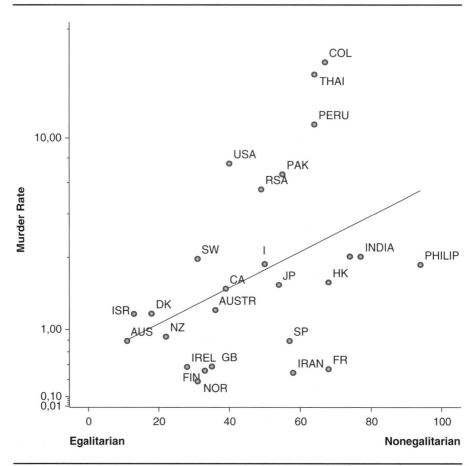

In the second part of the analysis, I explore how the institutional frameworks of democracies and autocracies interact with democratic/nondemocratic values to affect levels of lethal violence. These analyses are based on the time period between 1968 and 1972, for which all but one country could be classified either as a democracy or autocracy according to the classification system described above. The following results and tables are based on a very small sample; however, they demonstrate distinct interactions between institutional framework, values, and violent crime. The mean rate of lethal violent crime for democracies is 2.8 in contrast to 6.1 for autocracies, which is only significant at the $p < .1$ level. However, Table 2 for individualistic values and Table 3 for egalitarian values show that less violent societies are more likely to be democracies, both by institutional framework and the measure of democratic values. Democracies consistently have

FIGURE 3
INDIVIDUALISM/COLLECTIVISM
AND LETHAL VIOLENT CRIME, 1960-2000

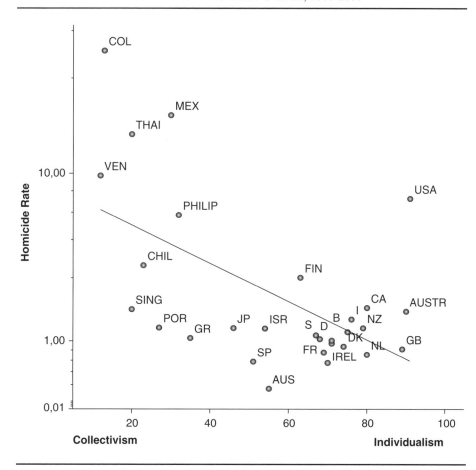

high levels of individualistic and egalitarian values, while autocracies and party bureaucracies are dominated by more collectivistic and authoritarian patterns. The practices and institutional framework of autocracies are geared toward preserving and exploiting group differences and power differentials in society, and both are linked to high rates of lethal violence. Countries with low rates of lethal violence are concentrated in democracies with high individualism and high egalitarianism, while countries with high rates are concentrated in nondemocratic countries ranking low on individualism and egalitarianism.

This very distinctive clustering demonstrates the impact of the individualistic and egalitarian culture of democracy and how this value pattern is nested within the institutional framework. Democracies with high individualism and egalitarianism and comparably low levels of lethal violent crime are mostly Western

FIGURE 4
EGALITARIANISM (POWER DISTANCE)
AND LETHAL VIOLENT CRIME, 1960-2000

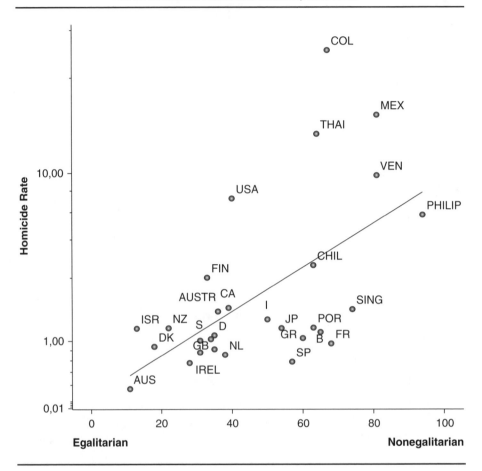

democracies, with the notable exception of the United States. Democracies with low levels of individualism are mostly non-Western democracies. India shows the typical pattern of low individualism and high rates of violent crime, while Japan is characterized by the atypical pattern of low individualism and low violence. The impact of non-Western traditions is obvious in both of these cases. Among the autocracies, Spain shows the pattern of high individualism and low rates of violent crime typically found for other West European countries, while South Africa has—despite high levels of individualism[12]—a high rate of lethal violent crime. Notwithstanding its authoritarian regime, Spain had already adapted structurally and culturally to the other European countries, which might account for its later mostly smooth transition toward democracy and a very short period

TABLE 2
LETHAL VIOLENT CRIME AND INDIVIDUALISTIC VALUES IN DEMOCRACIES
AND AUTOCRACIES, 1968-1972 (N = 26)

	Democracies		Autocracies	
	Individualism High	Individualism Low	Individualism High	Individualism Low
Murder rate high	3 (20%)	1 (33%)	1 (50%)	5 (83%)
Murder rate low	12 (80%)	2 (67%)	1 (50%)	1 (17%)
Total	15	3	2	6

NOTE: Individualism high/low: above/below median. Murder rate high/low: above/below median.

TABLE 3
LETHAL VIOLENT CRIME AND EGALITARIAN VALUES
IN DEMOCRACIES AND AUTOCRACIES, 1968-1972 (N = 26)

	Democracies		Autocracies	
	Egalitarian Values High	Egalitarian Values Low	Egalitarian Values High	Egalitarian Values Low
Murder rate high	4 (27%)	2 (67%)	1 (50%)	5 (83%)
Murder rate low	11 (73%)	1 (33%)	1 (50%)	1 (17%)
Total	15	3	2	6

NOTE: Egalitarian values high/low: above/below median. Murder rate high/low: above/below median.

of increasing violence (LaFree and Drass 2002). South Africa's high level of violence is presumably related to the social and economic discrimination during apartheid. It should be noted that these results are biased toward democracies because the former communist countries with distinct egalitarian (though not necessarily individualistic) value patterns are not included in the sample.

Structural inequality affects lethal violent conflicts within both democratic and autocratic societies. In democracies, structural inequality generates tensions between values and structural patterns that endanger the inclusionary project and produce violent crime. The impact of structural inequality might be attenuated by the more authoritarian value patterns that prevail in autocracies. The same measures of structural inequality as described above were used here, income inequality and economic discrimination. Table 4 shows how income inequality affects the level of violent crime in democracies and autocracies. Less than one-third of democratic countries have a high level of inequality, and the majority of democra-

TABLE 4
LETHAL VIOLENT CRIME AND INCOME INEQUALITY (GINI INDEX)
IN DEMOCRACIES AND AUTOCRACIES, 1968-1972 ($N = 26$)

	Democracies		Autocracies	
	Inequality High	Inequality Low	Inequality High	Inequality Low
Murder rate high	2 (40%)	3 (23%)	5 (83%)	1 (50%)
Murder rate low	3 (60%)	10 (77%)	1 (17%)	1 (50%)
Total	5	13	6	2

NOTE: Income inequality (Gini) high/low: above/below median. Murder rate high/low: above/below median.

tic societies with low levels of income inequality have low rates of lethal violence. The impact of income inequality is, however, ambiguous for democracies. More than half can retain low levels of violent crime even under conditions of high inequality; however, this conclusion is based on very small numbers. The pattern is more distinct for autocracies, with the majority of autocratic countries having high levels of income inequality and nearly all having high rates of lethal violence.

[T]he more that countries adopt individualistic and egalitarian values, the lower their levels of lethal violent crime.

Economic discrimination is an indicator of exclusionary inequality that mainly affects ethnic minorities. As Mann (2005) has argued, autocracies are more successful in containing ethnic conflict and violence. In contrast, economic discrimination in democracies should increase tensions and imbalances. Results in Table 5 illustrate this point. For economic discrimination, the pattern becomes slightly more distinct for democracies, and economic discrimination, which is in such sharp contrast to the project of liberal inclusion, produces a high level of violence where it prevails in democracies. However, no clear pattern emerges with autocracies. According to Table 5, economic discrimination does not significantly increase violent conflicts in an institutional and cultural environment that stresses subordi-

TABLE 5
LETHAL VIOLENT CRIME AND ECONOMIC DISCRIMINATION
IN DEMOCRACIES AND AUTOCRACIES, 1968-1972 ($N = 26$)

	Democracies		Autocracies	
	Discrimination High	Discrimination Low	Discrimination High	Discrimination Low
Murder rate high	3 (60%)	2 (18%)	3 (75%)	3 (75%)
Murder rate low	2 (40%)	11 (82%)	1 (25%)	1 (25%)
Total	5	13	4	4

NOTE: Economic discrimination high/low: above/below mean. Murder rate high/low: above/below median.

nation and nonegalitarian values, while it does increase tensions in an egalitarian institutional and cultural context. This generally corroborates Mann's argument, and we may conclude that even if nonegalitarian values are conducive to higher levels of violent crime, they nonetheless are capable of attenuating the tensions that arise from ingrained economic discrimination of ethnic minorities in autocracies.

Conclusion: Is There a Comparative Advantage of Democratic Values?

The arguments and analyses presented here can be taken only as a first step toward a systematic exploration of comparative advantages and disadvantages of democracies and autocracies in generating and containing violence. However, the development of core democratic values like individualism and egalitarianism appear to offer a comparative advantage to democracies in maintaining low levels of violence. The results of these analyses illustrate this conclusion in two ways. First, the more that countries adopt individualistic and egalitarian values, the lower their levels of lethal violent crime, though egalitarian values do not achieve this without egalitarian structures. Second, the concentration and clear pattern of clustering of democratic, individualistic, and egalitarian values and more egalitarian structures within democracies indicate that strong democratic institutions produce strong democratic practices and values, and both are related to lower levels of violence. If, however, economic discrimination prevails in democracies, the tensions between egalitarian values and actual discrimination generate higher levels of violence, pointing to comparative disadvantages of democracies. The same dynamic processes seem to be at work in autocracies—however, in the opposite direction. The clustering of collectivistic and authoritarian values as well as of structural inequality within autocracies indicates strong tendencies of enhanc-

ing cultural and structural inequality, which both generate the higher levels of
violence observed for these societies. But these same patterns and practices provide
a comparative advantage for autocracies in containing violent crime in the case of
high economic discrimination.

---

*As Alexis de Tocqueville . . .
might have argued, democratic
values have a high potential to realize
their comparative advantages in
restraining violent crime if they are
fostered by democratic practices
and institutions.*

As shown in Table 1, the core values of democracies can also create comparative disadvantages for democratic societies in restricting violent crime.
Individualistic and egalitarian values generate tensions within democracies and
act as anomic stressors within their cultural, institutional, and structural patterns.
A number of studies corroborate this point. LaFree and his colleagues (LaFree
and Drass 2002; LaFree and Tseloni 2006 [this volume]) have shown that mature
democracies experienced increasing trends of lethal violent crimes, and "booms"
were observed for several mature democracies during the second half of the
twentieth century. Several causal factors might have been responsible for generating tensions in democracies that increased violent crime. Egalitarian value patterns in mature democracies were confronted with rising social inequality and, in
particular in the democracies in Europe, with increasing levels of economic discrimination through the influx of large numbers of immigrants. Market individualism was not balanced by welfare and other institutions. As individualistic value
patterns shifted toward more extreme forms of self-expression and hierarchical
self-interest in mature Western democracies, patterns of control were loosened
and vital social bonds dissolved. Using data from the three waves of World Values
Survey from 1970 to 2000, Inglehart and Welzel (2005) showed that in particular
the most mature democracies have the highest scores on self-expression values.
During the transition to democracy, the core democratic values of individualism
and free choice might generate specific comparative disadvantages. Pridemore and
Kim (2006 [this volume]) showed with homicide victimization data from Russian

regions that levels of violent crime are higher where the new democratic values of individual freedom and choice pose severe threats to the collectivistic values of the past, however compromised these might have been.

As Alexis de Tocqueville—taking his typically optimistic stance on the future of democracy—might have argued, democratic values have a high potential to realize their comparative advantages in restraining violent crime if they are fostered by democratic practices and institutions; they risk, however, turning these advantages into comparative disadvantages. Democratic societies differ widely in terms of their value patterns, practices, and institutions, as do autocracies. Comparisons between democracies with high and low levels of violence and analogous comparisons between autocracies will help to identify those built-in mechanisms that impact on levels of violent crime in each type of society. Furthermore, a systematic comparison between democracies and autocracies within regions of similar value patterns will help to develop more precise knowledge about the role of democratic values in restraining violent crime. Such studies will enhance our ability to address the problems of high levels of violent crime during the transition toward democracy.

Appendix
Hofstede's Value Dimension

Hofstede (1984, 1997) obtained four value dimensions—Individualism/Collectivism, Power Distance, Avoidance of Uncertainty, and a gender factor. For each dimension, a scale was computed and standardized. The scales were checked against the specific conditions of the national branches and the composition of the workforce within each subsidiary. In particular, the dimension of Individualism/Collectivism has since then become a widely used measure of cross-cultural differences (Kim et al. 1994; Triandis 1995; Triandis and Trafimov 2001).

For the developing countries at that time, they represent the more modernized cultural patterns of the younger age brackets and of the established or emerging middle classes, but much less the values of older generations or the more traditional rural population. Nonetheless, the dimensions clearly differentiate between Western, industrialized countries and developing countries, in particular Individualism/Collectivism. The value dimensions are based on value patterns and cultural practices that are related to work and the organization of work. Work-related values refer to achievement as well as to practices within social hierarchies. Therefore, they provide a suitable foundation for the measurement of individualistic and egalitarian orientations.

The value dimension Individualism/Collectivism represents at its extreme "high individualism" personal challenge and accomplishment, (emotional) independence from family and group relationships, and a general cosmopolitan mentality. This is contrasted to group-related accomplishments, (emotional) dependence on groups and organizations, and a more local mentality represented by high collectivism. In all

Western industrialized societies including Australia and New Zealand, high individualism is the dominating value pattern, while in Latin American and Islamic countries, mostly collectivistic orientations prevail. Asian societies have a medium to stronger collectivistic orientation. Individualism is strongly related to structural indicators of the process of individualization: education, social security, and general social equality as well as equality of genders (Hofstede 1980, 237; Karstedt 2001a).

Power Distance represents cultural values related to social hierarchies, stratification, and social inequality. Low scores indicate a predominance of egalitarian values, high scores elitist and authoritarian value patterns. Western industrialized countries—with the exception of Latin European countries (e.g., France and Italy)—rank at the lower end of the scale, while Latin American and Asian countries are characterized by a comparably high power distance. High social inequality and lack of social mobility (indicated by the level of education and education expenditures) correspond to this value pattern. In addition, societies with a high power distance are male dominated and patriarchal (indicated by low proportions of women in secondary education and of women in the professional and technical workforce; Hofstede 1980, 306-7; Karstedt 2001a). The following table gives an overview of the country base of the analyses.

Country	Power Distance	Individualism
Argentina	49	46
Australia	36	90
Austria	11	55
Belgium	65	75
Brazil	69	38
Canada	39	80
Chile	63	23
Colombia	67	13
Denmark	18	74
Finland	33	63
France	68	71
Great Britain	35	89
Germany (Federal Republic of)	35	67
Greece	60	35
Hong Kong	68	25
India	77	48
Iran	58	41
Ireland	28	70
Israel	13	54
Italy	50	76
Japan	54	46
Mexico	81	30
Netherlands	38	80
Norway	31	69

(continued)

Appendix (continued)

Country	Power Distance	Individualism
New Zealand	22	79
Pakistan	55	14
Peru	64	16
Philippines	94	32
Portugal	63	27
South Africa	49	65
Singapore	74	20
Spain	57	51
Sweden	31	71
Switzerland	34	68
Taiwan	58	17
Thailand	64	20
Turkey	66	37
United States	40	91
Venezuela	81	12

Notes

1. Estimates for the victims of genocide and mass killings as distinguished from war deaths range from 60 to 150 million for the twentieth century alone (Valentino 2004, 1), with most estimates at about 80 million, and some considerably higher (Rummel 1998). Most genocide scholars agree that this makes the twentieth century the most violent in human history.

2. Mechanisms according to Elster (1989) link chains of events; they describe specific causal chains.

3. Transitional democracies often lack this solid foundation in a dense network of associations and interactions of citizens, which communism had destroyed in the countries of Eastern and Central Europe (Gellner 1994), resulting in "civilizational incompetence" (Sztompka 1993) and defective or low-intensity democracies (Nowotny 2002; Gibson and Duch 1994; Muller and Seligson 1994).

4. I use liberal inclusion as an empirical and historical concept and argue that democracies actually achieve (and need to achieve) inclusion to some and varying extent. In this way my argument profoundly differs from Young's (2000) normative argument.

5. Toqueville, however, never commented on the big divide in the democracy of the United States between its African, then-slave population, and white population (Cohen 2001). See Roth (2004) for an analysis of homicide rates in the seventeenth- and eighteenth-century United States.

6. Several authors, most prominently Rothstein and Stolle (2002), have argued that institutions create trust.

7. Muller and Seligson (1994) found that ethnic fractionalization decreased levels of democratic development.

8. In reality, official measures gloss over the glaring inequalities in terms of access to consumer goods, education, Western goods, and lifestyles in these countries (see for an overview Karstedt 2003).

9. South Africa seems to be an example of a country that achieved inclusion by "repressive segregation," which makes it a unique case in this respect.

10. Anatoli Pristawkin (2000), the former chairman of the Commission for Clemency of Russia, gives a gripping account of the unimaginable levels of powerlessness, lawlessness, and anomie in Russia before and during the transition.

11. It has to be taken into account that murder rates should be lower by definition; nonetheless, the data mirror the considerable increase in violent crime during this period.

12. The value orientations were mainly measured among the white population. The rating as a nondemocratic state is due to the apartheid regime.

References

Archer, Donald, and Rosemary Gartner. 1984. *Violence and crime in a cross-national perspective.* New Haven, CT: Yale University Press.

Caldeira, Teresa P. R., and James Holston. 1999. Democracy and violence in Brazil. *Comparative Studies in Society and History* 41 (4): 691-729.

Cohen, David. 2001. *Chasing the red, the white and the blue: A journey in Tocqueville's footsteps through contemporary America.* New York: Picador.

Durkheim, Emile. 1897/1979. *Suicide: A study in sociology.* Translated by John A. Spaulding and George Simpson. New York: Free Press.

———. 1900. Deux lois de l'évolution pénale. *L'Année Sociologique* 4:65-95.

———. 1900/1957. *Professional ethics and civic morals.* Translated by Cornelia Brookfield. New York: Routledge.

Eisner, Manuel. 1997. *Das Ende der zivilisierten Stadt. Die Auswirkungen von Modernisierung und urbaner Krise auf Gewaltdelinquenz.* Frankfurt, Germany: Campus.

———. 2001. Modernization, self-control and lethal violence. The long-term dynamics of European homicide rates in theoretical perspective. *British Journal of Criminology* 41:618-38.

———. 2003. Long-term historical trends in violent crime. In *Crime and justice. An annual review of research*, vol. 30, ed. M. Tonry, 83-142. Chicago: University of Chicago Press.

———. 2005. Modernity strikes back? The latest increase in interpersonal violence (1960-1990) in historical perspective. Presented at the 4th Workshop on Interpersonal Violence, Rotterdam, the Netherlands.

Elster, John. 1989. *Nuts and bolts for the social sciences.* Cambridge: Cambridge University Press.

———. 1999. *Deliberative democracy.* Cambridge: Cambridge University Press.

Gellner, Ernest. 1994. *Conditions of liberty: Civil society and its rivals.* New York: Penguin.

Gibson, James L., and Raymond M. Duch. 1994. Postmaterialism and the emerging Soviet democracy. *Political Research Quarterly* 47:5-39.

Gurr, Ted R. 1977. Crime trends in modern democracies since 1945. *Annales Internationales de Criminologie* 16:41-86.

———. 1993. *Minorities at risk. A global view of ethnopolitical conflicts.* Washington, DC: United States Institute of Peace.

———. 2000. *People versus states. Minorities at risk in the new century.* Washington, DC: United States Institute of Peace.

Hagan, John, Gabriele Hefler, Gerd Classen, Klaus Boehnke, and Hans Merkens. 1998. Subterrenean sources of subcultural delinquency beyond the American dream. *Criminology* 36:309-42.

Hagan, John, and Daniela Radoeva. 1998. Both too much and too little: From elite to street crime in the transformation of the Czech Republic. *Crime, Law & Social Change* 28:195-211.

Held, David. 2005. *Models of democracy.* 2nd ed. Cambridge, UK: Polity.

Hirschman, Albert O. 1988. *Engagement und Enttaeuschung.* Frankfurt, Germany: Suhrkamp. (Originally published as *Shifting involvements: Private interest and public action*, Princeton, NJ: Princeton University Press, 1982)

Hofstede, Geert. 1980/1984. *Culture's consequences: International differences in work-related values.* 1st and 2nd ed. Beverly Hills, CA: Sage.

———. 1997. *Cultures and organizations: Software of the mind.* New York: McGraw-Hill.

Holmes, Stephen. 1993. *The anatomy of antiliberalism.* Cambridge, MA: Harvard University Press.

Huggins, Martha, Mika Haritos-Fatouros, and Philip G. Zimbardo. 2002. *Violence workers: Police torturers and murderers reconstruct Brazilian atrocities.* Berkeley: University of California Press.

Inglehart, Ronald. 1997. *Modernization and postmodernization: cultural, economic, and political change in 43 societies.* Princeton, NJ: Princeton University Press.

Inglehart, Ronald, and Christian Welzel. 2005. *Modernization, cultural change and democracy.* Cambridge: Cambridge University Press.

Inkeles, Alex, ed. 1993. *On measuring democracy. Its consequences and concomitants.* New Brunswick, NJ: Transaction Publishers.

Jaggers, Keith, and Ted Gurr. 1995. Tracking democracy's third wave with the Polity III data. *Journal of Peace Research* 32:469-82.

Jain, Semantha. 1975. *Size distribution of income. A compilation of data.* Washington, DC: World Bank.

Karstedt, Susanne. 1999. Social transformation and crime: A crisis of deregulation. In *The rule of law after communism. Problems and prospects in East-Central Europe*, ed. M. Krygier and A. Czarnota. Aldershot, UK: Ashgate.

———. 2001a. Die moralische Staerke schwacher Bindungen: Individualismus und Gewalt im Kulturvergleich. *Monatsschrift fuer Kriminologie und Strafrechtsreform* 84:226-43.

———. 2001b. The production of trust in modern societies: A cross-national study of cultural and structural factors. Paper presented at the 35th Congress of the International Institute of Sociology, Krakov, Poland.

———. 2003. Legacies of a culture of inequality: The Janus face of crime in post-communist countries. *Crime, Law and Social Change* 40:295-320.

———. 2005. Individualisme et Violence: Modernisation Extrême ou Re-Traditionalisation de la Société? Une Comparaison Interculturelle. *Déviance et Société* 29:273-84.

———. Forthcoming. Democracy, democratization and violence: European and international perspectives. In *Cultures of violence in Europe: Historical and contemporary perspectives*, ed. S. Body-Gendrot and P. Spierenburg. Dordrecht, the Netherlands: Kluwer.

Keane, John. 2004. *Violence and democracy.* Cambridge: Cambridge University Press.

Kim, Uichol, Harry C. Triandis, Cigdem Kagitbaci, Sang-Chin Choi, and Gene Yoon, eds. 1994. *Individualism and collectivism. Theory, method and applications.* Cross-Cultural Research and Methodology Series, vol. 18. Thousand Oaks, CA: Sage.

Klages, Helmut. 1984. *Wertorientierungen im Wandel. Rückblick, Gegenwartsanalyse, Prognosen.* Frankfurt, Germany: Campus.

LaFree, Gary. 1998. *Losing legitimacy. Street crime and the decline of social institutions in America.* Boulder, CO: Westview.

LaFree, Gary, and Kenneth A. Drass. 2002. Counting crime booms among nations: Evidence for homicide victimization rates 1956-1998. *Criminology* 40:769-800.

LaFree, Gary, and Andromachi Tseloni. 2006. Democracy and crime: A multilevel analysis of homicide in forty-four countries, 1950-2000. *Annals of the American Academy of Political and Social Science* 605:26-49.

Lauth, Hans-Joachim, Gert Pickel, and Christian Welzel. 2000. *Demokratiemessung. Konzepte und Befunde im internationalen Vergleich.* Wiesbaden, Germany: Westdeutscher Verlag.

Lederman, Daniel, Norman Loayza, and Anna Menéndez. 2002. Violent crime: Does social capital matter? *Economic Development and Cultural Change* 50:509-39.

Los, Maria. 1988. *Communist ideology, law and crime.* London: Macmillan/New York: St. Martin's.

———, ed. 1990. *The second economy in Marxist states.* New York: St. Martin's.

———. 2003. Post-communist fear of crime and the commercialization of security. *Theoretical Criminology* 6 (2): 165-88.

Mann, Michael. 1970. The social cohesion of liberal democracies. *American Sociological Review* 35:423-39.

———. 2005. *The dark side of democracy. Explaining ethnical cleansing.* Cambridge: Cambridge University Press.

Mendez, Juan E. 1999. Problems of lawless violence: Introduction. In *The (un)rule of law and the underprivileged in Latin America,* ed. J. E. Mendez, G. O'Donnell, and P. S. Pinheiro. South Bend, IN: University of Notre Dame Press.

Mendez, Juan E., Guillermo O'Donnell, and Paulo S. Pinheiro, eds. 1999. *The (un)rule of law and the underprivileged in Latin America.* South Bend, IN: University of Notre Dame Press.

Messner, Steven F. 1982. Societal development, social equality and homicide: A cross-national test of a Durkheimian model. *Social Forces* 61:225-40.

———. 2004. An institutional-anomie theory of crime: Continuities and elaborations in the study of social structure and anomie. In *Soziologie der Kriminalität.* Special vol. 43 of *Kölner Zeitschrift für Soziologie und Sozialpsychologie*, ed. D. Oberwittler and S. Karstedt. Wiesbaden, Germany: Westdeutscher Verlag.

Messner, Steven F., and Richard Rosenfeld. 1994. *Crime and the American dream.* Belmont, CA: Wadsworth.

———. 1998. Social structure and homicide. In *Homicide: A sourcebook of social research,* ed. M. D. Smith and M. A. Zahn. New York: Russell Sage.

Muller, Edward N., and Mitchell A. Seligson. 1994. Civic culture and democracy: The question of causal relationships. *American Political Science Review* 88:635-52.

Nowotny, Thomas. 2002. Markets, democracy and social capital. *Österreichische Zeitschrift für Politikwissenschaft* 31:217-29.

O'Donnell, Guillermo, Jose V. Cullel, and Osvaldo M. Iazetta. 2004. *The quality of democracy*. South Bend, IN: University of Notre Dame Press.

Pharr, Susan, Robert Putnam, and Richard Dalton. 2000. A quarter-century of declining confidence. *Journal of Democracy* 11:5-25.

Pridemore, William A. 2003. Measuring homicide in Russia: A comparison of estimates from the crime and vital statistics reporting systems. *Social Science & Medicine* 57:1343-54.

Pridemore, William A., ed. 2005. *Ruling Russia: Law, crime, and justice in a changing society*. Lanham, MD: Rowman & Littlefield.

Pridemore, William Alex, and Sang-Weon Kim. 2006. Democratization and political change as threats to collective sentiments: Testing Durkheim in Russia. *Annals of the American Academy of Political and Social Science* 605:82-103.

Pristawkin, Anatoli. 2000. *Ich flehe um Hinrichtung. Die Begnadigungskommission des russischen Präsidenten*. München, Germany: Luchterhand.

Przeworski, Adam, Michael E. Alvarez, Jose Antonio Cheibub, and Fernando Limongi. 2000. *Democracy and development. Political institutions and well-being in the world, 1950-1990*. Cambridge: Cambridge University Press.

Rodrigues, Corinne Davis. 2006. Civil democracy, perceived risk, and insecurity in Brazil: An extension of the systemic social control model. *Annals of the American Academy of Political and Social Science* 605:242-63.

Rosenfeld, Richard, Steven F. Messner, and Eric P. Baumer. 2001. Social capital and homicide. *Social Forces* 80:283-309.

Roth, Randolph. 2004. American homicide: A political and psychological hypothesis. Presented at the 3rd Workshop on Interpersonal Violence, Brussels.

Rothstein, Bo, and Dietlind Stolle. 2002. How political institutions create and destroy social capital. An institutional theory of generalized trust. Presented at the Project on Honesty and Trust, Workshop 2, Collegium Budapest, Budapest, Romania.

Rummel, Rudolph J. 1997. *Power kills. Democracy as a method of nonviolence*. New Brunswick, NJ: Transaction Publishers.

———. 1998. *Statistics of democide*. Muenster, Germany: LIT.

Sampson, Robert, and Don J. Bartusch. 1998. Legal cynicism and (subcultural?) tolerance of deviance: The neighborhood context of racial differences. *Law & Society Review* 32:777-804.

Sampson, Robert J., Stephen W. Raudenbush, and Felton Earls. 1997. Neighborhoods and violent crime: A multilevel study of collective efficacy. *Science* 277:918-24.

Savolainen, Jukka. 2000. Inequality, welfare state, and homicide: Further support for the Institutional Anomie Theory. *Criminology* 38:1021-42.

Steinberg, John, ed. 2001. *Crime wave. The South African underworld and its foes*. Witwatersrand, South Africa: Witwatersrand University Press.

Sztompka, Piotr. 1993. Civilizational incompetence: The trap of post-communist societies. *Zeitschrift fuer Soziologie* 22:85-95.

Taylor, Chris L., and Derek A. Jodice. 1983. *World handbook of political and social indicators*. 3rd ed. New Haven, CT: Yale University Press.

Tilly, Charles. 1992. *Coercion, capital and European States, AD 990-1992*. Oxford, UK: Blackwell.

———. 2004. *Contention and democracy in Europe, 1650-2000*. Cambridge: Cambridge University Press.

Tocqueville, Alexis de. 1835-1840/2000. *Democracy in America*. Chicago: Chicago University Press.

Triandis, Harry C. 1995. *Individualism and collectivism*. Boulder, CO: Westview.

Triandis, Harry C., and David Trafimov. 2001. Cross-national prevalence of collectivism. In *Individual self, relational self, collective self*, ed. C. Sedikides and M. B. Brewer. Ann Arbor, MI: Taylor and Francis.

Tyler, Tom R. 1990. *Why people obey the law*. New Haven, CT: Yale University Press.

———. 2003. Procedural justice, legitimacy, and the effective rule of law. In *Crime and justice: A review of research*, vol. 30, ed. M. Tonry. Chicago: University of Chicago Press.

Tyler, Tom R., and Steven Blader 2000. *Cooperation in groups: Procedural justice, social identity, and behavioral engagement*. Philadelphia: Psychology Press.

Valentino, Benjamin. 2004. *Final solutions. Mass killing and genocide in the 20th century*. Ithaca, NY: Cornell University Press.

Waldmann, Peter. 2002. *Der anomische Staat. Über Recht, öffentliche Sicherheit und Alltag in Lateinamerika*. Opladen, Germany: Leske + Budrich.

———, ed. 2003. *Diktatur, Demokratisierung und soziale Anomie*. München, Germany: Vögel.

Welzel, Christian. 2002. *Fluchtpunkt Humanentwicklung. Über die Grundlagen der Demokratie und die Ursachen ihrer Ausbreitung*. Wiesbaden, Germany: Westdeutscher Verlag.

Welzel, Christian, and Ronald Inglehart. 2005. Demokratisierung und Freiheitsstreben. Die Perspektive der Humanentwicklung. *Politische Vierteljahresschrift* 46:62-85.

Young, Iris M. 2000. *Inclusion and democracy*. Oxford: Oxford University Press.

Democratization and Political Change as Threats to Collective Sentiments: Testing Durkheim in Russia

By
WILLIAM ALEX
PRIDEMORE
and
SANG-WEON KIM

Durkheim argued that acute political crises result in increased homicide rates because they pose a threat to sentiments about the collective. Though crucial to Durkheim's work on homicide, this idea remains untested. The authors took advantage of the natural experiment of the collapse of the Soviet Union to examine this hypothesis. Using data from Russian regions ($N = 78$) and controlling for measures of anomie and other covariates, the authors estimated the association between political change and change in homicide rates between 1991 and 2000. Results indicated that regions exhibiting less support for the Communist Party in 2000 (and thus greater change in political ideals because the Party had previously exercised complete control) were regions with greater increases in homicide rates. Thus, while democratization may be a positive development relative to the Communist juggernaut of the past, it appears that the swift political change in Russia is partially responsible for the higher rates of violence there following the collapse of the Soviet Union.

Keywords: Russia; democratization; political change; crime; violence; homicide

In this study, we drew upon Durkheim's (1897/ 1979) ideas on threats against collective sentiments to examine the association between political change and homicide rates in Russia. Democratization and marketization[1] in Russia during the 1990s represented a significant shift away from the group-oriented norms of the past, thus presenting a clear threat not only to the deeply ingrained socialist ideology and norms of the Soviet era but also to long-standing Russian cultural traditions and values that had

NOTE: This research was supported by grant no. R21 AA0139581 awarded by the National Institutes of Health, National Institute on Alcohol Abuse and Alcoholism. Points of view do not necessarily represent the official position of NIH/NIAAA. We thank Nina Andrianova and Evgenii Andreev for help with the Russian data. The first author thanks the Davis Center at Harvard University, where he was a research fellow when the analyses for this article were carried out. An earlier version of this article was presented at the 2005 World Congress on Criminology in Philadelphia.

DOI: 10.1177/0002716206286859

privileged the collective over the individual. The political changes were accompanied by a sharp increase in violence, and Russia's homicide victimization rate of about thirty per one hundred thousand residents is nearly five times higher than in the United States and is among the highest in the world (Pridemore 2003a). Russia is a vast nation, however, and homicide levels and trends vary widely. Initial research suggested that several structural variables—including poverty, single-parent households, and aggregate alcohol consumption—are associated with the cross-sectional variation of Russian homicide rates (Pridemore 2005). Similar variables were shown also to have influenced the *change* in regional homicide rates during the 1990s (Andrienko 2001). Furthermore, Chamlin, Pridemore, and Cochran (2005) and Kim and Pridemore (2005) used interrupted time-series methods and change models, respectively, to test explicitly Durkheim's hypothesis that rapid social change leads to societal deregulation and anomie and, in turn, to higher homicide rates. Both studies found consistent support for these ideas.

[I]t appears that the swift political change in Russia is partially responsible for the higher rates of violence there following the collapse of the Soviet Union.

Each of the studies mentioned above focused on the effects of socioeconomic factors and did not consider political characteristics. Yet both theory and empirical

---

William Alex Pridemore is on the criminal justice faculty at Indiana University, where he is also an affiliate faculty member of the Russian and East European Institute. He is also a member of the National Consortium on Violence Research. His main research interests include (1) social structure and violence, (2) the impact of the social/political/economic transition and of alcohol consumption on the cross-sectional and temporal variation of homicide and suicide rates in Russia, and (3) far right-wing culture and crime in the United States. He is the editor of Ruling Russia: Law, Crime, and Justice in a Changing Society; *and his recent articles have appeared in* American Journal of Public Health, Journal of Quantitative Criminology, Journal of Research in Crime and Delinquency, *and* Social Science and Medicine.

Sang-Weon Kim is in the Department of Police Science faculty at Dong-Eui University in Busan, South Korea. His main research interests include social structure and homicide in Russia, especially testing various forms of anomie theory as potential explanations for the increase in homicide rates in the country. His recent publications have appeared in British Journal of Criminology, Social Science Quarterly, *and* Journal of Criminal Justice.

evidence suggest it is unwise to ignore such issues. For example, recent studies have shown the various ways in which the political features of a society can influence criminal justice and rates of interpersonal violence (Stucky, Heimer, and Lang 2005; Stucky 2003; Villarreal 2002). Furthermore, distinct from the effects on violence of rapid social change and anomie, Durkheim argued that during periods of acute political crisis, interpersonal violence will increase due to the threat to collective sentiments posed by the crisis.

[B]oth theory and empirical evidence suggest it is unwise to ignore [political characteristics].

DiCristina (2004, 81) noted that the "sentiments about collective things" hypothesis, although crucial to Durkheim's work on homicide, has only rarely been acknowledged in the theoretical literature and has gone unaddressed empirically.[2] We believe the collapse of the Soviet Union and the subsequent transition toward democracy provided a unique opportunity to test this hypothesis, and our study was an attempt to begin to fill the void, especially since Durkheim himself argued that the strength of these sentiments are a key determinant of societal homicide rates (see chap. 10 in *Professional Ethics and Civic Morals* [1900/1957], titled "Duties in General, Independent of Any Social Grouping—Homicide," and *Suicide* [1897/1979, 356-58, 368-69]).

Theory

Durkheim's (1897/1979, 356-57; 1900/1957) two main theses about homicide were that homicide rates would decrease as (1) the "religion of humanity" became stronger over time as the result of gradual societal development and the shift to social bonds based on "complementary differences" or "exchange relations" (see DiCristina 2004, 85) and (2) collective sentiments weakened and became fewer in number over time (Durkheim 1897/1979, 356-57; 1900/1957). Although these ideas were based on the *level* of development in a society and assumed relatively slow evolutionary change, Durkheim also argued that the *rate* of change was important. Contrary to slow steady development, according to Durkheim, rapid change would lead to an anomic division of labor, social deregulation (Durkheim 1893/1984), and a greater number of *anomic* homicides (e.g., see Durkheim 1897/1979, 356-57), while threats to the collective would lead to a greater number of *altruistic* homicides (Durkheim 1897/1979, 357-58, 368-69).

Durkheim (1897/1979) outlined four basic types of suicide: egoistic, altruistic, anomic, and fatalistic. He stated that extreme individuation (which he believed leads to egoistic suicide) did not cause homicide, and he did not discuss fatalism in relation to homicide, thus leaving anomic and altruistic homicides. In general, the former can be expected to occur usually as a result of social conditions accompanying increased egoism or individuation *in the absence of* well-defined norms and values, while the latter are expected to be associated with strong sentiments about the collective and its protection.

The hypotheses related to development and to anomie have received considerable attention in the criminological literature, including the empirical literature on social structure and homicide, but the hypotheses related to sentiments about collective things, and threats to them, remain largely unaddressed. This absence represents a key gap in the literature. For example, although Durkheim believed that the development of the religion of humanity would help lead to a reduction in homicide rates over time, he argued that a long-term decrease in homicide would be due less to this respect for individual dignity and more to the weakening of collective sentiments (Durkheim 1900/1957, chap. 10). Specifically, he stated that "if homicide is diminishing, it is rather that the mystic cult of the State is losing ground than that the cult of the human being is gaining" (Durkheim 1900/1957, 115). In one of the few tests of this hypothesis, Karstedt (2001) found that nations that exhibited stronger collectivistic relative to individualistic norms had significantly higher homicide rates. Durkheim's views on this issue likely came from his stress more generally throughout his work (see especially *Division of Labor in Society* [1893/1994]) on the importance of the collective conscience. Subtle erosion of sentiments about collective things over long periods of time may not represent a concrete challenge to a society, especially if a new form of solidarity and new types of social bonds arise, but an acute and immediate threat to the solidarity based on these sentiments might well present a crisis, especially if the threat is against a collective belief that is emotionally charged. Such "deeply written" or "cherished" (also translated as "deeply engraven") beliefs can include those related to religion or other "sacred" collective objects or social symbols such as culture, the state, the family, and work.

Durkheim (1893/1984) explicitly afforded things such as tradition and the state a religious character and discussed how he expected the religiosity associated with them to decline as the division of labor increased. Such cherished collective sentiments were abundant in Russia, where we find (1) ancient cultural traditions, including those that privileged the group over the individual (see Kharkhordin 1999); and (2) three-quarters of a century of top-down socialism rife with ideological symbols and icons reminiscent of religion. The omnipresent Soviet state was not only a manifestation of the latter, but was also citizens' sole provider of nearly all the tangible things required for well-being, including health care, education, employment, and goods and services.

Durkheim (1900/1957) was clear in his belief that sentiments inspired by the collective (including the "cult of the State") are "stimulants to murder" (p. 115), which "is why political beliefs . . . often in themselves carry the seeds of homicide" (p. 116). Mentioning strong sentiments about politics, religion, and family together in the same paragraph in *Suicide*, Durkheim (1897/1979, 356) argued that "where family spirit has retained its ancient strength, offences against the family are regarded as sacrilege . . . [and w]here religious faith is very intense it often inspires murders and this is also true of political faith." Thus during times of political crisis (Durkheim 1897/1979, 353)—and during times of rapid political change that present an acute threat to the state and to long-standing traditions, and thus to collective sentiments—we should expect an increase in homicide rates. It follows that where political change and threats to collective sentiments are generally present, those areas experiencing greater change in political faith should be those areas where increases in homicide rates are greater.

It is important to note that while Durkheim spoke of threats to collective things, the type of violence he expected was not group-related or organized violence to protect the collective (i.e., calculated murders directed at a specific threat). On the contrary, he clearly believed that "the evolution of the trend of homicide . . . is better brought out by the curve of unpremeditated murder" (Durkheim 1897/1979, 349). This is probably because he more generally restricted his ideas about homicide to unpremeditated murders since to him "homicide is inseparable from passion" (Durkheim 1897/1979, 356). Thus, while our data did not allow us to discern between premeditated and unpremeditated homicide, it was more appropriate to test this aspect of his theory with data on interpersonal violence, as we did, and not group-related or organized crime and violence.

In this study, we tested the short-term aspect of Durkheim's hypothesis related to threats against collective sentiments. The large-scale natural experiment of the sudden collapse of the Soviet Union provided a rare opportunity to test this hypothesis, and the 1990s Russian political landscape presented unique measurement possibilities in relation to political change (we elaborate on both, especially the latter, in the Discussion section below). We argue that swift political change in Russia represented a political crisis. That is, the transition toward democratization and marketization—which stress individual freedoms, goals, rights, and responsibilities—represented a clear departure from and threat to (1) the Soviet state and all it represented and (2) deeply seated Russian cultural traditions and a lifestyle that privileged the group over the individual long before the Soviets arrived (Kharkhordin 1999).[3] Although these changes were occurring generally in Russia, their pace varied substantially throughout the vast nation. Thus, specifically, we tested the hypothesis that regions facing greater political change would be regions that experienced the greatest increases in homicide rates.

Data and Method

The unit of analysis in this study was the Russian region. There are eighty-nine of these regions, which are administrative units roughly equivalent to states or provinces. Data from the contiguous Ingush and Chechen Republics were considered unreliable for several reasons, including the ongoing war in the area, so they were excluded from this analysis. Data from nine of the smaller regions (each called an autonomous *okrug*, or district) were covered by the larger regions in which they are embedded. Note that data were not lost or missing from these regions but instead were simply included in the data from the larger region of which they are a part. This left seventy-eight cases for analysis (i.e., the entire sample of regions minus the Chechen and Ingush Republics).

The use of regions as units of analysis is important. Nearly all comparative political and social research within Russia employs these regions. In their study of electoral competition in Russia, for example, Moraski and Reisinger (2003, 280) stated that "Russia's regions are important polities with much influence over their residents' lives." The authors went on to state that "regional politics may well promote progress toward democracy for Russia as a whole or serve as a brake on such progress" (p. 280), which is a key theoretical issue at stake in this study. Finally, an important methodological issue is variation, and Moraski and Reisinger showed "that the regions vary significantly in electoral democratization . . . unlike during the Soviet era, when political institutions, policies, and mass behavior were kept relatively uniform" (p. 281).

The measure of violence in this study was the change in regional homicide victimization rates between 1991 (the final year of the Soviet Union's existence) and 2000.[4] We used the residual change score instead of the raw change score because it reflects the amount of change in a region's homicide rate unexplained by its initial levels (Bohrnstedt 1969). Thus, in this study, ΔHomicide2000 = Homicide2000 − (α + β × Homicide1991). Furthermore, because all of the regions were used to estimate the regression from which the residuals were drawn, the residual change scores reflect the developments of the entire ecological system under study (Morenoff and Sampson 1997). In other words, the score on the dependent variable for a specific region not only controls for that region's homicide rate in 1991 but also takes into account the changes in homicide rates between 1991 and 2000 in all of the other regions. This is important since we know from prior research that for the past several decades the spatial patterning of homicide in Russia has shown consistently lower rates in the Northern Caucasus and higher rates east of the Ural Mountains (Pridemore 2003a; Shelley 1980; Shkolnikov 1987; see also Stickley and Mäkinen 2005). Pridemore (2003b) described and compared Russian homicide estimates provided by the vital statistics and police reporting systems, concluding that the former provided significantly more reliable estimates of the overall number of homicides than the latter. We therefore used the age-standardized death rate (per one hundred thousand residents) due to homicide as our measure of the main dependent variable. The data employed here were prepared for the first author from vital statistics data from the Russian State Committee on Statistics.[5]

We used "political change" as a proxy for Durkheim's more abstract collective sentiments. Notice here a major assumption: we did not have a measure of collective sentiments, and thus we assumed rapid political change creates threats to these sentiments, which in turn heighten passions and lead to higher homicide rates. While we recognize that the statement that political change threatens sentiments about the collective is a proposition to be tested in itself, assumptions such as this are common in nearly every study of social structure and homicide, and we wish to make ours explicit here. Below, we present arguments about why we believe this to be a logical assumption, especially in Russia.

In our measurement of this concept, we began by recognizing Communist Party hegemony during the Soviet era, which resulted in essentially 100 percent of the vote being cast for Party candidates. We then obtained measures of the proportion of all voters who cast their ballots for Communist Party of the Russian Federation (CPRF) or Liberal Democratic Party of Russia (LDPR) candidates in the 1999 Duma and 2000 presidential elections.[6] As detailed in the Discussion section below, these were the two main opposition parties in Russia that called for a return to something resembling Communist or Soviet rule. An index was created that summed the z-scores for these four measures (i.e., CPRF vote in 1999 and 2000 and LDPR vote in 1999 and 2000).[7] Thus, the smaller a region's score on this index, the smaller its vote for these opposition parties, and therefore the greater the amount of political change in the region since the collapse of the Soviet Union (because Communist support was assumed to be nearly universal during the Soviet era, at least in terms of voting). This measure was reverse-coded so it could be interpreted in terms of the main concept under examination here, political change (i.e., dissipation of Communist Party electoral strength). We note that a unique set of political circumstances existed during the 1990s (until Vladimir Putin was elected president in 2000) that made this measure a strong indicator of political change. Specific political shifts since that time, however, mean that similar measures from subsequent elections probably would not tap the same sentiments we measured here. We elaborate on these unique circumstances (and their disappearance following the 2000 election) in the Discussion section below.

Several controls were employed in an attempt to isolate the effects of political change on changes in homicide rates. These controls come from prior structural-level research on homicide in Russia, the more general literature on the structural covariates of homicide, and from what we know about those most likely to have voted for the Communist Party in the Russian parliamentary and presidential elections. First, recent research testing another Durkheimian theory about rapid social change, social deregulation, anomie, and homicide showed that Russian regions facing the strongest negative effects of socioeconomic change during the 1990s were regions where homicide rates increased the most during this time (Kim and Pridemore 2005). Thus, we included as a control Kim and Pridemore's (2005) negative socioeconomic change index, which gauged regional changes over the 1990s in population, privatization, unemployment, poverty, and foreign capital investment (in their creation of the index, the authors coded these measures in such a way that privatization and foreign capital investment were positive).

Second, in the one cross-sectional model included in this analysis, we included the proportion of the regional population living below the poverty line in 1999 as a measure of poverty. This was done not only because area measures of poverty are the most consistent covariate of homicide rates in the social structure and homicide literature (see Messner and Rosenfeld 1999; Pridemore 2002b) but also because the Communist Party was popular among the poor during the election cycle under examination (March 2001). Similarly, measures for educational level of the population and the proportion of the population living in urban areas were included as controls because they were likely confounded with CPRF voting. That is, not only might these variables have an influence on homicide rates themselves, but those with a lower education and those living in rural areas were more likely to vote for the Communist Party and "against reform and reformers" (Slider, Gimpelson, and Chugrov 1994, 718; March 2001; also see chapters in Hesli and Reisinger [2003] and in Wyman, White, and Oates [1998]).[8] It was also important to control for the proportion living in urban areas because Durkheim (1897/1979, 353) argued that homicide rates in rural areas were higher due to stronger sentiments about the collective in rural areas and greater respect for the body and the individual in urban areas (see Durkheim [1897/1979, 293], where he argued that "gross and violent" acts conflict "with the gentleness of urban manners and the regard of the cultivated classes for the human body").[9] Education was measured as the number of people enrolled in college per one thousand residents, and urbanization as the proportion of the regional population living in cities with more than one hundred thousand residents (data for all three of these measures were obtained from Goskomstat [2001]).

Andrienko (2001) and Pridemore (2002a) have shown alcohol consumption to be associated with the growth of crime and violence in Russia and with the spatial distribution of regional homicide rates in the country, respectively. Thus, we used Pridemore's (2002a) proxy for heavy drinking, which was the regional age-standardized rate (per one hundred thousand) of deaths due to alcohol poisoning (examples of and reasons for using this proxy in Russia are explained elsewhere: Chenet et al. [2001]; Shkolnikov, McKee, and Leon [2001]; Shkolnikov and Meslé [1996]). Finally, prior research has shown that homicide rates in the regions east of the Ural Mountains are currently (Pridemore 2003b) and have been historically (Shelley 1980; Shkolnikov 1987) significantly higher than in the rest of the nation. Therefore, we included a dummy variable for those regions located in this area.

We note that the measures of alcohol consumption, education, and urbanization did not represent change scores between 1991 and 2000, although the dependent variable did. While this presents a problem with model estimation, we did not have access to all data for all variables in the final years before the breakup of the Soviet Union. We recognize this as a limitation but thought it better to employ these controls using available data rather than ignoring them completely, especially because some may be confounded with voting for the CPRF and LDPR.

We discuss our attempts to minimize this limitation in the discussion of model sensitivity below.

[W]hat disappeared with the Soviet Union was not simply an abstract ideology or government, but a provider and an icon, a way of life fused with the longer history and traditions of Russian culture.

Finally, the Chukot and Jewish Autonomous Okrugs were missing observations on 1991 homicide rates, so 1992 rates were substituted when creating the residual change scores. Two of the variables—education and percentage urban—had skew statistics greater than twice their standard errors, and thus we logarithmically transformed their values to more closely approximate a normal distribution. Four of the regions had no cities with more than one hundred thousand people, so 1 was added to each score before taking the log since the natural logarithm of 0 is undefined. With one exception (discussed below), all models were estimated using ordinary least squares regression. Common exploratory data analysis techniques were employed and regression diagnostics and tests of model sensitivity were carried out.

Results

Brief definitions and descriptive statistics for each variable are shown in Table 1. Means and standard deviations in this table are for each variable before log transformations were carried out. The table shows that the mean regional homicide victimization rate in 2000 was about thirty per one hundred thousand residents. The table also shows that, on average, regional homicide rates increased by nearly fourteen per one hundred thousand between 1991 and 2000, which represented a greater than 80 percent increase. Looking at absolute changes, every region except one (Kursk Oblast, in which the homicide rate decreased by less than one per one hundred thousand residents) experienced an increase in its homicide rate during this period. The mean regional proportion of the vote going to the CPRF and LDPR (as a percentage of those who voted) in the presidential elections

TABLE 1
BRIEF DEFINITIONS AND DESCRIPTIVE STATISTICS FOR
DEPENDENT AND INDEPENDENT VARIABLES ($N = 78$)

Variable	Description	Mean	SD
ΔHomicide	1991 homicide victimization rate subtracted from 2000 homicide rate	13.6	8.6
Homicide 2000	2000 homicide victimization rate	30.1	17.5
Political change	Z-scored index of political change (see text for description)	0.0	2.5
SE change	Index of negative socioeconomic change (see text)	1.4	1.1
Alcohol	Proxy (see text): Number of deaths per one hundred thousand residents due to alcohol poisoning in 2000	28.7	17.5
Education	Number of students enrolled in higher education per one thousand residents in 2000	27.0	13.8
Urban	Proportion of population living in cities with more than one hundred thousand residents in 2000	39.0	16.5
Poverty	Proportion of population living below subsistence minimum in 1999	42.7	16.2
East	Dummy variable for those regions located east of the Ural Mountains	—	—

NOTE: The change score for homicide in this table is the raw change score. In model estimation, the change score was the residual when 2000 rates were regressed on 1991 rates (see text). SE = socioeconomic

in 2000 was 32.6 percent, and in the parliamentary elections in 1999 was 32.1 percent (not shown in the table). Note that these are regional means, not the actual proportion of the vote for these parties in the country as a whole.[10]

Results of model estimation are shown in Table 2. Models 1 through 3 employed the residual change score as the dependent variable, while model 4 used the 2000 homicide rate as the dependent variable. Model 1 was a baseline model estimated without the inclusion of political change. As expected, the negative socioeconomic change index, the proxy for heavy drinking, and regional location east of the Urals were all positively and significantly associated with the change in homicide rates between 1991 and 2000. Model 2 was the same as model 1, but included the political change index. The results indicated support for Durkheim's prediction. That is, holding constant the other variables in the model, regions that experienced greater political change (and thus, we assume, greater threats to sentiments about the collective) between 1991 and 2000 were regions where homicide rates increased the most. The inferences drawn for the other variables remained unchanged with the addition of the political change

TABLE 2

RESULTS FOR ΔHOMICIDE RATES AND 2000 HOMICIDE RATES REGRESSED ON POLITICAL CHANGE AND CONTROL VARIABLES ($N = 78$)

Variable	Model 1: DV = ΔHomicide			Model 2: DV = ΔHomicide			Model 3: DV = ΔHomicide			Model 4: DV = 2000 Homicide		
	b	SE	p	b	SE	p	b	SE	p	b	SE	p
Constant	8.25	6.33	.196	9.24	6.13	.137	8.53	1.38	<.001	13.39	11.78	.260
Political change	—	—	—	0.79	0.32	.017	0.67	0.37	.075	1.71	0.59	.005
SE change	2.13	0.80	.009	2.06	0.77	.009	2.07	0.84	.015	—	—	—
Alcohol	0.19	0.05	<.001	0.18	0.04	<.001	—	—	—	0.43	0.08	<.001
Log education	−3.17	2.11	.139	−3.87	2.07	.065	—	—	—	−3.58	3.77	.346
Log urban	1.52	1.16	.195	1.78	1.13	.119	—	—	—	1.23	2.05	.549
Poverty	—	—	—	—	—	—	—	—	—	0.11	0.09	.227
East	6.59	1.81	<.001	8.48	1.91	<.001	7.85	2.16	.001	24.58	3.36	<.001
Adjusted R^2		.41			.45			.25			.56	

NOTE: DV = dependence variable; SE = socioeconomic

index, with the possible exception of education, which had a p-value of .065 in model 2.[11]

Model sensitivity

Aside from the normal regression diagnostics routinely employed, further precautions were taken to test the sensitivity of these findings to the peculiarities of the model resulting from data limitations. First, since the controls for heavy drinking, education, and urban did not represent change scores, a reduced model was estimated in which they were excluded. The results are shown as model 3 in Table 2. The p-value in this model for the political change index was .075. This does not allow for strong conclusions, but given the sample size, the absence of potential confounders from the model, and the unidirectional hypothesis, this is in line with expectations. The inferences drawn for the other two variables in model 3 remained the same as in previous models. Second, technically the political change index was not a change score because it represented outcomes from the 1999 and 2000 elections (and thus has only measures from time 2 not time 1). The initial response to this is that it *does* reflect change since in the past the Communist Party exerted hegemonic control over the political realm and received virtually 100 percent of the vote. Nevertheless, to address this limitation, an alternative model was estimated in which the dependent variable was the regional homicide rate in 2000. In this model, the negative socioeconomic change index was dropped because it represented a change score, though the other controls from earlier models were included since they were measured in 2000. Furthermore, a measure of poverty was included since it is often found to be associated with area homicide rates and since it is likely confounded with the vote for the opposition parties. The findings are presented as model 4 in Table 2. The results revealed that the effect size for the political change index in this model was substantially higher than in previous models and that the inferences drawn remained the same as in previous models.[12]

Discussion

Several prior structural-level studies have employed voter turnout to represent various concepts potentially related to crime and violence, including civic engagement (Chamlin and Cochran 1995; Rosenfeld, Messner, and Baumer 2001), political disaffection (Callahan 1998), and level of conformity with norms (Coleman 2002). For whom an electorate votes, however, may be an even more important indicator of larger social forces than voter turnout, especially in the midst of a political transition. In the case of Russia, the shift was from a totalitarian past toward democracy and a free market. The former state had not only provided cradle to grave benefits for its citizens, some of whom were dependent upon this largesse and thus more vulnerable to the forces of economic transition, but also instilled (or at least forced) among many an almost religious deference. Thus, what disappeared with the Soviet Union was not simply an abstract ideology or government, but a provider and an icon, a way of life fused with the longer history and traditions of Russian culture.

In his review and critique of the contemporary theoretical and empirical literature on Durkheim's theories of homicide, DiCristina (2004, 81) stated clearly that "no empirical study of Durkheim's theory has directly tested his proposition concerning the effect of collective sentiments on homicide. In fact . . . few descriptions of Durkheim's theory even acknowledge this core proposition. This is a serious oversight."[13] In this context, it appears as if DiCristina was speaking mainly of the expected decrease in homicide over the long term as a result of the decline in the number and strength of such sentiments. In our study, we tested for the first time a related version of Durkheim's hypothesis that DiCristina (pp. 69-70) also discussed: political crisis (in our case, rapid political change) represents a threat to collective things, which is expected to incite passions and thus increase homicide (see Durkheim 1897/1979, 352-55).

Taking advantage of the unique research and measurement opportunities presented by the large-scale natural experiment of the dissolution of the Soviet Union and the subsequent democratization and marketization in Russia, we found support for this hypothesis. Specifically, regions that experienced the greatest amount of political change during the 1990s were regions where homicide rates increased the most, even after controlling for the effects of rapid socioeconomic change. The results of prior research (Kim and Pridemore 2005) showing an association between socioeconomic change (i.e., the "anomie" hypothesis) and the change in regional homicide rates in Russia are strengthened by our study, given their replication in a model that includes a control for the "collective things" hypothesis. Furthermore, while *we* do not take a strong stance on the issue, and while political and socioeconomic change are not mutually exclusive, in Durkheimian terms the homicides due to the deregulation resulting from rapid socioeconomic change would be labeled anomic and those resulting from political change or crisis would be labeled altruistic since the latter result from threats to sentiments about the collective (see chap. 5 in book 2 of Durkheim's *Suicide* [1897/1979] as well as pp. 357-58 and 368-69).

[W]hile there may be alternatives to Durkheim's hypothesis when explaining our results, an idealized vision of Soviet communism and its vestiges is not one of them.

Although they did not directly test Durkheim's hypothesis, other scholars recently have found similar results. For example, Villarreal (2002) studied the connection between political characteristics and homicide in Mexico, another nation experiencing an uneven transition to democracy. He found a positive association between electoral competition at the local level and homicide rates. The author concluded that in societies that possess strong patronage networks (which Russia certainly did, given the history and entrenchment of the Communist Party), political changes that threaten the former political order result in increased rates of violence. Though Villarreal did not interpret his findings in Durkheimian terms, his results were consistent with those presented here, and in places his wording closely parallels Durkheim's. In another study, Kondrichin's (2000) research on Belarus, reported in a Russian-language journal, found an inverse correlation between a region's vote for a Communist candidate and its homicide rate. The results of these studies, as well as our own, suggest that where there is less (rapid) movement away from the past there is less of a political crisis and less threat to sentiments about collective things (DiCristina 2004); and where there is less threat to these sentiments, homicide rates are lower. All of this coincides with Karstedt's (2001) findings of higher homicide rates in nations with stronger collectivistic values.

The radical political change experienced by Russian citizens cannot be overstated. Socialist ideology was infused into every aspect of daily life, and the Communist Party was deeply entrenched not just nationally but at the local level and in multiple aspects of daily life such as education and employment. Furthermore, by design Soviet institutions created narrow and homogenized interests and desires, not to mention dependence on the state. Yet while vestiges of state socialism and the Communist Party certainly remain and in some aspects are still quite strong, the political break from the past could have hardly been swifter or sharper. The "shock therapy" that instituted market reforms was radically at odds with the former centrally planned economy in its most fundamental assumptions. The same is true for group protection and the dependence engendered by the Soviets in their relation to the new individual rights, responsibilities, and diversity of democracy. These profound changes, together with the dramatic and publicly visible events of the time, by their very nature represented a direct assault on and break from the past (Bunce 1998, 192-93, 200-201). Slow evolutionary change allows strong sentiments to dissipate, erode, and be replaced, thereby leaving the original sentiments (and the "things" themselves) to fade into the past. On the other hand, rapid political change occurs in a context where the collective things are still present and the sentiments about them still strong, thus perhaps engendering interpersonal violence via the mechanisms described by Durkheim.

One alternative explanation for our findings is that the conditions in regions with a greater vote for the Communist Party are similar in structure and institutional strength (as opposed to sentiments) to the communist past and thus exert more social control, thereby resulting in smaller increases in homicides. While we do not have a measure of social control in our analysis, and while several of the regions with higher vote totals for the Communist Party in the presidential and parliamentary elections also had governors who were members of or sensitive to the Communist Party, it is important to understand the limits of this explanation. First, the belief that rates of violent crime were significantly lower in Soviet Russia than in Western nations was propaganda and patently false. Pridemore (2003a) has employed newly available mortality data to track Russian homicide victimization rates over time and found that they were as high as or higher than in the United States for at least the past several decades. Karstedt's (2001) findings about collectivistic value structures and higher violence rates mentioned earlier are also relevant here. Second, the high level of corruption and low morale among the police in post-Soviet Russia are not due solely to present conditions, but are rooted in the (police) culture of the Soviet era (Beck and Robertson 2005). Similarly, regions governed by CPRF politicians likely possess fewer reasons (and demand) for police transparency and responsibility than more democratic regions. Furthermore, even where Communist Party candidates received a large proportion of the vote or won local mayoral or gubernatorial elections, the regions were not truly communist in structure and institutions, at least as thought of during the Soviet era. Finally, several studies have shown a strong link in Russian regions "between democratic success and success in solving key economic and social problems" (Moraski and Reisinger 2003, 297). Those regions that resist democratic and economic reforms and maintain high levels of firm-level barter, subsidies, and social spending have been unable to attract business and thus build a strong tax base to support their policies in the long run (Konitzer-Smirnov 2003), which has led to a reduction in standards of living and an increase in dependency in these regions. All this suggests that while there may be alternatives to Durkheim's hypothesis when explaining our results, an idealized vision of Soviet communism and its vestiges is not one of them.

Given the topic of this special issue of the journal, we should note that the results of our study are more about the effects on changing homicide rates of rapid political change generally, not necessarily democratization specifically. In discussing democracy, transition, and crime, for example, Karstedt (2003) made a similar point: that it is the failure to democratize rather than democratization that is responsible for rising crime rates in several post-Soviet countries. She noted specifically the failure of these nations to develop a functioning civil society, along with other deficiencies such as continuing distrust of the legal system, as a cause of crime. Similarly Karstedt (1999) focused on the crisis of *deregulation* (i.e., the lack of regulation, or at least the dissolution of the former mode of regulation) in her discussion of social transformation and crime as opposed to how specific characteristics of democratization and democracy lead to higher crime rates. And as mentioned earlier, Karstedt (2001) found that nations in which respondents scored higher on the individualistic and egalitarian values associated with democracy had *lower* rates of violence than nations in which respondents scored higher on collectivistic values. Thus, while it is true in the case of Russia that the initial change was from Soviet socialism and a centrally planned economy toward democracy and a free market, our analysis does not allow us to conclude that there is something special about the transition to *democracy* that is important, but rather it is the *rapid change* that appears to be the operative mechanism. Future comparative research may find that the conditions accompanying the Russian transition are in fact common to democratizing nations, and thus there truly may be something special about becoming a democracy that in the short term leads to increased levels of crime. On the other hand, other paths to democracy may not result in increased rates of crime; or we may find that Russia is not truly becoming a democracy and that what led to increased crime rates was state failure, social and legal deregulation, and the criminogenic conditions engendered by rapid change in the political economy.

Unique natural experiment and measurement opportunities

Certain specific and unique elements made Russia an appropriate case study to test this previously unexamined Durkheimian theory, and a fleeting political context made this study feasible and allowed us to create a valid measure of political change. First, some of the foundational theories of sociology and structural-level criminology were created in an attempt to understand the causes and effects of social change. However, scholars are usually stuck with slow-moving cases as examples or, even further from theoretical tenets but often necessary, using cross-sectional studies to compare cases possessing a range of scores on a particular variable and assuming these differences represent linear development. In Russia, we have a natural experiment in socioeconomic and political change associated with democratization and marketization that has had a profound influence on Russian society and social institutions, thereby presenting scholars with a large-scale case study of the effects of rapid social change on a society.

Second, a unique set of circumstances made our measure of political change appropriate for the period under study, but following the 2000 presidential election, changes in the political landscape made this specific indicator suspect. During the 1990s, the Communist Party (and to a lesser extent the LDPR) was clearly the place to turn not only for ideological communists but for those dissatisfied with the transition. The Party was most popular among people (e.g., the poor, uneducated, and pensioners) and in places (e.g., rural areas and regions with failing farms and unproductive heavy industry) left behind by the sweeping changes (March 2001). Further distinguishing the Communist Party as the antichange party (and party of the past) was Yeltsin's virulent anticommunist position, as well as the Party's own strong stance of anti-Westernism.

The Russian homicide rate more than tripled between 1988 and 1994.

The CPRF took advantage of the popular dissatisfaction with marketization by stressing economic issues in its campaigns and running on a strongly patriotic and nationalist platform, for example, calling for the state to "return to citizens their guaranteed socioeconomic rights" and to again become "the main guarantor of social justice" (as quoted in Cook 2005, 51). Similarly, the Party continued to call for the protection of the "culture, language, beliefs, and customs of all Russian people" while declaring itself the refuge of "patriots" who had experienced "pain" and "humiliation" as a result of the Soviet downfall (Kommunisticheskaya Partiya Rossiskoi Federatsii 2005). Throughout the elections of the 1990s and until 2000, the Communist Party created broad coalitions of socialist and nationalist opposition organizations (McFaul 1997). The Party was the main victor in the 1995 Duma election (garnering about one-third of all seats); its presidential candidate, Gennady Zyuganov, received 32 percent (to Yeltsin's 35 percent) in the first round of the 1996 presidential election, which Zyuganov lost in the runoff (but still received 40 percent of the vote); and the Communist Party again won the largest faction in the 1999 Duma elections, securing 50 percent more seats than its closest rivals (114 compared to 73 for Unity and 67 for Fatherland–All Russia).

Following the 1999/2000 election cycle, however, several developments converged to decrease the popularity of the Communist Party and to make a measure such as ours a much weaker indicator of political change. Even in the 1999 Duma election, the CPRF ranked at the bottom in attracting new voters, those who had previously voted for other parties, and young Russians (Colton and McFaul 2003; March 2001), yet the Party ran on the same platform in 2003. Furthermore, before the 2003 Duma election President Putin increased electoral competition on the Left by working with communist splinter parties that were pro-Kremlin, and he also orchestrated a widespread media campaign aimed at discrediting the Communist Party. All this resulted in a sharp drop in the number of Duma seats won by Party candidates. President Putin enjoyed enormous popularity during his first term, during which he seized control of the media, continued to build a superpresidential system (see Sakwa 2005a), and co-opted elites across the political system (as well as symbols and ideas—such as patriotism, self-reliance, and Soviet references—that had previously "belonged" to the CPRF).[14] The perennial Communist Party presidential candidate, Gennady Zyuganov, withdrew from the 2003 presidential election because of Putin's insurmountable lead, and the replacement candidate received only 14 percent of the vote. In the 2003/2004 election cycle, the Communist Party not only failed to gain new voters, but also lost votes from specific regions and demographic groups that had previously provided solid support. Recent surveys also suggest that even citizens who maintain hope for a return to a Soviet-style economy believe Russia should be friendly toward the West, which is in contrast to the Party's distinctly anti-Western platform. Thus, while the CPRF still has a voice, it is muted, and the Party no longer fills the distinctive ideological niche it did during the 1990s.

Conclusion

The Russian homicide rate more than tripled between 1988 and 1994. Although the rate decreased somewhat from its 1994 peak and stabilized, in 2000 it was still twice as high as it had been a decade earlier. Prior research has established compelling evidence for Durkheim's anomie/social deregulation hypothesis as an explanation for increases in both national-level (Chamlin, Pridemore, and Cochran 2005) and regional-level (Kim and Pridemore 2005) homicide rates. This study examined another important, though rarely tested, aspect of Durkheim's ideas about change, finding support for the hypothesis that rapid political change (or political crisis) has separate and distinct effects on homicide rates.

Durkheim's overarching thesis concerning societal development and solidarity should lead us to expect a decrease in violence in the long run because of the strengthening of the religion of humanity, or moral individualism. Similarly, during gradual societal development, the weakening of the power of the collective, and thus of the strength of passions and collective sentiments, should lead to fewer homicides. According to Durkheim (1897/1979, 353), however, short-term political crises or threats to the collective (more generally, see pp. 352-55) will incite passions that result in increased violence. Soviet Russia was hardly an undeveloped society representative of Durkheim's mechanical solidarity. To the contrary, it was technologically advanced, possessed a developed (if forced) division of labor, and exhibited certain values that highlighted individuality (Karstedt 2003; Kharkhordin 1999). Nevertheless, it is fair to argue that long-standing Russian cultural traditions included strong bonds based on collective sentiments, and the Soviet era resulted in ideologically rooted and exaggerated sentiments about the collective. Such cherished beliefs, according to Durkheim, are bound to elicit heightened passions when threatened.

We have provided initial support for this hypothesis here, and the results were made even stronger by controlling for the negative effects of rapid socioeconomic change, thereby distinguishing two different mechanisms through which different aspects of change (socioeconomic and political) can influence rates of interpersonal violence. So while we would expect democratization, political competition, and the development of civil society to be healthy (especially relative to the Soviet juggernaut of the past) and, in the long run, to result in lower rates of violence, the process is not without considerable accompanying growing pains. In Russia, at least, it appears that the threats to sentiments about the collective resulting from swift political change was partially responsible for the increase in the Russian homicide rate, which is now among the highest in the world.

Notes

1. By "democratization" in Russia, we refer to developments such as building civil society, competitive elections, governmental transparency, and privileging the protection of individual rights instead of protecting the state. By "marketization" in Russia, we refer to movement away from state ownership and toward private ownership and entrepreneurship, away from a centrally planned command economy toward a free market and a demand economy, and creating the legal framework necessary to secure business transactions. While democratization and marketization often go hand in hand and are hard to separate in the discussion of political economy, they are not necessarily interchangeable, with China (and increasingly Russia) being a good example of a move toward a relatively free market in the midst of a decidedly undemocratic political system. Similarly, most free markets were originally established in nondemocratic societies (e.g., nineteenth-century Germany, the United Kingdom, and France). In this article, we focus on the democratization aspect of these changes, given our focus elsewhere on the effects of the social and economic features of the transition on changes in homicide rates (Pridemore and Kim 2005).

2. Following DiCristina's (2004) usage throughout his article, we use the phrase "sentiments about collective things" (or alternatively "sentiments about the collective" or "collective sentiments"). Tangible examples of these "things" and of "collective sentiments" include religion, family, community, and the state, which are visible symbols of more abstract concepts such as culture, tradition, daily routines, and way of life.

3. In her discussion of social transformation and crime, Karstedt (1999, 309) aptly described this shift as a "transformation of one 'mode of regulation' to another." The earlier mode resulted not only from the cultural traditions of the collective in Russia but also the forced homogeneity, uniformity, and overregulation of society by the Soviets. Russia was thus faced with a paradigmatic shift from the social protection of the past to the economic and political liberalization of the present and the diversity it allowed (see also Karstedt 2003).

4. While political and economic change in the Soviet Union began in the mid-1980s to late 1980s, there are several reasons for choosing 1991 as the key initial year for analysis of change. The changes of the 1980s were qualitatively different than those following the dissolution of the Soviet Union. While liberalizing, the former sought to retain the underlying political and economic framework, while the latter resulted in a paradigmatic shift that required discarding this framework. Furthermore, examination of available socioeconomic

time-series data reveals that they remained relatively stable until the collapse of the Soviet Union, then changed rapidly. Similarly, while homicide rates did go up at the end of the 1980s, they were increasing from the abnormal lows that occurred during the antialcohol campaign (Pridemore 2003a). Finally, the formal shifts toward democratization and a free market officially and legally began in 1992.

5. Russia used the abridged Soviet coding system to classify cause of death until 1999, when it began using International Classification of Diseases (ICD) codes—10th revision. The case definition of homicide in the Soviet system was the same as that in the ICD codes. Soviet and Russian mortality data in general (Anderson and Silver 1997) and for violent death (Wasserman and Värnik 1998) have been subjected to multiple validation procedures with positive results (see also Värnik et al. 2001). The Russian Mortality Database, 2003, was provided to first author by Dr. Evgueni Andreev and Nina Andrianova, based upon Goskomstat data.

6. Although in strict political terms the Liberal Democratic Party of Russia (LDPR) might be considered a nationalist party on the opposite end of the spectrum of the Communist Party, it appealed to similar sentiments in terms of a return to state socialism and authoritarian rule (Cook 2005). Most important, it was a key player in the so-called "red-brown" coalitions that targeted market reforms and were vehemently anti-Yeltsin. As noted in the Model Sensitivity section, an alternative measure that included only the Communist Party of the Russian Federation (CPRF) vote yielded the same results as the index including the LDPR.

7. See Solnick (1998) and Konitzer-Smirnov (2003) for examples from the Russian Area Studies literature of research employing the vote for the Communist Party and/or the LDPR as measures of the strength of oppositionist sentiment and similar theoretical concepts.

8. Individual-level political research on postcommunist transitions shows that older generations, especially pensioners, are more likely to vote for communist successor parties (Moraski and Reisinger 2003, 286). Unlike the United States, however, homicide victimization rates in Russia are higher among older people (even into their fifties and sixties) than among younger cohorts (Pridemore 2003a), so it is unclear theoretically how this would influence the outcome in Russia.

9. Assuming that Durkheim was correct in this assertion, this is another example where the evidence suggests Russia, at least more closely than most Western nations, fits Durkheim's notion of stronger bonds based on sentiments about the collective. That is, in Russia the association between urbanization and homicide rates is not what we expect given the literature on homicide in the United States. On average, homicide rates in small cities and rural Russia are higher than urban rates, though recent evidence suggests this gap is closing (Chervyakov et al. 2002).

10. At the national level, the CPRF received 24.3 percent and the LDPR 6.0 percent of the vote in the 1999 Duma election. In the 2000 presidential election, the Communist Party candidate, Gennady Zyuganov, received 29.2 percent and the LDPR candidate, Vladimir Zhirinovsky, received 2.9 percent.

11. Given the unidirectional hypotheses, one-tailed tests would be appropriate for all variables. We report p-values for two-tailed tests, however, to err on the conservative side.

12. Furthermore, given that the distribution of the regional homicide rates in 2000 was substantially skewed, model 4 was reestimated employing negative binomial regression, which is a more reliable remedy to this limitation than a log transformation of the dependent variable (Hannon and Knapp 2003; Osgood 2000). Results are not shown here, but the inferences drawn for each of the variables, including the political change index, remained the same. Finally, all of the models discussed thus far were reestimated using only the vote for the CPRF since it received a much greater proportion of the vote (based upon regional means: a greater than ten to one margin in 2000 and nearly a four to one margin in 1999) and was often considered a coalition representing various opposition voices, and since the LDPR was nationalist in ideology and viewed as more of a fringe party. Similarly, since the Russian political system is dominated by the executive, which leads to differential voter turnout and party preference in presidential elections relative to elections for local representatives (Freedom House 2004), models were estimated using an index that represented only the 1999 Duma election. When employing these alternative measures, the inferences drawn for the effects of political change on change in homicide rates remained the same as those discussed thus far for the political change index, nor were there any substantial changes to the results for the other variables in the various models.

13. While several studies have borrowed from Durkheim in various ways, we generally agree with DiCristina (2004) about the lack of tests of the specific hypothesis he mentioned here and our test of a variant of it. However, we note that while cross-sectional and not necessarily testing *threats* to collective

sentiments, Karstedt's (2001) work testing Durkheimian hypotheses via the use of Hofstede's cultural dimensions of collectivism is one possible exception.

14. Furthermore, it is safe to say that under President Putin (especially his second administration), there has been some political backsliding and a stagnation in the transition toward democracy. This also plays out in the results from the 2003/2004 election cycle (see Hale, McFaul, and Colton 2004; Sakwa 2005b), though these issues are beyond the scope of the current article.

References

Anderson, Barbara A., and Brian D. Silver. 1997. Issues of data quality in assessing mortality trends and levels in the New Independent States. In *Premature death in the new independent states*, ed. José L. Bobadilla, Christine A. Costello, and Faith Mitchell, 120-55. Washington, DC: National Academy Press.

Andrienko, Yuri. 2001. Understanding the crime growth in Russia during the transition period: A criminometric approach. *Ekonomicheskiy Zhurnal Vyshey Shkoly Ekonomiki* 5:194-220.

Beck, Adrian, and Annette Robertson. 2005. Policing in post-Soviet Russia. In *Ruling Russia: Law, crime, and justice in a changing society*, ed. William A. Pridemore, 247-60. Lanham, MD: Rowman & Littlefield.

Bohrnstedt, George W. 1969. Observations on the measurement of change. *Sociological Methodology* 1:113-33.

Bunce, Valerie. 1998. Regional differences in democratization: The east versus the south. *Post-Soviet Affairs* 14:187-211.

Callahan, David. 1998. Ballot blocks: What gets the poor to the polls? *American Prospect* 39 (9): 68-75.

Chamlin, Mitchell B., and John K. Cochran. 1995. Assessing Messner and Rosenfeld's institutional anomie theory: A partial test. *Criminology* 33:411-29.

Chamlin, Mitchell B., William A. Pridemore, and John K. Cochran. 2005. An interrupted time series analysis of Durkheim's social deregulation thesis: The case of the Russian Federation. Paper presented at the International Union for Scientific Study of Population, Tours, France.

Chenet, Laurent, Annie Britton, Ramune Kalediene, and Jadvyga Petrauskiene. 2001. Daily variations in deaths in Lithuania: The possible contribution of binge drinking. *International Journal of Epidemiology* 30:743-48.

Chervyakov, Valerii V., Vladimir M. Shkolnikov, William A. Pridemore, and Martin McKee. 2002. The changing nature of murder in Russia. *Social Science & Medicine* 55:1713-24.

Coleman, Stephen. 2002. A test for the effect of conformity on crime rates using voter turnout. *Sociological Quarterly* 43:257-76.

Colton, Timothy, and Michael McFaul. 2003. *Popular choice and managed democracy: The Russian elections of 1999 and 2000*. Washington, DC: Brookings Institution Press.

Cook, Linda J. 2005. Russian political parties, the Duma, and the welfare state. In *Ruling Russia: Law, crime, and justice in a changing society*, ed. William A. Pridemore. Lanham, MD: Rowman & Littlefield.

DiCristina, Bruce. 2004. Durkheim's theory of homicide and the confusion of the empirical literature. *Theoretical Criminology* 8:57-91.

Durkheim, Emile. 1893/1984. *The division of labor in society*. Translated by W. D. Halls. New York: Free Press.

———. 1897/1979. *Suicide: A study in sociology*. Translated by John A. Spaulding and George Simpson. New York: Free Press.

———. 1900/1957. *Professional ethics and civic morals*. Translated by Cornelia Brookfield. New York: Routledge.

Freedom House. 2004. *Nations in transit: Democratization in East Central Europe and Eurasia*. Lanham, MD: Rowman & Littlefield.

Goskomstat. 2001. *Rossiiskoi statisticheskii ezhegodnik* [Russian statistical yearbook]. Moscow: Goskomstat.

Hale, Henry E., Michael McFaul, and Timothy Colton. 2004. Putin and the "delegative democracy" trap: Evidence from Russia's 2003-04 elections. *Post-Soviet Affairs* 20:285-319.

Hannon, Lance, and Peter Knapp. 2003. Reassessing nonlinearity in the urban disadvantage/violent crime relationship: An example of methodological bias from log transformation. *Criminology* 41:1427-48.

Hesli, Vicki, and William Reisinger, eds. 2003. *The 1999-2000 elections in Russia: Their impact and legacy*. Cambridge: Cambridge University Press.

Karstedt, Susanne. 1999. Social transformation and crime: A crisis of deregulation. In *The rule of law after communism: Problems and prospects in East-Central Europe*, ed. Martin Krygier and Adam Czarnota. Brookfield, VT: Ashgate.

————. 2001. Die moralische Stärke schwacher Bindungen: Individualismus un Gewalt im Kulturvergleich [The moral strength of weak ties: A cross-cultural comparison of individualism and violence]. *Monatsschrift fuer Kriminologie und Strafrechtsreform* 84:225-43.

————. 2003. Legacies of a culture of inequality: The Janus face of crime in post-communist countries. *Crime, Law, and Social Change* 40:295-320.

Kharkhordin, Oleg. 1999. *The collective and the individual in Russia: A study of practice*. Berkeley: University of California Press.

Kim, Sang-Weon, and William A. Pridemore. 2005. Poverty, socioeconomic change, institutional anomie, and homicide. *Social Science Quarterly* 86:1377-98.

Kommunisticheskaya Partiya Rossiskoi Federatsii. 2005. Ofitsialnii sait KPRF [Official Web site of the Communist Party of the Russian Federation]. www.kprf.ru.

Kondrichin, Sergei V. 2000. Regional'naya differentsiatsiya elektoral'nykh, urovnya samoubiistv i smertnosti ot nasil'stvennykh prichin: k voprosu ob etnogeneze sotsial'nogo povediniya [Regional differences in electoral turnout and the level of suicide and deaths from violent causes: On the question of the genesis of social behavior]. *Sotsiologicheskii Zhurnal* 3-4:98-117.

Konitzer-Smirnov, Andrew. 2003. Incumbent electoral fortunes and regional economic performance during Russia's 2000-2001 regional executive election cycle. *Post-Soviet Affairs* 19:46-79.

March, Luke. 2001. For victory? The crises and dilemmas of the Communist Party of the Russian Federation. *Europe-Asia Studies* 53:263-90.

McFaul, Michael. 1997. *Russia's 1996 presidential election: The end of polarized politics*. Stanford, CA: Hoover Institution Press.

Messner, Steven F., and Richard Rosenfeld. 1999. Social structure and homicide: Theory and research. In *Homicide: A sourcebook of social research*, ed. M. Dwayne Smith and Margaret A. Zahn. Thousand Oaks, CA: Sage.

Moraski, Bryon J., and William M. Reisinger. 2003. Explaining electoral competition across Russia's regions. *Slavic Review* 62:278-301.

Morenoff, Jeffrey D., and Robert J. Sampson. 1997. Violent crime and the spatial dynamics of neighborhood transition: Chicago, 1970-1990. *Social Forces* 76:31-64.

Osgood, D. Wayne. 2000. Poisson-based regression analysis of aggregate crime rates. *Journal of Quantitative Criminology* 16:21-43.

Pridemore, William A. 2002a. Vodka and violence: Alcohol consumption and homicide rates in Russia. *American Journal of Public Health* 92:1921-30.

————. 2002b. What we know about social structure and homicide: A review of the theoretical and empirical literature. *Violence & Victims* 17:127-56.

————. 2003a. Demographic, temporal, and spatial patterns of homicide rates in Russia. *European Sociological Review* 19:41-59.

————. 2003b. Measuring homicide in Russia: A comparison of estimates from the crime and vital statistics reporting systems. *Social Science & Medicine* 57:1343-54.

————. 2005. Social structure and homicide in post-Soviet Russia. *Social Science Research* 34:732-56.

Pridemore, William A., and Sang-Weon Kim. 2005. Negative socioeconomic change and homicide in transitional Russia. Paper presented to the Homicide Research Working Group annual meetings, Orlando, FL.

Rosenfeld, Richard, Steven F. Messner, and Eric P. Baumer. 2001. Social capital and homicide. *Social Forces* 80:283-309.

Sakwa, Richard. 2005a. Presidential power: The struggle for hegemony. In *Ruling Russia: Law, crime, and justice in a changing society*, ed. William A. Pridemore. Lanham, MD: Rowman & Littlefield.

————. 2005b. The 2003-2004 Russian elections and prospects for democracy. *Europe-Asia Studies* 57:369-98.

Shelley, Louise. 1980. The geography of Soviet criminality. *American Sociological Review* 45:111-22.

Shkolnikov, Vladimir M. 1987. Geograficheskie faktori prodolzhitelnosti [Geographical factors of length of life]. *Izvestiya AN USSR, Geographical Series* 3:225-40.

Shkolnikov, Vladimir M., Martin McKee, and David A. Leon. 2001. Changes in life expectancy in Russia in the mid-1990s. *Lancet* 357:917-21.

Shkolnikov, Vladimir M., and France Meslé. 1996. The Russian epidemiological crisis as mirrored by mortality trends. In *Russia's demographic "crisis,"* ed. J. DaVanzo, 113-62. Santa Monica, CA: Rand.

Slider, Darrell, Vladimir Gimpelson, and Sergey Chugrov. 1994. Political tendencies in Russia's regions: Evidence from the 1993 parliamentary elections. *Slavic Review* 53:711-32.

Solnick, Steven. 1998. Gubernatorial elections in Russia, 1996-1997. *Post-Soviet Affairs* 14:48-80.

Stickley, Andrew, and Ilkka Henrik Mäkinen. 2005. Homicide in the Russian Empire and Soviet Union: Continuity or change? *British Journal of Criminology* 45:647-70.

Stucky, Thomas D. 2003. Local politics and violent crime in U.S. cities. *Criminology* 41:1101-36.

Stucky, Thomas D., Karen Heimer, and Joseph B. Lang. 2005. Partisan politics, electoral competition and imprisonment: An analysis of states over time. *Criminology* 43:43-76.

Värnik, Airi, Danuta Wasserman, Ene Palo, and Liina-Mai Tooding. 2001. Registration of external causes of death in the Baltic States, 1970-1997. *European Journal of Public Health* 11:84-88.

Villarreal, Andres. 2002. Political competition and violence in Mexico: Hierarchical social control in local patronage structures. *American Sociological Review* 67:477-98.

Wasserman, Danuta, and Airi Värnik. 1998. Reliability of statistics on violent death and suicide in the Former USSR, 1970-1990. *Acta Psychiatrica Scandinavica* 394(suppl.):34-41.

Wyman, Matthew W., Stephen White, and Sarah Oates, eds. 1998. *Elections and voters in post-Communist Russia*. Cheltenham, UK: Edward Elgar.

Democracy and Intellectual Property: Examining Trajectories of Software Piracy

By
NICOLE LEEPER
PIQUERO
and
ALEX R. PIQUERO

Social scientists interested in criminal activity have generally neglected the topic of democracy, while researchers interested in the topic of democracy have virtually ignored criminal activity. This confluence of neglect has been especially obvious in research on intellectual property (IP) theft. In this study, the authors examine the interrelationship between democracy and IP theft—specifically software piracy. Piracy data from eighty-two countries between the years 1995 and 2000 are used to examine how democratization relates to rates of software piracy. The authors use trajectory methodology to identify distinct offender groups, which vary in their rates of software piracy. The current research has two specific goals: (1) to identify distinct trajectories of software piracy offenders at the international level and (2) to examine how these groups vary according to several measures of democratic strength. The authors hypothesize that more democratic countries (including those that have strong political and civil liberties) will have lower software piracy rates.

Keywords: democracy; intellectual property; piracy; trajectory analysis

Democracy has been linked to many social issues and problems including corruption (Sung 2004); war (Bremer 1992); organized crime (Allum and Siebert 2003); felon disenfranchisement; punishment practices; and crime, including homicide, violence generally (Keane 2004) and political violence in particular (Powell 1982; Krain 1998).[1] A limited amount of research has examined the reciprocal relationship between democracy and crime. One strand of research indicates that crime is likely to threaten democratic institutions by (1) encouraging political entities to scale back personal freedoms; (2) reducing social capital in communities by weakening trust and lowering levels of civic participation; (3) exacerbating economic, racial, and ethnic cleavages and disparities; and (4) making it more difficult to maintain social order, thereby threatening economic well-being and development (LaFree 2003). A second strand of research has argued that democracy is actually

DOI: 10.1177/0002716206287015

criminogenic, at least in the short term, in transitioning societies such as Russia during the 1990s (see Kim and Pridemore 2005).

Although some research has examined the interrelationships between democracy and crime, we are aware of no study to date that has specifically examined the impact of democracy on rates of intellectual property theft. Intellectual property (IP) refers to the creative ideas or innovations that result from intellectual activity and creation (Piquero 2005). Four categories of IP are generally recognized: copyright, patents, trademarks, and trade secrets. Of interest to the current study is the violation of the copyright realm of IP. Copyrights deal largely with forms of creativity concerning mass entertainment (World Intellectual Property Organization [WIPO] 2001, 40), including novels, music, song lyrics, motion pictures, plays, choreography, and computer software. The unauthorized copying of copyrighted material for commercial purposes and the unauthorized commercial dealing in copied materials is often called piracy (WIPO 2001, 51). When computer software, movies, video games, music, or other copyrighted works are copied, publishers and authors are denied economic returns on their IP.

IP theft has received some research attention in the legal and business literatures but very little attention in the social science literature. While the few existing studies on the relationship between democracy and crime have generally focused on violent crime (in large part due to the reliability of homicide data), this should not preclude an investigation of the possible link between democracy and other crime types. IP, in particular, lies in a unique position to aid in understanding the relationship between democracy and crime due to what is believed to be its important effect on economic activity for both individuals and nations (Ronkainen and Guerrero-Cusumano 2001). We suspect that democracy will relate to IP theft primarily because the democratic countries, which provide their citizens with the strongest personal and civil liberties, also produce large quantities of IP. As such, strong democratic countries stand to benefit the most from the creation and implementation of strict laws against IP theft. Such democracies

Nicole Leeper Piquero is an assistant professor in the Department of Criminology, Law and Society at the University of Florida. Her current research focuses on the etiology of white-collar crime, personality dimensions and traits associated with white-collar and corporate crime decision making, and white-collar crime victimization. Her work has appeared in Justice Quarterly, Law and Society Review, Journal of Criminal Justice, Trends in Organized Crime, *and* Youth & Society. *She recently completed a project for the National Institute on Justice on intellectual property theft.*

Alex R. Piquero is a professor of criminology, law and society and the 2005 Magid Term Professor in the College of Liberal Arts and Sciences at the University of Florida, a member of the National Consortium on Violence Research, and a member of the MacArthur Foundation's Research Network on Adolescent Development and Juvenile Justice. He is recipient of the American Society of Criminology's 2002 Cavan Young Scholar Award, of the University of Florida's 2004 Teacher of the Year Award, and of the American Society of Criminology's 2005 E-Mail Mentor of the Year Award. His research interests include criminological theory, criminal careers, and quantitative research methods; and his work has appeared in Criminology, Journal of Research in Crime and Delinquency, Journal of Quantitative Criminology, Criminology & Public Policy, Sociological Methods & Research, *and* Journal of Adolescent Research.

have a vested interest in protecting IP, and because they are the driving force behind the development of IP laws, they are also likely to exhibit fewer infractions.

The WIPO (2001, 41) contends that "intellectual creation is one of the basic prerequisites of all social, economic, and cultural development." According to the WIPO, the lack of protection of IP rights hampers or provides disincentives for individuals to freely create and develop innovations. The fear is that if individuals do not feel that they can protect (and profit from) their IP, they will no longer create and develop innovations, thus discouraging technological, cultural, and intellectual advances. One way to create a productive and prosperous environment is to provide individuals with economic incentives for continuing to advance ideas and innovations.[2] According to the WIPO model, to protect economic interest and promote innovation and advancement, it is important to protect IP from piracy and theft.

On the other hand, it has been argued that WIPO is a legislative body that is controlled by and espouses a Western business philosophy that is not universally accepted (Shore et al. 2001; Steidlmeier 1993). In fact, Drahos (2002; also see Drahos and Braithwaite 2001/2002) argues that the development of international IP standards has been largely dictated and coerced into action by the strategic behavior of big business firms in the United States. This is evident in the Trade-Related Aspects of Intellectual Property Rights (TRIPS) agreement established in 1994 (see Drahos 2002). The TRIPS agreement establishes the rules to govern the rights of IP as part of worldwide trade negotiations (i.e., requiring a minimum standard of protection of IP), provides effective enforcement of these rights, and outlines dispute resolution. While TRIPS was designed to create a bargaining atmosphere of sovereign equals, this ideal is not always met. The negotiation process essentially eliminated the active participation of industrializing countries in designing the TRIPS agreement (Drahos 2002). Drahos and Braithwaite (2001/2002) argue that TRIPS is the product of duress by economically powerful states against weaker states, that industrializing states receive few reciprocal benefits and many more adverse consequences because of the agreement.

Rates of IP theft vary, with the highest rates found among industrializing countries (Rapp and Rozek 1990; Ronkainen and Guerrero-Cusumano 2001, 59). Unlike *mala in se* crimes, regulation and protection of IP is not equally distributed nor easily agreed upon. As such, attitudes toward and outrage against IP theft vary dramatically along both economic and cultural lines. Protection of IP has been found to significantly vary across countries with industrialized, mostly Western countries most likely to regard IP rights as a serious matter (Ronkainen and Guerrero-Cusumano 2001; Swinyard, Rinne, and Keng Kau 1990). Ronkainen and Guerrero-Cusumano (2001, 60) argue that the lack of protection by industrializing countries (which tend to be less democratic) is due both to the lack of appropriate legislation and to the fact that industrializing nations want to ensure the availability of products to their citizens, even if they are copies.

More generally, there is general disagreement about the seriousness and criminal status of copyright violations. As Altbach (1988, 62) notes, Third World and many Asian nations have been critical of copyright laws, claiming "that it is a Western concept which was created to maintain a monopoly over the distribution and production of knowledge and knowledge-based products." Countries holding this view do not place high priority on protecting IP rights because economically they cannot afford to limit exposure to new advances (such as pharmaceuticals) and technologies or because of fundamental cultural beliefs that "do not generally support the notion of protecting proprietary creative work" (Swinyard, Rinne, and Keng Kau 1990, 657).

Regardless of how we interpret the amount of protection needed for IP rights, one thing is certain: the costs of IP theft are staggering, with the highest total dollar amount losses incurred by highly industrialized countries such as the United States (Ronkainen and Guerrero-Cusumano 2001). Maher and Thompson (2002, 765) report that the theft of intellectual property in the United States costs well over $300 billion, with high-technology corporations frequently victimized. Of course, estimating the exact costs of IP theft is not an easy task with each industry (e.g., music, motion picture, software) calculating its own losses. But while precise estimates vary, everyone agrees that the total losses incurred are huge. For example, worldwide estimates on the annual dollar amount of software pirated range from $7.5 to $17 billion (Gopal and Sanders 1997, 29). Meanwhile, in the United States alone, the music industry places the value of the sales of pirated recordings at $4.6 billion for 2002 (International Federation of the Phonographic Industry [IFPI] 2003), and the motion picture industry estimates that $1.25 billion was lost between 1998 and 2002 due to audiovisual piracy (not including the impact from Internet piracy nor losses stemming from signal theft [Motion Picture Association [MPA] 2003]). This study focuses on one specific form of copyright violation, software piracy: a part of one of the most innovative and fastest-growing industries, one that has been especially hard hit by piracy (Ronkainen and Guerrero-Cusumano 2001) and one that incurs very high monetary losses (Maher and Thompson 2002).

The Case of Software Piracy

Of all forms of IP theft, software piracy has also garnered the most research attention. Definitions of software piracy usually "include the sharing and duplication of program floppy disks and the misappropriation of application licenses for networks" (Hinduja 2001, 370). Estimates of software piracy focus on how much of the existing software are unauthorized copies. It has been suggested that as much as 50 to 90 percent of all software packages in use have been illegally copied (Christensen and Eining 1991, 68; Taylor and Shim 1993). In fact, software piracy is believed to be so widespread that in some environments, such as universities, businesses, and government, the behavior has become socially acceptable (Sims, Cheng, and Teegen 1996; Cheng, Sims, and Teegen 1997; Hinduja 2001; Christensen and Eining 1991).

Most attempts to understand the causes of software piracy have focused on individual-level variables and have relied on interviews of undergraduate and

graduate students. Some early studies attempted to identify demographic characteristics that would allow for the creation of a software pirate profile (see review
in Piquero 2005). The most commonly examined correlates have been gender, age,
level of schooling, and level of computer usage. Results regarding gender were
inconclusive; however, younger individuals, those with more years of schooling,
and those who use the computer more often were more likely to report engaging
in software piracy (see Piquero 2005). Another line of research has focused on
ethics and morality. Evidence indicates that many college students view software
piracy as both acceptable and normal and report that they regularly engage in it
(Cohen and Cornwell 1989; Solomon and O'Brien 1990). The same holds true for
others working in the academic community (Seale, Polakowski, and Schneider
1998; Shim and Taylor 1989; Taylor and Shim 1993).

*Data for eighty-two countries
from 1995 to 2000 are examined through
a trajectory analysis, a methodological
approach that is designed to identify distinct
offender groups (or groups of countries) that
vary in rates of software piracy.*

Researchers have been quick to recognize the global impact of software piracy
and have focused on comparative studies of student samples. For example, Kini,
Ramakrishna, and Vijayaraman (2003) investigated attitudes toward software
piracy and demographics of students in Thailand, while Swinyard, Rinne, and
Keng Kau (1990) compared attitudes of U.S. students with those from Singapore.
Results from this latter study showed that while students from Singapore were
more knowledgeable about software copyright laws than North Americans, their
attitudes were less supportive of those laws and they were more likely to pirate
software than North Americans. Additionally, the students from Singapore were
more strongly influenced by the benefits of their actions on self, family, or community than by the legality of copying software. In contrast, the U.S. subjects
were more influenced by the legality of the decision than by the benefits of the
decision. Shore et al. (2001) were the first to use more than two countries for
comparison. After examining attitudes of students from the United States, New
Zealand, Hong Kong, and Pakistan, they found that (1) software ethics were
country-dependent, (2) softlifting[3] and piracy were distinct ethical problems, and

(3) cultural dimensions and piracy were significantly related. Although these cross-national studies have been beneficial, they provide little information about the macro-level correlates that may relate to rates of software piracy across countries, specifically the role of democracy.

Current Focus

Data for eighty-two countries from 1995 to 2000 are examined through a trajectory analysis, a methodological approach that is designed to identify distinct offender groups (or groups of countries) that vary in rates of software piracy. This study has two specific goals: (1) to identify distinct trajectories of software piracy offending countries and (2) to examine how these trajectories vary according to strength of democratic institutions. We expect more democratic countries (including those that have strong political and civil liberties) to have lower software piracy rates. This cross-national comparative analysis is important because few studies exist regarding the cross-national connections between crime, criminal justice, and democratic institutions (LaFree 2003) and with IP (and more specifically software piracy) in particular. In addition to providing the first empirical analysis of software piracy using the trajectory methodology, we also present the first application of the trajectory methodology using country-level data.

Method

All social, behavioral, and biological processes evolve over time, and social scientists refer to the evolution of an outcome over time as a "developmental trajectory" (Nagin 2005, 1). A trajectory is a collection of units (i.e., people, countries) that resemble one another on an outcome of interest. For example, if three trajectory groups emerge from a data analysis, the units in one group are more likely to resemble one another than they are to resemble those in the other two groups. It is important to note that the trajectory methodology does not assume the existence of developmental trajectories of a specific form before the statistical analysis begins; instead, the method provides the capacity for testing the number and form of trajectories that best characterize the individual trends in the data (Nagin 2005, 2). Once the distinctive trajectories are identified, characteristics of the groups can be linked to understand what variables might account for qualitative differences across groups in their developmental course (Nagin 2005, 2).

Mixture, trajectory, or group-based models are useful for modeling the variation that exists in the outcome of interest (Jones, Nagin, and Roeder 2001). The technique employed here is the group-based procedure developed by Nagin and Land (1993) and recently programmed into the SAS computer package by Jones, Nagin, and Roeder (2001). This approach is best viewed as descriptive because rather than assuming the existence of trajectories of a specific form prior to data analysis, it allows groups/trajectories to emerge from the data. Thus, the methodology allows us to determine whether there are meaningful subgroups in the piracy data and, if so, what these piracy trajectories look like. To date, most trajectory analyses have been conducted among individuals; as such, this study presents the first application of the trajectory methodology at the country level of analysis. Appendix A contains a more detailed description of the modeling procedure.

Variables

Outcome variable. The principal outcome variable is software piracy rates, defined as the volume of software pirated as a percentage of total software installed in each country, annually, between 1995 and 2000.[4] These data come from the Sixth Annual Business Software Alliance Global Software Piracy Study (Business Software Alliance 2001). The survey involves the reconciliation of two data sets, the demand for new software applications (i.e., installed applications) and the legal supply of new software applications (i.e., shipped applications). An earlier version of the data was used by Ronkainen and Guerrero-Cusumano (2001). Appendix B contains a detailed description.

Independent variables. Based on previous research and following the work of Ronkainen and Guerrero-Cusumano (2001), a number of variables were used as correlates of IP violation. We divide these independent variables into market, involvement/opportunity, and democracy factors.

Market factors. These factors include the economic development and business environment in a particular country. Two specific variables are used. First, to capture the ability and willingness to pay for the authentic product (Ronkainen and Guerrero-Cusumano 2001) as well as a country's economic power, we use the gross domestic product (GDP in millions of 1987 U.S. dollars) of each country measured in 1995 from the World Bank's World Development Indicators database. We hypothesize an inverse relationship between GDP and rates of piracy.

Second, to measure the extent of enforcement of laws and regulations generally (Ronkainen and Guerrero-Cusumano 2001), and the degree of business corruption in particular, we use the Corruption Perceptions Index (CPI), obtained from Transparency International (www.transparency.org). The CPI relates to the perceptions of the degree of corruption as seen by businesspeople, including senior business persons and managers, as well as risk analysts, and ranks countries in terms of the degree to which corruption is perceived to exist among public officials and politicians. The CPI focuses on corruption in the public sector and defines corruption as the abuse of public office for private gain. The surveys used in compiling the CPI include perceptions of the misuse of public power for private benefit, with a focus, for example, on bribe taking by public officials in public procurement. The sources do not distinguish between administrative and political corruption. We use the 2003 measure, which originally ranged from 0 *(high corruption)* to 10 *(low corruption)*. We recoded the 2003 measure so that lower values indicated low corruption and higher values indicated high corruption (range 0-10). We expect high levels of corruption to be associated with high levels of software piracy.[5]

Involvement/opportunity factors. These factors describe a particular country's opportunities for the distribution and use of software piracy. We include two opportunity variables, the number of personal computers (per one thousand population; International Telecommunications Union [ITU]) and the number of persons (per one thousand population) within a country that access the Internet (CIA World Factbook 2005, http://www.cia.gov/cia/publications/factbook/). According to the ITU, communication data come from an annual questionnaire sent to tele communication authorities and operating companies (http://www.itu.int/ITU-D/ict/statistics/WTI_2003.pdf, accessed October 14, 2005). These data are supplemented by annual reports and statistical yearbooks of telecommunication ministries, regulators, operators, and industry associations. Data on Internet users are based on nationally reported data. In some cases, surveys have been carried out that give a more precise figure for the number of Internet users. However, surveys differ across countries. For example, countries that did not have surveys generally based their estimates on derivations from reported Internet service provider subscription counts, calculated by multiplying the number of subscribers by a multiplier. Data on personal computers (PCs) show the estimated number of PCs, derived from an annual questionnaire supplemented by other sources.[6] We hypothesize that high-piracy countries are poor countries and that citizens in poor countries have fewer computers and more economic incentives to pirate/steal software.[7]

Democracy factors. These variables measure a country's level of democracy and/or degree of civil and political liberties/rights.[8] These include the 1999 Democratic Institutions Rating Index, obtained from the Polity IV Project (Gleditsch 2003), which ranges from –10 *(fully autocratic)* to +10 *(fully democratic)*; the 1995 Political Rights Index, obtained from Freedom House (Freedom House 1996), which originally ranged from 1 *(highest degree of freedom)* to 7 *(lowest degree of freedom)*; and the 1995 Civil Liberties Index, obtained from Freedom House (Freedom House 1996), which originally ranged from 1 *(highest degree of freedom)* to 7 *(lowest degree of freedom)*. To keep the interpretation consistent across the two types of democracy measures (i.e., the Democratic Institutions Rating Index and the two Freedom House indices), we recoded the Freedom House indicators so that 1 represented the *lowest degree of freedom* and 7 represented the *highest degree of freedom*. For these two final variables, because 1995 data were unavailable for Cyprus, Puerto Rico, and Hong Kong, data from 1999 to 2000 were substituted. We hypothesize that more democratic countries (including those with higher levels of political and civil rights) will have lower rates of software piracy.

Table 1 presents descriptive statistics for all variables used in this study. Here, it can be seen that the average piracy rate is decreasing over time. Also, data from the CPI suggest that, on average, countries appear to occupy middle range values. Furthermore, data indicate that, on average, the countries in our sample score highly on the civil and political freedom scales. Finally, the descriptive information

TABLE 1
DESCRIPTIVE STATISTICS ($N = 82$)

Variable	Mean	SD	Min	Max
Piracy rate 1995	74.646	17.911	26.00	99.00
Piracy rate 1996	69.914	19.075	27.00	99.00
Piracy rate 1997	65.780	19.010	27.00	98.00
Piracy rate 1998	63.951	19.848	25.00	97.00
Piracy rate 1999	60.561	18.663	25.00	98.00
Piracy rate 2000	58.085	17.948	24.00	97.00
Average piracy rate (1995-2000)	65.489	18.413	25.67	98.00
Total GDP, 1995 (millions of $U.S.)	257,242.4	741,188.671	2,270	5,452,500
Corruption Perceptions Index, 2003	5.021	2.386	0.30	8.60
Democratic institutions rating, 1999	5.704	6.015	–10.00	10.00
Personal computers per one thousand population	136.919	145.828	3.70	498.76
Internet users per one thousand population	207.951	176.481	5.46	601.25
Freedom House political rights, 1995	5.049	2.036	1.00	7.00
Freedom House civil liberties, 1995	4.790	1.765	1.00	7.00

from the Democratic Institutions Ratings Index suggests that, on average, the countries in the sample scored more highly on the democracy side of the democracy-autocracy scale.

Results

We used trajectory analysis to determine the number of distinct piracy groups present in the data. The Bayesian Information Criterion (BIC) statistics (see Appendix A for complete explanation) indicated that the statistical fit of the model to the data improved as the number of trajectories increased from one to six. It is important to note that the identification of six trajectories does not necessarily mean that only six groups exist in the population; instead, "the aim is to identify as simple a model as possible that displays the distinctive features of the population distribution of trajectories" (Nagin and Tremblay 2005).[9] In other words, the model that best represented the distinct number of piracy trajectories was selected and is presented throughout.

FIGURE 1
SOFTWARE PIRACY TRAJECTORIES (1995-2000),
EIGHTY-TWO COUNTRIES WORLDWIDE

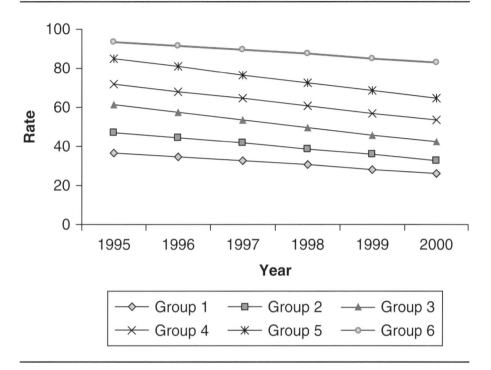

Piracy trajectories

To aid in the substantive interpretation of the software piracy trajectories opti-mally identified and estimated in the data, the trajectories of expected (i.e., pre-dicted on the basis of estimated model parameters) piracy rates for each group implied by the model are plotted in Figure 1.

The six trajectories in this figure all share an important commonality as well as an important difference. The commonality evident in this figure is that over time, all trajectory groups are decreasing in rates of software piracy, with some groups evinc-ing a sharper slope decline than others (e.g., compare the rapid slope declines of groups 3 and 5 to the much slower decline of group 6, shown at the top of Figure 1). Although several reasons could explain these declining trends, they may simply signal that adjustments are being made to this new technology and that eventually it will become more fully regulated. The main difference evident in Figure 1 is the intercept-level differences (i.e., the initial point of the trend line) at the first data point (1995). These differences continue to exist over time, albeit shrinking some-what between groups 1 through 5, but not group 6, whose piracy trajectory remains relatively stable, with a slight trend decrease, over the six-year period.

Another way of thinking about how the trajectories changed over time is to provide an estimate of the percentage change from 1995 to 2000 in the average piracy rate for the predicted values. These calculations indicate that the percentage change from 1995 to 2000 for groups 1 (low rate group) through 6 (high-rate group) were –27.15 percent (group 1), –30.61 percent (group 2), –31.23 percent (group 3), –25.42 percent (group 4), –23.84 percent (group 5), and –11.21 percent (group 6). The negative signs show that all piracy rates for all six groups decreased over time. But as the percentage change scores show, the high-rate group 6 evinced the lowest percentage change between 1995 and 2000.

Table 2 presents a list of the countries and the piracy trajectory to which they were assigned. We found considerable variation across the six groups in terms of the number of countries being represented. For example, the highest rate trajectory, group 6, is composed of 23.1 percent of the sample, while the lowest rate trajectory, group 1, is composed of only 7.3 percent of the sample. In between these two groups, the others are group 5 (25.7 percent), group 4 (19.6 percent), group 3 (13.3 percent), and group 2 (10.9 percent). A quick examination of Table 2 suggests that the low-rate piracy trajectory includes mostly countries that are fully democratic, high GDP (e.g., United States, United Kingdom, Germany), while the high-rate piracy trajectory includes countries that are less democratic, lower GDP (e.g., Indonesia, Kuwait, Vietnam). More generally, the trajectory groupings in Table 2 resemble a democracy continuum, moving on the left from fully democratic countries (those in piracy groups 1 and 2) to less democratic countries (piracy groups 3 and 4) and finally to the least democratic countries (piracy groups 5 and 6). We will return to these distinctions in greater detail later.

Model estimates and assignments

For each country (and subsequent latent class) the maximum posterior membership probability was computed.[10] Specifically, the model uses a procedure that sorts countries into the trajectory group to which they have the highest probability of belonging. Based on model coefficient estimates, the probability of observing each country's longitudinal pattern of offending is computed conditional on their being, respectively, in each of the latent classes. For example, if the United Kingdom has posterior probabilities of assignment to group 1 of .98 and .01 for groups 2 through 6, then the United Kingdom will be assigned to group 1. This procedure, of course, does not guarantee perfect assignment, but higher posterior probabilities raise confidence in the accuracy of the classification. The average assignment probabilities for each group in the current analysis are high (with all scores greater than .95), suggesting that the majority of countries can be assigned to a particular latent trajectory group with high probability. For example, the mean posterior probability for group 1 was .997, suggesting that the likelihood of assignment to that particular trajectory group was near perfect. Countries in group 1 were correctly assigned to the low-rate trajectory group because there is virtually no likelihood that they would have been assigned to any of the other five trajectory groups. Average posterior probability assignment for groups 2 through 6 were .995, .987, .999, .956, and .998, respectively.

TABLE 2
COUNTRY BY TRAJECTORY CLASSIFICATION

Group 1 (Low Rate)	Group 2	Group 3	Group 4	Group 5	Group 6 (High Rate)
Australia	Austria	Chile	Argentina	Costa Rica	Bahrain
Denmark	Belgium	Czech Republic	Brazil	Croatia	Bolivia
Germany	Canada	Israel	Colombia	Cyprus	Bulgaria
New Zealand	Finland	Italy	Hong Kong	Dominican Republic	China
United Kingdom	France	Netherlands	Hungary	Ecuador	El Salvador
United States	Japan	Portugal	Ireland	Egypt	Guatemala
	Norway	Puerto Rico	Korea	Greece	Indonesia
	Sweden	South Africa	Malta	Honduras	Kuwait
	Switzerland	Singapore	Mexico	India	Lebanon
		Slovakia	Poland	Jordan	Nicaragua
		United Arab Emirates	Reunion	Kenya	Oman
			Spain	Malaysia	Pakistan
			Taiwan	Mauritius	Paraguay
			Venezuela	Morocco	Qatar
			Zimbabwe	Nigeria	Romania
				Panama	Russia
				Peru	Thailand
				Philippines	Ukraine
				Saudi Arabia	Vietnam
				Slovenia	
				Turkey	
				Uruguay	

What variables distinguish the trajectories?

Next, the variables that distinguish between the six piracy trajectories were examined. We expected that countries comprising the low-rate software piracy trajectories would be less corrupt, more democratic, have a higher GDP, have higher civil and political liberties, and have more computers and Internet users per one thousand population. The opposite was expected for those countries in the high-rate software piracy trajectories.

---

*[C]ountries with higher scores
on the democracy measure had lower
software piracy rates.*

An analysis of variance was performed (see Table 3) and revealed significant differences across all variables—all of which were in the expected direction. Countries with a higher GDP have a lower software piracy rate. Specifically, the low-rate piracy groups (i.e., groups 1 and 2) have the highest average GDP, while the two high-rate piracy groups (groups 5 and 6) have the lowest average GDP. With regard to the CPI, the low-rate software piracy group (group 1) had the lowest level of corruption, while the high-rate software piracy group (group 6) had the highest corruption levels. Low-rate software piracy countries were likely to be more democratic, while high-rate software piracy countries were likely to be less democratic. The results regarding PC ownership and Internet usage indicate that the low-rate software piracy group had the most personal computers per 1,000 population as well as the most Internet usage per 1,000 population, while the two highest-rate software piracy groups (groups 5 and 6) had lower numbers of personal computers and Internet usage.[11] These results are striking: the highest-rate software piracy group (group 6) averaged 40 personal computers and 91 Internet users per 1,000 population, while the lowest-rate software piracy group (group 1) averaged 407 personal computers and 496 Internet users per 1,000 persons. With regard to the political rights and civil liberties indices, the results show that the high-rate software piracy group had the lowest political and civil rights while the low-rate software piracy group had the highest political and civil rights. Across all comparisons, the other four groups (2 through 5) were always in between the two extreme groups, with group 2 always being closer to group 1 (lower-rate software piracy groups) and group 5 always being closer to group 6 (higher-rate software piracy groups).

In a further analysis aimed at distinguishing between the different trajectories, we next averaged the piracy rates across the six years to produce more reliable

TABLE 3
ANALYSIS OF VARIANCE RESULTS OF INDEPENDENT VARIABLES AND TRAJECTORY GROUP ASSIGNMENT ($N = 82$)

Variable	Group 1 (Low Rate)	Group 2	Group 3	Group 4	Group 5	Group 6 (High Rate)	F-Value	Eta
Corruption Perceptions Index, 2003	1.383	1.688	3.820	5.446	6.286	6.626	24.978*	.794
Democratic institutions rating, 1999	10.000	9.888	7.333	7.090	3.368	2.823	3.674*	.469
GDP, 1995 (millions of $U.S.)	1,359,905.0	599,052.8	139,531.0	132,539.0	47,931.95	84,569.87	4.533*	.500
Personal computers	407.895	340.212	188.576	160.890	52.913	40.386	24.526*	.831
Internet users	496.555	442.911	306.797	251.501	99.775	91.002	20.836*	.804
Political rights, 1995	7.000	7.000	6.000	5.500	4.318	3.473	9.516*	.623
Civil liberties, 1995	6.833	6.777	5.454	5.214	4.090	3.315	13.915*	.694

*$p < .05$.

TABLE 4
CORRELATIONS WITH AVERAGED PIRACY RATES

Variable	Correlation
GDP, 1995	−.410°°
Corruption Perceptions Index, 2003	.759°°
Democratic institutions rating, 1999	−.475°°
Personal computers	−.786°°
Internet users	−.775°°
Freedom House political rights, 1995	−.620°°
Freedom House civil liberties, 1995	−.701°°

°°$p < .01$.

estimates. We then estimated correlations with the six-year piracy averages and the independent variables.[12] These results are presented in Table 4 and are consistent with the hypotheses that more democratic countries (including those with more political and civil liberties) had lower software piracy rates.

A unique aspect of our analysis was its application of the trajectory methodology to software piracy at the country level of analysis.

Because correlations between key independent variables and the average piracy rate do not control for rival causal variables, we also present two ordinary least squares regression analyses in which we include control variables and predict the average software piracy rate. In the first, we use the total GDP, the Consumer Price Index, the number of PCs per one thousand population, the number of Internet users per one thousand population, and the democratic institutions rating to predict the average software piracy rate. To gauge the sensitivity of the democracy measure, in a second regression model we replace the democratic institutions rating with a scale of the two Freedom House political and civil liberties measures (summed for the analysis). The results are shown in Table 5.

The results for model 1 in Table 5 indicate that three of the five variables exert a significant effect on the average software piracy rate. Consistent with our

TABLE 5
ORDINARY LEAST SQUARES REGRESSION ANALYSIS PREDICTING
AVERAGE SOFTWARE PIRACY RATE ($N = 82$)

Variable	Model 1 (Beta)	Model 2 (Beta)
Gross domestic product	−.142°	−.158°
Corruption Perceptions Index	.488°	.364°
Personal computers	−.095	−.140
Internet users	−.143	−.157
Democratic institutions rating	−.240°	
Freedom House civil/personal liberties		−.231°
R-squared	.780	.755

NOTE: Beta refers to standardized regression coefficient. All models included a constant (not shown).
°$p < .05$ (one-tailed).

hypothesis, countries with higher scores on the democracy measure had lower software piracy rates. Also, countries with a higher GDP have lower average software piracy rates, while countries with high corruption have a higher average software piracy rate. Neither of the two opportunity variables—PCs and Internet users—were significant predictors of the average software piracy rate. In model 2, we repeat the analysis except we insert the combined Freedom House civil/personal liberties measure in lieu of the democratic institutions rating. The results are substantively similar to those reported in model 1. Specifically, three of the five variables exert a significant effect on the average software piracy rate: GDP, CPI, and the combined Freedom House civil/personal liberties measure. Consistent with our expectations, countries with more civil/personal liberties have a lower average software piracy rate. As was the case earlier, countries with a higher GDP have a lower average software piracy rate, while countries with more corruption have a higher average software piracy rate.

Discussion

In this article, we set out to examine the relationship between several common measures of democracy and one form of IP theft, software piracy. To examine this question, we collected data on software piracy for eighty-two countries from 1995 to 2000, as well as a series of variables that included democracy measures. A unique aspect of our analysis was its application of the trajectory methodology to software piracy at the country level of analysis. Our approach allowed for a descriptive examination of how groups of countries varied from one another in longitudinal trends in software piracy. After assigning countries to six different software piracy trajectories, we examined whether measures of democracy distinguished between the software piracy groups net of a set of control variables.

The trajectory analysis identified six distinct software piracy trajectories. Common to all six trajectory groups was a flat or slowly declining trajectory of software piracy between 1995 and 2000. While no trajectory group showed an increase in software piracy over time, the highest rate trajectory group (group 6) exhibited a high (around 90 percent) flat software piracy rate. Noticeable declines in software piracy were evident for several of the trajectory groups, most notably group 5, whose piracy rate declined from 85 percent in 1995 to 70 percent in 2000.

Across all variables, the low-rate software piracy groups were always more democratic and had more political and civil liberties, whereas the high-rate software piracy groups were always less democratic and had lower political and civil liberties.

We also examined how the various software piracy trajectory groups differed on a number of key indicators. Across all variables, the low-rate software piracy groups were always more democratic and had more political and civil liberties, whereas the high-rate software piracy groups were always less democratic and had lower political and civil liberties. Additionally, in multiple regression analysis, the democratic measures still had a significant effect on the software piracy rate even after controlling for GDP, corruption, and two opportunity variables (number of personal computers and number of Internet users).

What is it about the high-rate trajectory groups that lead them to evince very high software piracy rates for the period spanned by our data? Some have suggested that cultural differences between the West and East contribute to differing views regarding IP rights. Swinyard, Rinne, and Keng Kau (1990) argue that Western cultures are more supportive of IP laws because of a preoccupation with individual freedoms and rights—to the point that individual benefits are valued more than societal gains. Eastern cultures, on the other hand, stress the importance of society as a whole over any single individual. Thus, members of Eastern cultures are more likely to believe that new technological developments made by individuals should be shared with society for the greater good and not simply for individual profit. These varying views contribute to the perceptual differences not only in how IP should be monitored, regulated, and enforced but also in motivational influences toward the advancement of knowledge and knowledge-based products.

On this score, we also examined whether Eastern countries were more likely to evidence higher software piracy rates than non-Eastern (Western) countries. This analysis showed that the average piracy rate of Eastern countries was 67.84, while among non-Eastern countries it was 64.96, a nonsignificant difference. One potential confound is the inclusion of Japan and Singapore as Eastern countries. While these countries are technically considered to be located in the far-eastern realm, they tend to operate more like non-Eastern (Western) countries. When they are removed from the analysis, the average piracy differences become more apparent. Specifically, the average piracy rate among non-Eastern countries remained 64.96, while the rate among Eastern countries increased to 71.25, a trend that was approaching significance.

Drahos and Braithwaite (2001/2002) have argued that some countries, primarily industrializing, less powerful countries, are being coerced by highly industrialized, more powerful countries into abiding by IP laws. Conflict perspectives in criminology (Taylor, Walton, and Young 1973; Greenberg 1981; LaFree 2005) suggest that cross-national patterns of unequal development, economic inequality, and unemployment may account for growing crime differences between highly industrialized core nations and developing peripheral nations. While conflict perspectives (e.g., Vold, Bernard, and Snipes 1998) have usually been applied to predict that powerful groups will further their own interests by controlling legislative bodies and influencing the creation of laws at the national level, it could be argued that rich countries are doing something similar with copyright laws at the international level. As such, countries with less power will be subject to laws enacted by countries with more power (e.g., Wallerstein 1974, 1991; Neuman and Berger 1988). And as we have already seen, more democratic countries generally fall into the powerful group category, while most nations transitioning to democracy fit into the less powerful group category (Drahos 2002).[13]

Thus, from a conflict viewpoint, rich and powerful democratic countries produce large quantities of IP. As such, they benefit most directly from the creation and implementation of strict laws against the theft of their IP property. These powerful democracies, therefore, have a vested interest in protecting IP, and because they were the driving force behind the development of IP laws, they are also likely to exhibit fewer infractions. The law (i.e., TRIPS) protects the interests of the powerful groups (i.e., democratic countries) that directly benefit from its enforcement. Considered in this context, conflict theory may provide a useful connection between democracy and IP theft. Because of their large-scale production of IP, democratic countries, which tend to be rich, have a vested interest in protecting IP laws. By using the law as a vehicle to protect IP, they have, as the data show, far fewer IP infractions.

What are we to make of the fact that GDP and the democracy measures were both significant in our multivariate analysis? The negative effect of GDP shows that compared to richer nations, poorer nations have higher IP infractions, which supports a conflict argument. But the fact that the democracy indicators were still significant suggests that something else is also going on—that democracy matters above and beyond GDP. While GDP may not be a sufficient control for power in the conflict sense, the analyses shows that democracy relates to IP theft even after GDP is controlled.

Because of data limitations, only a partial analysis of the relationship between democracy and software piracy could be considered. First, because only six years of data for eighty-two countries were available, future efforts should strive to collect a longer time series of data for more countries. Second, it would be interesting to examine how transitional democracies deal with the software piracy problem and how they enforce intellectual property laws. Finally, our study was limited to one type of piracy. Hence, we might find different patterns of piracy for other piracy forms, such as music and movie piracy, as well as piracy of luxury items such as designer purses/handbags, sunglasses, and perfume/cologne. Billions of dollars have been lost on these forms of piracy worldwide, and it would be useful to examine whether the countries identified as high rate with regard to software piracy also emerge as high rate for other forms of piracy.

According to Alford (1996/1997, 145), serious IP protection requires political and economic pluralism and independent legal institutions capable of vigorously enforcing citizens' rights. The problem in the high-rate countries is that citizens do not have much autonomy to develop and pursue their own ideas and the means to protect such interests from intrusion. Reichman (1996/1997) argues that until industrializing countries absorb the world's knowledge base, they cannot become producers of IP in their own right. On this score, Friedman (2005) has recently argued that there is a revolution in the works that will change all of this. Specifically, he argues that through technology, the world is being "flattened," which is to suggest that all of the knowledge centers on the planet are being connected together into a single global network that is ushering in a new era of prosperity and innovation (p. 8), which will undoubtedly include IP.

In closing, this analysis showed that democracy and software piracy interrelate in interesting ways. Democratic countries as well as the democratic principles of strong civil and political liberties seem to offer a buffer against software piracy, while nondemocratic countries appear to exacerbate piracy by having restricted market access to certain products.[14] This restricted access to legitimate products, which might be seen as politically innocuous in other contexts (Netanel 1996, 350), provides opportunities for exploitation of copyrighted materials to fill the void (Dudas 2004). Hopefully, future research will build upon this preliminary work by extending the database in terms of years covered, countries involved, and types of piracy acts assessed to better understand the relationship between democracy and IP theft.

Appendix A

Because the data are continuous yet bounded (0-100 percent), the censored normal distribution is appropriate (Jones, Nagin, and Roeder 2001). Following prior research (Nagin 2005), the Bayesian Information Criterion (BIC) is used to evaluate model fit. BIC, or the log-likelihood evaluated at the maximum likelihood estimate less one-half the number of parameters in the model times the log of the sample size (Schwarz 1978), favors more parsimonious models than likelihood ratio tests when used for model selection. Following previous research (D'Unger, Land, and McCall 1998), an iterative procedure is used in identifying meaningful groups. The approach taken begins with a one-group model and continues along the modeling space to two, three, and more groups, until the BIC is maximized (i.e., when the fit estimates reach their best point and the addition of additional trajectories does not result in a meaningful fit improvement). D'Unger, Land, and McCall (1998, 1627) explain that "this statistical criterion favors model parsimony by extracting a penalty for complicating a model (by adding parameters) that increases with the log of the sample size. Furthermore, this BIC (or Schwarz) criterion for model selection embodies the intuitive notion that, when the analyst complicates a model by adding parameters, the payoff in terms of a decrease in the log maximized-likelihood function of the model should be larger than this penalty."

Appendix B

According to the Business Software Alliance (BSA; 2001, 7-8), demand- and supply-based information were obtained from several sources. With regard to demand, personal computer (PC) shipments for the major countries were estimated from proprietary and confidential data supplied by BSA member companies. The data were compared and combined to form a consensus estimate, which benefited from the detailed market research available to these member companies. From market research provided by member companies, International Planning and Research (IPR), an international consulting firm specializing in providing solutions for planning and research problems facing corporations, which has developed PC software piracy estimates by country for the BSA since 1995, determined the number of software applications installed per PC shipment and developed ratios for four shipment groups: (1) home-new shipments, (2) non-home-new shipments, (3) home-replacement shipments, and (4) non-home-replacement shipments. Because piracy rates can vary among applications, grouping the software applications into three tiers and using specific ratios for each tier further refined the ratios. The tiers used were general productivity applications, professional applications, and utilities. These were chosen because they represent different target markets, different price levels, and, it is believed, different piracy rates.

Software applications installed per PC shipped have been researched and estimated using four dimensions: (1) home versus nonhome, (2) new PCs versus replacement PCs, (3) level of technological development, and (4) software application tier. An estimate of total installed software applications was calculated by country for each software tier. This produced a figure for total worldwide software installed in 2000, both legal and illegal. With regard to supply, for the 1995 and 1996 piracy studies, the primary source of data for software shipments was the Software and Information Industry Association (SIIA) Data Program. However, the SIIA Data Program ceased operation in 1997. IPR's approach was to utilize the member companies of BSA to develop piracy study sponsors who would volunteer their proprietary shipment data to the study under nondisclosure agreements for the purpose of constructing an accurate estimate of the software industry's 2000 shipments. This became the primary source of software shipment data. Because the SIAA data program was active until early 1997, IPR is able to continue using it to provide historical estimates of the software industry and can calibrate the results of the data collection from their sponsors in determining software shipments for the total industry. This has been IPR's cross-check and led BSA to believe that the data collection provided reliable and consistent estimates. The data were collected by country and by software application. For the study, only business software applications were used; hence, seven consumer software applications were excluded: recreation, home creativity, home education, integrated, personal finance, reference software, and tax programs. The twenty-six business software applications included were databases, presentations graphics, project management, spreadsheets, word processors, accounting, c languages, curricular, desktop publishing, other languages, professional drawing and painting, programming tools, application utilities, calendars and scheduling, clips, communications, education administration and productivity, electronic mail, fonts, forms, general business, Internet access and tools, personal and business productivity, personal information managers (PIMs), system utilities, and training. The collected software shipment data represent the software shipments of most U.S. companies.

To estimate the entire U.S. software shipments, IPR used an uplift factor reflecting an estimate of shipments by companies participating in the study as a percentage of software shipped by all U.S. software publishers. To estimate the entire worldwide software shipments, IPR applied a second uplift factor, based on an estimate of software shipped by U.S. companies as a percentage of software shipped by all software publishers. Thus, two factors were constructed. Factor 1 includes software shipped by the piracy study–participating companies as a percentage of software shipped by all U.S. software publishers, and factor 2 included software shipped by U.S. software publishers as a percentage of software shipped by all software publishers. By applying these two factors, BSA was able to estimate the total legal market of software shipments for all companies. IPR believes that certain software shipments in the data collected from participating companies are reported for one country, but the software is exported and used in another country. To account for this and to eliminate this effect from the piracy study as much as possible, net import estimates were developed on a country-by-country basis. The difference between software applications installed (demand) and software applications legally shipped (supply) equals the estimate of software applications pirated. These were calculated by country for 2000. The piracy rate was defined as the volume of software pirated as a percentage of total software installed for each country. The "rest of region" data were used to develop piracy estimates outside of major markets. The methodology for the piracy study provides total world shipments with country information for the major countries and aggregated information for smaller countries. For these additional countries, a PC shipment estimate was acquired, either through member company internal data or from published sources. These data were used to split apart the "rest of region" total for the countries within each region. Wherever possible, separate software shipment data were used to split the software shipments within the "rest of region" countries. This resulted in piracy estimates that varied by country within the region. Where these data were unavailable, the additional countries have the same piracy rate as the region. To ensure a high level of confidence, member companies of BSA reviewed the results of the study, and their input was used to validate and refine the study assumptions.

Notes

1. We recognize that there are several different conceptions and operationalizations of democracy. After Barber (1984, 117), we defined a "strong democracy" as one that emphasizes a "participatory process of ongoing, proximate self-legislation and the creation of a political community capable of transforming dependent, private individuals into free citizens and partial and private interests into public goods." This definition is similar to Moran's (2001, 379-80) comprehensive definition of democratization as a process typified by "the vote as a basis for constitutional mechanisms for the transfer of power; political competition through parties; guaranteed individual liberties; freedoms to form public organizations and private organizations."

2. For an interesting discussion of this, see Friedman (2005).

3. Softlifting refers to the unauthorized copying of copyrighted material in which there is no monetary gain such as pirating for personal use (Shore et al. 2001).

4. More generally, software piracy can be defined as the illegal copying and distribution of software.

5. We employ the 2003 Corruption Perceptions Index (CPI) because it contained the most complete information for the largest number of countries. Additionally, since 1995, when the CPI was first conducted, more information via more surveys and more countries have been included. The 1999 and 2003 CPIs are very highly correlated ($r = .97$).

6. It is difficult to obtain precise information on both Internet users and personal computers (PCs) at the country level. Unfortunately, aside from the International Telecommunications Union's (ITU's) data, we are unaware of any other reliable source for these variables.

7. We also considered a country's membership in organizations that monitor and advocate intellectual property protection. We obtained information on whether each of the countries in our database were members of the World Intellectual Property Organization (WIPO). We suspect that countries that are members of the WIPO, because they have specific interests in intellectual property, will have lower piracy rates. However, the majority of countries in our data were members of the WIPO (except for Taiwan and Hong Kong). Because of this, we were unable to use this variable in the analysis.

8. We also collected a number of alternative measures for democracy (i.e., Human Rights Index, Democracy Index, Property Rights Index), and subsequent analysis with those measures revealed similar conclusions as those presented in the text and tables. Because of space constraints, we do not report these results here. Furthermore, we concentrated on the democratic institutions rating and the Freedom House political and civil rights indices because they are well-established measures for democracy.

9. A table containing the final parameter estimates for the six-class model is available upon request.

10. A posterior probability of group membership/assignment collectively measures a specific country's likelihood of belonging to each of the model's trajectory groups. They are referred to as posterior probabilities because they are computed postmodel estimations using the model's estimated coefficients (Nagin 2005, 78).

11. At first glance, this may seem like a contradiction: if few people in the group 6 countries have PCs, what are they doing with all of this pirated software? We believe that these countries are producers—and not necessarily consumers of the pirated software.

12. The authors would like to thank David Greenberg for this suggestion.

13. To be sure, one must be careful to differentiate between democracy (which is typically about internal relationships within society) and conflict arguments (which can also be about relations between societies).

14. According to Netanel (1996, 348), "Democratic civil society and citizenship rely heavily on the widespread distribution of knowledge." Moreover, "Since democratic education encourages independent thinking through active learning, the access to existing knowledge must involve an opportunity to reformulate ideas and transform expressive works, as well as simply to contemplate them. Copyright supplies a vital incentive for authors and publishers to contribute to the store of knowledge" (p. 349).

References

Alford, William P. 1996/1997. Making the world safe for what? Intellectual property rights, human rights and foreign economic policy in the post-European cold war world. *Journal of International Law and Politics* 29:135-52.

Allum, Felia, and Renate Siebert, eds. 2003. *Organized crime: The challenge to democracy*. London: Routledge.

Altbach, Philip G. 1988. Economic progress brings copyright to Asia. *Far East Economic Review* 139 (9): 62-63.

Barber, Benjamin R. 1984. *Strong democracy: Participatory politics for a new age*. Berkeley: University of California Press.

Bremer, Stuart. 1992. Dangerous dyads: Conditions affecting the likelihood of interstate war, 1816-1965. *Journal of Conflict Resolution* 36:309-41.

Business Software Alliance (BSA). 2001. *Sixth Annual BSA Global Software Piracy Study*. May. Washington, DC: International Planning and Research Corporation.

Cheng, Hsing K., Ronald R. Sims, and Hildy Teegen. 1997. To purchase or to pirate software: An empirical study. *Journal of Management Information Systems* 13 (4): 49-60.

Christensen, Anne L., and Martha M. Eining. 1991. Factors influencing software piracy: Implications for accountants. *Journal of Information Systems* 5 (spring): 67-80.

Cohen, Eli, and Larry Cornwell. 1989. A question of ethics: Developing information systems ethics. *Journal of Business Ethics* 8:431-37.

Drahos, Peter. 2002. Developing countries and international intellectual property standard-setting. *Journal of World Intellectual Property* 5 (5): 765-89.

Drahos, Peter, and John Braithwaite. 2001/2002. Intellectual property, corporate strategy, globalisation: TRIPS in context. *Wisconsin International Law Journal* 20 (3): 451-80.

Dudas, Jon W. 2004. Statement of Jon W. Dudas, Acting Under Secretary of Commerce for Intellectual Property and Acting Director of the United States Patent and Trademark Office, before the Committee on Judiciary, United States Senate. March 23. http://www.uspto.gov/web/offices/com/speeches/2004 mar23.htm (accessed August 25, 2005).

D'Unger, Amy V., Kenneth C. Land, and Patricia L. McCall. 1998. How many latent classes of delinquent/ criminal careers? Results from mixed Poisson regression analyses. *American Journal of Sociology* 103 (6): 1593-1630.

Freedom House. 1996. *World Survey of Economic Freedom 1995-1996: A Freedom House study*. New Brunswick, NJ: Transaction Publishers.

Friedman, Thomas L. 2005. *The world is flat: A brief history of the twenty-first century*. New York: Farrar, Straus, and Giroux.

Gleditsch, Kristian Skrede. 2003. Modified Polity P4 and P4D data, version 1.0. http://weber.ucsd.edu/ ~kgledits/Polity.html.

Gopal, Ram D., and G. Lawrence Sanders. 1997. Preventive and deterrent controls for software piracy. *Journal of Management Information Systems* 13 (4): 29-47.

Greenberg, David F., ed. 1981. *Crime and capitalism: Readings in Marxist criminology*. Palo Alto, CA: Mayfield.

Hinduja, Sameer. 2001. Correlates of internet software piracy. *Journal of Contemporary Criminal Justice* 17 (4): 369-82.

International Federation of the Phonographic Industry (IFPI). 2003. *The record industry commercial piracy report, 2003*. London: IFPI.

Jones, Bobby L., Daniel S. Nagin, and Kathryn Roeder. 2001. A SAS procedure based on mixture models for estimating developmental trajectories. *Sociological Methods and Research* 29:374-93.

Keane, John. 2004. *Violence and democracy*. Cambridge: Cambridge University Press.

Kim, Sang-Weon, and William A. Pridemore. 2005. Social change, institutional anomie, and serious property crime in transitional Russia. *British Journal of Criminology* 45:81-97.

Kini, Ranjan B., H. V. Ramakrishna, and B. S. Vijayaraman. 2003. An exploratory study of moral intensity regarding software piracy of students in Thailand. *Behaviour and Information Technology* 22 (1): 63-70.

Krain, Matthew. 1998. Contemporary democracies revisited: Democracy, political violence, and event count models. *Comparative Political Studies* 31 (2): 139-64.

LaFree, Gary. 2003. Criminology and democracy. *The Criminologist* 28 (1): 1-5

———. 2005. Evidence for elite convergence in cross-national homicide victimization trends, 1956-2000. *Sociological Quarterly* 46:191-211.

Maher, Megan K., and Jon Michael Thompson. 2002. Intellectual property crimes. *American Criminal Law Review* 39 (2): 763-816.

Moran, J. 2001. Democratic transitions and forms of corruption. *Crime, Law, and Social Change* 36:379-93.

Motion Picture Association (MPA). 2003. *2003 piracy fact sheets: US overview.* Los Angeles: MPA Worldwide Market Research.

Nagin, Daniel S. 2005. *Group-based modeling of development.* Cambridge, MA: Harvard University Press.

Nagin, Daniel S., and Kenneth C. Land. 1993. Age, criminal careers, and population heterogeneity: Specification and estimation of a nonparametric, mixed poisson model. *Criminology* 31:327-62.

Nagin, Daniel S., and Richard E. Tremblay. 2005. Developmental trajectory groups: Fact or a useful statistical fiction? *Criminology* 43 (4): 873-904.

Netanel, Neil W. 1996. Copyright and a democratic civil society. *Yale Law Journal* 106 (2): 283-387.

Neuman, W. Lawrence, and Ronald J. Berger. 1988. Competing perspectives on cross-national crime: An evaluation of theory and evidence. *Sociological Quarterly* 29:281-313.

Piquero, Nicole Leeper. 2005. Causes and prevention of intellectual property crime. *Trends in Organized Crime* 8 (4): 40-61.

Powell, G. Bingham. 1982. *Contemporary democracies: Participation, stability, and violence.* Washington, DC: Congressional Quarterly Press.

Rapp, Robert, and Richard P. Rozek. 1990. Benefits and costs of intellectual property protection in developing countries. *Journal of World Trade* 6 (2): 75-102.

Reichman, Jerome H. 1996/1997. From free riders to fair followers: Global competition under the TRIPS agreement. *New York University International Journal of Law and Politics* 29:11-93.

Ronkainen, Ilkka A., and Jose-Luis Guerrero-Cusumano. 2001. Correlates of intellectual property violations. *Multinational Business Review* 9:59-65.

Schwarz, Gideon. 1978. Estimating dimensions of a model. *Annals of Statistics* 6:461-64.

Seale, Darryl A., Michael Polakowski, and Sherry Schneider. 1998. It's not really theft! Personal and workplace ethics that enable software piracy. *Behaviour and Information Technology* 17 (1): 27-40.

Shim, J. P., and G. Stephen Taylor. 1989. Practicing manager's perception/attitude toward illegal software copying. *OR/MS Today* 16:30-33.

Shore, Barry, A. R. Venkatachalam, Eleanne Solorzano, Janice M. Burn, Syed Zahoor Hassan, and Lech J. Janczewski. 2001. Softlifting and piracy: Behavior across cultures. *Technology in Society* 23:563-81.

Sims, Ronald R., Hsing K. Cheng, and Hildy Teegen. 1996. Toward a profile of student software pirates. *Journal of Business Ethics* 15:839-49.

Solomon, S. L., and J. A. O'Brien. 1990. The effect of demographic factors on attitudes toward software piracy. *Journal of Computer Information Systems* 30:40-46.

Steidlmeier, Paul. 1993. The moral legitimacy of intellectual property claims: American business and developing country perspectives. *Journal of Business Ethics* 12 (2): 157-64.

Sung, Hung-En. 2004. Democracy and political corruption: A cross-national comparison. *Crime, Law, and Social Change* 41:179-94.

Swinyard, W. R., H. Rinne, and A. Keng Kau. 1990. The morality of software piracy: A cross-cultural analysis. *Journal of Business Ethics* 9:655-64.

Taylor, G. Stephen, and J. P. Shim. 1993. A comparative examination of attitudes toward software piracy among business professors and executives. *Human Relations* 46:419-33.

Taylor, I., P. Walton, and J. Young. 1973. *The new criminology.* London: Routledge & Kegan Paul.

Vold, George B., Thomas J. Bernard, and Jeffrey B. Snipes. 1998. *Theoretical criminology.* 4th ed. New York: Oxford University Press.

Wallerstein, Immanuel. 1974. *The modern world-system.* Vol. 1, *Capitalist agriculture and the origins of the European world-economy in the sixteenth century.* New York: Academic Press.

———. 1991. *Geopolitics and geoculture: Essays on the changing world-system.* Cambridge: Cambridge University Press.

World Intellectual Property Organization (WIPO). 2001. *WIPO intellectual property handbook: Policy, law, and use.* WIPO Publication no. 489(E). Geneva, Switzerland: WIPO.

SECTION TWO:

Building Democratic Societies: The Role of Criminal Justice

War Crimes, Democracy, and the Rule of Law in Belgrade, the Former Yugoslavia, and Beyond

By
JOHN HAGAN
and
SANJA KUTNJAK
IVKOVIĆ

The creation and operation of the International Criminal Tribunal for the Former Yugoslavia (ICTY) is an advance in the rule of law and arguably part of a larger process of the globalization of democratic norms. Yet support for the ICTY is increasingly influenced by local processes in which these norms are contested by indigenous parties and forces. We explore this issue with regard to support of Serbs living in and outside of Serbia for the ICTY in comparison to local courts. Serbs in Belgrade are distinctive in insisting that war criminals be tried in their places of origin, while Serbs in Sarajevo and Vukovar agree with other groups in these settings that war criminals should be tried in the locations where their crimes occurred. This is compelling evidence of the localized influence of cultural norms on ethnic and national group members in post–war crime settings.

Keywords: war crimes; democracy; rule of law; ICTY; ethnicity; legal cynicism; liberal legalism

The International Criminal Tribunal for the Former Yugoslavia (ICTY) has been in existence for more than a decade and is widely

John Hagan is John D. MacArthur Professor of Sociology and Law and senior research fellow at the American Bar Research Foundation. His most recent books are Justice in the Balkans: Prosecuting War Crimes at The Hague Tribunal (University of Chicago Press, 2003) and Northern Passage: American Vietnam War Resisters in Canada (Harvard University Press, 2001), which received the 2004 Albert J. Reiss Jr. Award from the Crime, Law and Deviance Section of the American Sociological Association.

Sanja Kutnjak Ivković is an assistant professor in the College of Criminology and Criminal Justice at the Florida State University. Trained both in criminology (Ph.D., University of Delaware) and criminal law (S.J.D., Harvard Law School), her research interests are courts, policing, and comparative and international criminology and criminal justice. Her most recent book is Fallen Blue Knights: Controlling Police Corruption (Oxford University Press, 2005). Her research has appeared in journals such as the Journal of Criminal Law and Criminology, Law and Society Review, Law and Social Inquiry, Law and Policy, and Stanford Journal of International Law.

DOI: 10.1177/0002716206287088

ANNALS, AAPSS, 605, May 2006

regarded as the most important advance in transnational human rights and criminal law enforcement since the International Military Tribunal following World War II in Nuremberg (Wilson 2005). The success of the ICTY in helping to reestablish the rule of law across the former Yugoslavia is further seen as a precondition for the redevelopment of social, political, and economic institutions and the reintegration of the states of the former Yugoslavia among the democratic nations of Europe. Some would go beyond this to identify the process involved as part of a "new world order" (Slaughter 2004). Yet if the work of the ICTY is an advance in the rule of law and part of a larger process of the globalization of democratic norms, it is also still influenced by processes of localization in which these norms are contested by indigenous parties and forces (Dezalay and Garth 2002). The challenge is to understand these intersecting and often competing processes.

A dominant view is that the everyday work of institutions such as the ICTY (see Kutnjak Ivković 2001; Hagan 2003; Hagan and Levi 2004, 2005, forthcoming) represents a sustained effort to establish international standards of procedural fairness and due process through the development of judicial and courtroom practices reflecting the ideals of liberal legalism (Bass 2000). Even from this view of the advancement of international criminal law, however, there is a clear awareness of the limits of this norm creation process, especially in localized settings. This is reflected in the recent concession by the ICTY that a former soldier accused of rape and torture during the 1992 to 1995 war in Bosnia, Radovan Stankovic, be transferred from The Hague and tried for war crimes in Sarajevo (Wood 2005). Recent research indicates that Bosnians have moved from an earlier position of strong support for the work of the ICTY to a more recent position of skepticism that questions the political neutrality of ICTY judges, leading to the insistence that future cases involving Bosnian victims be tried in indigenous rather than international tribunals (Kutnjak Ivković and Hagan forthcoming).

It is important to recognize that the decline in public confidence of Bosnians in the capacity of the ICTY to dispense justice is not distinctive to the contemporary period in the former Yugoslavia. Suzanne Karstedt (1998, Figures 3 and 7) observes a striking German parallel in the declining satisfaction with denazification programs after 1945 in postwar Germany and increasing opposition after 1989 to lustration procedures in the former German Democratic Republic. This is despite the fact that at the outset in 1945 and 1989 Germany, as more recently in Bosnia, there were strong demands for criminal proceedings against high-ranking authorities. With the passage of time, however, public satisfaction with the recently developed judicial institutions in all these settings declined.

Each of the party states to the wars in the former Yugoslavia has initiated cases in its own national courts involving minor figures in war crimes. Among these, the Bosnian efforts are probably the best known. Less is known in comparison about Serbian attitudes and activities addressing war crimes. What is known is sufficient to conclude that the Serbian public attitude is not supportive of the ICTY or its self-conception as a liberal legal institution embodying the rule of law. One analyst,

Michael Parenti (2000, 128), succinctly summarizes a viewpoint sympathetic to the former Yugoslavia:

> The International Criminal Tribunal for the Former Yugoslavia was set up by the United Nations Security Council in 1993 at the bidding of Madeline Albright and the US government. It depends on NATO countries for its financial support, with the United States as the major provider, and it looks to NATO to track down and arrest the suspects it puts on trial. Although located in The Hague, this tribunal has no connection to the World Court and no precedent in international law or the UN Charter. It hardly qualifies as any kind of independent judiciary body.

If the ICTY is to accomplish its liberal legal goals of establishing procedural fairness and due process not only in practice, but also in terms of its public perception, it will be important to understand the extent to which Parenti's view prevails among Serbs, as well as among others in the former Yugoslavia. This article explores Serbian attitudes toward the ICTY in Belgrade and more broadly in comparison to attitudes of various groups in other major cities in the former Yugoslavia.

From Liberal Legalism

It is no minor matter when international criminal law is used, directly or indirectly, to unseat a head of state who has been ostensibly democratically elected. Slobodan Milosevic was the first sitting head of government to be indicted by an international criminal tribunal, and his indictment by the ICTY surely played a significant role in his removal from elected office.

The first chief prosecutor of the ICTY, Richard Goldstone, freely acknowledged his discomfort when confronted with questions about the selection of the former Yugoslavia as the site for the first international tribunal since Nuremberg. His successor, Louise Arbour, had to answer subsequent questions about why this particular elected official was the first to be indicted by an international tribunal in the process of being removed from office. Goldstone (2000, 122-23) observed of his part in this process that

> a decent and rational person is offended that criminal laws should apply only to some people and not others in similar situations. I felt distinctly uncomfortable when, in October 1994, in Belgrade, I was asked by the Serb minister of justice why the United Nations had established a War Crimes Tribunal for the former Yugoslavia when it had not done so for Cambodia or Iraq. Why were the people of the former Yugoslavia being treated differently? Was this an act of discrimination? The only answer I could give was that the international community had to begin somewhere, but that if there was no follow-through and if other equivalent situations in the future were not treated comparably, then the people of the former Yugoslavia could justifiably claim discrimination.

Goldstone might also have answered that intervention was necessary to help reestablish a functional democracy in the former Yugoslavia. Yet for such intervention to be successful in advancing democracy, it is not only necessary to meet procedural and due process standards in doing so but also to be broadly *perceived* as meeting these standards by members of the public who identify with both the victims and the parties accused of perpetrating crimes against them (Lind and Tyler 1988; Tyler 1994).

Because international war crimes are so often ignited by ethnic and national hatred, there is a persistent and contrasting perception of prejudice and discrimination in attempts to legally address these disputes. We have already noted that the ICTY is seen by some as an Anglo-American and European–inspired legal justification for NATO's intervention in the former Yugoslavia and therefore as inherently biased against the Serbs (Parenti 2000). Others argue that neither the former Yugoslavia nor the ICTY should be prejudged in this way. For example, a prominent contemporary historian, Mark Mazower (2000, 128-29), argues in defense of the citizens of the former Yugoslavia that the war in the 1990s "represented the extreme force required by nationalists to break apart a society which was otherwise capable of ignoring the mundane fractures of class and ethnicity." It is unclear what role, if any, contemporary ethno-national tensions play in the ICTY and in the response of citizens and victims to its actions in the new and old state settings.

In the former Yugoslavia, there may be no declared "victors," but below we will argue that there may nonetheless be "defeated" and "defended" parties. The war in Bosnia and Herzegovina was ended without a declaration of victory through the Dayton Peace Agreement of 1995. This may make the ICTY a substitute for military conflict, with court outcomes symbolically calibrating who are considered the defeated and defended through the sentencing of convicted offenders representing former warring parties (see also Chambliss and Seidman 1971/1982, 236). This source of conflict may also make the respective parties especially sensitive to their perceptions of the justness of these court outcomes.

Beyond this, the liberal legalism of international criminal law is well known for the conflicts associated with its institutional politics. The creation of the ICTY was itself criticized for its origin in the narrow membership of United Nations' Security Council rather than the more diverse and representative General Assembly (Robertson 1999). The United Nations also was criticized for perpetuating a policy of "moral equivalency" that failed to respond militarily to Serbian aggression in a timely way, while also delaying action in creating and sustaining the ICTY (Guest 1995; see also Power 2002). Picking the first ICTY prosecutor, Richard Goldstone, was a highly politicized and conflicted process that took more than a year (Scharf 1997; Goldstone 2000). The selection of judges for the ICTY, "no two of whom may be nationals of the same State" (Statute of the Tribunal 1993, Article 12), is also a highly politicized process that requires balancing a wide range of international interests and demands for representation (Neier 1998). This selection process often has little to do with the settings in which war crimes occur—which may or may not be a good thing—but which in either event is a source of conflict in relation to the parties involved, who will usually want their own nations represented.

Hannah Arendt (1965) provided a classic record of the conflicts involved in Israel's resistance to international liberal legalism with its decision to try Adolf

Eichmann in an Israeli court in Jerusalem. This decision was defended by Prime Minister David Ben-Gurion's dismissal of a more universal jurisdiction and by his assertion that "Israel does not need the protection of an International Court" (p. 272). It included Arendt's own defense against the charge of the retributive purpose that the trial's death sentence for Eichmann produced: "Hence, to the question most commonly asked about the Eichmann trial: what good does it do?, there is but one possible answer: It will do justice" (p. 254). Yet the political conflict and uncertainty that this trial left in its wake greatly troubled Arendt, and she in the end endorsed the institutions of international liberal legalism, at least to the extent that she observed that the Jerusalem court "should have either sought to establish an international tribunal or tried to reformulate the territorial principle in such a way that it applied to Israel" (p. 262). These sources of conflict in Jerusalem may be no less prominent today in the former Yugoslavia.

All of the above conflicts threaten to potentially undermine what in the comparative politics of law literature is called "diffuse support" for the ICTY. This literature has long seen the diffuse support for the U.S. Supreme Court expressed by citizens as a finding to be explained and compared with responses to other national and transnational courts (Casey 1974). Diffuse support is understood as conferring legitimacy and as rationally calculated in the sense that it can be diminished by decisions that conflict with majority opinion (Caldeira 1986), especially in transitional settings where new courts, on one hand, lack a cushion of historical embeddedness and are susceptible to legitimacy shortfalls, and, on the other hand, are established as institutions of new nationalist governments and thus are enjoying the confidence of the regime supporters (Gibson and Caldeira 1995, 1998). Of course, in addition to the difference of historical longevity, there is also in the international context the pull of national sovereignty, and it is the jurisdictional challenge to sovereign immunity that is the ultimate source of contention in the indictment of national military and political figures by the ICTY.

Finally, in addition to the comparative politics research on support for courts, there is also a significant and growing literature on the perception of criminal (in)justice. To date, such work is concentrated almost entirely within the United States and focused on the American criminal justice system, especially the perception of this system by African Americans compared to whites. This research provides unequivocal evidence that African Americans disproportionately perceive actions of the American police and courts as unjust (Hagan and Albonetti 1982; Weitzer 1999; Brooks 2000; Brooks and Jeon-Slaughter 2001; see also Wortley, Hagan, and Macmillan 1997). Even within the United States, however, this research literature has failed to keep pace with demographic shifts, for example, providing few studies of Latino perceptions of the justice system (see Brooks and Jeon-Slaughter 2001; Hagan, Shedd, and Payne 2005).

In an intriguing contrast with the optimistic concept of legal liberalism, Sampson and Bartusch (1998) suggest use of the concept of "legal cynicism" to capture the "anomie about law" and apparent skepticism of American minority group members for the criminal justice system. Beyond this, they add the concept of "cognitive landscapes" to make the point that these perceptions vary across the contours formed in relation to individuals, groups, and places where perceptions of justice are formed. While Sampson and Bartusch devote their attention to contextualizing American neighborhood and ghetto experiences, we believe the conceptualization they provide has broader application.

To ultimately achieve the goals of democratization and the rule of law, of course, confidence in judicial independence is essential.

Linking their work to earlier research by Kapis (1978), Sampson and Bartusch argue (1998, 783) that individual and group perceptions are grounded in structural landscapes that define defeated and defended peoples and settings. Their fundamental hypothesis is that structural settings "where inability to influence the structures of power that constrain lives is greatest, also breed cynicism and perceptions of legal injustice." In the 1990s aftermath of their sense of defeat in the wars in the former Yugoslavia first at the hands of NATO, and then the Tribunal, Serbia is likely one such place. However, Sampson and Bartusch's perspective goes further in predicting that sensitivity to inequities of political and power relationships is preeminently contextual and not reducible to the groups and individuals themselves.

The implication of this prediction is that it is the structural landscape of Serbia's current national circumstance that determines its localized attitudes toward the ICTY. Serbs who are removed from the localized structural circumstances of this defeat in Serbia—for example, living among the defended in Bosnia or Croatia—may not be similarly embittered. The historian quoted above, Mark Mazower (2000), suggests reasons for predicting as much in the Balkan settings that have prided themselves on their defense of ethnic tolerance. Sampson and Bartusch's (1998) conclusion is that there is an ecological structuring to normative orientations or "cognitive landscapes" that is essential to understanding perceptions of justice, and we argue in this article that this is the case as much or even more in international than in domestic settings. In addition, we go one step further in suggesting that in this international setting it is skepticism about the independence of the Tribunal judiciary that accounts for the Serbian disapproval of the ICTY. To ultimately achieve the goals of democratization and the rule of law, of course, confidence in judicial independence is essential.

The Cognitive Landscape of the Conflict
in the Former Yugoslavia

We can provide here only a brief account of the ICTY (see also Hagan 2003) to set the foundation for understanding how this institution is seen from several parts of the former Yugoslavia. The prosecution has asserted in ICTY cases that three wars in the former Yugoslavia took the following toll in the 1990s: at least several thousand deaths and 170,000 deportations in the early 1990s in Croatia, followed in the mid-1990s by more than 7,000 deaths and 200,000 to 300,000 deportations in Bosnia, leading in the late 1990s to more than 4,000 deaths and 750,000 deportations in Kosovo. As leader of the former Yugoslavia, Slobodan Milosevic is charged with aiding these events by supporting local Serb leaders in Croatia, Bosnia, and Kosovo, while further creating government ministries in the former Yugoslavia to form links with these leaders outside Serbia. By 1991, Milosevic had laid the groundwork for the wars that would follow.

Following Croatia's secession from the former Yugoslavia in 1991, several areas of Croatia dominated by Serbs separated from Croatia, and local Serbian leaders used military and paramilitary units from the former Yugoslavia to murder, detain, and deport Croats and other non-Serbs, in the process largely destroying the city of Vukovar and heavily damaging the city of Dubrovnik. The Croats were able to later push back militarily against the Serbs and took the opportunity to themselves control portions of Bosnia. Colonel Tihomir Blaskic was an early defendant prosecuted and convicted by the ICTY for his role in guiding Croatian operations in central Bosnia, although the charges and his sentence were substantially reduced when it became apparent that the evidence against him was actually rather dubious.

Bosnia was the second theater of operations, and when the Muslims and Croats in Bosnia voted to separate from the former Yugoslavia, Radovan Karadzic simultaneously declared the formation of an independent Republika Srpska, or Serbian Republic of Bosnia, and became its president. The ethnic cleansing of Prijedor, the Siege of Sarajevo, and the massacre of Srebrenica, under the direction of Karadzic and General Ratko Mladic, were three of the most devastating of the Bosnian Serbian aggressions against the Bosnian Muslims. When the Tribunal was unable to apprehend Karadzic and Mladic, it had to content itself in the nearer term by prosecuting figures like Esad Landzo, a guard in a detention camp. Later, General Radislav Krstic was arrested by U.S. forces in Bosnia and convicted for his role in the Srebrenica genocide.

Kosovo was the scene of the final war, coming to a climax with NATO bombing in early 1999, which Milosevic claimed as the pretext for the deportation of one-third of the Kosovo Albanian population. The events in Kosovo led finally to the ICTY indictment of Milosevic in the spring of 1999. It took until the summer of 2001 to get Milosevic removed from office, arrested, and transferred to the Tribunal, and at the time of this writing Karadzic and Mladic still remain at large.

This abridged historical introduction to the Tribunal indicates that its work is not likely to be seen similarly in different parts of the former Yugoslavia. To use

Sampson and Bartusch's (1998) metaphor, the case-based historical edges and contours of the ICTY are sufficiently varied to make it a vivid institutional landscape onto which the sentiments of the various parties can be cognitively projected. To borrow further from Sampson and Bartusch's conceptualization, the Serbs constitute the defeated party in Tribunal cases, while the Bosnians and Kosovars are the defended parties, and the Croats find themselves located somewhere in between. This pattern becomes more conspicuous as the Tribunal accumulates its judgments, and in the process the Tribunal itself has assumed an important role in writing a legal war history of the former Yugoslavia. As the historian Robert Donia (2004, 11) notes, "These chambers have produced histories that are not only credible and readable, but indispensable to understand the origins and course of the 1990s conflicts in the former Yugoslavia." Richard Wilson (2005, 941) goes further in observing that "international tribunals such as the ICTY are altering the relationship between law and history."

In drafting this history, the judgments of the ICTY are helping to reshape the cognitive landscape of the former Yugoslavia. Public opinion surveys (International Institute for Democracy and Electoral Assistance 2002) reveal a pattern of responses to the ICTY that range from high regard in Kosovo (83 percent approval), through acceptance in Bosnia (51 percent approval), to rejection in Serbia and Republika Srpska (4 to 8 percent approval). As Karsted's (1998) research in post–World War II and post–cold war Germany anticipates, this pattern of approval has since declined in Bosnia (Kutnjak Ivković and Hagan forthcoming) but has not descended to the levels found in Serbia and Republika Srpska. These varied levels of support form the broad contours of the Tribunal cognitive landscape. Richard Wilson (2005, 941-42) suggests that, in particular, we should hardly be surprised by the low approval in Serbian areas, arguing that "any historical account which punctures nationalist mythologies is likely to be rejected as long as a region is dominated by nationalist politicians who have regularly denied responsibility for mass atrocities." As recently as the fall of 2002, the Republika Srpska government was in deep denial of its responsibility, insisting, for example, that only about a thousand Bosnian Muslim soldiers, rather than seven to eight thousand Bosnian Muslim civilians, had been killed at Srebrenica.

Sampson and Bartusch's (1998) point is that such policies of denial in relation to events like the Srebrenica massacre will have a radiating cultural impact that collectively influences the cognitive landscape of public opinion. Of course, this is what cultural propaganda is all about, and it is the kind of fuel that can drive genocidal violence in the first place. If this view of the cognitive landscape of attitudes toward efforts at international criminal justice is correct, we should be able to see testable signs of its operation. For example, we should find that the effects of such cultural policies and pronouncements are localized in their influence to the place of their origin and not more globally endemic or generic to the groups involved. That is, we should find that the Serbs in places like Belgrade are most affected in their views, while elsewhere in the former Yugoslavia the effect of being Serbian might be culturally diffused and mitigated by countervailing cultural beliefs and victimization experiences shared with the locally defended rather than defeated groups. This is the kind of thesis that we go on to assess next.

Method and Results

Surveys were conducted in 2003 and 2004 in the cities of Sarajevo (Bosnia, n = 473), Belgrade (Serbia, n = 500), Vukovar (Croatia, n = 501), and Pristina (Kosovo, n = 500). Nearly two thousand interviews were conducted overall. In Belgrade, Pristina, and Vukovar, it was possible to use census data to conduct randomly selected household interviews. In Sarajevo, neither telephone nor household sources of information were sufficiently developed to establish unbiased sampling frames. In these limiting circumstances, the respondents were sampled from the streets, coffee shops, and department stores of the central business district of the city. Potential respondents were approached and asked whether they would like to participate in a study of the ICTY.

Systematic bias in our sampling could have influenced responses to our surveys. For example, there are indications that our respondents are better educated than the general populations of the cities involved. Better-educated respondents may have been more willing to take part because they are better informed about the ICTY and because they are more comfortable with the survey methodology. However, our multivariate models show no effect of the respondents' educational level on their opinions about the ICTY and its decisions (see also Kutnjak Ivković and Hagan forthcoming).

Table 1 presents an overview of the sampled respondents in the four cities. The samples are about equally made up of men and women. The greatest variation in age is in Pristina, where nearly half of the sample is younger than thirty-five, and just over one-fifth of the respondents are older than fifty. This is likely because the mass deportation from Kosovo exacted an especially heavy toll on middle-aged and elderly persons with chronic health problems (see Burkholder, Spiegel, and Salma 2001). Meanwhile, consistent with its cosmopolitan reputation, the Sarajevo sample has the highest education, with 97 percent having high school graduation or higher. As expected, Sarajevo also has the largest Muslim population (65.5 percent), Belgrade the largest Serbian population (90.7 percent), Vukovar the largest Croatian population (60.3 percent), and Pristina the most Albanians (97.8 percent). Still, it is useful for our purposes that there are notable numbers of Serbs in Vukovar (32.7 percent) and in Sarajevo (11.4 percent). The simultaneous concentration of Serbs in Belgrade and the dispersion of Serbs in Sarajevo and Vukovar make it possible for us to consider the localized as contrasted with globally generic impact of Serbian nationalist cultural messages.

Finally, the victimization measures included at the bottom of Table 1 make it clear that although Belgrade may occupy a "defeated" position in the legal judgments of the ICTY, they are also the least likely to have been victimized by the war itself; the respondents in Vukovar and Pristina fall somewhere in between,

TABLE 1
RESPONDENTS' DEMOGRAPHIC CHARACTERISTICS AND VICTIMIZATION
STATUS (IN PERCENTAGES)

	Sarajevo (n = 473)	Belgrade (n = 500)	Vukovar (n = 501)	Pristina (n = 500)	χ^2	Phi/ Cramer's V
Gender					12.4**	.079
Women	44.2	49.8	54.3	53.6		
Age					103.4***	.163
Eighteen to thirty-five	25.3	33.6	27.7	49.2		
Thirty-six to fifty	36.7	27.8	26.7	29.6		
Older than fifty	38.0	38.6	45.5	21.1		
Education					169.8***	.208
Below high school	3.4	17.9	35.1	28.2		
High school	80.3	67.6	53.7	55.6		
College	16.3	14.5	11.2	16.2		
Nationality					3,652.0***	.786
Croats	18.9	1.2	60.3	0.0		
Muslims	65.5	1.8	0.6	1.0		
Serbs	11.4	90.7	32.7	0.0		
Albanians	0.0	0.0	0.0	97.8		
Others	4.2	6.3	6.4	1.2		
Victimization status						
Personally victimized[a]	82.2	17.6	54.6	49.2	405.3***	.457
Witnessed[b]	73.8	18.9	29.6	17.3	446.4***	.478
Family victimized[c]	89.4	28.6	64.7	52.5	380.1***	.441
Neighbors victimized[d]	94.7	41.9	81.1	72.1	360.1***	.432

a. The question was worded as follows: "Do you consider yourself a victim of war crimes or crimes against humanity?" The possible answers were "yes" and "no."
b. The question was worded as follows: "Have you witnessed a war crime or a crime against humanity?" The possible answers were "yes" and "no."
c. The question was worded as follows: "Has a member of your family or a close friend been a victim of war crimes or crimes against humanity?" The possible answers were "yes" and "no."
d. The question was worded as follows: "Has an acquaintance or a fellow citizen been a victim of a war crime or a crime against humanity?" The possible answers were "yes" and "no."
**$p < .01$. ***$p < .001$.

while the sample in Sarajevo suffered massively (with 82.2 percent reporting personal victimization in Sarajevo, compared to only 17.6 percent in Belgrade). By these measures, Sarajevans were uniquely in need of the kind of compensatory legal "defense" invoked in Sampson and Bartusch's (1998) framework.

The results in the far left column of Table 2 provide our first indication of approval and disapproval of the ICTY as the appropriate jurisdiction for war

TABLE 2
RESPONDENT DESIGNATIONS OF APPROPRIATE
JURISDICTION (IN PERCENTAGES)

	International Criminal Tribunal for the Former Yugoslavia (ICTY)	Local Courts Where Crimes Committed	Local Courts of the Offenders' Country	Victims' Families	χ^2	Cramer's V
Whole sample (N = 1,974)	41.5	28.3	20.1	10.2		
Sarajevo (n = 473)	44.1	44.7	1.1	10.1	946.8°°°	.417
Belgrade (n = 500)	18.4	6.3	67.5	7.8		
Vukovar (n = 501)	34.3	44.1	14.8	6.8		
Pristina (n = 500)	65.1	16.7	2.7	15.5		
Croats (n = 368)					10.2°	.166
Sarajevo (n = 86)	38.4	53.5	1.2	7.0		
Vukovar (n = 282)	28.0	52.1	11.3	8.5		
Serbs (n = 571)					185.9°°°	.403
Sarajevo (n = 53)	35.8	52.8	1.9	9.4		
Belgrade (n = 375)	18.4	6.1	68.5	6.9		
Vukovar (n = 143)	47.6	25.9	22.4	4.2		

NOTE: The question was worded as follows: "Who should try the persons accused of war crimes committed in the territory of the former Yugoslavia?" The possible answers were "a) the courts on the territory of Croatia and Bosnia and Herzegovina where the crimes have been committed; b) the courts of the offender's country or country whose army force he was a member of; c) the International Tribunal in The Hague; d) the families of the victims; e) other _____."
°p < .05. °°°p < .001.

crimes cases. This table presents results by the four cities in which the interviews took place and then displays the results for Croats and Serbs (the two groups that are sufficiently distributed beyond one setting to make analysis possible) across several cities. The ICTY receives the most support in Pristina (65.1 percent), the city that was most recently in need of defense and least able to organize criminal proceedings itself, while the ICTY receives the least support in Belgrade (18.4 percent), with Vukovar (34.3 percent) and Sarajevo (44.1 percent) in between. The middle portion of the left-hand column of Table 2 further reveals that Croats are not enthusiastic in their support but nonetheless rather similar in their response to the ICTY (28 and 38.4 percent support, respectively) in Sarajevo and Vukovar. This makes it all the more striking to see in the bottom portion of Table 2 that Serbs living in Sarajevo (35.8 percent) and Vukovar (47.6 percent) are about twice as likely to support the ICTY as are Serbs living in Belgrade (18.4 percent).

TABLE 3
RESPONDENT DESIGNATIONS OF APPROPRIATE JURISDICTION
FOR KARADZIC AND MLADIC (IN PERCENTAGES)

	International Criminal Tribunal for the Former Yugoslavia (ICTY)	Bosnia and Herzegovina Courts	Serbian Courts	Victims' Families	χ^2	Cramer's V
Whole sample ($N = 1,974$)	50.8	24.2	13.1	11.9		
Sarajevo ($n = 473$)	40.9	45.4	1.1	12.6	906.6°°°	.421
Belgrade ($n = 500$)	23.4	10.1	59.8	6.6		
Vukovar ($n = 501$)	55.2	24.8	6.4	13.6		
Pristina ($n = 500$)	73.8	12.7	0.4	13.1		
Croats ($n = 365$)					21.4°°°	.242
Sarajevo ($n = 88$)	35.2	53.4	1.1	10.2		
Vukovar ($n = 277$)	50.2	27.1	2.5	20.2		
Serbs ($n = 475$)					139.2°°°	.383
Sarajevo ($n = 53$)	35.8	49.1	3.8	11.3		
Belgrade ($n = 288$)	23.2	11.1	59.0	6.6		
Vukovar ($n = 134$)	60.4	20.9	15.7	3.0		

NOTE: The question was worded as follows: "In your opinion, who should try Radovan Karadzic and Ratko Mladic?" The possible answers were "a) courts in Bosnia and Herzegovina; b) courts in Serbia/the Serb Republic; c) the International Tribunal in The Hague; d) the families of the victims; e) other _____."
°°°$p < .001$.

The remainder of Table 2 considers the support other possible jurisdictional locations receive as alternative settings to the ICTY. The lower part of the second column of Table 2 shows how similar Serbs interviewed in Sarajevo are to Croats living in Sarajevo and Vukovar in supporting the location of cases in the local courts where the crimes were committed. Just more than half of the Serbs living in Sarajevo and more than half of the Croats living in Sarajevo and Vukovar approve of trying cases in these jurisdictions. In sharp contrast, more than a two-thirds majority of the Serbs (68.5 percent) interviewed in Belgrade believed that the appropriate jurisdiction was in the local courts of the offender's country. The implication is that the Serbs interviewed in Belgrade were distinctive in their desire to have cases involving Serbs as defendants tried in Serbia, and these same Serb respondents in Belgrade (only 6.1 percent) were extremely unlikely to want Serbian defendants tried in the local courts (i.e., mostly Bosnia or Kosovo) where the crimes were committed.

Tables 3 through 5 examine whether the results we have considered thus far are conditional on the identity of particular defendants who might be tried. Table 3 considers Karadzic and Mladic, the Bosnian Serb political leader and military

TABLE 4
RESPONDENT DESIGNATIONS OF APPROPRIATE JURISDICTION
FOR BLASKIC (IN PERCENTAGES)

	International Criminal Tribunal for the Former Yugoslavia (ICTY)	Croatian Courts	Bosnia and Herzegovina Courts	Victims' Families	χ^2	Cramer's V
Whole sample (N = 1,974)	47.5	17.4	25.9	9.2		
Sarajevo (n = 473)	44.5	4.9	1.1	12.6	429.1°°°	.293
Belgrade (n = 500)	28.3	39.7	22.8	9.2		
Vukovar (n = 501)	35.0	24.7	33.9	6.4		
Pristina (n = 500)	76.5	6.2	6.8	10.5		
Croats (n = 318)					11.7°°	.191
Sarajevo (n = 88)	39.8	11.4	40.9	8.0		
Vukovar (n = 230)	26.1	27.8	37.4	8.7		
Serbs (n = 519)					59.9°°°	.240
Sarajevo (n = 54)	35.2	5.6	48.1	11.1		
Belgrade (n = 332)	28.0	40.7	22.3	9.0		
Vukovar (n = 133)	51.9	18.0	26.3	3.8		

NOTE: The question was worded as follows: "In your opinion, who should have tried Tihomir Blaskic?" In the 2003 version we added the explanation, "In your opinion, who should have tried Tihomir Blaskic (the Commander of the Regional Headquarters of the HVO Armed Forces [Croatian Defense Council] in central Bosnia as of June 1992)?" The possible answers were the same: "a) courts in Croatia; b) courts in Bosnia and Herzegovina; c) the International Tribunal in The Hague; d) the families of the victims; and e) other _____." Because only a few respondents selected answers "families of victims" and "courts in Croatia," they were omitted from the 2000 cross-ethnicity analysis.
°°p < .01. °°°p < .001.

commander indicted, but not yet arrested, for their involvements in the siege of Sarajevo, the Srebrenica massacre, and beyond. Karadzic and Mladic are certainly the most notorious of the currently unarrested figures in the former Yugoslavia. The results in Table 3 largely replicate the patterns in Table 2, although it is of interest that the overall level of support for the ICTY shows some increase in approval as the appropriate jurisdiction for these notable figures.

TABLE 5
RESPONDENT DESIGNATIONS OF APPROPRIATE JURISDICTION
FOR LANDZO (IN PERCENTAGES)

	International Criminal Tribunal for the Former Yugoslavia (ICTY)	Croatian Courts	Bosnia and Herzegovina Counrts	Victims' Families	χ^2	Cramer's V
Whole sample (N = 1,974)	49.9	7.4	32.6	10.4		
Sarajevo (n = 473)	43.0	15.0	32.5	9.5	309.8°°°	.260
Belgrade (n = 500)	30.4	2.3	55.5	11.8		
Vukovar (n = 501)	43.8	3.6	43.4	9.1		
Pristina (n = 500)	76.7	4.8	7.7	10.9		
Croats (n = 265)					28.7°°°	.329
Sarajevo (n = 87)	34.5	24.1	34.5	6.9		
Vukovar (n = 178)	36.5	3.4	48.3	11.8		
Serbs (n = 455)					74.2°°°	.286
Sarajevo (n = 53)	32.1	24.5	32.1	11.3		
Belgrade (n = 324)	30.2	2.5	55.2	12.0		
Vukovar (n = 78)	60.3	2.6	32.1	5.1		

NOTE: The question was worded as follows: "In your opinion, who should have tried Esad Landzo?" In the 2003 version we added the explanation, "In your opinion, who should have tried Esad Landzo (a guard at the Celebici concentration camp)?" The possible answers were the same: "a) courts in Croatia; b) courts in Bosnia and Herzegovina; c) the International Tribunal in The Hague; d) the families of the victims; and e) other _____." Because only a few respondents selected answers "families of victims" and "courts in Croatia," they were omitted from the 2000 cross-ethnicity analysis.
°°°$p < .001$.

Indeed, whereas just more than 40 percent of the full sample supports the ICTY's jurisdiction in the abstract (Table 2: 41.5 percent), this overall support reaches a majority level for Karadzic and Mladic (Table 3: 50.8 percent), and Sarajevo is the only setting where support declines slightly. There is a slight increase in support for the idea of trying Karadzic and Mladic at the ICTY even among Serbs in Belgrade (from 18.4 to 23.2 percent). Still, Serbs in Belgrade overwhelmingly think Karadzic and Mladic (59 percent) should be tried in their own jurisdiction.

Table 4 considers Colonel Blaskic, formerly a colonel in the HVO (Croatian Defense Council), and the jurisdiction for his trial on war crimes committed in Bosnia. Perhaps the most striking finding in this table is that the largest proportions of Croats, be they interviewed in Sarajevo or Vukovar, indicate that they believe Blaskic should have been tried in Bosnia (40.9 and 37.4 percent), while Serbs in Belgrade (but not elsewhere, it should be noted) are most likely to believe that Blaskic should have been tried in Croatia (40.7 percent). The point, of course, is that Serbs in Belgrade express stronger support for local jurisdiction of this Croatian defendant than do Croats in Vukovar or Sarajevo. To this extent, Serbs in Belgrade are thus consistent in their defense of the principle of local, sovereign jurisdiction, beyond the cases of their own fellow citizens.

Table 5 considers the case of the Bosnian Serb guard at the Celebici concentration camp, Esad Landzo. This case produces the largest expression of support across groups and settings for the local jurisdiction of the Bosnian courts. Indeed, a majority of the Serbs interviewed in Belgrade (55.2 percent) supported local Bosnian jurisdiction in this case. The largest exception to support for local jurisdiction was in Pristina (Kosovo), where fully three-quarters of those interviewed (76.7 percent) supported the jurisdiction of the ICTY in this case. This high level of residual support for the ICTY in Pristina would seem to confirm the strength of continuing suspicion among Kosovars about the practices of local courts (see Wilson 2006 [this volume]).

[E]ven though there is often an obvious and pressing need in wartime and soon after for international legal assistance, the further challenge is to manage the tempo and terms of a return to local legal institutions.

While the tables provide evidence of variation across specific cases, with some indication of greater support for the ICTY's international jurisdiction in major cases involving figures like Karadzic and Mladic, and more support for local national jurisdiction in less important cases involving figures like Landzo, the most salient finding is that Serbs interviewed in Belgrade (and much less so elsewhere) are least supportive of the ICTY not only for their own citizens' cases but also for the citizens of other jurisdictions in the former Yugoslavia—regardless of whether the defendant is of major or minor importance. Serbs in Belgrade are

TABLE 6
PERCEPTIONS ABOUT THE POLITICAL INDEPENDENCE
OF THE INTERNATIONAL CRIMINAL TRIBUNAL
FOR THE FORMER YUGOSLAVIA (ICTY)

	Mean	F-Test/t-Test
Whole sample (N = 1,974)	10.9	
Sarajevo (n = 475)	10.5	145.4°°°
Belgrade (n = 500)	12.4	
Vukovar (n = 501)	10.1	
Pristina (n = 500)	9.5	
Croats (n = 278)		0.3
Sarajevo (n = 86)	10.4	
Vukovar (n = 192)	10.4	
Serbs (n = 572)		70.2°°°
Sarajevo (n = 54)	10.6	
Belgrade (n = 439)	12.4	
Vukovar (n = 89)	9.7	

NOTE: Four items composing the ICTY political independence scale ask about judges' ability to resist political pressure, judicial independence, national bias, and the role played by political factors in judicial decisions. The alpha reliability coefficient for this scale is .70. The scale ranges from 4 (indicating perceptions about the ICTY's political neutrality) to 16 (indicating perceptions about the ICTY's political lack of neutrality).
°°°p < .001.

not alone in their preference for local jurisdiction, with citizens of Sarajevo also supportive of their own Bosnian jurisdiction; but the Serbs interviewed in Belgrade are certainly the least supportive of the ICTY.

We ultimately wanted to consider if this strong localized response to the ICTY by Serbs in Belgrade could be explained by the suspicions of these respondents about the lack of political independence of judges at the ICTY. Earlier we noted that decisions written by judges at the Tribunal have played an important role in creating a history of the wars in the former Yugoslavia that in particular holds Serbian political and military figures accountable for death and displacement. We created a scale of perceived judicial political independence to measure variation in respondents' views of the political neutrality of judges at the ICTY. Four items comprising the ICTY judicial neutrality scale ask about judges' ability to resist political pressure, judicial independence, national bias, and the role played by political factors in judicial decisions. The alpha reliability coefficient for this scale is .70. When we coded the scale to assign higher values for lack of political neutrality or political independence, we found that Serbs in Belgrade scored highest (12.4), while Serbs in Vukovar (9.7) scored among the lowest, with Serbs in Sarajevo scoring in between (10.6). As shown in Table 6

($F = 70.2$, $p < .001$), the differences in these scale scores are high in statistical significance.

[Interviewees in Sarajevo and Belgrade concur] that war crimes offenders from the wars in the former Yugoslavia can now more appropriately be tried in local, national courts, rather than at the ICTY.

Table 7 presents a final logistic regression analysis. The initial results in this table parallel those presented earlier in Table 2 in showing that the Serbs in Belgrade (i.e., the omitted comparison category), compared to the Serbs in both Sarajevo ($B = -0.91$, $p < .001$) and Vukovar ($B = -1.39$, $p < .001$), are more likely to believe that a jurisdiction other than the ICTY is preferable. When the scale measuring lack of political neutrality or independence is added to the equation, these effects are both reduced below statistical significance and nearly entirely eliminated ($B = -0.05$ and -0.18, $p < .10$). The final column in the table reports results from an equation that further includes measures of perceived judicial fairness in decisions ($B = -2.07$, $p < .001$) and procedures ($B = -1.25$, $p < .05$), as well as a focus on deterrence as a purpose in sentencing ($B = 1.04$, $p < .01$). Each of these variables is also a significant predictor of preferring a jurisdiction other than the ICTY, and inclusion of these variables explains some of the influence of the lack of perceived judicial neutrality/independence (reduced from .63 to .26), but this influence remains highly statistically significant ($p < .01$).

Discussion and Conclusions

Fundamentally, to be seen as legitimate, legal justice must ultimately also be seen as local justice, and this is a compelling democratic premise underlying the venerable American politician Tip O'Neill's (1994) observation that "all politics is local." Global legal institutions may need to be particularly sensitive to this localized democratic norm. So that, even though there is often an obvious and pressing need in wartime and soon after for international legal assistance, the further challenge is to manage the tempo and terms of a return to local legal institutions. Karstedt (1998) made this point before for two instances in twentieth-century

TABLE 7

LOGISTIC COEFFICIENTS FROM THE REGRESSION OF APPROPRIATE JURISDICTION ON SERBIAN RESPONDENTS' ATTITUDES AND BACKGROUND CHARACTERISTICS

	Model 1		Model 2		Model 3		Model 4	
	B	SE	B	SE	B	SE	B	SE
Sample[a]								
Sarajevo	-0.91**	.316	-0.79*	.335	-0.05	.405	-0.47	.518
Vukovar	-1.39***	.332	-1.52***	.231	-0.18	.338	-0.21	.409
Fairness of decisions[b]							-2.07***	.458
Fairness of procedures[c]							-1.25*	.507
Punishment purpose[d]							1.04**	.325
Political scale[e]					.63***	.069	.26**	.087
Victim status[f]			-.20	.228	-.22	.287	-.13	.348
Education[g]								
Less than high school			.52	.368	.59	.495	.21	.620
High school			-.01	.282	.04	.339	.01	.403
Gender[h]			-.07	.201	-.09	.255	-.26	.306
Age[i]								
Older			.46	.246	.43	.314	.35	.368
Middle-aged			.06	.254	-.03	.315	.09	.380
Constant	1.49	.167	-2.2	.363	-6.1***	.791	-3.70***	.964
Model χ^2 (df)	44.57*** (2)		53.62*** (8)		158.99*** (9)		218.53*** (12)	

NOTE: The question was worded as follows: "Who should try the persons accused of war crimes committed in the territory of the former Yugoslavia?" The possible answers were "a) the courts on the territory of Croatia and Bosnia and Herzegovina where the crimes have been committed; b) the courts of the offender's country or country whose army force he was a member of; c) the International Tribunal in The Hague; d) the courts of the families of the victims; e) other _____." The dependent variable is coded as follows: 0 = ICTY; 1 = other forms of decision makers.

a. Sample is coded as follows: 0 = Belgrade; 1 = Sarajevo; and 2 = Vukovar.

b. Fairness of decisions is coded as follows: 0 = fair; 1 = unfair.

c. Fairness of procedures is coded as follows: 0 = fair; 1 = unfair.

d. Punishment purpose is coded as follows: 0 = retribution; 1 = deterrence (special and general).

e. Political scale ranges from 4 to 16.

f. Victim status is coded as follows: 0 = not a victim; 1 = victim.

g. Education is coded as follows: 0 = college; 1 = less than high school; 2 = high school.

h. Gender is coded as follows: 0 = males; 1 = females.

i. Age is coded as follows: 0 = younger than thirty-five; 1 = older than fifty; 2 = between thirty-six and fifty.

$^\circ p < .05$. $^{\circ\circ} p < .01$. $^{\circ\circ\circ} p < .001$.

German history, and we have shown that it appears true again most recently in the former Yugoslavia.

Kosovo interviewees to a surprising degree are in agreement that the ICTY has an important role to play with regard to war crimes in the former Yugoslavia. Perhaps equally surprising is the consensus in both Sarajevo and Belgrade that war crimes offenders from the wars in the former Yugoslavia can now more appropriately be tried in local, national courts, rather than at the ICTY. They also share a view that a key reason this is the case is because judges at the ICTY are believed to lack political neutrality and independence.

Beyond this preliminary agreement, however, there are also important differences. For example, the dominant view in Sarajevo is that the appropriate venue for war crimes prosecutions is the jurisdiction where the victimization occurred, while the prevailing view in Belgrade is that the appropriate jurisdiction is where the offender is from. Furthermore, while Sarajevo public opinion is multiethnic in that it is not sharply divided along ethno-national lines, Belgrade public opinion is essentially monoethnic.

[U]timately settings and persons who have experienced major crimes by, as well as against, their people will wish to reclaim an indigenous role in the restoration of locally experienced justice.

In spite of superficial agreement among respondents in Belgrade and Sarajevo that war crimes jurisdiction should shift away from the ICTY, there are apparent differences of views. We have identified these differences as a source of what Sampson and Bartusch (1998) call legal cynicism, a public perspective that competes with the goals of liberal legalism and suggests a local source of divergent contours in the cognitive landscape of international criminal justice. These contours are drawn along the lines of the competing interests of what can be regarded as the defended (i.e., Bosnian) and the defeated (i.e., Serbian) parties in the underlying dispute. A particularly notable aspect of the contours of this landscape is the predicted difference between Serbian views in Belgrade and elsewhere. Serbs in Belgrade are distinctive in insisting that war criminals be tried in their places of origin, while Serbs in Sarajevo and Vukovar agree with other groups in these settings that war criminals be tried in the settings where their crimes occurred. This is compelling evidence of localized cultural norms operating among ethnic group members in war crime settings.

It seems likely that there is a predictable sequence to international efforts to restore a democratic sense of criminal justice in war crime settings and that ultimately settings and persons who have experienced major crimes by, as well as against, their people will wish to reclaim an indigenous role in the restoration of locally experienced justice. Hannah Arendt (1965) concluded as much nearly a half century ago in her classic book on Eichmann in Jerusalem. The challenge, Arendt ultimately concluded, is to find a liberal legal balance between local, national, and international inclinations. Finding this balance point is as much an empirical as an ideological matter, and it may inevitably involve conflict as well as consensus.

References

Arendt, Hannah. 1965. *Eichmann in Jerusalem: A report on the banality of evil*. New York: Penguin.

Bass, Gary. 2000. *Stay the hand of vengeance: The politics of war crimes tribunals*. Princeton, NJ: Princeton University Press.

Brooks, Richard. 2000. Fear and fairness in the city: Criminal enforcement and perceptions of fairness in minority communities. *Southern California Law Review* 73:1219-73.

Brooks, Richard, and Hackyung Jeon-Slaughter. 2001. Race, income and perceptions of the U.S. court system. *Behavioral Sciences and the Law* 19:249-64.

Burkholder, Brent, Paul Spiegel, and Peter Salma. 2001. Methods of determining mortality in the mass displacement and return of emergency-affected populations in Kosovo, 1998-1999. In *Forced migration and mortality*, ed. Holly Reid and Charles Keely. Washington, DC: National Academy of Sciences.

Caldeira, Gregory. 1986. Neither the purse nor the sword: Dynamics of public confidence in the Supreme Court. *American Political Science Review* 80:1209-26.

Casey, Gregory. 1974. "The Supreme Court and Myth: An Empirical Investigation." *Law and Society Review* 8: 385-419.

Chambliss, William, and Robert Seidman. 1971/1982. *Law, order and power*. Reading, MA: Addison Wesley.

Dezalay, Yves, and Bryant Garth. 2002. *Global prescriptions: The production, exportation, and importation of a new legal orthodoxy*. Ann Arbor: University of Michigan Press.

Donia, Robert. 2004. Encountering the past: History at the Yugoslav War Crimes Tribunal. *Journal of the International Institute* [online edition], nos. 2-3.

Gibson, James, and Gregory Caldeira. 1995. The legitimacy of transnational legal institutions: Compliance, support, and the European Court of Justice. *American Journal of Political Science* 39:459-89.

———. 1998. Changes in the legitimacy of the European Court of Justice: A post-Maastrict analysis. *British Journal of Political Science* 28:63-91.

Goldstone, Richard. 2000. *For humanity: Reflections of a war crimes investigator*. New Haven, CT: Yale University Press.

Guest, Ian. 1995. *On trial: The United Nations, war crimes and the former Yugoslavia*. Washington, DC: Refugee Policy Group.

Hagan, John. 2003. *Justice in the Balkans: Prosecuting war crimes in The Hague Tribunal*. Chicago: University of Chicago Press.

Hagan, John, and Celesta Albonetti. 1982. Race, class and the perception of criminal injustice in America. *American Journal of Sociology* 88:329-55.

Hagan, John, and Ron Levi. 2005. Crimes of war and the force of law. *Social Forces* 83:1499-1534.

———. Forthcoming. Swaying the hand of justice: Regime change at the International Criminal Tribunal for the former Yugoslavia. *Law & Social Inquiry*.

Hagan, John, Carla Shedd, and Monique Payne. 2005. Race, ethnicity, and youth perceptions of criminal injustice. *American Sociological Review* 70:381-407.

International Institute for Democracy and Electoral Assistance. 2002. New regional opinion survey shows the public in South East Europe care more about domestic than international issues. Press Release, April 4.

Kapis, Robert. 1978. Black ghetto diversity and anomie: A sociopolitical view. *American Journal of Sociology* 83:1132-53.

Karstedt, Susanne. 1998. Coming to terms with the past in Germany after 1945 and 1989: Public judgments on procedures and justice. *Law & Policy* 20:15-56.

Kutnjak Ivković, Sanja. 2001. Justice by the International Criminal Tribunal for the Former Yugoslavia. *Stanford Journal of International Law* 37:255-346.

Kutnjak Ivković, Sanja, and John Hagan. Forthcoming. The politics of punishment and the Siege of Sarajevo: Toward a conflict theory of perceived criminal (in)justice. *Law & Society Review*.

Lind, E. Allan, and Tom Tyler. 1988. *The social psychology of procedural justice*. New York: Plenum.

Mazower, Mark. 2000. *The Balkans*. London: Weidenfeld & Nicolson.

Neier, Aryeh. 1998. *War crimes: Brutality, genocide, terror, and the struggle for justice*. New York: Times Books/Random House.

O'Neill, Tip. 1994. *All politics is local and other rules of the game*. With Gary Hymel. New York: Crown.

Parenti, Michael. 2000. *To kill a nation: The attack of Yugoslavia*. London: Verso.

Power, Samatha. 2002. *"A problem from hell": America and the age of genocide*. New York: Basic Books.

Robertson, Geoffrey. 1999. *Crimes against humanity: The struggle for global justice*. London: Penguin.

Sampson, Robert, and Dawn Bartusch. 1998. Legal cynicism and (subcultural?) tolerance of deviance: The neighborhood context of racial differences. *Law & Society Review* 32:777-804.

Scharf, Michael. 1997. *Balkan justice*. Durham, NC: Carolina Academic Press.

Slaughter, Ann Marie. 2004. *A new world order*. Princeton, NJ: Princeton University Press.

Statute of the Tribunal. 1993. Report of the Secretary-General Pursuant to Paragraph 2 of U.N. Security Council Resolution 808, U.N. GAOR, 48th Sess., 3175th mtg., arts. 2-5, U.N. Doc. S/2-5704 (1993), reprinted in 32 I.L.M. 1159, 1192-93 (1993). http://www.un.org/icty/legaldoc/index.htm (accessed July 20, 2004).

Tyler, Tom. 1994. Governing amid diversity: The effect of fair decision-making procedures on the legitimacy of government. *Law & Society Review* 28:809-31.

Weitzer, Ronald. 1999. Racialized policing: Perceptions in three neighborhoods. *Law & Society Review* 34:301-27.

Wilson, Jeremy M. 2006. Law and order in an emerging democracy: Lessons from the reconstruction of Kosovo's police and justice systems. *Annals of the American Academy of Political and Social Science* 605:152-77.

Wilson, Richard. 2005. Judging history: The historical record of the International Criminal Tribunal for the former Yugoslavia. *Human Rights Quarterly* 27:908-42.

Wood, Nicholas. 2005. Bosnia: U.N. transfers first war crimes suspect to a local court. *New York Times*, September 30, p. A8.

Wortley, Scot, John Hagan, and Ross Macmillan. 1997. Just des(s)erts? The racial polarization of perceptions of criminal injustice. *Law & Society Review* 31:637-76.

Law and Order in an Emerging Democracy: Lessons from the Reconstruction of Kosovo's Police and Justice Systems

By
JEREMY M. WILSON

"Nation-building" is an increasingly frequent activity of Western governments and the United Nations, with Kosovo an important recent example. This study examines the reconstruction by the United Nations of Kosovo's internal security infrastructure from 1999 to 2004. It analyzes United Nations and other activities to build democratic police and justice systems. Through a model of security reconstruction, it examines in detail the primary security challenges facing Kosovo, the specific efforts the United Nations made to address these challenges, the ultimate effectiveness of the reconstruction in establishing stability and rule of law, and the linkages between reconstruction efforts and democracy. It concludes with several lessons for improving the effectiveness of such efforts in the future.

Keywords: Kosovo; nation-building; internal security; police; justice; democracy; United Nations

"Nation-building" has become an increasingly frequent activity of the United Nations and Western governments. Such operations, undertaken after major combat to support peace and democracy, involve the deployment

Jeremy M. Wilson is an associate behavioral scientist at the RAND Corporation, the Willett Chair in Public Safety in the Center for Public Safety at Northwestern University, and an adjunct professor in the Heinz School of Public Policy and Management at Carnegie Mellon University. His research focuses on police administration, internal security, and violence. His recent and forthcoming books include Establishing Law and Order after Conflict, State and Local Intelligence in the War on Terrorism, and Community Policing in America. His other recent research includes examinations of local homicide patterns, gun violence interventions, community policing measurement, police-community problem solving, and creating a global counterterrorism network. He received his Ph.D. in public administration from The Ohio State University.

NOTE: I would like to thank Gary LaFree, Susanne Karstedt, and Clifford Grammich for their thoughtful suggestions and editorial prowess throughout the development of this article. Their assistance significantly improved that which is presented in the following pages.

DOI: 10.1177/0002716206286783

of international military forces and include comprehensive efforts to rebuild a society's security, political, and economic sectors. In some cases, such operations occur in a benign security environment with little or no resistance. In others, such as Somalia, Afghanistan, and Iraq, significant violence and insurgent activity accompany nation-building efforts.

In an analysis of nation-building activities in nine nations (Panama, El Salvador, Somalia, Haiti, Bosnia, East Timor, Kosovo, Afghanistan, and Iraq), Jones et al. (2005) offered some evidence that long-term prospects for democratic governance and stability depend especially upon viable police, security forces, and justice structures to deal with the most salient internal threats from insurgents, organized criminal organizations, and local militia. In this work, I examine UN and other efforts to establish security in Kosovo following combat between the North Atlantic Treaty Organization (NATO) and Yugoslav forces there in 1999. I assume that studying the development of Kosovo's internal security infrastructure can highlight ways to improve future efforts to support the establishment of democratic institutions in failed states.

In particular, this research focuses on how well nation-building efforts in Kosovo have established stability and rule of law. By establishing "stability," I mean the development of a stable environment in which violence-prone groups such as insurgents or criminals are subordinated to legitimate governmental authority, reintegrated into society, or defeated. A stable environment is one in which the population is free from major threats to their safety and where national and international actors are able to rebuild political, economic, and other key governance institutions. Under "rule of law," I include courts, legislatures, legal statutes and codes, executive agencies, and independent nongovernmental organizations (NGOs) such as bar and civic associations. The rule of law serves to protect people against anarchy as well as from arbitrary exercise of power by public officials and allows people to plan their daily affairs with confidence.

The remainder of this article provides a brief history of the Kosovo operation and how the UN set up Kosovo's internal security infrastructure, including three fundamental challenges the UN had to confront in establishing stability and rule of law. I then offer a model of rebuilding internal security, which I use to explore Kosovo's reconstruction process and how the UN addressed critical security threats. I conclude with some implications of this case study for similar situations in the future.

Background and Security Challenges

On June 9, 1999, following seventy-seven days of NATO air strikes, NATO and the Federal Republic of Yugoslavia signed a military technical agreement that led to the immediate withdrawal of Yugoslav army and police forces from Kosovo (NATO 1999). The United Nations Security Council subsequently authorized a fifty-thousand-strong NATO-led Kosovo Force (KFOR) composed of military from thirty contributing countries organized into five multinational brigades, one each led by the United States, the United Kingdom, France, Germany, and Italy. Additionally, the UN Security Council established the United Nations Interim

Administration Mission in Kosovo (UNMIK) to oversee the civilian administration of the territory.

UNMIK divided the provision of public security in Kosovo into three elements: KFOR, UNMIK international civilian police (CIVPOL), and an indigenous Kosovo Police Service (KPS) (UNMIK 2001). From the beginning, civil (as opposed to military) authority was principally responsible for law and order. CIVPOL maintained daily security and was tasked with developing and deploying the KPS. Full policing responsibilities were to be transferred to the KPS by the end of 2005 (UNMIK 2003). The role of NATO's KFOR was (and continues to be) to provide law and order where CIVPOL lacked the capacity to ensure security.

Among the security challenges to overcome in Kosovo, my review suggests that three are particularly important: organized crime, corruption, and ethnic conflict. I contend that the perceived legitimacy of and confidence in the democratic police and justice institutions that UNMIK seeks to establish will likely be a function of its ability to address these challenges.

Kosovo's multifaceted organized crime problem is manifest in several trafficking problems. Kosovo is both a destination and point of transfer for women and children being trafficked for prostitution (UNMIK 2003). As in other countries experiencing democratic transition, Kosovo also has a drug-trafficking problem (Jones et al. 2005). UNMIK (2003) claimed that roughly 80 percent of heroin consumed in Western Europe travels through the former Yugoslav Republic of Macedonia and Kosovo. Kosovo must also grapple with weapons trafficking, including that by the Kosovo Liberation Army (KLA), a remnant of the Kosovo independence movement (UNMIK 2003).

Kosovo's corruption problem has included many high-ranking public administrators taking bribes and engaging in other unethical behavior since reconstruction efforts began in 1999. Organized criminals developed strong ties to former KLA members and existing political parties, through which they bribed and intimidated judges and prosecutors (U.S. Agency for International Development and the Organization for Security and Cooperation in Europe 2001), weakening public confidence in Kosovo's security infrastructure. Preventing corruption is made difficult by the fact that for some, its long tradition in Kosovo has strengthened its usefulness as a simple means to an end (Spector, Winbourne, and Beck 2003).

Ethnic discrimination and tension are deeply rooted in Kosovo's history and have often led to violence in the past. Reducing ethnic conflict lies in integrating the Serb and Albanian populations. Progress depends on integrating both groups into an institutional and social fabric that can reduce tension between them (International Crisis Group 2000).

A Model of Reconstructing Internal Security

To evaluate the process of reconstructing internal security in Kosovo, I use a model developed by Jones et al. (2005). As shown in Figure 1, this model depicts success in achieving stability and rule of law as a function of initial conditions, inputs, and outputs.

FIGURE 1
MODEL OF REBUILDING INTERNAL SECURITY

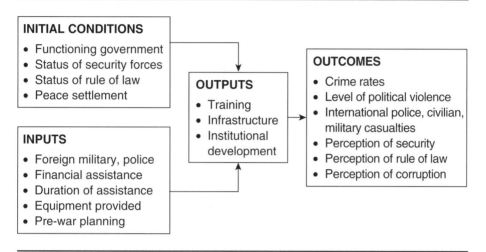

NOTE: Adapted from Jones et al. (2005, 8).

Initial conditions are those prevalent at the beginning of reconstruction. At least four of these can significantly affect reconstruction of internal security. The first is a functioning central government that, as defined by Weber (1958, 78), has a "monopoly of the legitimate use of physical forces within a given territory." Literature and practice of the past decade have shown the importance of good governance in promoting economic development as well as pluralist, democratic, and effective political institutions (Einhorn 2001; World Bank 2000). The second is the existence and effectiveness of the security forces. The third, rule of law, requires an effective justice system and security forces at the beginning of reconstruction. Rule of law institutions are difficult to strengthen through external assistance because they are deeply embedded in the social fabric, contribute to legitimizing the state, and are heavily influenced by the cultural norms and values that shape institutions in any society (Fukuyama 2004, 59). The final initial condition is a peace agreement or formal surrender, which can significantly increase the likelihood of stability by convincing the combatants to shed their forces and surrender conquered territory.

Critical internal security inputs in the model include the external means for providing security and stability. First, the number and type of intervening troops affect how well the new security structure can defeat and deter insurgents, patrol borders, secure roads, combat organized crime, and conduct general law enforcement functions such as policing streets. Timing of troop arrival is also critical, particularly immediately after major combat in which external intervention may enjoy some popular support and international legitimacy and when potential insurgents and resisters have had insufficient time to organize. Second, financial assistance for training indigenous police, army, and justice personnel; providing equipment;

running ministries and courts; and building infrastructure (e.g., police stations, court houses, prisons)[1] affect security and stability. Third, the duration of assistance similarly contributes to training, equipping, and mentoring of police and other security forces as well as building and refurbishing infrastructure. Some research suggests that successful nation-building requires at least five years (Dobbins et al. 2003, 2005). Fourth, knowledge regarding the availability of equipment is necessary to ascertain if troops have the tools required to conduct their security functions (e.g., weapons, computers, desks). Finally, prewar planning, including standard best practices and their applicability to local cultures and requirements, can help ensure that appropriate levels of funds, equipment, personnel, and trained and configured military and police forces are available.

Outputs are the first-order results of the assistance program. They may include the number of (1) indigenous trained troops, police, judges, prosecutors, and corrections officers; (2) police stations, courts, prisons, and other infrastructure facilities built or refurbished; and (3) ex-combatants who have completed a demobilization, demilitarization, and reintegration program. Outputs may also include difficult to quantify elements such as institutional development and reform of security ministries. Institutional development includes improving the institutional capacity of the recipient organization, whether a ministry or a security force, to perform its internal security mission. It may also include establishing democratic security institutions that serve individual citizens rather than the government, are accountable to the law rather than the government, protect human rights, and are transparent in their activities (Bayley 2001).

Outcomes of success include internal security functions that ensure stability and the rule of law. They are conditions that directly affect the public. Outcomes are not what governments and international institutions do, but the consequences of their efforts. Without the ability to measure performance, policy makers lack adequate means for judging success and failure in ongoing crises and for making midcourse corrections. Measurable outcomes include crime rates, levels of political violence and insurgency, and public perception of security, rule of law, and corruption.

Below, I review how the United Nations and its partners rebuilt Kosovo's internal security framework and responded to the fundamental security challenges shown in the above model.

Initial Security Conditions

The conflict in Kosovo originated with the suspension of Kosovo autonomy and oppression of ethnic Albanians by former Yugoslav President Slobodan Milosevic (Daalder and O'Hanlon 2001). Kosovo had enjoyed semi-independence as an autonomous province of Serbia, granted by the former communist government in 1968 and reaffirmed in the 1974 constitution.

In 1989, Milosevic implemented direct rule from Belgrade and sought to take power from the ethnic Albanians and place control of Kosovo in Serbian hands (Hagen 1999). This included a prohibition on ethnic Albanians serving as judges, prosecutors, and legal educators. Ethnic Albanians responded by forming a parallel society with its own public infrastructure and animated by nonviolent nationalist separatism (Hagen 1999). Given their exclusion from the legal system, ethnic Albanians returned to using traditional alternative dispute resolution mechanisms and reconciliation councils, essentially a form of arbitration overseen by village elders. These councils are credited with solving approximately one thousand blood feuds throughout the 1990s (U.S. Agency for International Development and the Organization for Security and Cooperation in Europe 2001).

Support among Yugoslavia's Albanians for Kosovo's independence grew as Yugoslavia collapsed and the KLA gained strength. The emergence of the KLA in turn provided justification for Milosevic's ethnic cleansing of Kosovo, including the displacement of several hundred thousand Kosovar Albanians and the murder of many others (Hagen 1999).

As conditions worsened in Kosovo, the UN Security Council adopted Resolution 1199 on September 23, 1998, which demanded an immediate end to hostilities, a withdrawal of security units used for civilian repression, and an international monitoring team. In October 1998, Milosevic agreed to cease civilian attacks and to extract security forces from Kosovo. The Organization for Security and Cooperation in Europe (OSCE) deployed the Kosovo Verification Mission, comprising two thousand unarmed monitors (including five hundred police officers), to verify implementation of the agreement (Perito 2004). Nevertheless, Milosevic later ordered intensified military assaults (Solana 1999), and in February 1999 NATO brought the Serbs and the KLA together for negotiations at Rambouillet, France. Although an agreement was developed and signed by the Albanian Kosovars on March 18, Milosevic, who had been deploying Serbian forces to the Kosovo area during the talks, refused to sign (Solana 1999). On March 24, 1999, NATO initiated Operation Allied Force and began a bombing campaign over Kosovo and Yugoslavia. Milosevic yielded to NATO's demands on June 9, 1999, after eleven weeks of intensifying battle. This paved the way for the United Nations Mission in Kosovo.

Reconstruction of the Internal Security Infrastructure

UNMIK organized its administration around four pillars: humanitarian assistance, civil administration, democratization and institution building, and reconstruction and economic development. Originally, CIVPOL (responsible for providing interim public security and developing the KPS) and the UNMIK Department of Justice (responsible for rebuilding and operating the judiciary and penal systems) were part of the civil administration pillar. But because the police and justice institutions lacked overall coordination, UNMIK, when later phasing out the humanitarian assistance pillar, created a new police and justice pillar that brought together CIVPOL and the UNMIK Department of Justice (UNMIK 2003). The UNMIK police organization was responsible for law enforcement, whereas the UNMIK Department of Justice oversaw all issues pertaining to justice and corrections.

The UN Secretary General charged the UNMIK Department of Justice with creating an unbiased, independent, and multiethnic judiciary (UNMIK 2003). Established in July 1999, the UNMIK Department of Justice (originally named the Department of Judicial Affairs) has four sections: the Judicial Development Division, the Penal Management Division, the International Judicial Support Section, and the Office of Missing Persons and Forensics (UNMIK 2003). An independent Kosovo Judicial and Prosecutorial Council comprising both international and Kosovar members is responsible for recommending to UNMIK judicial candidates for appointment.

UNMIK and the KFOR constructed the Kosovo Protection Corps, the final component of Kosovo's internal security system. This organization was designed as a civil defense organization, tasked with reconstruction of nonmilitary facilities, search and rescue missions, disaster response, humanitarian relief, and infrastructure repair (Solana 1999).

Police provision

As in other nation-building efforts (e.g., El Salvador, Haiti, Bosnia, East Timor), international police in Kosovo assisted indigenous police in providing service. As of March 2004, forty-six countries were contributing to UNMIK CIVPOL, with the United States (11 percent), India (10 percent), Germany (9 percent), and Jordan (8 percent) providing the largest shares of CIVPOL officers (United Nations Security Council S/2004/348, April 30, 2004). UNMIK CIVPOL has two official goals: to establish law and order and to develop, implement, and ultimately transfer law and order responsibilities to a professional KPS (UNMIK 2001).

Upon withdrawal of Yugoslav forces, UNMIK deployed CIVPOL personnel almost immediately but in small numbers (Perito 2004). Within the first few weeks after the formal conflict ended, many CIVPOL personnel were transferred to Kosovo from Bosnia. Though unarmed, these officers created an immediate civil police presence. The KFOR provided security where civilian authorities could not. The difficulties of establishing an international police presence were threefold. First, it took time for the international police officers to arrive in Kosovo (Dobbins et al. 2003). Second, it took time to test and train international police officers at UNMIK's Induction Training Center. Finally, once on site, CIVPOL officers lacked basic equipment such as vehicles and radios and even administrative supplies such as office space, desks, and stationery (International Crisis Group 2000).

UNMIK CIVPOL initially numbered about 1,800 officers in 1999: 95 officers per 100,000 Kosovo residents (Perito 2002). Figure 2 shows that by 2000, CIVPOL officer strength had increased to its current level of about 4,450: 237 officers per 100,000 residents (Jane's Information Group 2004). UNMIK distributed its CIVPOL officers among three basic functions: traditional law enforcement (66 percent), special police units including paramilitary forces and a canine unit (25 percent), and border enforcement (9 percent) (UNMIK 2003).

Well prior to the beginning of reconstruction, the U.S. Department of Justice's International Criminal Investigative Training Assistance Program (ICITAP) began detailed planning for indigenous police in Kosovo (U.S. Department of Justice 2004).

FIGURE 2
POLICE STRENGTH IN KOSOVO, 1999-2004

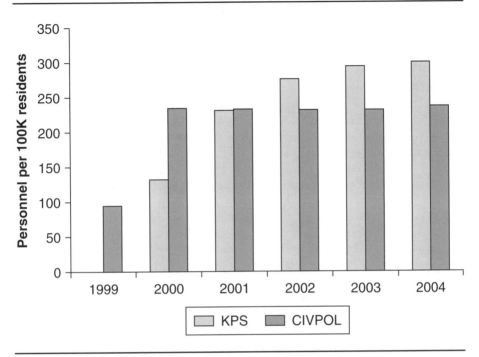

NOTE: KPS = Kosovo Police Service; CIVPOL = international civilian police.

Many of the international police monitors with the Kosovo Verification Mission had helped to establish security in Bosnia, Haiti, Eastern Slavonia, and other areas; ICI-TAP drew upon and benefited from their experience. Together, they developed extensive plans for a first-responder system, incorporating elements of a police function but also much broader in scope. The idea was to create a general response system that could dispatch persons with training in areas such as first aid, human rights, and conflict resolution to riots, natural disasters, and other crisis situations. Other plans also detailed the creation and training of a new police force.

The OSCE was originally to have primary responsibility for civil administration, including establishing rule of law and constructing and operating the new police force, but the UN Security Council gave overall responsibility to UNMIK just after combat operations ended (Perito 2004). With little time to construct plans of its own, UNMIK adopted the plans developed earlier by ICITAP and OSCE. Under this arrangement, UNMIK recruited officers and OSCE trained them.

UNMIK began recruiting KPS officers in June 1999. In September, OSCE established the Kosovo Police Service School in Vushtrri (UNMIK 2003). By the time it became fully operational in March 2000, two hundred international police instructors from twenty-two OSCE member states staffed the school (Perito 2004). The official purpose of the school is to recruit and train professional KPS officers who act according to democratic police principles as instilled through ICITAP's training program (OSCE 2003; Perito 2004). The total amount of training offered to KPS recruits has increased considerably since the school was established, with the requirement as of 2004 being twenty weeks of basic training and fifteen weeks of field training (OSCE 2004b).

The Kosovo Police Service School graduated its first class with 176 recruits in October 1999 and contributed to a steady increase in the number of deployed KPS officers. In 2000, there were 2,516 KPS officers on the job in Kosovo; by 2004, there were 5,704 (United Nations Security Council S/2000/1196, December 15, 2000; S/2004/71, January 26, 2004; S/2004/348, April 30, 2004). As shown in Figure 2, the number of KPS officers surpassed CIVPOL officers in 2002. The growth of KPS over this time suggests that UNMIK made progress toward its main objective, the transfer of police authority to a professionally trained indigenous police force. Compared to other recent nation-building operations such as those in Afghanistan and Iraq, Kosovo has enjoyed a higher ratio of CIVPOL and national police to the total population and in general, the international teams have been more successful in training police (Jones et al. 2005). Jones et al. (2005) also determined that of the nine case studies they examined, Kosovo had the highest level of economic assistance for the overall mission (not just for internal security). They determined that Kosovo's annual aid per capita over the first two years of reconstruction was US$526, whereas it was US$225 for Iraq and US$30 for Afghanistan over a similar period.

UNMIK has also undertaken three other initiatives to address organized crime and related problems such as drug trafficking and weapons smuggling. First, it created several organizational units throughout the Police and Justice Pillar that focus on these issues, including a Central Intelligence Unit, Kosovo Organized Crime Bureau, Sensitive Information and Operations Unit, Trafficking and Prostitution Investigation Unit, Victim Advocacy and Assistance Unit, and an interim secure facility. However, the limited information on these units makes it impossible for me to assess their individual effectiveness.

Second, UNMIK has implemented various forms of legislation aimed at combating organized crime and improving criminal procedure.[2] Of particular importance is the Provisional Criminal Code of April 6, 2004, which upholds international human rights standards and proscribes terrorism, trafficking in persons, and organized crime (UNMIK 2004b). Finally, UNMIK (2003) has established cross-border police information sharing through cooperative agreements with Serbia, Albania, and the former Yugoslav Republic of Macedonia.

Corruption of public officials may also pose a serious threat to Kosovo's security. In 2002 and 2003, police made several high-profile arrests of those involved in corruption. For example, in September 2002, UNMIK CIVPOL arrested the director of the property registration office for the Pristina municipality, who was accused of registering illegal property transfers and demanding bribes to register legitimate property transfers (UNMIK 2002). UNMIK (2002) estimated that twelve thousand (of a total of fifteen thousand) property transfers recorded in this office between 2000 and 2002 were of questionable legality. Other notable arrests for corruption have included the director of the public housing authority in Pristina and the director of the vehicle registration office for Pec (UNMIK 2002).

To improve its effectiveness in combating corruption, UNMIK created the Financial Inspection Unit within the Police and Justice Pillar in January 2003. Ten financial inspectors, from the Italian Guardia di Finanza, comprise this unit. Their primary purpose is to conduct random audits of any entity receiving public funds (UNMIK 2003). The new provisional criminal code also encompasses international conventions regarding corruption (UNMIK 2004b).

Because of the potential for interethnic conflict in Kosovo, UNMIK has sought to create a multiethnic KPS that reflects the ethnic composition of the population. In 2000, the ethnic distribution of Kosovo was 88 percent Albanian, 7 percent Serbian, and 5 percent other (Statistical Office of Kosovo 2003). In 2003, the composition of the KPS was 84 percent Albanian, 9 percent Serbian, and 7 percent other (UNMIK 2003). Such balance will not necessarily prevent ethnic hostility or even bias by the KPS, but such integration may have symbolic importance that can enhance public trust in democratic governance.

Still, while UNMIK's attempts to address Kosovo's major security challenges may help instill public confidence in fledgling democratic institutions, the actual effectiveness of these efforts will likely have a greater impact on public support for democracy. As Bayley (1999) contended, the police (and presumably the justice system) cannot create democracy, but they can facilitate or impede it.

Justice system

When UNMIK began its mission in Kosovo, the police were unable to ensure public safety, and there was no judicial system to conduct trials or prisons to incarcerate criminals (UNMIK 2003). There is now a tiered court structure for criminal and other cases, including twenty-four municipal courts for adjudicating less serious criminal cases (i.e., typically those carrying no more than a five-year penalty); district courts that adjudicate cases falling outside the jurisdiction of the municipal courts and provide review of cases initiated in the municipal courts; and the Kosovo Supreme Court, the court of last resort for all Kosovo (OSCE 2004a).

Within two weeks of their arrival, UNMIK staff created the Joint Advisory Council on Judicial Appointments (later replaced by the Advisory Judicial Commission), which began appointing judges and prosecutors. By June 30, 1999, UNMIK had appointed nine judges and prosecutors who served as a mobile judicial unit with jurisdiction over all Kosovo (Strohmeyer 2001). As of May 2004, the Special Representative of the UN Secretary General had appointed more than 320 judges (UNMIK 2004a). Establishing a court system helped Kosovo respond to its security challenges as those arrested for organized crime, corruption, and violence could now be brought to justice.

The initial code of law these prosecutors and judges enforced was that of Yugoslavia and Serbia prior to NATO intervention (Hartmann 2003). However, Albanian Kosovars detested this code because it had been applied in a discriminatory fashion against them in the previous decade. UNMIK therefore revoked the earlier code and replaced it with the 1989 law that had been in effect during Kosovo's autonomy within Serbia.

But ethnic politics complicated the application of the law. The Kosovar judiciary primarily comprised ethnic Albanians because Serbs refused to accept appointments as judges and prosecutors out of fear or general resentment (Hartmann 2003). UNMIK had a somewhat greater challenge developing a multiethnic judiciary than it had in integrating the KPS; as of 2003, Serbians comprised only 4 percent of judges and prosecutors though they were about 7 percent of the population and 9 percent of the KPS (UNMIK 2003). Furthermore, experienced observers claim that the judiciary, 91 percent Albanian, failed to apply the law equally between the ethnic Albanians and Serbs because of community pressure, fear of ostracism or harm against self or family, or other bias (Hartmann 2003). This perceived ethnic disparity in the application of the law, as well as ethnic unrest in Mitrovica in February 2000 that included riots and interethnic violence, led the Special Representative of the UN Secretary-General to assign international judges and prosecutors to work in conjunction with the local judiciary (Hartmann 2003; UNMIK 2003). UNMIK presumed judges and prosecutors from other countries would not exhibit ethnic bias and would be less susceptible to corruption and pressure. By May 2000, non-Kosovars were permitted to serve in all five judicial districts (and not just that encompassing Mitrovica); by July 2003, there were sixteen non-Kosovar judges and ten non-Kosovar prosecutors serving the Kosovo court system (UNMIK 2003).

This initial infusion of non-Kosovar judges and prosecutors failed to stop many miscarriages of justice because Kosovar judges could still outvote the non-Kosovars who sat on panels with them. This led to the December 2000 creation of "64" panels, named for Regulation 2000/64 that permits the Special Representative of the UN Secretary-General to assign specific cases to a panel of three professional judges of whom at least two are non-Kosovar rather than the standard five-judge panel comprising two professional and three lay judges (UNMIK 2000). One notorious case ultimately assigned to a 64 panel involved an eyewitness identifying a suspect who used an automatic weapon to shoot Serbs socializing outside of a grocery store, murdering three (including a four-year-old child) and injuring five. The KFOR had previously arrested this former KLA member three times (twice for threatening Serbs), only to see the suspect released by an Albanian judge after an Albanian prosecutor dropped charges (Hartman 2003).

Another shortcoming in the justice system is a growing backlog of cases. At the end of 2001, there was a backlog of 33,538 civil and criminal cases; this backlog grew to 81,900 cases at the end of 2003 (OSCE 2004a). Contributing to this problem is a lack of judges (thirty-seven posts were vacant in 2003) and the unequal distribution of cases to judges (seven courts received more than 300 complex cases per judge, while seven others received less than 150 per judge).[3] Additional problems identified by the OSCE (2004a) include noncompliance with established time frames and failure of necessary parties to attend proceedings, and numerous rights violations, such as the right to be tried by a tribunal established by law (in some cases, two-judge rather than three-judge panels were used), right to an impartial tribunal (in some cases, judges assumed the role of absent prosecutors, and some retrials were heard by the same, initial panel of judges), right to a public trial (in some cases, date and place of hearings were not made public), and the right to cross-examine witnesses (in some cases, witnesses' prior statements were read when they did not appear in court). The OSCE (2004a) anticipated that some (though not all) of these issues would be resolved with the April 2004 implementation of the Provisional Criminal Procedural Code of Kosovo, designed to improve efficiency and protect those being processed through the criminal justice system.

In addition to having to reestablish a judicial system, UNMIK also had to rebuild a correctional system. Many prisons were damaged or destroyed, and guards fled along with the Yugoslav security forces, transferring prisoners to unknown locations in Serbia (Strohmeyer 2001). The Penal Management Division of the UNMIK Department of Justice was tasked with recruiting non-Kosovar experts, operating Kosovo's correctional system, devising a strategy to transfer correctional authority to the Kosovo Correctional Service, and helping to reform the legal framework of the prison system to ensure that it met international standards (UNMIK 2003). In November 1999, the Penal Management Division assumed responsibility for the Prizren Detention Center. Since then, it has assumed responsibility for and restored four detention facilities in Pristina, Mitrovica, Gnjilane, and Pec/Paja and two prisons in Dubrava and Lipljan (UNMIK 2003). Dubrava is the largest facility, housing 67 percent of all Kosovo inmates in 2003 (UNMIK 2003).

The opening of these facilities has considerably increased Kosovo's capacity to incarcerate offenders, which could improve security through incapacitation of chronic offenders. Figure 3 shows that prison capacity in Kosovo nearly tripled between 2000 and 2003, increasing from 497 to 1,358 (United Nations Security Council S/2000/538, June 6, 2000; S/2000/1196, December 15, 2000; S/2002/62, January 15, 2002; S/2002/1126, October 9, 2002; S/2003/996, October 15, 2003). During this same time, the number of correctional officers quadrupled from 350 to 1,416 (United Nations Security Council S/2000/538, June 6, 2000; S/2000/1196, December 15, 2000; S/2003/113, January 29, 2003; S/2003/996, October 15, 2003).

Correctional instructors at the Vushtrri Police Academy train recruits for the Kosovo Correctional Service. Non-Kosovar corrections officers have replaced CIVPOL (i.e., non-Kosovar police) at the prisons and continue to assist the administrators of the Kosovo Correctional Service. UNMIK has developed a multiethnic correctional staff that is now actually more ethnically diverse than either the total or the incarcerated minority population of Kosovo. Thus, in 2003, Kosovo Correctional Service staff constituted 85 percent Albanians, 11 percent Serbs, and 4 percent others; while Albanians constituted 90 percent, Serbs 7 percent, and others 3 percent of Kosovo's prison population (UNMIK 2003).

The number of inmates in Kosovo prisons has grown with the space to house and staff to supervise them. As shown in Figure 3, the number of prisoners incarcerated increased by 244 percent from 2000 to 2003 (United Nations Security Council S/2000/538, June 6, 2000; S/2001/926, S/2002/62, January 15, 2002; S/2003/996, October 15, 2003). By 2003, the correctional system was operating at about 89 percent capacity. About one in three inmates was incarcerated for murder, with an additional one-third being held for robbery or theft (UNMIK 2003).

FIGURE 3
PRISON CAPACITY, CORRECTIONAL OFFICERS, AND INMATES, 2000-2003

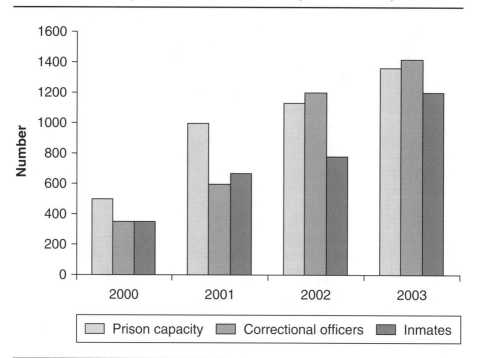

Defense sector

UN Security Resolution 1244 (1999) called for an international security force to be deployed to Kosovo, which led to the creation of the KFOR. KFOR's official purpose was to ensure a safe and secure environment that would facilitate the return of refugees and the implementation of UNMIK's mandate (Perito 2004). Entering Kosovo on June 12, 1999, KFOR maintained responsibility for conducting patrols, maintaining public order, crowd control, information gathering, antiterrorism activities, and gathering intelligence on organized crime (Perito 2004).

As Yugoslav military and police forces withdrew from Kosovo, the KLA sought to assume power. One of KFOR's principal tasks upon arrival was to demilitarize the KLA, a task facilitated through a June 21, 1999, agreement. Under this agreement, the KLA accepted a ninety-day demilitarization and reintegration process in which it relinquished ten thousand weapons, 5.5 million rounds of ammunition, and twenty-seven thousand grenades (International Crisis Group 2000). To speed up the demilitarization, UNMIK and KFOR created the Kosovo Protection Corps, a mostly unarmed civilian emergency service that provides rescue missions, disaster relief, and infrastructure repair. Many demilitarized KLA members assumed responsibilities in the Kosovo Protection Corps. The Kosovo Protection Corps currently employs more than three thousand persons and approximately two thousand reserves (United

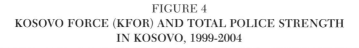

FIGURE 4
KOSOVO FORCE (KFOR) AND TOTAL POLICE STRENGTH
IN KOSOVO, 1999-2004

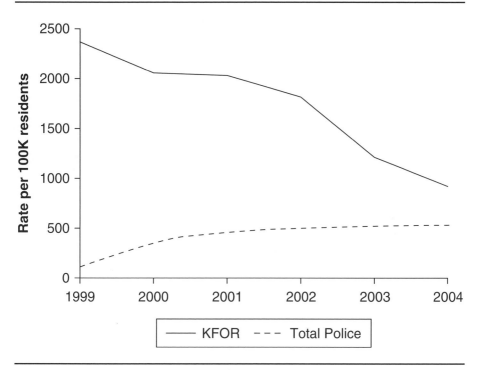

Nations Security Council S/2004/348, April 30, 2004; Jane's Information Group 2004). Although the KLA relinquished a large stock of arms and the KFOR commander certified that it had adequately demilitarized (Dobbins et al. 2003), the KFOR later discovered stockpiles of weapons, which led Jane's Information Group (2004) to conclude that the KLA still maintain an armed capability.

Figure 4 shows that KFOR's size has diminished from 45,000 troops in 1999 to 17,500 in 2004, or from 2,368 per 100,000 residents to 921 (Dobbins et al. 2003). Through an examination of the first five years of nation-building efforts in nine recent cases, Jones et al. (2005) concluded that Kosovo had the most troops per resident for each comparison year. Figure 4 visually demonstrates that the KFOR presence has decreased as police strength has increased. This is consistent with the conclusion that KFOR is succeeding in transferring responsibility for law and order to civilian police.

Success in Establishing Security

Security may help strengthen emerging democracies by increasing public confidence in the effectiveness of police and justice institutions and ensuring that people can freely participate in democratic processes without fear of harm or reprisal. According to Jones et al. (2005), among recent attempts to establish law and order in emerging democracies, Kosovo is one of the most successful. We may gauge the effectiveness of the internal security and justice systems in a number of ways, but reliable indicators of success are limited. I have collected information on four types of law and order success measures: return of refugees, rule of law and civil liberties, crime, and corruption. I discuss below each measure and its relationship to security and democracy.

Return of refugees

Whether instability leads to the displacement of indigenous people may depend on variables such as the likelihood of improved conditions, the targets of violence, existence of better conditions in nearby nations, and the ability to emigrate elsewhere. Prior to NATO's intervention, conditions were not improving in Kosovo, ordinary citizens faced discrimination and death, and surrounding countries provided a viable opportunity for refuge. Many ethnic Albanians therefore chose to flee Kosovo. Growing trust in the democratic institutions that established the security may enhance the public's willingness to embrace democracy and its principles (Bayley 1999). Accordingly, I use the extent to which refugees return when a democratic government assumes administration as one indicator of how safe and secure citizens feel in relation to the new state authority.

UNMIK has done well in creating a police and correctional system that reflects Kosovo's population but has been less effective in creating a judiciary that includes Serbs.

By NATO (1999) estimates, about 90 percent of Kosovo's population had been expelled from their homes by May 1999. Refugees numbered more than 430,000 in Albania, 230,000 in the former Yugoslav Republic of Macedonia, 64,000 in Montenegro, 21,500 in Bosnia, and 61,000 in other countries. In addition, within Kosovo, about 580,000 persons were homeless and an additional 225,000 were missing.

Following the NATO intervention, refugees quickly returned. Within the first three weeks of June 1999, approximately 480,000 refugees had returned to Kosovo (Ramet 2000), or about 23,000 per day. By August 1999, about 90 percent of

Albanian Kosovars who fled Kosovo during the previous year had returned. However, there was less success with the Serbian population: by the end of July 1999, roughly 40 percent of the 2,000 Serbs living in Kosovo had fled under Albanian pressure (Ramet 2000).

Rule of law and civil liberties

I use perceptions of rule of law and civil liberties as measures of safety and security. They indicate the extent to which the public feels it can conduct daily activities free from an arbitrary and capricious legal system. Properly functioning justice institutions may enhance citizen trust in democratic governance (Bayley 1999), thereby increasing public participation in civic life. Conversely, poorly implemented justice institutions may inhibit trust in democracy (Bayley 1999). Structure and personnel are not enough to ensure an efficient, effective, and equitable justice system. The initial establishment of a justice system did not prevent Kosovar judges from acting in a discriminatory fashion or neglecting proper procedures. These abuses indicate the need to ensure that those assigned to specific positions are properly trained and remain objective in their application of the law. Future planners attempting to reconstruct internal security in emerging democracies should consider employing international staff trained in the provisional legal codes until indigenous personnel can effectively resume their responsibilities.

Kosovo provides an example of a stabilization and reconstruction effort in which the UN and its partners secured a peace treaty between conflicting parties and attempted to develop a functioning criminal justice system early in the process.

The Freedom in the World database offers some relative indication of the rule of law in varying nations including Kosovo, summarizing information on freedom of expression and belief, judicial independence, civilian control of police, and protection from police terror or torture and unjustified imprisonment (Freedom House 2004). Ratings range from 1, indicating *substantial civil liberties and a functioning rule of law*, to 7, indicating *no civil liberties and little or no functioning rule of law*. In the first year of reconstruction, Freedom House rated Kosovo's rule of law and civil liberties as being the worst possible (i.e., 7). This rating has improved

FIGURE 5
KOSOVO CRIME RATES, 2000-2002

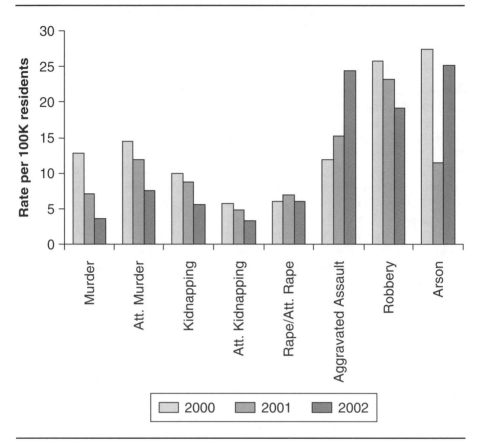

modestly since then, to a 5 by the fifth year, indicating reconstruction efforts have helped to enhance individual freedom, personal security, and procedural justice.

Crime

Crime is perhaps the most direct measure of safety and security. Crime reduction not only reduces the number of citizens who are victimized but may also lessen fear of crime and improve confidence in the public institutions that are charged with handling it (LaFree 1998). As shown in Figure 5, official crime data collected by the UN's civilian police (UNMIK 2002) indicate rates of many violent crimes, such as murder, have decreased in the first three years of reconstruction. Of course, these data may be subject to weaknesses such as underreporting associated with official crime statistics (Mosher, Miethe, and Phillips 2002; Schneider and Wiersema 1990). Given the general agreement that the rigor and consistency of

FIGURE 6
MURDER VICTIMS BY ETHNICITY, 2000-2002

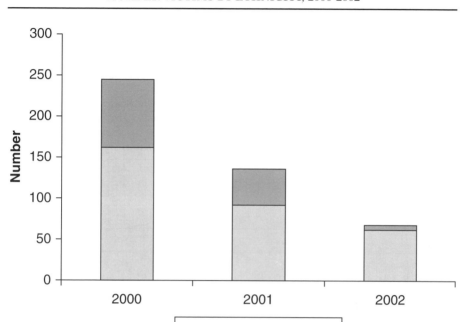

murder reporting is greater than that for other crimes (Blumstein 2000; Smith and Zahn 1998), murder trends are especially important for tracking stability. Immediately after the intervention, up to fifty murders were being reported per week in Kosovo (Ramet 2000). By contrast, the number of murders in Kosovo decreased dramatically following the intervention: from 245 in 2000 to 68 in 2002, or from 13 per 100,000 residents to 4.

Figure 5 further shows that over this same period, the rates of attempted murder, kidnapping, attempted kidnapping, robbery, and arson dropped. These figures suggest that shortly after the Kosovo intervention, many forms of violence decreased. Some rates of crime, however, remained the same or increased. The frequency of aggravated assault doubled in this period, while that of rape remained roughly the same. Although it appears that violent crime overall fell during the first few years of reconstruction, it is not clear from these data that this trend can be attributed to the NATO intervention.

Data on murder by ethnicity may provide some indication of how the population of crime victims compares to the overall population. In 2000, persons of minority ethnicity (i.e., non-Albanian) comprised 12 percent of the Kosovo population but 34 percent of murder victims (UNMIK 2003). By 2002, minorities were only 9 percent of murder victims. Figure 6 presents these trends over time. So while there is some indication of declining rates of murder involving ethnic

FIGURE 7
TERRORISM IN KOSOVO, 1998-2004

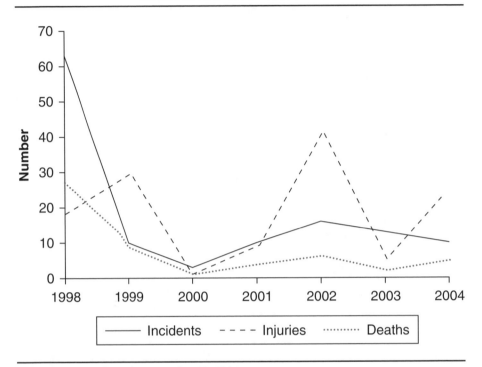

NOTE: Data are through September 23, 2004.

minority victims, the numbers are too small and the time frame too short to allow definitive conclusions.

As a specific form of violent crime, the extent of terrorism can also be used to gauge the security environment. I obtained terrorism data from the RAND-MIPT Terrorism Incident Database, a compilation of open-source material that is used to monitor worldwide terrorism incidents. This database defines terrorism as violence, or the threat of violence, calculated to create an atmosphere of fear and alarm, designed to coerce action, and intended to produce effects beyond the immediate physical damage of the cause, having long-term psychological repercussions on a particular target audience (RAND-MIPT 2005). The number of terrorism incidents fell in 1999 and remained at about the same level in 2004.[4] Figure 7 depicts this and further illustrates that terrorism-related deaths and injuries in 2004 are also near their levels in 1999. Yet between 2000 and 2002, the targets and tactics surrounding the terrorist incidents broadened considerably (RAND-MIPT 2005). Although the identities of specific perpetrators are unknown and the number of incidents too small to permit generalization, the circumstances surrounding these incidents suggest a continued concern regarding Albanian-Serb relations and political and governmental progress.

It appears that considerable progress was made in reducing traditional forms of crime during the first three years of the Kosovo operation. This could be explained by the increase in police levels to detect crime and enforce the law, judges and prosecutors to process criminal cases, and prison capacity and correctional staff to incapacitate and manage those found guilty of crimes, but there is no way to be certain. The limited data prohibit me from ruling out other explanations for these variations, such as changes in reporting, general trends in crime, other events that occurred, or developments in other sectors of the nation-building process (e.g., the economy or health and education institutions). Furthermore, the explosive interethnic violence that occurred from March 17 to 20, 2004, provides additional reasons for concern. Over these three days, 19 persons were murdered and 954 persons were injured; 730 houses belonging to minorities and 42 Serbian Orthodox churches and monasteries were damaged or destroyed; 65 UNMIK CIVPOL, 58 Kosovo Police Service, and 61 Kosovo Force personnel were injured; and 3,800 Serbs were displaced (United Nations Security Council S/2004/348, April 30, 2004).

Corruption

UNMIK did not address corruption suppression in the Police and Justice Pillar as explicitly as it addressed organized crime. Nevertheless, official corruption or even the perception of it may undermine the trust the public has in its government and civil service. Democratic institutions that effectively prevent corruption may, with persistence, facilitate democracy. In a cross-national study of corruption, Montinola and Jackman (2002) concluded that countries that transition to democracy may first experience heightened levels of corruption, which, if not suppressed, can inhibit the democratization process.

Perhaps the most vexing security threat
facing Kosovo is the . . . interethnic strife
[that permeates its history].

Objective data on the extent of corruption are not available. However, Spector, Winbourne, and Beck (2003) examined the issue by conducting a public opinion survey of 505 respondents and interviewing major stakeholders in anticorruption efforts, such as government staff, international administrators, donors, civil society organizations, business officials, and mass media representatives. They found that corruption, defined as the misuse of public office for private gain (including such acts as bribery, extortion, fraud, embezzlement, influence peddling, favoritism, and nepotism), is less of an issue in Kosovo than other countries in the region, concluding that

> despite public opinion and discussions in the mass media that presume very high levels of public corruption, it does not appear that corruption is a pervasive force in the governance process [or that] it . . . significantly undermine[s] the capacity of the government to perform its duties and deliver services in a fundamental way. (p. 2)

This is not to say that public corruption does not exist. Spector, Winbourne, and Beck (2003) provided two additional reasons why corruption is likely to remain an important issue in Kosovo. First, UNMIK has often not been transparent in its functions, leading many Kosovars to assume improprieties within it. Second, Kosovars perceive that compared to public institutions, private institutions are more corrupt. In particular, Spector, Winbourne, and Beck found that respondents perceived the private institutions of businesses, hospitals, and law firms to be among the most corrupt of all institutions. Yet in terms of public institutions, they also found that more than half the respondents rated corruption "high" or "very high" for customs, and about one-third had the same perception of political party leaders. Nonetheless, even these findings must be interpreted with caution. Spector, Winbourne, and Beck claimed to have surveyed a representative sample of the public, but they offered little discussion of their sampling frame, nonresponse rates, or the specific content of individual survey questions. This makes it difficult to assess the validity of their findings. Overall, then, available information does not demonstrate conclusively whether UNMIK was successful in curbing corruption. Instead, it indicates that improvement is necessary in terms of suppressing perceived and actual corruption as well as the need for better data collection efforts to assess corruption suppression progress.

Conclusions and Lessons

Kosovo provides an example of a stabilization and reconstruction effort in which the UN and its partners secured a peace treaty between conflicting parties and attempted to develop a functioning criminal justice system early in the process. The UN coalition quickly implemented a structure for the police and judicial systems, deployed increasing numbers of police officers and judicial officials, enhanced prison capacity, and attempted to counter important security threats through various organizational and legal vehicles.

This review noted three main challenges to the development of Kosovo's security and described specific ways in which UNMIK has addressed them. Perhaps the most vexing security threat facing Kosovo is the ongoing interethnic strife. Integrating the Serb and ethnic Albanian populations appears to be a critical component of Kosovo's future. A key way in which UNMIK has addressed this issue is by creating a multiethnic criminal justice system. UNMIK has done well in creating a police and correctional system that reflects Kosovo's population but has been less effective in creating a judiciary that includes Serbs. Should this failure render the judiciary ineffective, it may also undo whatever progress law enforcement is able to make in establishing law and order and building trust in Kosovo's democratic institutions. The difficulty of forming an unbiased judiciary in Kosovo suggests that future reconstruction efforts should pay particular attention to the equity and effectiveness of all institutions charged with law and order responsibilities. Nonetheless, relative to other recent cases of nation-building, Kosovo stands out as one of the more successful attempts to reconstruct a complete justice system (Jones et al. 2005).

A multiethnic police and justice system may help to establish a more equitable application of law and serve as an example for other public institutions, but it will not resolve interethnic differences by itself. Instead, such a system can only help reduce interethnic disparities and violence through effective prevention and enforcement of rule of law. In this endeavor, UNMIK has been, at best, partially successful.

[I]nternal security reconstruction efforts in Kosovo have been more successful at establishing law and order [than in many other places].

Addressing issues such as ethnic discrimination takes time, planning, assistance, and persistence. Developing and implementing a criminal justice system is a necessary but not sufficient component for reconstructing security and justice. It is also important to address the underlying causes of unrest. Establishing a formal peace treaty among the conflicting parties is a first step in resolving a conflict. President Milosevic signed a military technical agreement that required Yugoslav military and police forces to withdraw to end conflict. The signing of peace treaties usually represents a period of relatively low levels of hostility because, at the moment of signing, they represent the parties' will to end the violent phase of their conflict (Doyle and Sambanis 2000; Walter 2002). They also facilitate international involvement in the form of loans and foreign aid (Dobbins et al. 2003, 2005; Doyle and Sambanis 2000; Walter 2002). Formal surrenders can also increase the likelihood of stability. The destructive defeat of a regime undermines its credibility and demonstrates that it can no longer deliver vital services to the population. These lessons were largely ignored in Iraq and Afghanistan, where the United States and its allies did not secure either a peace treaty or a formal surrender. The broader lesson is to direct sufficient diplomatic and military resources toward negotiating peace treaties among warring parties in cases of civil war and formal surrenders from defeated powers in cases of interstate war. A peace agreement or formal surrender can help convince combatants to demobilize and demilitarize, while a lack of one creates little impetus for opposing factions to do so. Not having a peace agreement or surrender has contributed to greater challenges such as those posed by warlords and regional commanders in Afghanistan and by militia and insurgents in Iraq (Jones et al. 2005).

Compared to many other places, internal security reconstruction efforts in Kosovo have been more successful at establishing law and order. The rule of law improved over the course of reconstruction, and the level of violence decreased. Why was Kosovo comparatively effective? According to Jones et al. (2005), the chances of success in these nation-building exercises are strongly affected by conditions at the beginning of reconstruction. Compared to other nation-building exercises, the amount of financial assistance, duration of assistance, size of international military and police, and size of national police (and the proportion of them trained) for Kosovo were consistently high. Kosovo had the highest level of civilian police forces of nine recent nation-building cases (Jones et al. 2005), and the police forces were armed and given arrest authority. This provides some evidence that traditional law enforcement may be better left to civilian authority. While it is important to ensure that military authorities are ready to assume public security responsibilities after major combat, it is also important to recognize the importance of a strong civilian police force. In Kosovo, carabinieri and gendarmerie forces were put under civilian, not military, authority. This contrasts with recent U.S. practices in Iraq and Afghanistan. Military and civil police have different training, purposes, and expertise, and it is important for both to be part of an international security force (Perito 2004).

A final lesson is the critical need for data regarding reconstruction. It is important to develop and use outcome-based metrics to define program success and managerial performance. Data can help determine progress toward achieving goals and identify what may be facilitating or impeding progress. Relative to other recent operations, more data are available regarding the inputs in Kosovo and the resultant outcomes. Such data enhance evaluations of reconstruction. Even in Kosovo, however, data were seriously limited. These limitations included a lack of consistent data over time, the length of time for data to become available, differing estimates of the same variable, and minimal detail regarding criminal offenses. It is no doubt difficult for occupying forces to collect data while consumed with reconstruction activities. Nonetheless, the success of operations can be improved if decision makers couple data collection plans with their operational objectives so that performance can be gauged and midcourse corrections made.

Planning for future operations based on past experience can help reduce the overall trauma associated with these complex and important efforts. It is important to enhance the ability to establish law and order in emerging democracies for many reasons. Most important is the need to protect citizens from all forms of crime. Forming a safe and secure environment also contributes to the conduct of other nation-building activities and to the overall transition to democracy.

Police and justice institutions are some of the most visible and heavily used public entities. They are the institutions of the democratic government with which ordinary citizens interact most frequently. Consequently, public support for democracy is likely to be associated with the extent to which citizens trust their police and justice institutions and believe them to be legitimate and effective.

Notes

1. Financial assistance has some limitations, and more is not always better. In industrializing countries, governments do not always have the capacity to spend large amounts of money. Furthermore, corruption may reduce the viability of financial assistance.

2. Specifically, these included trafficking in persons, possession of weapons, unauthorized border and boundary crossing, terrorism, protection of injured parties and witnesses, witness cooperation, organized crime, covert and technical measures of surveillance and investigation, use of written records in criminal proceedings, criminal code, and criminal procedure code.

3. The Organization for Security and Cooperation in Europe (2004a) did not provide a precise definition of what exactly constituted a complex case but indicated that such cases include investigation, criminal cases, juvenile cases, civil cases, inheritance, and noncontentious cases.

4. The data for 2004 only account for incidents through September 23, 2004. During the January to September time frame, eleven terrorism incidents occurred in 2002, and there were ten incidents in 2004. This suggests that the total number of incidents in 2004 may be somewhat close to the number of incidents in 2002.

References

Bayley, David H. 1999. Compendium of participants' views. In *Civilian police and multinational peacekeeping—A workshop series: A role for democratic policing*, ed. James Burack, William Lewis, and Edward Marks. Washington, DC: National Institute of Justice.

———. 2001. *Democratizing the police abroad: What to do and how to do it*. Washington, DC: National Institute of Justice.

Blumstein, Alfred. 2000. Disaggregating the violence trends. In *The Crime Drop in America*, ed. Alfred Blumstein and Joel Wallman, 13-44. New York: Cambridge University Press.

Daalder, Ivo H., and Michael E. O'Hanlon. 2001. *Winning ugly: NATO's war to save Kosovo*. Washington, DC: Brookings Institution Press.

Dobbins, James, Seth G. Jones, Keith Crane, Andrew Rathmell, Brett Steele, Richard Teltschik, and Anga Timilsina. 2005. *The UN's role in nation-building: From the Congo to Iraq*. MG-304-RC. Santa Monica, CA: RAND.

Dobbins, James, John G. McGinn, Keith Crane, Seth G. Jones, Rollie Lal, Andrew Rathmell, Rachel Swanger, and Anga Timilsina. 2003. *America's role in nation-building: From Germany to Iraq*. MR-1753-RC. Santa Monica, CA: RAND.

Doyle, Michael W., and Nicholas Sambanis. 2000. International peacebuilding: A theoretical and quantitative analysis. *American Political Science Review* 94:779-801.

Einhorn, Jessica. 2001. The World Bank's mission creep. *Foreign Affairs* 80:22-35.

Freedom House. 2004. *Freedom in the World 2004: The annual survey of political rights and civil liberties*. New York: Freedom House.

Fukuyama, Francis. 2004. *State-building: Governance and world order in the 21st century*. Ithaca, NY: Cornell University Press.

Hagen, William H. 1999. The Balkans' lethal nationalisms. *Foreign Affairs* 78:52-64.

Hartmann, Michael E. 2003. *International judges and prosecutors in Kosovo: A new model for post-conflict peacekeeping*. Special Report 112. Washington, DC: U.S. Institute of Peace.

International Crisis Group. 2000. *Kosovo report card.* Washington, DC: International Crisis Group.

Jane's Information Group. 2004. *Jane's Sentinel Security Assessments, Serbia and Montenegro, Kosovo* special profile. http://www.janes.com (accessed April 2004).

Jones, Seth G., Jeremy M. Wilson, Andrew Rathmell, and K. Jack Riley. 2005. *Establishing law and order after conflict.* MG-374. Santa Monica, CA: RAND.

LaFree, Gary. 1998. *Losing legitimacy: Street crime and the decline of social institutions.* Boulder, CO: Westview.

Montinola, Gabriella R., and Robert W. Jackman. 2002. Sources of corruption: A cross-country study. *British Journal of Political Science* 32:147-70.

Mosher, Clayton J., Terance D. Miethe, and Dretha M. Phillips. 2002. *The mismeasure of crime.* Thousand Oaks, CA: Sage.

North Atlantic Treaty Organization (NATO). 1999. *NATO's role in relation to the conflict in Kosovo.* http://www.nato.int/kosovo/history.htm (accessed May 2005).

Organization for Security and Cooperation in Europe (OSCE). 2003. *Kosovo Police Service School.* Pristina, Kosovo: OSCE.

———. 2004a. *Kosovo: Review of the criminal justice system: The administration of justice in the municipal courts.* Pristina, Kosovo: OSCE.

———. 2004b. *New class of cadets to graduate from OSCE Kosovo Police School.* Pristina, Kosovo: OSCE.

Perito, Robert M. 2002. *The American experience with police in peace operations.* The Academic Series. Clementsport, Nova Scotia, Canada: The Canadian Peace Keeping Press, Pearson Peacekeeping Centre.

———. 2004. *Where is the lone ranger when we need him? America's search for a postconflict stability force.* Washington, DC: United States Institute of Peace.

Ramet, Sabrina. 2000. *KFOR's record in Kosovo.* Meeting Report 219. Washington, DC: Woodrow Wilson International Center for Scholars.

RAND-MIPT (National Memorial Institute for the Prevention of Terrorism). 2005. Terrorism Incident Database. www.tkb.org.

Schneider, Victoria W., and Brian Wiersema. 1990. Limits and use of the Uniform Crime Reports. In *Measuring crime: Large-scale, long-range efforts,* ed. Doris L. MacKenzie, Phyllis J. Baunach, and Roy R. Roberg, pp. 21-48. Albany: State University of New York Press.

Smith, M. Dwayne, and Margaret A. Zahn. 1998. *Studying and preventing homicide: Issues and challenges.* Thousand Oaks, CA: Sage.

Solana, Javier. 1999. NATO's success in Kosovo. *Foreign Affairs* 78:114-20.

Spector, Bertram I., Svetlana Winbourne, and Laurence D. Beck. 2003. *Corruption in Kosovo: Observations and implications for USAID.* Washington, DC: Management Systems International.

Statistical Office of Kosovo. 2003. *Living Standard Measurement Survey, 2000.* Pristina: Statistical Office of Kosovo.

Strohmeyer, Hansjorg. 2001. Collapse and reconstruction of a judicial system: The United Nations missions in Kosovo and East Timor. *American Journal of International Law* 95:46-63.

United Nations Interim Administration Mission in Kosovo (UNMIK). 2000. Regulation No. 2000/64: On Assignment of International Judges/Prosecutors and/or Change of Venue (December 15, 2000). http://www.unmikonline.org/regulations/2000/reg64-00.htm.

———. 2001. *Civilian police—Mandate & tasks.* www.unmikonline.org/civpol/mandate.htm (accessed May 2005).

———. 2002. *Police report for 2002, a year of transition.* United Nations Civilian Police: UNMIK. Pristina, Kosovo: Commissioner's Press Office.

———. 2003. *Pillar 1: Police and justice, presentation paper.* www.unmikonline.org/justice/documents/pillarI_report_jul03.pdf (accessed May 2005).

———. 2004a. *PDSRSG swears in two court presidents and six other Kosovo judges.* http://www.unmikonline .org/press/pressr04.htm (accessed May 2005).

———. 2004b. SRSG's remarks on the entry into force of the Provisional Criminal Code and the Provisional Criminal Procedure Code. www.unmikonline.org/press/2004/pressr/pr1163.pdf (accessed June 2005).

United Nations Security Council. Various dates. S/1998/1199 (September 23, 1998); S/2000/538 (June 6, 2000); S/2000/1196 (December 15, 2000); S/2001/926 (October 2, 2001); S/2002/62 (January 15, 2002);

S/2002/1126 (October 9, 2002); S/2003/113 (January 29, 2003); S/2003/996 (October 15, 2003); S/2004/71 (January 26, 2004); S/2004/348 (April 30, 2004). http://www.un.org/Docs/sc/.

U.S. Agency for International Development, and the Organization for Security and Cooperation in Europe. 2001. *Judicial Assessment Mission II.* Washington, DC: U.S. Agency for International Development.

U.S. Department of Justice. 2004. *Project overviews: Kosovo.* www.usdoj.gov/criminal/icitap/kosovo.html (accessed June 2005).

Walter, Barbara F. 2002. *Committing to peace: The successful settlement of civil wars.* Princeton, NJ: Princeton University Press.

Weber, Max. 1958. Politics as a vocation. In *From Max Weber: Essays in sociology,* ed. H. H. Gerth and C. Wright Mills, 77-128. New York: Oxford University Press.

World Bank. 2000. *Reforming public institutions and strengthening governance.* Washington, DC: World Bank.

The Right to Unionize, the Right to Bargain, and the Right to Democratic Policing

By
MONIQUE MARKS
and
JENNY FLEMING

This (normative) article explores the importance of police unions in the quest for democratic policing. The authors argue that if we are to expect police to behave democratically, it is important for police themselves to experience democratic engagement within the organizations in which they work. That is, if police are expected to defend democracy, they should not be denied basic democratic rights such as the right to collective bargaining and the right to freedom of association. The authors contend that police unions, through networking with other social justice groupings and through encouraging democratic practice, constitute a real forum for the promotion of democratic policing. For this potential to be reached, however, police unions need to identify with broader labor movement trends toward community unionism.

Keywords: police labor rights; community unionism; democratic policing

This article explores the importance of police unions in the quest for democratic policing. We argue that if we are to expect police to behave

Monique Marks is a research fellow at the Regulatory Institutions Network (RegNet) at the Australian National University. Prior to joining RegNet, she was a senior lecturer in the Sociology Department at the University of KwaZulu Natal in South Africa. Her research interests include police reform, police labor relations, youth politics, and ethnographic encounters. Her recently published book is Transforming the Robocops: Changing Police in South Africa (2005).

Jenny Fleming is a fellow at the Regulatory Institutions Network (RegNet) in the Research School of Social Sciences at the Australian National University in Canberra, Australia. She is a former research fellow with the Key Centre for Ethics, Law, Justice and Governance at Griffith University, Brisbane, Australia, from which she holds a doctorate. She is the coeditor with I. Holland of Motivating Ministers to Morality (2001, Ashgate) and Government Reformed: Values and New Political Institutions (2003, Ashgate) and publishes widely on police management, police unionism, and criminal justice administration. Her research interests include police labor relations, police-government relations, and the politics of criminal justice.

NOTE: The authors would like to acknowledge the support of the Australian Research Council for parts of this article (Grant nos. LP0346987 and LP0348682).

DOI: 10.1177/0002716206287181

democratically, it is important for police themselves to experience democratic engagement within the organizations in which they work. In the literature, democratic policing is often discussed with reference to accountability structures and processes, civilianization, policing outcomes and performance measurement, and community participation and partnerships. However, there is almost no mention of the labor and social rights of police employees.

> *[I]f we are to expect police to behave democratically, it is important for police themselves to experience democratic engagement within the organizations in which they work.*

We argue that if police are expected to defend democracy, they should not be denied basic democratic rights such as the right to collective bargaining and the right to freedom of association. Through being part of collective representative organizations, police may begin to appreciate the significance of freedom of association. Through engaging in collective bargaining processes, police may acknowledge the rights of social groupings to engage in collective action. Yet despite the link between organizational police democracy (the democratic internal workings of these organizations) and societal democracy (where citizens are able to participate in decision-making processes and where basic human rights are protected), the social and labor rights of the police are often constrained by regional, national, and international regulatory frameworks.

Like other trade unions, police unions can be narrowly self-interested, focusing their energies on workplace improvement and status enhancement. Unions also have the tendency, as Robert Michels cautioned almost a century ago, to become highly bureaucratized, resulting in rank-and-file union members "inevitably be[ing] controlled by a tiny minority . . . [and] thwart[ing] democratic aspirations within trade union structures" (Burgmann and Burgmann 1998, 63). These tendencies may seriously inhibit the democratic potential of the trade union movement but should not be cause for pessimism. As Alvin Gouldner has observed (cited in Burgmann and Burgmann 1998, 63), an "iron law of democracy" operates as effectively as Michels's "iron law of oligarchy." As Burgmann and Burgmann noted,

Trade unions are among the most democratic organisations in our society, certainly more democratic in general than corporations, parliamentary parties and governments. (1998, 63)

Indeed, trade unions (including police unions) have, over time and across continents, demonstrated a real concern with democratic rights and with social justice agendas.

Through being part of collective representative organizations, police may begin to appreciate the significance of freedom of association.

In a number of instances, unions are "broadcasting agendas for social change" and aligning themselves with social movements for racial justice, gender equality, and urban change (Johnston 2000, 139-40; Robinson 2000). In many cases, these unions are building on hitherto obscured but "strong histor[ies] of democratic and militant unionism and intelligent and progressive union leadership" (Wooding, Levenstein, and Rosenberg 1997, 126). A case in point is the Police and Prisons Civil Rights Union (POPCRU) in South Africa. Based on this case as well as data about police unions in Europe and in America, we contend that police unions potentially constitute a real vehicle for the promotion of democratic policing. For this potential to be reached, however, police unions need to identify with broader labor movement trends toward community unionism. This form of unionism promotes strong alliances with social justice groupings as a means for building union profiles and influence and for achieving positive public interest agendas (Tattersall 2004). This networking may also play a role in preventing police unions from oligarchical tendencies because leaders will have to look outward in setting their agendas and in doing so call upon the active support of their members.

This article takes a normative approach. It incorporates existing knowledge about police unions while constructing future paths that we believe police unions could and should take. Normative judgments tell us what ought to be the case (Mayhew 2000). These judgments are generally based on hypothetical directives, using empirical data, where possible, to "throw a flood of light on the discovery of norms and obligations" (Walhout 1957, 48). The premise of the normative approach taken in this article is as follows: democracy is built through active participation of citizens in decisions that affect their lives and through "opposition to entrenched patterns of unjustified inequality" (Sklansky 2005b, 1808). Police officers are most likely to cherish the rules and ideals of democracy if the organization in which they work promotes internal political participation at both the individual and collective level and if police representative organizations engage with social justice issues.

Global Trends in Trade Unionism

Trade unions can be thought of as, to borrow a term from Tom Nairn (1997), "Janus-faced" organizations. They have the potential both to advance social justice agendas and to be narrowly concerned with their own vested interests (Hyman 2000; Prasad and Snell 2004). In recent decades, trade unions have displayed their vested interest face more often than they have revealed their social justice features (Levi 2003; Hyman 2000). Bureaucratic conservatism has shaped much of the direction taken by the trade union movement in recent years.

The challenge for the trade union movement in the twenty-first century is for unions to overcome this conservatism and to reinvigorate and "redefine their role as a sword of justice" (Hyman 2000, 1). Change is necessary for two reasons. First, engaging in more social justice issues provides unions with an opportunity for much needed revival. Second, through being involved in social justice issues, trade unions will increase their capacity to mobilize a broad range of civil society actors in pursuit of their public interest agendas. Some scholars suggest that the trade union movement offers a social democratic alternative to global neoliberalism (Lambert 2000; Adler and Webster 2000). But to be able to achieve these objectives, trade unions must

> be part of a major social movement in which organised labour plays a crucial role while acting as a reciprocal participant in a larger network of social activists. An increasing number of unions—although still too few—are democratising internally, engaging in issues of economic and social justice for others as well as themselves. (Levi 2003, 60)

How unions identify themselves, what agendas they decide to promote, and whom they forge alliances with are all contingent on a number of factors. These include the political opportunity structure at the local, national, and global level; the characteristics of union members and supporters; the extent to which unions are viewed as valuable within networks of influence; the vision of union leaders; and, importantly for this article, the frameworks of international regulatory organizations such as the International Labor Organization (ILO).

Trade unions have been central to democratic transitions in the Pacific region, Asia, and Southern Africa. In these regions, trade unions were forced to respond to multiple challenges resulting from interlinked economic and political crises. Political instability compelled trade unions to "focus their attention on broader issues related to democracy and human rights" (Prasad and Snel 2004, 268; see also von Holdt 2002; Lambert 2000; Muhsin 2005).

Trade unions are not only important proponents of social justice in regions of the world struggling to create democratic institutions and practices. Even in established democracies, trade unions retain a democratic impetus (for example, see Burgmann and Burgmann 1998). Waterman (2004) suggested that

> while examples of autocratically run and bureaucratic trade unions, some well known, exist in many countries, it remains true, nonetheless, that the trade union movement as a whole is by far and away the most democratic institution in every society and certainly the only major democratic international movement worldwide. (p. 5)

Waterman also acknowledged the oligarchical tendencies within trade unions. However, he maintained that the large membership base of trade unions (from subordinated groupings) and the geographic reach they have provide them with the *potential* to deepen and broaden support for democratic principles. Trade unions are, moreover, often the only mass democratic organizations in a given society capable of organizing large numbers of citizen groupings across the boundaries of nation-states.

Trade union scholars are beginning to consider ways that trade unions can break out of their bureaucratic conservatism to implement new programs within a broad social justice framework through (re)engaging more strategically and ideologically with community-based groupings. Unionists and scholars refer to "community unionism" (Wills 2001; Tattersall 2004) to denote a form of trade unionism where unions develop new models of organizing through reaching out to groups with interests beyond the workplace. Johnston (2000, 140), writing of trade unions in the United States, talked about trade unions as moving toward "social movement unionism" where the unions are prepared to build new alliances and employ more confrontational tactics in promoting gender justice, immigrant rights, and urban social change. These trade unions are trying new strategies, building new coalitions, and rethinking their agendas. They are also mobilizing and representing "working people beyond the boundaries of the bargaining unit, in dealings not limited to employers and on issues not limited to the scope of recognition" (p. 142).

Governments are also starting to take stock of the important role that trade unions can play in governance networks. For example, in South Africa, the National Economic Development and Labour Council (NEDLAC) was established by the democratic government in 1995, ushering in a new era of inclusive decision making and consensus seeking in the economic arena. NEDLAC represents four constituencies—organized labor, government, business, and the community. Its aim is to prevent unilateral decision making. The social partners in NEDLAC have key roles to play in developing effective policies to promote urgently needed economic growth, increased participation in economic decision making, and social equity on a sustained basis (see http://www.nedlac.org.za/).

In Britain, following the election of the New Labour government in 1997, "trade unions have become increasingly important agents in local and regional development and governance" (Pike, O'Brien, and Tomaney 2004, 103). Trade unions are now viewed as important stakeholders, shaping legislation and creating opportunities for trade unions to engage directly in local and regional development issues, to expand their own agendas beyond the shop floor, to build alliances with other local and regional organizations, and to challenge traditional ways of organizing.

The Spirit of Police Unions

Police unions, much like other unions, can be both conservative and forward looking in their outlook. They have also, over time, demonstrated real oligarchic tendencies as their agendas have become increasingly conservative and as leaders have become entrenched within individual police unions.[1] Perhaps more than any other union, police unions attract much controversy and evoke strong reactions from academics, police managers, and the public. Goldstein (1979) best summarized the divergent responses to police unions:

> Some see the [police] unions as the natural enemies of change; as committed to protecting the hard earned gains reflected in the status quo. Others see the unions as a new and potentially dynamic force for positive change, especially as they press for more democratic police organisations. (p. 312)

Police managers and supervisors view police unions as disruptive entities within highly disciplined organizations (Halpern 1974). Policing scholars condemn them as obdurate organizations (Fogelson 1977; O'Malley 2005). Politicians regard them anxiously as powerful interest groupings able to (improperly) influence public perceptions and voting patterns (Kadleck 2003; Barker and Carter 1994; Finnane 2002). Even those who ideologically support the police union movement as an avenue for worker participation within the police organization "object to the often conservative content of their policy proposals" (Reiner 1978, 151). Police unions, like other trade unions, have taken on the character of "business unionism" (Voss and Sherman 2000) where union representatives spend most of their time promoting members' welfare and routinely supporting them in disciplinary hearings or in legal matters (Fleming and Marks 2004; Swanton 1982).

Some, however, recognize police unions as important social agencies with the capacity to positively influence policing trends (Sklansky 2005a; O'Malley 2005; Fleming, Marks, and Wood 2006). Police stakeholder groups in Canada have come to realize that "if police mangers foster respectful and collaborative relations with police unions/associations, there will be less likelihood of labor conflict and less reason for the association/union to take extraordinary measures to present their issues" (Biro et al. 2000, 15). They recognize that police associations/unions may provide police managers with the only forum by which to communicate with police members and as a vehicle for gaining support for change processes. Police unions, in their view, can provide platforms for the formulation of policies oriented to greater professionalism and to improving partnerships with communities and other stakeholders. In addition, their involvement in decision-making processes within police organizations has led to a weakening of "management rights, powers and traditional autocratic authority" (Hewitt 1978, 218), thereby creating more participatory and democratic processes within police organizations (Fleming and Marks 2004).

The democratic challenge that police unions present within police organizations was recognized in the early 1970s by William Ker Muir. Muir (1977), through his study of Oakland police, discovered that police are more likely to have a capacity for tolerance and an affinity for deliberation and compromise if their workplaces embrace these values internally. For the most part, though, the democratic impetus of police unions is seldom recognized in the literature, and yet a number of police unions have taken the lead in promoting more just, equitable, and effective policing.

Perhaps the best example of such a police union is POPCRU in South Africa. POPCRU was formed in 1989 during a period of defiance on the part of the mass democratic movement against apartheid. POPCRU has consistently pushed management for more transparent and even-handed policing. POPCRU was launched when a group of black police officers in the Eastern Cape province came together in defiance of brutal apartheid policing (Hopkins 2004). While POPCRU does practice business unionism, it has maintained a democratic policing agenda. At its 2004 General Conference, a number of key resolutions were articulated that reflect POPCRU's concern with both the internal democratization of the South African Police Service and with the furtherance of democratic policing within communities. In that forum, POPCRU resolved to allocate resources to speed up the transformation in the criminal justice system, to advance the equitable redistribution of police resources, to embark on a campaign to eradicate police corruption, to push for the targeting of women for leadership positions within the Police Service, to challenge the unilateral behavior of police employers and managers, and to campaign to narrow the wage gap between high-ranking and rank-and-file police (POPCRU 2004).

In 1997, POPCRU affiliated to the progressive trade union federation in South Africa and has since engaged in campaigns aimed at "defending the interests of communities against unpopular socio-economic policies" (Marks and Fleming 2004). POPCRU's commitment to democratic governance has been recognized by international human rights organizations. In August 2004, Shizue Tomoda, one of the ILO's technical specialists, wrote a letter to POPCRU's president:

> I am confident that under your leadership POPCRU will grow further and will be an important instrument in the promotion of truly democratic labour relations not only in South Africa but also in the neighbouring countries in the region and eventually the entire continent. POPCRU's commitment to the principle of good governance and quality service delivery is a model for any public service anywhere in the world. Viva POPCRU![2]

POPCRU is not the only police union pursuing democratic governance agendas. The European Confederation of Police (EUROCOP) is an association of police unions across Europe. It has twenty-seven member organizations. Since January 2004 EUROCOP has been a participant in the Council of Europe. Through this participation, EUROCOP is able to directly approach government delegations to the Council of Europe. EUROCOP has a number of missions related to the development of European policing and is committed to "the promotion of fairness and equal opportunities in the police service, its own bodies and its member organizations" (EUROCOP 2004, 3).

EUROCOP has supported police officers throughout Europe who wish to unionize. In February 2005, EUROCOP held a conference devoted to the policing of a unified Europe. The conference looked at the constructive role that police unions could play in the planning of reform and transition processes within the police (see http://www.eurocop-police.org/events/eurocop/20050228-riga/20050228-riga.htm).

EUROCOP, representing unionized police officers in Europe, has charted a democratic policing pathway. While EUROCOP was established in 2002, it draws on a long history of democratic police unionism in Europe. As Berkley (1969, 46-51) reminded us, as early as the 1960s, "highly developed" police unions in France, Sweden, Germany, and the United Kingdom were demonstrating a progressive outlook. Berkley provided several examples of how police unionism facilitated the creation of the "democratic policeman."

In Australia, too, police unions have shaped the reform agenda in very direct ways and initiated a number of important reviews of police organizations (Fleming and Marks 2004). These reviews have largely centered on resourcing and working conditions. However, some of the police unions have taken up broader reform agendas.

The New South Wales Police Association's involvement in the Royal Wood Commission (established in 1994 to examine the existence or otherwise of entrenched police corruption in the New South Wales Police [Wood 1997]) and the subsequent reform agenda, for example, have been much remarked on. It made extensive submissions supporting radical change, including integrity testing and greater external oversight (Fleming and Lewis 2002, 92). The Northern Territory Police Association (NTPA) also played a central role in exposing that territory's resource problem, particularly within remote Aboriginal areas. The territory's government publicly lauded its contribution. The NTPA went further to advocate mechanisms for equalizing the treatment of Aboriginal Community Policing Officers (Fleming, Marks, and Wood forthcoming).

At the local level, evidence indicates that police union members are reported to have closer links with community groupings than those police who are not unionized. Magenau and Hunt (1996) argued that police unionization in the United States "has increased the political power of the rank and file, relative to other network partners." While they criticized police unions' law enforcement agendas, their data confirm that union officers have better police-community relations than nonunionized police. This finding, they said, is consistent with other work on public sector unions that indicates that these unions identify with and promote public interest agendas. Rank-and-file behavior is then more consistent with community preferences. This public interest agenda is also evident in the demands of police union members for governments to release the findings of public reports, even when these may reflect poorly on the police organization (*Portland Press Herald* 2005).

Police Unions, Collective Bargaining, and Democratic Policing

In a recent handbook for assessing police performance in democratizing countries, Bruce and Neild (2005) insisted that police themselves must be treated as citizens if we are to expect them to behave democratically toward other citizens. They effectively draw the link between the internal democratization of police organizations and the external democratization of police conduct. According to them, "the fact that police are citizens, means they are entitled to the rights, privileges and benefits of citizenship" (p. 41). They argued that central to recognizing the police as citizens is their right to decent conditions of service, the right to form employee representative organizations, and the right to engage in collective bargaining (p. 43).

As early as 1947, an Australian historian and civil libertarian, Brian Fitzpatrick, made a similar point. Fitzpatrick asserted that if police had full political rights—including the right to unionize—"it would be harder for them to be used in the service of political repression." Fitzpatrick defended the rights of police to unionize as "consistent with the advancement of democracy and good governance" (see Finnane 2002, 131-32).

For Fitzpatrick, democratic police reform and more participatory police management practices are synonymous. Berkley (1969) concurred with Fitzpatrick:

> The trade union tends to make the policeman think of himself [*sic*] as a trade unionist, and thereby to identify with what is usually a pro-democratic, and somewhat left of center sector of democratic society. This is important, since policemen often experience a pull to the right. . . . Thus, the trade union can act as a countervailing force which keeps the police in the mainstream of democratic society. (pp. 46-47)

In the past three decades, attempts have been made to shift toward more corporate and participatory management styles coinciding with "the emerging consensus around a service-based, consumerist-approach to policing" (Reiner 1992, 267). Police managers have come to recognize the value of rank-and-file participation. They now view police members as entrepreneurs rather than employees (O'Malley 2005). Through more participatory management practices, police managers and supervisors are now required to promote, rather than restrict, creativity and problem-solving approaches (Birzer 1996). The technologies (problem solving, negotiation, consultation, partnership building) are also seen as crucial to community policing agendas that have been adopted by the police across the world. Participatory management is aimed at direct forms of participation by *individual* police.[3]

While community-oriented policing may call for more participatory styles of management, there are also intraorganizational rationales for introducing such management practices, especially during periods of organizational change. Like any work-based organization, it is crucial to bring all members of the police organization on board in times of transition. Change must make sense to those on the front line. If this does not occur, rank-and-file police officers are likely to feel threatened by change (Goldstein 1990; Van Heerden 1982; Washo 1984; Sykes 1986; Cowper 2004; Marks 2005).

Participatory management practices are not the only innovation required in police organizations for police to be responsive, creative, and collaborative. The right to more indirect forms of participation is just as important if police are to feel that they can effectively engage in codetermination processes. It is through collective representation that police officers (like other employees) are empowered to influence and shape decision-making processes within police organizations—something that is extremely difficult to achieve as individuals given the hierarchical nature of police organizations. It is through participating via collective representative organizations (like trade unions) that individual members are afforded the opportunity to be informed and heard, to be involved in codetermination processes, and to negotiate important decisions that affect them individually and collectively (Peccei and Guest 2002).

The right of police officers to engage in direct and indirect forms of participation is crucial to rights-based awareness on the part of the police. Police are more likely to respond toward the public in democratic and fair ways if they themselves experience the benefits of democratic labor and social rights in their own organizational lives (Berkley 1969, 46-47). Put slightly differently, for police cultural knowledge about rights to be transformed and then reinforced, police themselves must be able to directly experience the benefits of newly awarded citizen rights so that shifts in cultural knowledge can occur.

Rights awareness is not the only democratic benefit of police unionization. Police unions can play a number of other positive roles to advance democratic policing. Police unions can "serve as a necessary internal check against bureaucratic usurpation" (Gammage and Sacks 1972, 102). Through their engagement, police unions pose a challenge to the culture, decision-making processes, and traditionally austere atmosphere of public police agencies (Guyot 1979; Burpo 1971). Through collective bargaining activity, police unions serve to restrict the unilateral decision making on the part of police management (Levi 1978).

The unions should not be viewed as a thorn in the side of police managers or employers. Through (direct and indirect) participatory labor processes, employees are more likely to feel they have a positive stake in the policies, outcomes, and strategies of the organization (O'Brien 1994; Berkley 1969, 46). For these reasons O'Malley (2005, 8) has suggested that "police unionism should perhaps be moved to the forefront of our analysis of contemporary transformations in policing."

Regulating Police Labor Rights—National and International Legislative Frameworks

Nation-states

The legislative frameworks of sovereign nations largely determine the right of the police to unionize and to bargain collectively. These national frameworks are themselves dependent on a number of national dynamics including broad labor law legislation (at all levels of government), party political standpoints, social movement environments, and the configuration of police organizations. Police unions are most likely to be present in countries where

- freedom of association and collective bargaining rights are recognized,
- liberal or progressive political ideologies dominate,
- social movement organizations operate freely and civic engagement is encouraged, and
- hierarchical bureaucratic traditions within police organizations are challenged.

Where collective bargaining and freedom of association is proscribed, governments (and police management) argue that access to such rights will negatively affect the operational efficiency of the police. In these countries, government and police managers maintain that awarding police the rights to collective bargaining and freedom of association will diminish discipline and emasculate the chain of command (see below).

Police are denied the right to unionize and to bargain collectively in most African and Asian countries, many South American countries, and many Eastern European countries. The countries in which police are denied basic labor rights are usually emerging democracies, countries characterized as "weak states," or countries with authoritarian governmental approaches. In recent years, police who have been denied the right to unionize and to bargain collectively have made attempts to challenge national prescriptions. In so doing, they have turned to police unions in nearby countries for assistance. Police in Lesotho, Zambia, and Botswana, for example, have called upon the South African police union, POPCRU, to assist them in convincing police authorities and managers about the benefits of police unionization (see Hopkins 2004). The Papua New Guinea Police Association has called upon the Police Federation of Australia to assist with capacity building and entrenching the rights of the police in that country. Other organized forums of police officers have looked toward international labor regulatory bodies, such as the ILO, for assistance.

The ILO

The ILO is a key international body and a specialized agency of the United Nations responsible for promoting international efforts to improve working conditions, living standards, and equitable treatment of workers. One of the primary goals of the ILO is to formulate international labor standards in the form of conventions. A convention defines standards and provides a model for nations to follow. The ILO provides best practice benchmarks and aspirational norms.

It is a common belief that the ILO has no legal authority to enforce its recommendations on governments that are found to have violated basic ILO conventions. That belief is not entirely correct. An article in the ILO constitution permits the organization to take whatever action it deems necessary to bring about compliance with its core standards.[4] However, it is a strong ILO custom to use moral suasion and the threat of weaker nations earning the disfavor of strong nations such as the United States or the European Union to persuade a government to reconsider its actions that are contradictory to basic international standards (Adams 2006).

The central role of the ILO, then, is to bring pressure to bear on countries that do not comply with internationally accepted core labor standards (Biffl and Isaac 2002). The ILO is therefore a key player in the "webs of influence" (Braithwaite and Drahos 2000) in the sphere of labor-management relations and employee rights. In the absence of an international authority like the ILO prepared to enforce specific labor standards, countries are free to pursue their own particular legislation and practices that may fall outside of international conventions.

In its official documentation, the ILO states that freedom of association and the right to collective bargaining are basic employment rights and are crucial to building democracy in any given country (ILO 2004). However, those police groupings that have turned to the ILO for assistance in acquiring these rights have been disappointed. Police groups from Argentina who have been mobilizing for labor rights are a good example of this.

In late 2003, two organized groupings of police members in Buenos Aires (Argentina) approached the ILO Body on Freedom of Association to review a decision by the Argentine government denying police members the right to unionize.[5] The case emerged following attempts by the low–ranking Buenos Aires' police officers to form and register a police union (Obeid and Weisenberg 2003). These police officers argued that a police union would "not only improve police working conditions, but would also help curb the 'police mafia' and 'trigger happy' officers who are responsible for hundreds of deaths each year" (see Latinamericapress.org, http://www.communitiesbychoice.org/printme.cfm?ID=1226&print=1). The Buenos Aires police hierarchy responded by opposing unionization and expelling "agitators" from the police. Similar responses occurred in other provinces of Argentina. Police authorities argued that police union activities "seriously affected discipline and responsibility for assignment of duties" (ILO 2003b, 4).

The government of Argentina, in making its case for the prohibition of police unions, made reference to the ILO's core labor conventions. It argued that its decision was in accordance with ILO Convention No. 87, which deals with freedom of association, and Convention No. 98, which deals with the right to collective bargaining. Argentina is a member state of the ILO and has ratified both Convention No. 87 and Convention No. 98. The Argentine government argued in its defense that these two conventions stipulate that relevant labor rights are not immediately applicable to the security forces. Instead, they pointed out, the ILO stipulates that national legislative frameworks should determine these labor rights, allowing for restrictions in the interests of national security or public order.

The Argentine government's reference to the ILO conventions was accurate. Conventions 87, 98, 151, and 154 do not automatically apply to the police and the military.[6] Unsurprisingly, then, when the case was referred to the ILO, the Committee on Freedom of Association concluded in favor of the Argentine government (ILO 2003b, 6).

The determination by the ILO, and the fact that it buttressed the limitations stipulated by the Argentine government, is significant for two reasons. In the first instance, the exclusionary clauses, as they currently stand, lump together the police and the military. In so doing, they reinforce characterizations of police organizations as militarized and as operating primarily with state interests in mind. This is problematic given that global trends in policing indicate that for police to operate in ways that are democratic and community oriented, clear distinctions need to be made between the functions and identity of the police and the military (Waddington 1999; della Porta and Reiter 1998).

Second, in deferring authority to national states in regard to police labor rights, the ILO is inadvertently safeguarding the agendas of governments characterized by autocratic rule, corrupt practices, and low levels of civic engagement. The market economy and domestic political maneuvers have not facilitated improved police employee rights, particularly in places like Africa and Latin America. Indeed, relying on the quality of domestic institutions and policies may seriously curtail what police may view as their "citizen" rights, in turn, negatively affecting the capacity of police members to contribute to the democratization of policing.

While an international network of police unions is attempting to persuade the ILO to review its conventions as they pertain to police, such changes are unlikely in the near future. The ILO is not an independent entity. It is the collective sum of all the member states, which includes representatives from trade unions, employers, and government. Inherent within this body are all the shortcomings and inefficiencies found in such bodies—many of which are opposed to police unionization. As Shizue Tomoda of the ILO points out,

> As long as a large number of member states feel that it is proper for police labour rights to be regulated by national laws, the ILO Secretariat can do little to change the status quo.[7]

The ILO does revise its conventions from time to time. However, this only takes place when member states are ready for such revisions, which is not the case at present in regard to extending police labor rights. In the absence of such revisions, the ILO develops codes of practice. Such codes of practice promote, for example, social dialogue within the public service, including the public emergency services. In January 2003, the ILO held a Joint Meeting on Public Emergency Services and the meeting (which included police labor and management representatives) adopted a document titled "Guidelines on Social Dialogue for Public Emergency Services in a Changing Environment" in which fundamental labor rights such as freedom of association and the right to bargain collectively are promoted. While not legally binding, these guidelines do indicate a real attempt on the part of the ILO to engender a labor rights framework within this occupational sector (ILO 2003a).

A change in the ILO conventions would arguably provide a more robust reference point for those who promote police labor rights. But even if the ILO were to amend its conventions, the regulatory capacity of the organization is limited (Elliot 2000). The ILO can only resort to dialogue, moral suasion, and technical assistance in enforcing labor standards and conventions. In addition, most ILO members have not ratified most standards, leading many commentators to suggest that "the minimum standards were often set too high by the original members of the Western European club" (Braithwaite and Drahos 2000, 234). Many countries in the world still fail to comply with the basic conventions on freedom of association and the right to collective bargaining. Yet the ILO conventions are used to justify exclusions from certain rights—a target for "blame diversion," as we saw in the Argentine case.

As an international organization, the ILO has significant influence in regard to facilitating normative orders and practices for workplaces in both the private and public sector. Developing countries and countries whose governments prefer "union-free" environments[8] may lack the institutional arrangements (and willingness) to develop and apply core labor standards on their own (Biffl and Isaac 2002). The ILO remains an important reference point for national governments in devising regulatory systems for police labor rights.

Police Unions, the Labor Movement, and Community Unionism

Even if regulatory frameworks facilitated police unionization, there is no guarantee that police unions would not succumb to the iron law of oligarchy—pursuing narrow conservative agendas and rejecting forward-thinking participative leadership. Much depends on whether these unions are willing to pursue the new trends within the trade union movement. This, to some extent, depends on whether police unions in the first instance identify with the broader trade union movement.

In many ways, police unions are best identified as industry-based organizations or trade unions, viewing their key role as representing the workplace interests of their members. They engage in collective bargaining and are prepared to employ confrontational tactics when consultative processes fail (Finnane 2002; Fleming and Lafferty 2001). But the question remains, Are police like other workers? The answer to this would be both yes and no. On one hand, as Reiner (1978, 151) put it, "Their condition and experience may incline them toward unionism." Indeed, police organizations have a comparative advantage with regard to police union potential. While technology has supplemented and continues to supplement some fields of policing, policing remains a labor-intensive industry. Where police unions do exist, they represent almost 100 percent of the members of the police organization— a real achievement given the decline of trade union membership internationally (Fleming and Peetz 2005; Finnane 2002; Farber 2005; Marks 2000).

On the other hand, police identities are profoundly shaped and reproduced through public symbols and icons that represent the constabulary as "central to the production and reproduction of order and security" (Loader 1997, 3) and the reproduction of dominant interests (Hall et al. 1978). There is, therefore, a tension between the police identifying with the broader labor movement and their being required to function as "reproducers of order" (Ericson 1982; Fleming and Marks 2004).

Reciprocal relations between the labor movement and police unions may require police unions to adopt a stronger union-community approach in the future.

The extent to which police unions identify and align themselves with the trade union movement is contingent on historical trajectories of the trade union movement, police union leadership, police subcultures, labor law legislation, police labor regulations, and the types of networks that police unions are part of. Interviews with police union officials in Australia revealed a deep ambivalence in identifying with the labor movement. This ambivalence was derived from a preoccupation with police professionalism and a conviction on the part of police union leaders that their social base is extremely conservative. Their preoccupation with organizational maintenance has resulted in a reluctance to generate internal discord by aligning with more far-reaching agendas than those that directly pertain to police workplace conditions (Fleming and Marks 2004).

The Police Federation of Australia has a formalized affiliation with the national trade union federation. But many police unions view the premise of this relationship as strategic rather than ideological. While an alliance with the labor movement is seen as strategically advantageous, this does not dramatically shape the self-identity of the police unions and their members. Australian police unions clearly indicated that they were unlikely to take up a range of the issues on the agenda of the broader labor movement, like, for example, gay rights issues or antiwar campaigns (Fleming and Marks 2004).

The ambivalence of Australian police union leaders is also evident in Canada. According to David Griffin, chief executive officer of the Canadian Professional Police Association,[9] in the provinces of Nova Scotia, New Brunswick, and Saskatchewan, the police associations see themselves as unions and are part of the larger public sector union body. In Ontario (where police associations are prohibited from affiliating with any trade union) however, municipal police associations view themselves largely as professional bodies and tend not to align themselves with the interests of organized labor.[10]

Strategically, then, police unions would be well advised to take stock of new trends in the union movement.

Police unions in some countries do align themselves with the broader trade union movement. In South Africa, as mentioned earlier, POPCRU is an affiliate of the national trade union federation (Marks 2000, 2005). One of the resolutions taken by POPCRU at its 2004 national congress was "to constantly struggle to assert a working class and pro-poor perspective within the alliance" (POPCRU 2004, 16). In Brazil, the police union has on occasion publicly demonstrated solidarity with the labor movement. In 1997, the union joined forces with the Landless Workers' Movement and the Workers' Council in a campaign in protest of the government's neoliberal policies (*Weekly News Update on the Americas* 1997).

It is difficult to generalize about police union identities and strategic alliances. But what can be said with certainty is that police are as concerned about working conditions and wages as any other employees (Reiner 1978, 5). Even if not for ideological reasons, police unions are likely to look toward the labor movement as a source of support for their campaigns and as a source of inspiration for their tactics. Strategically, then, police unions would be well advised to take stock of new trends in the union movement. Reciprocal relations between the labor movement and police unions may require police unions to adopt a stronger union-community approach in the future.

The current global socioeconomic climate may compel police unions to associate more closely with other public sector unions. Public sector unions the world over are on the defensive with neoliberal governance and the entrenching of the regulatory state (Braithwaite and Drahos 2000). The increasing pluralization of policing through privatization, civilianization, and responsibilization will lead to significant changes in public police organizations and may compromise police union membership rates. As police unions battle to assert (and protect) the primacy of the public police in the policing industry, they may well cast an eye to other public sector unions for solutions to these new governance arrangements.

Should they choose this path, the new discourse that police unions are likely to share with other public sector unions in their fight against new governance arrangements would center on citizen rights to publicly accountable and professional service delivery. Police unions would then have to demonstrate that the services the public police provide are more accountable, more equitable, more democratic, and more professional than those of private police and civic police groupings.

The future challenge for police unions will be to find a balance between responding to traditional industrial concerns (which will always be a primary focus) and promoting democratic policing and social justice agendas. One way to do this would be to consider the route of community unionism. This will mean showing both faces of police unions—their vested interest face and their social justice face. David Griffin (2001) of the Canadian Professional Police Association has put this challenge:

> In order for 21st century police associations or unions to be effective, they must engage in strategic activities which position the organisation as an influential and respected stakeholder on issues concerning the safe and effective delivery of police services to their communities. (p. 17)

The rights of the police as citizens to freely associate and to collectively bargain are likely to increasingly be intertwined with the rights of the broader citizenry.

Conclusion

In the ensuing years, the face of public police agencies will change dramatically. Contract employment and an emphasis on performance measurement will probably replace tenured employment. Civilians will continue to be employed in police organizations in nonoperational functions. Female and minority group representation is likely to increase within police organizations. Police are likely to be better educated and more aware of their individual rights and more concerned with issues of equal treatment and even affirmative action (Grabosky 2001; Griffin 2001). Consequently, they may become even more demanding of police employers with regard to working conditions, wages, benefits, and rights. The right to join police associations/unions and to engage in collective bargaining is likely to be viewed increasingly as a basic right of police members. However, the challenge for police unions is to align their rights with the democratic rights of those they police and to promote a police professionalism that is characterized by equitable, just, and effective service delivery.

The ILO, as a key international regulatory body, would do well to take heed of the organizing capacity of this sector of workers as well as the potential democratic advantages that could flow from police labor rights.

The past few decades have witnessed major reform movements within police organizations aimed at a more democratic police profession (Marenin 2004). However, both within academic and police discourse, democratic policing inevitably means "making the police answerable to democracy, not bringing the benefits of democracy to police officers themselves" (Sklansky 2005a, 1). Of course, this is not surprising given that where police have acted undemocratically, there are concerns that police should be reined in and made more accountable. We do not disagree with the need for police to be held accountable for their behavior both within police organizations and within the communities they serve. As we have suggested above, however, awarding police the rights of freedom of association and collective bargaining could facilitate the (further) democratization of policing. After all, in those jurisdictions where police have been allowed to organize and bargain collectively, civil disorder has not broken out. Through being able to freely form and join police labor organizations and engage in collective bargaining, police members are able to directly influence the governance of policing. Through collective bargaining processes, police are able to develop skills in problem solving and negotiation, both viewed as key to democratic policing. By being part of collective organizations, police members may begin to appreciate the importance of the right to freedom of association and freedom of expression generally, cornerstones of democratic societies.

Growing networks of police union representatives regionally and internationally will ensure that police unionization will continue to thrive. The ILO, as a key international regulatory body, would do well to take heed of the organizing capacity of this sector of workers as well as the potential democratic advantages that could flow from police labor rights. But change in conventions pertaining to police labor rights will only occur if member state constituencies agree to this. In this regard, member states of the ILO who maintain that police labor rights should be curtailed should be encouraged to reconsider these views.

The limited capacity of the ILO to regulate police labor relations will mean that police employees and managers will need to turn to regional groupings and international networks of police representative organizations and advocates of police labor rights in developing fairer labor practices for police. In the short and medium term, the ILO could provide technical support to police who wish to form police unions and to engage in social dialogue with police managers and employers. This is already occurring to a limited extent in Southern and East Africa where the ILO is currently organizing technical workshops for the police focusing on labor law reform and collective bargaining skills.[11]

If police unions are to positively contribute to the democratization of policing and to broader social justice programmers, they must not be pushed into the margins of scholarly works or left alone to fight for their existence in hostile national milieus.

As we have pointed out, police labor organizations are not inherently progressive organizations, and they tend to focus on narrow vested interests. If they are to be taken seriously in police governance arrangements, they need to respond creatively to newly configuring social, political, and economic environments. If they are to be seen as legitimate organizations worthy of support from civic groupings and from government agencies, they will have to think seriously about their own definitions of professionalism and how they can contribute to the democratization of policing. Police unions will have to become, to borrow a term from Martin Godfrey (2003, 29), "swords of justice" rather than "protectors of vested interests." In so doing, they would need to consider aligning themselves with the broad labor movement, reaching out to community organizations, and expanding their agendas to include "issues of democracy, human rights and social justice not only in the context of labor relations but also in the larger society" (cited in Webster and Lambert 2003, 4).

As Tattersall (2004) has pointed out,

> The process of reaching out is not only useful to maximise a union's capacity to achieve objective victories, but is also essential for unions to again be the central agents for improving the livelihood of working people, both inside and outside the workplace . . . [such relationships] require a significant depth of commitment and participation by unions. (pp. 19, 2)

Police unions *are* important stakeholders in the policing landscape, but they are not the only ones that need to demonstrate participation and commitment in building community relationships. If police unions are to positively contribute to the democratization of policing and to broader social justice programs, they must not be pushed into the margins of scholarly works or left alone to fight for their existence in hostile national milieus. The challenge, then, is not only directed at police unions but also at international regulatory organizations and scholars of the police to seriously engage with police unions so such organizations are able to contribute positively to debates on the future of policing and the realization of democratic citizen frameworks.

Notes

1. Less typically of oligarchic trade unions, police unions often resort to confrontational tactics in achieving their goals.

2. This letter was given to one of the authors by the general secretary of the Police and Prisons Civil Rights Union (POPCRU).

3. It is worth bearing in mind, as David Sklansky (2005a) rightly pointed out, that participatory management may be implemented as a means of thwarting policing unionism, not promoting it.

4. In fact, that provision has only been used once, against Burma for engaging in forced labor (personal communication, Roy Adams, December 2005).

5. For more detail on the Argentine story, see Marks and Fleming (forthcoming).

6. Article 9 (1) says, "The extent to which the guarantees provided for in this Covention (87) shall apply to the armed forces and the police shall be determined by national laws and regulations." In short, the International Labor Organization (ILO) does not say the provisions do not apply, rather that it is up to each state to decide the extent to which they do apply.

7. E-mail correspondence with Shizue Tomada, ILO Secretariat, March 19, 2004.

8. Adams (2001) argues the "union-free" philosophy is well and alive in North America. This school of thought proclaims that unions have no place in well-managed enterprises.

9. E-mail correspondence dated May 10, 2005.

10. E-mail correspondence with Dale Kinnear, Director of Labour Services, Canadian Professional Police Association, May 19, 2005.

11. E-mail correspondence with Jane Hodges, ILO labour law specialist, January 28, 2004.

References

Adams, Roy J. 2001. Human rights in employment: Implications of the international consensus for management teaching and practice. *Journal of Comparative International Management* 4 (1): 22-32.
———. 2006. America's "union-free" movement in light of international human rights standards. In *Justice on the job: Perspectives on the erosion of collective bargaining in the United States*, ed. Richard Block, Sheldon Friedman, Michelle Kaminski, and Andy Levin. Kalamazoo, Michigan: W.E. Upjohn Institute for Employment Research.
Adler, Glenn, and Eddie Webster, eds. 2000. *Trade unions and democratization in South Africa, 1985-1997*. International Political Economy Series. New York: St. Martin's.
Barker, Thomas, and David L. Carter, eds. 1994. *Police deviance*. Cincinnati, OH: Anderson.
Berkley, George E. 1969. *The democratic policeman*. Boston: Beacon.
Biffl, Gudrun, and Joe Isaac. 2002. How effective are the ILO's labour standards under globalisation? Paper presented at the IIRA/CIRA 4th Regional Congress of the America's Centre for Industrial Relations, University of Toronto, June 25-29.

Biro, Frederick, Peter Campbell, Paul McKenna, and Tonita Murray. 2000. *Police executives under pressure: A study and discussion of the issues.* Police Futures Group, Study Series no. 3. Ottawa, Ontario: Canadian Association of Chiefs of Police Publication.

Birzer, Michael L. 1996. Police supervisors in the 21st century. *FBI Law Enforcement Bulletin* 65 (6): 5-11.

Braithwaite, John, and Peter Drahos. 2000. *Global business regulation.* Cambridge: Cambridge University Press.

Bruce, David, and Rachel Neild. 2005. The police that we want: A handbook for oversight of the police in South Africa. Resource Center Publications and Articles. http://www.soros.org/resources/articles_publications/publications/police_20050125 (accessed November 15, 2005).

Burgmann, Meredith, and Verity Burgmann. 1998. *Green bans, red union environmental activism and the New South Wales Builders Labourers' Federation.* Sydney, Australia: University of New South Wales Press.

Burpo, John. 1971. *The police labor movement: Problems and perspectives.* Springfield, IL: Charles C Thomas.

Cowper, Thomas J. 2004. The myth of the military model of leadership in law enforcement. In *Contemporary policing: Controversies, challenges and solutions,* ed. Quint Thurman and Jihong Zhao. Los Angeles: Roxbury Publishing.

della Porta, Donatella, and Herbert Reiter. 1998. *Policing protest: The control of mass demonstrations in Western democracies.* Minneapolis: University of Minnesota Press.

Elliot, Kimberley A. 2000. The ILO and enforcement of core labour standards. *International Economics Policy Briefs* 6:1-7.

Ericson, Richard. 1982. *Reproducing Order: A Study of Police Patrol Work,* Toronto, Toronto University Press.

European Confederation of Police (EUROCOP). 2004. *The voice of police news in Europe.* March. http://www.eurocop-police.org/index.html (accessed November 4, 2005).

Farber, Henry S. 2005. Union membership in the United States: The divergence between the public and the private sectors. September. Working Paper no. 503, Industrial Relations Section, Princeton University, Princeton, NJ.

Finnane, Mark. 2002. *When police unionise: The politics of law and order in Australia.* Sydney, Australia: Institute of Criminology, University of Sydney.

Fleming, Jenny, and George Lafferty. 2001. Police unions, industrial strategies and political influence: Some recent history. *International Journal of Employment Studies* 9 (2): 131-40.

Fleming, Jenny, and Colleen Lewis. 2002. The politics of police reform. In *Police reform: Building integrity,* ed. Tim Prenzler and Janet Ransley, 83-96. Sydney, Australia: Federation Press.

Fleming, Jenny, and Monique Marks. 2004. Reformers or resisters: The state of police unionism in Australia. *Employment Relations Record* 4 (1): 1-14.

Fleming, Jenny, Monique Marks, and Jennifer Wood. 2006. Standing on the inside looking out: The significance of police unions in networks of police governance. *Australian and New Zealand Journal of Criminology* 39 (1).

Fleming, Jenny, and David Peetz. 2005. Essential service unionism and the new police industrial relations. *Journal of Collective Negotiations* 30 (4): 283-305.

Fogelson, Robert M. 1977. *Big-city police.* Cambridge, MA: Harvard University Press.

Gammage, Allen Z., and Stanley L. Sacks. 1972. *Police unions.* Springfield, MA: Charles C Thomas.

Godfrey, Martin. 2003. Employment dimensions of decent work: Trade-offs and complementarities. Discussion Paper DP/148/2003, International Institute for Labour Studies, Geneva, Switzerland.

Goldstein, Herman. 1979. *Policing a free society.* Cambridge, MA: Ballinger.

———. 1990. *Problem oriented policing,* New York: McGraw-Hill.

Grabosky, Peter. 2001. Crime control in the 21st century. *Australian and New Zealand Journal of Criminology* 34 (3): 221-34.

Griffin, David. 2001. Police association advocacy—A strategic priority: Police associations, political activism and public opinion. Paper presented at the Police Employment in 2001 Conference, Toronto, Canada, February 27.

Guyot, Dorothy. 1979. Bending granite: Attempts to change the rank structure of american police departments. *Journal of Police Science and Administration* 7 (3): 253-84.

Hall, Stuart, Charles Critcher, Tony Jefferson, John Clarke, and Brian Roberts. 1978. *Policing the crisis: "Mugging" the state and law and order.* London: Macmillan.

Halpern, Stephen C. 1974. *Police-association and department leaders: The politics of co-optation.* Lexington, MA: D.C. Heath.

Hewitt, William H. 1978. Current issues in police collective bargaining. In *The future of policing*, ed. Alvin W. Cohn, 207-23. Beverley Hills, CA: Sage.

Hopkins, Pat. 2004. *Justice for all: The first 15 years of POPCRU*. Cape Town, South Africa: Police and Prisons Civil Rights Union (POPCRU).

Hyman, Richard. 2000. *An emerging agenda for trade unions?* Labour Net Germany, http://www.labournet.de/index.html.

International Labor Organization (ILO). 2003a. Guidelines on social dialogue in public emergency services in a changing environment. Report from a joint meeting on public emergency in a changing environment, Geneva, Switzerland, January 27-31.

———. 2003b. ILO governing body on freedom of association: 332nd Report of the Committee on Freedom of Association. November. Geneva, Switzerland: ILO.

———. 2004. Organising for social justice. Report of the Director-General. International Labour Conference, 92nd Session, Report 1 (B), International Labour Office, Geneva, Switzerland.

Johnston, Paul. 2000. The resurgence of labor as citizenship movement in the new labor relations. *Critical Sociology*, 26 (1-2): 139-60.

Kadleck, Colleen. 2003. Police employee organisations. *Policing: An International Journal of Police Strategies and Management* 26 (2): 341-51.

Lambert, Rob. 2000. Trade unions, democracy and global change: South African Transitions. In *A review of trade unions and democracy in South Africa, 1985-1997*, ed. Glenn Adler and Eddie Webster. London: Macmillan.

Levi, Margaret. 1978. Conflict and collusion: Police collective bargaining. In *Police accountability: Performance measures and unionism*, ed. Richard C. Larson. Toronto, Canada: Lexington Books.

———. 2003. Organizing power: The prospects for an American labor movement. http://depts.washington.edu/pcls/OrganizingPower.pdf (accessed February 1, 2006).

Loader, Ian. 1997. Policing and the social: Questions of symbolic power. *British Journal of Sociology* 48 (1): 1-18.

Magenau, John M., and Raymond G. Hunt. 1996. Police unions and the police role. *Human Relations* 42 (6): 547-60.

Marenin, Otwin. 2004. Police training for democracy. *Police Practice and Research* 5 (2): 107-23.

Marks, Monique. 2000. Labour relations in the South African Police Service. In *Public service labour relations in a democratic South Africa*, ed. Glenn Adler. Johannesburg, South Africa: University of Witwatersrand Press.

———. 2005. *Transforming the robocops: Changing police in South Africa*. Scottsville, South Africa: University of KwaZulu-Natal Press.

Marks, Monique, and Jenny Fleming. 2004. As unremarkable as the air they breathe? Reforming police management in South Africa. *Current Sociology* 52 (5): 783-807.

———. Forthcoming. The untold story: the regulation of police labour rights and the quest for police democratisation. *Police, Practice and Research*.

Mayhew, David R. 2000. Political science and political philosophy: Ontological not normative. *Political Science and Politics* 22 (2): 192-93.

Muhsin, Abdullah. 2005. Iraqi labor unions and the war. April 27. http://politicalaffairs.net/article/articleview/1021/1/91/ (accessed November 15, 2005).

Muir, William K. 1977. *Police: Street corner politicians*. Chicago: University of Chicago Press.

Nairn, Tom. 1997. *Faces of nationalism: Janus revisited*. London: Verso.

Obeid, El Halli, and Laura L. B. Weisenberg. 2003. Case studies in social dialogue in the public emergency services—Argentina. ILO Sectoral Activities Programme Working Paper no. 193, Geneva, Switzerland, International Labor Organization.

O'Brien, Kevin M. 1994. Determinants of political activity by police unions. *Journal of Collective Negotiations* 23 (3): 265-78.

O'Malley, Pat. 2005. Converging corporatisation? Police management, police unionism, and the transfer of business principles. Paper presented the Centre for Market and Public Organisation, University of Bristol, UK, September.

Peccei, Ricardo, and David Guest. 2002. Trust, exchange and virtuous circles of cooperation: A theoretical and empirical analysis of operations at work. Research Paper 011, the Management Centre, Kings College, University of London.

Pike, Andrew, Peter O'Brien, and John Tomaney. 2004. Trade unions in local and regional development and governance: The Northern Trades Union Congress in North East England. *Local Economy* 19:102-16.

Police and Prisons Civil Rights Union (POPCRU). 2004. Constitutional Amendments, Resolutions and Programme of Action, Book 4, 5th National Congress, June.

Portland Press Herald. 2005. Police unions serve public by demanding investigation's results. October 10. http://pressherald.mainetoday.com/ (accessed November 15, 2005).

Prasad, Satendra, and Darryn Snell. 2004. The sword of justice: South Pacific trade unions and NGOs during a decade of lost development. *Development in Practice* 14:267-79.

Reiner, Robert. 1978. *The blue coated worker: A sociological study of police unionism.* London: Cambridge University Press.

———. 1992. *The politics of the police.* London: Harvester Wheatsheaf.

Robinson, Ian. 2000. Neoliberal restructuring and US unions: Toward social movement unionism? *Critical Sociology* 26 (1-2): 107-37.

Sklansky, David L. 2005a. Democratic policing inside and out. Manuscript.

———. 2005b. Police and democracy. *Michigan Law Review* 4:1699-1830.

Swanton, Bruce. 1982. *Protecting the protectors.* Canberra: Australian Institute of Criminology.

Sykes, Gary W. 1986. Automation, management and the police role: The new reformers? *Journal of Police Science and Administration* 14 (1): 24-30.

Tattersall, Amanda. 2004. Union-community coalitions and community unionism: Developing a framework for the role of union-community relationships in union renewal. Paper submitted to the International Colloquium on Union Renewal Conference HEC Montreal, Montreal, Quebec, Canada, November 18-20.

Van Heerden, T. J. 1982. *Introduction to police science.* Pretoria: University of South Africa Press.

von Holdt, Karl. 2002. Social movement unionism: The case of South Africa. *Work, Employment and Society* 16 (2): 283-304.

Voss, Kim, and Rachel Sherman. 2000. Breaking the iron law of oligarchy: Union revitalization in the American labor movement. *American Journal of Sociology* 106 (2): 303-49.

Waddington, Peter A. J. 1999. Police canteen (sub) culture. *British Journal of Criminology* 39:287-309.

Walhout, Donald. 1957. Is and ought. *Journal of Philosophy* 54 (2): 42-48.

Washo, B. 1984. Effecting planned change within a police organization. *The Police Chief*, November, pp. 33-35.

Waterman, Peter. 2004. Trade unions, NGOs and global social justice: Another tale to tell. Manuscript.

Webster, E., and R. Lambert. 2003. What is new in the new labour internationalism: A southern perspective. Paper presented at the seminar series in the Department of Sociology at the Rand Afrikaans University, Johannesburg, South Africa, March 7.

Weekly News Update on the Americas. 1997. "Open your eyes": Day of protest in Brazil. Issue 391, July 27.

Wills, J. 2001. Community unionism and trade union renewal in the UK: Moving beyond the fragments at last? *Transactions of the Institute of British Geographers* 26:465-83.

Wood, J. R. T. 1997. *Royal Commission into the New South Wales Police Service, final report.* Vols. 1-3. Sydney, Australia: New South Wales Police Integrity Commission.

Wooding, J., C. Levenstein, and B. Rosenberg. 1997. The Oil, Chemical and Atomic Workers International Union: Refining strategies for labor. *International Journal of Health Services* 27 (1): 125-38.

SECTION THREE:

*Democracy and the
Governance of Security:
Safe Societies and
Strong Democracy*

Policing, Recognition, and Belonging

By
IAN LOADER

In this article, the author reflects on the question of how policing institutions can help to foster and sustain the values and practices of democracy. The author's overarching concern is to outline and defend a conception of democratic policing that highlights the role of policing agencies in recognizing the legitimate claims of all individuals and groups affected by police actions and affirming their sense of belonging to a political community. From this perspective, the author offers a critique of certain prominent forms of what he calls "ambient policing" and aims to cast some new light on the issue of how policing contributes to—or undermines— citizen security in democratic societies.

Keywords: policing; security; political community; membership; democracy

Individuals do not fear only bodily torture and cruelty, they fear social oppression, marginalization and, worst of all, invisibility. They dread being intimidated, suppressed or exploited not only as individuals but also as members of disadvantaged groups.

—Tamir (1997, 302)

Over the past decade or so, we have witnessed a dramatic expansion in the number and scope of multinational police operations in postconflict societies and "weak" or "failed" states—from

Ian Loader is a professor of criminology at the University of Oxford and director of the Oxford Centre for Criminology. He has in recent years written extensively on the topics of policing and security and public sensibilities toward crime, order, and justice. His publications include Youth, Policing and Democracy *(1996, Palgrave);* Crime and Social Change in Middle England *(2000, Routledge, with Evi Girling and Richard Sparks); and* Policing and the Condition of England: Memory, Politics and Culture *(2003, Oxford University Press, with Aogan Mulcahy). He is currently working on a book— with Neil Walker—on the idea of security and its relationship to political community.*

NOTE: I would like to thank David Bradley, Martin Innes, Susanne Karstedt, Gary LaFree, Clifford Shearing, Richard Sparks, and Neil Walker for their comments on earlier versions of this article.

DOI: 10.1177/0002716206286723

Haiti and East Timor to Bosnia and Kosovo (Oakley, Dziedzic, and Goldberg 2002; Wilson 2006 [this volume]). One significant and revealing dimension of these operations is the claim—albeit often an ideological one—that the required police task involves not merely keeping a lid on crime and disorder or tracking down criminals but also promoting the rule of law, a culture of human rights, and what David Bayley (2001, 13) terms "democratic political development." What is revealing about this is the way in which policing institutions are saddled in these settings with liberal democratic purposes that are lost sight of, or even actively disputed, "back home" in contexts where democracy appears to be more securely in place. When, after all, did one last hear a U.S., or British, or Italian police officer proclaim that his or her job is to contribute to "democratic political development" or see protecting the rule of law and respect for human rights listed as one of the police's core functions?

When . . . did one last hear a U.S., or British, or Italian police officer proclaim that his or her job is to contribute to "democratic political development"?

I want in this article to bring under the spotlight, and subject to critical reflection, this often complacently taken-for-granted topic of how policing institutions contribute to the production and flourishing of the values and practices of democracy. In so doing, my guiding concern is to spell out a conception of democratic policing that views the overarching purpose of police institutions to be that of pursuing their crime control and social ordering tasks in ways that *recognize* the legitimate claims of all individuals and groups affected by police actions and affirm their sense of *belonging* to a democratic political community. Having done this, I address the question of the institutional mechanisms that are required to give practical effect to democratic policing so understood—mechanisms whose purpose is to ensure that the competing demands for order made in contemporary multicultural societies are responded to in ways that sustain, rather than undermine, considerations of equity and democracy.

The argument takes the form of three broad claims, each of which involves consideration of how—if one centers equity and democracy in this manner—one can best understand the nexus between policing and security. I begin by taking issue with contemporary forms of what I call "ambient policing." I argue that ambient police strategies—such as community, broken windows, and problem-oriented policing—radically misconstrue the contribution that policing institutions can make to security in democratic societies. These strategies rest, in particular, on a *shallow* but *wide* understanding of the police-security relation that runs the risk of making security institutions, practices, and discourse—and hence insecurity— a *pervasive* feature of everyday life.

I then outline an alternative perspective that extends and develops the idea that policing is a social institution whose routine ordering and cultural work communicates authoritative meanings to individuals and groups about who they are, about whether their voices are heard and claims recognized, and about where and in what ways they belong. These routine—identity denying and affirming— policing practices consequently play a significant part in reinforcing or else undermining the sense of security that flows from a feeling of effortless, confident membership of a political community (Margalit and Raz 1994, 118).

In developing and illustrating this perspective, I offer an account of the policing-security nexus that is *deep* (policing is, sociologically speaking, fundamental to people's sense of security) but *narrow* (police institutions should be reactive, minimal agencies of last resort) and consider the forms of institutional design and politics that are prerequisite to making security an *axiomatic*—rather than pervasive— ingredient of the lived social relations of democratic polities.

Ambient Policing, Pervasive Insecurity

In striving to understand the security work that policing institutions perform in multicultural democracies, we are faced with two contrasting developments. In one part of the woods, governmental and police actors appear to be confronting the demands and conflicts that attend the question of policing ethnically and socially diverse societies in ways that sustain considerations of equity and social justice. This is in part the outcome of the claims for recognition pressed upon police institutions by feminist, ethnic minority, and gay and lesbian movements over the past three decades. It has been fuelled by intermittent scandals concerning police mistreatment of ethnic minority individuals and groups—notably the beating of Rodney King in the United States and, in the United Kingdom, the professionally incompetent and institutionally racist conduct of the investigation into the murder of black teenager Stephen Lawrence. And it has been given new urgency by the conflicts around security and identity that have surfaced in the wake of 9/11 and the Madrid and London bombings. The result has been a move to address and improve the historically tense relations between the police and disadvantaged groups, albeit one that remains halting, uneven, and deeply contested.[1]

But these concerns stand in the shadow of a family of policing strategies that appeal to some powerful constituencies and their yearning for security, and resonate with certain deeply rooted popular sensibilities about the forms of policing that may best deliver it. Some of these—"quality of life," "broken windows," or "zero-tolerance" policing—draw inspiration and guidance from Wilson and Kelling's (1982) influential, if controversial, account of the connection between policing and neighborhood disorder (cf. Kelling and Coles 1996; Harcourt 2001). Others—"community," or "multiagency," or "problem-oriented" policing—proffer a critique of police reacting willy-nilly to calls from the public, proposing instead that they "join-up" with other agencies in search of holistic solutions to social problems of which crime and disorder are symptoms (cf. Goldstein 1990; Brogden and Nijhar 2005). Their latest incarnation in Britain—"reassurance" or "neighborhood" policing—aims to redress what is alleged to have become the insecurity-generating remoteness of police authority from everyday life (Innes 2004a). There are, to be sure, some significant differences between these approaches—matters of internal dispute that are not my concern in this article. But they also exhibit certain features in common sufficient for them to be considered together for present purposes under the heading of *ambient policing*. By this I mean strategies that share an express or implied commitment to raising overall numbers of policing operatives (whether employed by the police, the local state, or the private sector), coupled with a conception of the policing purpose that is expansive, proactive, and visible. So let us—taking an important recent article by Martin Innes (2004a) as our point of departure—critically examine the claims that underpin the theory and practice of ambient policing.

Innes (2004a) argued that four connected purposes and techniques underpin what in Britain has come to be known as "reassurance policing." First, to reduce the social distance that has developed between police and public. This is to be done by increasing the supply of visible, accessible, and familiar police authority (Povey 2001) and assembling neighborhood policing teams that can supply a policing service fitted to today's higher, more demanding customer expectations. Second, meeting public "needs and expectations" by identifying and targeting the problems that matter most to them and responding with proactive, multiagency, problem-solving interventions that aim to stimulate informal social control mechanisms with a view to coproducing strong, cohesive communities.[2] Third, creating an "extended police family" that joins up a range of policing (police, wardens, private security firms, antisocial behavior units) and other agencies (housing, social services, youth offending teams) in local social control activities coordinated by the public police (Johnston 2003). In this vein, Innes (2004a, 165) recommended the formation of "local control hubs" at the center of which will be the police constable—a vertical model of governing authority that responds to the pluralization of security providers by seeking to place the public police in a pivotal position as both providers and regulators—"coordinating and in effect steering the allocation of policing services" (p. 166). Fourth, seeking by these means to assemble a "total policing philosophy" (encompassing reassurance, crime management, public order strategy, intelligence gathering, national security, etc.), the specific purpose of which is to enhance neighborhood security through "perceptual interventions" (Ditton and Innes 2005) that alter both objective conditions inside neighborhoods and the ways in which problems are interpreted by individuals (Innes et al. 2004, 38).

In developing the argument that I have briefly summarized here, Innes (2004a) made two claims that, broadly speaking, I share: first, he proposed a concept of security that folds together an objective (or intersubjective) dimension concerned with the existence of threats in one's environment and a subjective dimension concerned with individuals' perception of the risks posed by that environment. Second, he brought into focus the symbolic dimensions of policing—the capacity of police practices to generate and communicate powerful social meanings (or what he called "control signals"). Yet Innes remained, in my view, insufficiently attentive to the full implications of these insights, for reasons I detail below. In addition, he deployed a further distinction—between "ontological" and "material" security—in ways that I find problematic. The former, he argued, is concerned with existential issues to do with identity and belonging (the question, "Who am I?")— matters, he strongly implied, that lie beyond the reach of policing. The latter has as its ambit "pragmatic" issues to do with threats to person and property (the question, "Am I safe?") and constitutes, for Innes, the organizing motif of neighborhood policing (pp. 158-59). For by increasing the supply of visible, active police authority, reassurance policing "signals the presence of a situated mechanism for the protection and restoration of social order should it be threatened. It gives the public an aura of protection in insecure times" (Innes et al. 2004, 222).

[Public demands for order are] not infrequently motivated by parochial desires for injustice, xenophobic antipathy toward others, or unattainable fantasies of absolute security.

Much may be said about these constitutive elements of Innes's (2004a) variant of ambient policing, as well as about the political and cultural conditions in which these police strategies have been mobilized and attracted support. But I want to limit my remarks to those aspects that are germane to my overarching purpose— that of deepening our understanding of how policing contributes to security in democratic societies. Here four critical observations are worth elucidating.

First, ambient policing tends too readily to presume that public demands for order (and for more, visible police protection) are entirely benign. This is an improbable depiction. That many individuals today are or feel insecure and make demands for greater policing resources can hardly be disputed. But these demands seldom take shape merely as measured calls for action based upon cool, sober calculations of risk. Rather, public sensibilities toward, and demands for, order are often laced with emotions (anger, resentment, fear, anticipated pleasure, etc.); situated in narratives about the trajectory of one's personal biography or the past, present, and possible futures of one's local or national community (Girling, Loader, and Sparks 2000); and not infrequently motivated by parochial desires for injustice, xenophobic antipathy toward others, or unattainable fantasies of absolute security (Markell 2003). When, in other words, people speak of crime and disorder, and make claims for this or that level of security provision, they are always also giving voice to a series of fears about, and hopes for, the political community in which they live and to the insecurities that flow from their sense of place within it. They may do so, moreover, in ways that are by no means conducive to what I have suggested is the overarching purpose of democratic policing, or—on the surface at any rate—consistent with the idea that security is a right available, by reason of their membership alone, to all members of that community.

[Ambient policing confuses] questions of democratic governance with those of proximity, visibility, and unmediated responsiveness and [collapses] the former into the latter.

Second, ambient policing assumes that the demands of consumers or citizens for particular styles and levels of policing can and ought to be met. This is an implausible aim. Such demands lay claim to resources that are finite and have to be funded and prioritized. They may articulate competing visions of what policing objectives and styles should be. They are often pressed by middle-class constituencies replete with economic and social capital in ways that risk distributing policing resources in inverse relation to crime risks (Hope, Karstedt, and Farrall 2001). And they make claims that are not easily sated in the terms in which they are presented—claims that all too easily result in a vicious, self-propelling circle whereby popular demands, and the numbers of police supplied in a bid to meet them, are both endlessly ratcheted up. Yet at the same time, demands for public policing express forms of solidarity toward strangers and an implicit attachment to the idea of public provision. They indicate, in turn, a prior commitment to putting security in common and pursuing it through democratic institutions and practices—a commitment to the exercise of "voice" rather than "exit" (Hirschman 1970). All this, rather than pointing in the direction of uncritically seeking to satisfy public demands for policing in the name of "citizen focus" or "consumer responsiveness," suggests that such demands are best recognized by being brought within institutional arrangements that subject them, and their supporting narratives and resource claims, to the scrutiny of democratic dialogue (Crawford 2006). Too much ambient policing discourse forgets this, confusing questions of democratic governance with those of proximity, visibility, and unmediated responsiveness and collapsing the former into the latter.[3]

Third, ambient police strategies evince little express concern with the interests of the routinely policed—those once graphically referred to as "police property" (Lee 1981). They tend to efface questions to do with public consent to, and the regulation of, police power and devote insufficient thought to the central paradox of policing and its consequences—namely, that as a monopolist of coercive resources, the police stand simultaneously as a guarantor of, and threat to, citizen security (Walker 2000, chap. 1). This is especially pronounced, and not especially surprising, in official discourse on neighborhood policing, with its rhetorical talk of "the law-abiding citizen" driving police reform (Home Office 2004, 43). But one finds the same omissions—and, implicitly, the same majority constituencies being mobilized and appealed to—in academic defenses of community and related forms of ambient policing. In these defenses, academics assume complacently that all social groups find policing interventions benign, welcome, and reassuring. Innes (2004a) risked reproducing, in other words, the silence about police disorder that has long been strikingly common among advocates of community, "broken windows" and other forms of ambient policing (Harcourt 2001, 138-39). In so doing, he proceeded as if some antique questions to do with constraining and regulating police power, and some still vexed problems pertaining to police relations with disadvantaged groups, have somehow been settled, or ceased to matter.

Fourth, advocates of ambient policing strategies radically misconstrue the contribution that policing most fundamentally makes to citizen security in a democracy. The police relation to security is, on this view, *shallow* but *wide*. It is "shallow" insofar as that contribution is limited to a claim to be able to protect persons, property, and neighborhoods from the threat of crime and disorder. Policing in this sense is oriented to answering the question, "How safe am I?" rather than toward any more encompassing notion of ontological security. It is "wide" because, conceived as such, the police's contribution to public security lies principally in the visible display and activation of police authority in local social relations. Security, on this view, depends on the unmediated presence of uniformed officers. The greater their numbers, the more visible, familiar, and active they are, the more secure individuals will be or, as important, feel. The problem here is that, by seeking to deliver security through the police-centered strategy of supplying greater visible policing, and making the police constable pivotal to community building and cohesion, ambient policing strategies risk making security a *pervasive* feature of social and political life—indeed, it is this in part that warrants the description of them as ambient.

Security may be said to be "pervasive" when it becomes the prevailing discourse for understanding social problems, the lens through which they are defined, examined, and acted upon. It is pervasive when it begins, in these ways, to acquire a certain colonizing force, or "everywhereness," when its claims and values (to take "tough" policing and punishment-centered measures to protect "us" from "them") prevail in areas of public life and policy (housing, or education, or youth work) where they have no proper business. When security becomes pervasive, it generally coincides with a sense of impatience and urgency; with calls for the unhindered, speedy hand and visible display of executive authority; with deepening levels of intolerance toward minority groups and practices; and with evident frustration at, and calls for the curtailment of, basic rights and liberties. When security practices and discourse take this form, one can usually be sure that individuals are, in fact, feeling insecure. The practices of pervasive security also generally do little to confront the conditions generating that insecurity and much that serves to fuel and deepen it. A vicious—insecurity-sustaining—circle is thereby joined.

Democratic policing supplies . . . a small but vital component of the resources of secure belonging.

In failing either to apprehend ambient policing as an outcome of this form of security politics, or to register its tendency to entrench further a dominant culture of pervasive security, Innes (2004a) failed to appreciate fully the import of the subjective dimension of security that he was otherwise so attentive toward. For once we encompass this dimension (and in so doing distinguish security from notions such as order, safety, and protection), one can see that public security inheres not only in individuals' relative immunity from threat ("Am I safe?"). Security inheres, rather, in the capacity of individuals and groups to feel at ease with the threats that their environment poses, such that they do not, on an everyday basis, have to think about how safe they are, or routinely concern themselves with the effectiveness of the security measures that are in place, or constantly be bothered with whether and how these may need to be bolstered. To be secure, as opposed to simply safe, is to be comfortable in, and with, one's environment and hence free from the burdens of recurring security work (Loader and Walker 2006). Ambient policing, for the reasons I have set out, risks reproducing social and political conditions that are inimical to these elements of what one may call *axiomatic* security. By treating security as an unmediated relation between police and citizen that requires the former to be routinely displayed in front of the latter, and by pandering to, rather than calling into question, popular fantasies of total security, ambient policing makes security pervasive in ways that, in the end, foster and sustain the very insecurity it purports to tackle.

Security, Recognition, and Belonging:
The Cultural Work of Policing
in Democratic Societies

A decent society must not develop or support on an institutional level any symbols that are directed explicitly or implicitly against some of the citizens of the state.
                                                                           —Margalit (1996, 161)

Security—I have suggested above and argued elsewhere (Loader and Walker 2006)—has both intersubjective and subjective dimensions. It has to do with the levels of trust one has in one's environment, whether in terms of the strangers one lives among, or the measures that are put in place to ensure the safety of person and property. The thresholds individuals develop for enabling them to feel routinely at ease with the threats posed by that environment depend not only on the "objective" scale of those threats but also on their sense of attachment to, and confident, effortless membership of, a political community. This sense of belonging is in large measure mediated by and through the institutions of that community and flows from the experience and expectation individuals have that those institutions recognize their legitimate rights, entitlements, and loyalties. Security, in short, is not only a matter of material risk. It has to do with the resources individuals and groups possess for managing the unease and uncertainty that the risks present in their environment generate—and these resources differ in amount according to people's sense of their place within that environment.

Two things follow from thinking about security in this "thick," sociological sense—one that has been touched upon already, a second that I want now to develop. First, that no helpful, or even meaningful, distinction can be drawn between "material" and "ontological" security—between the questions, "How safe am I?" and "Who am I?" Second, that the delivery and regulation of policing, far from having little to contribute to security in this "thick" sense, lies in fact at its "coal-face": being implicated in sociologically fundamental ways in people's social fears about "oppression, marginalization and, worst of all, invisibility" (Tamir 1997, 302) or, conversely, in the sense that their claims are being recognized, that they meaningfully belong as full citizens to the society in which they reside, and that in these respects they possess the resources necessary to be and remain secure. Democratic policing supplies, in other words, a small but vital component of the resources of secure belonging (see, also Karstedt 2006 [this volume]).

To press this point further, let us explore more fully the *cultural* work performed by policing institutions—the ways in which they generate not only social order but also social meaning. As one of the "active centers of the social order" (Geertz 1983, 122), state policing routinely produces and communicates an array of authoritative (if rarely uncontested) meanings regarding such matters as order/disorder, justice/injustice, normality/deviance, inclusion/exclusion, "us"/"them" (Loader and Mulcahy 2003, chap. 2). In so doing, it operates in ways that condition individual subjectivities and their constitutive dispositions (Harcourt 2001, chaps. 5-6)—helping to shape the manner in which people think, feel, and act in relation to problems of crime and disorder, their causes, and their effects. But policing also operates as a mediator of collective identity, a social institution through which recognition and misrecognition are relayed, a sender of resonant—sometimes coercive—signals about whose voices are to be heard or silenced, whose claims are to be judged legitimate, how and in what ways individuals and groups belong (Fraser 2003, 29). This is not only or mainly a matter of overt police symbolism, though—as the case of divided societies such as Northern Ireland attests—police oaths, uniforms, flag flying, and the like can be deeply vexed and highly charged matters (Ellison and Smyth 2000). Rather, it permeates all police talk and action (and police talk *as* action)—from the utterances and interventions of individual officers to the aggregate distribution of the burdens and benefits of policing among social groups. Every stop, every search, every arrest, every group of youths moved on, every abuse of due process, every failure to respond to call or complaint, every racist snub, every sexist remark, every homophobic joke, every diagnosis of the crime problem, every depiction of criminals—all these send small, routine, authoritative signals about society's conflicts, cleavages, and hierarchies, about whose claims are considered legitimate within it, about whose status identity is to be affirmed or denied as part of it (cf. Sparks and Bottoms 1995, 60). The police, in short, are both minders and *re*minders of community (Walker 2002, 315)—a producer of significant messages about the kind of place that community is or aspires to be.

Much contemporary analysis of the cultural dimensions of police—and by extension state—power tends, not improperly, to focus on its negative side—its repressive or exclusionary properties and effects. In so doing, it has brought more fully into view the fact that policing institutions are often systematically oriented to maintaining dominant societal interests and values (that is, "specific" as well as "general order" [Marenin 1982]) in ways that foster and reproduce insecurity among members of economically and socially disadvantaged groups. Two illustrations serve to make the point.

One can refer first to the ways in which policing institutions are elevated to the status of revered national symbols such that they become the object of almost sacred, uncritical devotion from certain majority constituencies. In some contexts, this valorization of the police (coupled often with a fierce determination to deny malpractice or condone abuses of police power) comes to be entangled with its role in defending "our" community, or culture, or nation against others—an outcome not infrequently associated with police coercion being directed at minority populations. The close, affective link between the Royal Ulster Constabulary and the Protestant majority in Northern Ireland is a good case in point here, as is the Rodney King case. But one can also highlight the ways in which the police are implicated in hegemonic national histories and dominant renditions of national identity in ways that expressly or implicitly denigrate or misrecognize minority—immigrant or indigenous—populations. The warm association made by elements of English society between the "bobby on the beat" and a nostalgic image of a lost white England is a notable instance of this—and arguably one from which ambient policing draws much of its cultural allure (Loader and Mulcahy 2003, chaps. 3-5). So too is the way in which the Mounties figure in representations of the founding and self-image of Canada that efface the historical experience of indigenous minority groups (Walden 1982). In each case, what one encounters is the use of the police as a symbol that forges and gives effect to a shared identification with a "national community," but in ways "liable to make members of the minority feel actively rejected by the society" (Margalit 1996, 160).

One may note, second, how routine police utterances and practices can operate to communicate powerful exclusion signals, practices that indicate that particular groups—teenage boys, or black males, or Muslims—are not to be considered full members of society. The patterns of oversuspicion and underprotection that have long marked police relations with disadvantaged groups send an oblique signal of just this kind. So too do discriminatory patterns of arrest, or stop and search, or the police's failure to deal properly with cases of male or racist violence, or police pronouncements associating this or that ethnic or social group with crime and disorder. These forms of misrecognition or denigration of "morally legitimate encompassing groups" (Margalit and Raz 1994) represent acts of symbolic violence that themselves contribute to the lack of belonging, and the attendant feelings of insecurity, experienced by members of such groups. But they also create an environment conducive to acts of material violence toward members of those groups (and hence insecurity in its intersubjective sense) by sending an authoritative signal that such individuals lie beyond the security concerns of "our" community, that they are not fully "one of us," that they are somehow "fair game." Jacob Levy (2000, 25) made this connection between symbolic and material violence extremely well:

> When we humiliate someone—either individually or as a member of some larger collective—we make subsequent cruelty to that person easier, for ourselves and for others. If a person or group of persons is routinely referred to, thought of, and treated as demons, objects, machines, animals, or otherwise subhuman, physical cruelty is a short leap away.

These cases offer what are well-documented instances of the ways in which policing can enact or support forms of cultural domination, nonrecognition, and disrespect (Fraser 2003) in ways that conduce to both objective and subjective insecurity. They demonstrate that certain "tough" styles of ambient policing can appear to reduce crime or produce order while contributing to public insecurity through unfair practices that undermine the sense of secure belonging felt by certain individuals and social or ethnic groups (Harcourt 2001). This, in turn, can erode or undermine the commitments of those groups to the common democratic institutions that can best foster forms of axiomatic security in multicultural democracies, leading them to eschew the difficult work of building and sustaining such institutions in favor of particularistic, parochial practices that aim to make members of such minorities safe in the absence of any confident sense of security.

Yet if one accepts this reading of the symbolic power of the police and its dele-terious effects (and plenty in the historical and contemporary record supports it), one is bound also to acknowledge that alternative readings and effects are possi-ble, that the cultural work of policing can be performed in ways that contribute positively to security conceptualized in sociological terms as a "thick" public good (Loader and Walker 2006). In exploring these alternative associations between policing and the social, one can make explicit and begin to thematize what is an obvious, but often occluded, dimension of the police-security nexus in democra-tic societies—namely, that the contribution of the former to the latter lies not in controlling crime or preventing disorder per se (for this can be done in ways that reduce police legitimacy and increase public insecurity), but in performing crime control and order maintenance tasks in ways that sustain the conditions of a democratic common life in which the security of all individuals and groups can best flourish. Once understood thus, three significant elements come into view.

It indicates, first, that human rights and controls on police power, on one hand, and arrangements for the democratic governance of policing agencies, on the other, are both vital to public security. The former are not unwarranted and unwanted burdens on the police, unnecessary curtailments of their capacity to "fight crime" effectively (accusations typically leveled in police, media, and lay discourse). Nor do such rights exist solely to protect individuals from the power of the state. They are, rather, preconditions for the police being able to con-tribute positively to citizen *security* in a democratic society and ought to be artic-ulated and defended as such. Similarly, regulatory mechanisms for ensuring public oversight of, and consent to, policing priorities and practices are neither secondary to, nor separable from, the "core" police tasks of controlling crime and disorder—as, for instance, is often said in the European policing arena where the development of seemingly "less pressing" accountability mechanisms routinely lags behind the "urgent" task of building new police agencies such as Europol inside the EU (den Boer 2002). Policing cannot adequately contribute to the realization and protection of political freedom, to sustaining forms of democratic common life, and in these terms to the security of citizens, without police gover-nance arrangements being treated and acted upon as an indispensable dimension of how policing in democratic societies is thought about and performed.

Second, it offers further reasons for thinking that democratic policing does not entail responding uncritically to publicly voiced "needs and expectations"; that such policing is not best theorized and practiced in terms of customer satisfaction; and that the encouragement and extension of a "consumer attitude" (Bauman 1990, 203-4) to policing, and commercial markets in security provision, is inimical to the production and maintenance of security as an axiomatic feature of social life. Policing agencies cannot, in socially and ethnically plural societies, become conduits for majority concerns and demands, attuned only or mainly to the claims of the wealthy, active, noisy, well connected, or organized. If policing is to be capable of recogniz-ing, rather than denigrating or silencing, the security claims of *all* citizens, and in this way fostering a sense of common belonging, the task is to create what Charles Taylor (2000, 281) suggestively called a "shared identity space"—institutional arenas in which competing demands can be listened to, argued about, and negotiated on a recurrent basis. Bringing the claims of anxious, disgruntled majorities and insecure, misrecognized minorities into common democratic processes of this kind may even help to dispel the forms of *ressentiment* that fuel the contemporary cultural politics of pervasive security (Tully 2000, 479).

Third, it emphasizes why the question of police relations with ethnic minority and other disadvantaged populations cannot be handled as if these are marginal or secondary to "core" police activity, hived off to specialist community or public relations divisions, or treated as episodic crises that have to be managed in order that normal business can be resumed. Any policing supplier that is to contribute meaningfully to public security in multicultural societies has to confront the question of its relations with disadvantaged groups on a continuing basis, such that it becomes institutionally embedded in policing agencies and their working cultures and central to the purposes of the regulatory bodies that scrutinize them. This is so with respect to addressing the pattern of oversuspicion and underprotection that has long characterized the distribution of policing benefits and burdens among ethnic minority and socially disadvantaged groups. It is also the case with respect to the fairness with which citizens are or are not treated in their encounters with policing operatives—questions of procedural justice that, as Tom Tyler (1990) has shown, are causally related both to people's compliance with the law and the degree of legitimacy they accord to the police and criminal justice agencies. Policing bodies that are committed to contributing positively to citizen security must, in short, be required to attend routinely to the distributive pattern and situational enactment of their coercive and symbolic power. Only by so doing can they become what John Keane (2004, 140) called "a public affirmation of civility."

I can now begin to condense these considerations into a revised, more sociologically plausible and normatively compelling, formulation of the policing-security nexus—one that recognizes the indispensable and positive contribution the state's capacity to deliver and regulate policing makes to citizen security (what one may call its necessary virtues) but understands that contribution in radically different ways to that which underpins ambient policing. This revised conception is best described as *deep* but *narrow*. The contribution policing makes to security is "deep" insofar as it can and does provide individuals with a powerful token of their membership of a political community in ways that afford them the material and symbolic resources required to manage, and feel relatively at ease with, the threats that they encounter in the settings of their everyday life. The public delivery and/or regulation of policing both expresses and gives effect to the idea of a society as an ongoing collective project that puts and pursues security in common, one that enables individuals to derive a stable identity and sense of security from their effortless, confident membership of, and attachment to, that political community. Policing, in other words, *does* in a limited but profound way help individuals to answer such questions as "Where do I belong?" "Who cares about me?" and, ultimately, "Who am I?"

The policing contribution to citizen security is "narrow" insofar as it does not require police actors to be supplied in ever-greater numbers, or to be displayed in front of, or known to, the citizenry. Rather, it flows from the confident, tacit assurance that policing institutions can be called upon to recognize and respond to public concerns in ways that demonstrate that (1) they are answerable to democratically negotiated priorities that all affected constituencies can see themselves as having played a part in authoring and (2) they respect the human rights and minority interests that are constitutive of the democratic common life that supplies its participants with their sense of shared identity and secure belonging. In other words, policing institutions contribute both to public security and to the getting and keeping of democracy as—and by remaining—constrained, reactive, rights-regarding agencies of minimal interference and last resort (Kinsey, Lea, and Young 1986, chap. 9). Their value in producing social order and solidarity is a mediated effect of the regulatory arrangements in place to ensure that police work is performed according to the above two stipulations, not something that flows from unmediated efforts to satisfy the demands of anxious citizen-consumers. This, I want to suggest, is how policing can best assist in making security, not an all-pervasive preoccupation of the insecure, but an axiomatic element of the lived social relations of democratic societies.

Axiomatic Security, Minimal Policing: Turning Vicious into Virtuous Circles

We cannot expect the outcome of democratic politics to be just in a society that contains large numbers of people who feel no sense of empathy with their fellow citizens and do not have any identification with their lot. This sense of solidarity is fostered by common institutions.

—Barry (2001, 79)

To make security axiomatic is, as I have indicated, to create conditions in which individuals possess an effortless, confident attachment to a political community in ways that enable them to feel routinely at ease with the threats posed by the settings of their everyday lives. It is to effect a situation in which individuals are able to "go on" in those settings without having to think routinely about how secure they are. Making security axiomatic thus depends not only or mainly on the production of safer environments—though the higher the levels of material threat posed by that environment, the more difficult it is to be or feel at ease within it. It has much more to do with individuals possessing the degree of tacit trust in the institutional arrangements that are put in place to provide for their security that enables their own security work to remain unobtrusive and unonerous—a matter of "practical" rather than "discursive" consciousness (Giddens 1984).

These conditions of objective and intersubjective security are only partially and unevenly to be found in late modern societies—notably, but by no means only, in the United States and Britain—that evince marked economic and social inequalities coupled with heightened levels of public consciousness toward crime

(Garland 2001). In these settings, the project of making security axiomatic confronts lived social relations and media and political cultures in which security has become, or been made, pervasive, as well as the vicious—insecurity-sustaining—circles that surface when social and political life assumes this form. The practices of pervasive security display a powerful tendency to atrophy the conditions of possibility for producing security in its more axiomatic sense, to prove and renew social anxiety, and to entrench and institutionalize insecurity in a manner that reproduces an ambient security politics.

Two such vicious circles warrant particular attention. Let us call the first an *authoritarian spiral*. It runs something like this. Individuals who live under conditions of pervasive insecurity tend to make demands for what they judge to be "tough" anticrime measures (more police, more police powers, crackdowns on this offence or those suspects, stiffer sentencing, harsher penal regimes, and so on) in ways that display impatience with informed democratic deliberation, seek to suspend or abandon basic rights, foster hostility toward minorities and outsiders, and risk melding their interests and identities with those of the state whose "protective" power they seek to mobilize. This process is vicious and circular because once such demands are met in the terms in which they are presented, it becomes difficult to create the political and cultural conditions wherein the pace of such measures can be slowed, or a change or reversal of direction effected—thereby effecting a potentially endless "ratcheting up" in police numbers, or incarceration rates, or curtailments of basic liberties. And if such actions are perceived to have "failed," or are ideologically depicted in those terms—because crime rates go up, or a child is abducted, or a group of youths run amok, or another terrorist outrage occurs—this overwhelmingly prompts calls for still "tougher" measures—only this time with a heavier dosage. A democracy- and liberty-eroding spiral is thus entered in ways it becomes hard to escape. A form of security politics gets entrenched that does much to put at risk democratic principles and basic rights, while doing little to make citizens either any safer or any more secure. As the "war on terror" is reminding us once again, anxious citizens make bad democrats (cf. Neumann 1957; Rorty 2004).

Let us call the second a *fragmentation spiral*. This runs broadly speaking like this. Individuals or social groups who feel insecure or unprotected by the state tend increasingly to search for alternative security solutions, either by organizing local forms of autonomous communal ordering (in corporate or residential enclaves or through citizen patrolling) or by turning to the market to purchase desired levels or types of security personnel and hardware (patrols, static guards, alarms, surveillance systems, etc.). The more widespread these practices become, the less willing such individuals and groups are to support, fund, and engage in dialogue about general forms of policing and security provision. This results in social fragmentation insofar as it erodes people's sense of being participants in an ongoing collective project whose members are committed to putting and pursuing security in common, which, in turn, undermines the "architecture of sympathy" (Sennett 2003, 200) through which this shared purpose takes practical shape. The security, and forms of political freedom, associated with the sense of belonging to, and identification with, a political community is thereby placed in jeopardy, and with it the collective capacity to forge and realize common purposes, including security purposes (Taylor 1995, chap. 7). Society fractures into a world of markets and tribes.

There is at present little shortage of evidence of these dynamics at work, as is attested by recent social analysis of the displacement of welfarist by penal modes of social ordering, on one hand (Parenti 1999; Pratt et al. 2005), and trends in the pluralization and commodification of security, on the other (Kempa et al. 1999; Crawford 2003). I have also argued that current preoccupations with ambient policing must in part be viewed as a response to the second of these trends, albeit one that sits rather too comfortably with the first. So how, then, can the vicious circles that characterize the practices of pervasive security be broken? Is it possible to envision more virtuous circles of the kind that will foster axiomatic security in multicultural democracies, and what forms of institutional design and politics may best facilitate their creation?

I can do no more in conclusion to this article than sketch in necessarily brief and abstract terms the outlines of an answer to these questions. That answer requires in my view that—while acknowledging and seeking to counter the negative propensities of the state, its heavy implication in contemporary practices of pervasive security—we also register the necessary and virtuous ordering work that the state can perform in helping to effect social relations in which security is more axiomatic. We need to spell out, in particular, the regulatory functions that the state is alone or best equipped to enact with respect to producing forms of policing that *recognize* the security claims of all citizens and respond to them in ways that sustain rather than undermine their sense of secure *belonging*. Several aspects of this ordering work are worth emphasizing by way of conclusion.

The state is best equipped, first of all, to act as a meta-authority over what has today become a diverse range of public, commercial, and citizen policing actors in ways that coordinate the allocation of policing resources, ensure that all policing agencies answer to democratically negotiated priorities, and call such agencies to account for their performance. This form of vertical governance of plural policing is best conducted, not by the public police in ways that inevitably muddy the distinction between regulator and provider (cf. Blair 2002; Innes 2004a), but by new- and old-fashioned forms of public political authority tasked with dedicated regulatory functions in the security field. The broad purpose of such authority is to allocate policing resources in ways that—in Phillip Pettit's (2001) terms—track the "common avowable interests" of all affected parties—by which he meant interests that "are conscious or can be brought to consciousness without great effort" (as opposed to being imputed by regulatory bodies), and the product of "cooperatively admissible" (rather than selfish or parochial) considerations (p. 156). This, in turn, requires institutional processes that eliminate "false negatives" (the legitimate but unheard and disregarded claims of citizens) by searching for and including in democratic deliberation every relevant candidate for determining how security resources can be distributed in ways consistent with it being a public good and remove "false positives" by rigorously scrutinizing and disallowing claims that cannot reasonably be encompassed in any negotiated conception of common interest (p. 156-60). The competing demands for order and protection made by different social and ethnic groups are each in this way recognized—in democratic processes that offer to all citizens what Nancy Fraser (2003, 36) termed "parity of participation."

But ensuring all affected constituencies are given a voice in forms of public deliberation about the distribution and control of policing does not require "that we consider every possible demand for recognition as morally legitimate or acceptable" (Honneth 2003, 171). The politics of recognition cannot and should not mean this. It is precisely the burden of republican political forms of the kind that Pettit (2001) advocated that such claims are subject to practices of justification in the light of certain principles of public justice (Loader 2000), rules of the game that—in the present case—permit only those outcomes that broadly sustain the forms of democratic common life and respect for human rights that are indispensable to the secure belonging of all citizens in ethnically and socially pluralistic societies (cf. Patten 1999). The task, as such, is not to pretend that all claims can be acceded, that all can or will be winners. It is, rather, to engage citizens in public dialogue about policing in ways that enable them to see that the security and political freedom of each and all is more likely to be nurtured and protected through their participation with others in forms of common deliberation (the specific outcomes of which they may not always concur with) than by pursuing their own safety as individual "sovereign consumers" in the marketplace; or clubbing together within particularistic communities; or falling for the seductive security promises of strong, superficially responsive rulers.

It is, in sum, not the purpose of regulatory arrangements that aim to give effect to more axiomatic forms of security to be the servant of partisan or parochial interests, or to satisfy without scrutiny demands for order that may be motivated by desires for injustice, or xenophobic fears of the alien and unknown, or fantasies of absolute or sovereign security (Markell 2003). Their purpose, instead, is to subject those desires to the power of reflection, to make plastic the apparently fixed interests and social identities that sustain them, to encourage greater acknowledgement of our mutual vulnerabilities and codependencies, and in these ways to subject demands for order (or greater, visible policing) to democratic governance. This mode of regulatory politics must, in so doing, appeal to and mobilize those motivational feelings of identification with, and belonging to, a common political community that presently exist among members of such communities, and seek to deepen and extend the expressions of solidarity with strangers, and commitments to the security and political freedom of *all* citizens, that are an immanent part of people's sense of allegiance to an ongoing collective project. If we take this as our lodestar, we can better orient ourselves toward creating the forms of minimal, rights-regarding policing that can, materially and symbolically, underpin the confident assurance individuals draw from being recognized as part of the "common public culture" of a democratic polity (Miller 1995), instead of playing critical witness to strategies of ambient policing that fail to deliver the good of security to citizens and misconstrue the ways in which police institutions can help foster and sustain the values and practices of democracy.

Notes

1. The term "disadvantaged groups" clearly effaces the specific histories, experiences, and internal divisions of the range of such groups—such as economically dispossessed young men, women, blacks, Asians, Hispanics, gay men, and lesbians—whose relationships with the police have tended historically to be tense and that have in recent decades become politically problematized. It nonetheless remains useful, for present purposes at least, in focusing analytic attention on what economically, politically, and socially marginalized populations share in common in relation to social institutions in general and the police in particular. With respect to the latter, this has tended to include the police's systematic failure to listen attentively to the concerns and demands of disadvantaged groups, coupled with patterns of resource deployment that entail that members of these groups are overpoliced as suspects and underprotected as victims.

2. The "signal crimes perspective"—described by Innes et al. (2004, vxxii) as the "theoretical engine" behind reassurance policing—is accorded particular importance here (see, further, Innes 2004b). Signal crimes theory claims that criminal and disorderly events differ in the meanings that are given within, and the impact they have upon, particular localities, with some events being salient because they change the way in which people think, feel, or behave (signal crimes) or signify the presence of other risks (signal disorders). Signal crimes theory purports to offer, in this regard, a conceptual rationale and methodological toolkit for intelligently determining those incidents that take the greatest toll on neighborhood security (Innes et al. 2004, chaps. 3-4; cf. Skogan 1990; Kelling and Coles 1996).

3. Several commentators have argued recently that the illiberal and unquenchable characteristics of public demands for order and punishment mean that democratic governments urgently need to find or preserve ways of insulating criminal justice systems from popular—and especially populist—pressures (Pratt 2006; Zimring and Johnson 2006 [this volume]). It is my belief that this liberal elitist strategy of preserving criminal justice by protecting it *from* democracy is wrong in principle and likely to prove counterproductive in practice. The burden of this article is, instead, to try to think about how to supplement necessary forms of insulation to fashion democratic policing institutions that recognize the claims of diverse publics and are therefore minimally credible to these publics as entities they have played a part in authoring, without succumbing to the demands of the loud, well-organized, and angry or ushering forth illiberal, majoritarian outcomes. For a discussion of this position that engages more directly and critically with the "insulation model," see Loader (2006).

References

Barry, B. 2001. *Culture and equality: An egalitarian critique of multiculturalism.* Cambridge: Polity.

Bauman, Z. 1990. *Thinking sociologically.* Oxford: Basil Blackwell.

Bayley, D. 2001. *Democratizing the police abroad: What to do and how to do it.* Washington, DC: National Institute of Justice.

Blair, I. 2002. The policing revolution: Back to the beat. *New Statesman*, September 23, pp. 21-23.

Brogden, M., and P. Nijhar. 2005. *Community policing: National and international models and approaches.* Cullompton, UK: Willan.

Crawford, A. 2003. The pattern of policing in the UK: Policing beyond the police. In *Handbook of policing*, ed. T. Newburn. Cullompton, UK: Willan.

———. 2006. Reassurance policing: Seeing is believing. In *Police and public*, ed. D. Smith and A. Henry. Cullompton, UK: Willan.

den Boer, M. 2002. Towards an accountability regime for an emerging police governance. *Policing and Society* 12 (4): 275-90.

Ditton, J., and M. Innes. 2005. The role of perceptual intervention in the management of the fear of crime. In *Handbook of crime prevention*, ed. N. Tilley. Cullompton, UK: Willan.

Ellison, G., and J. Smyth. 2000. *The crowned harp: Policing Northern Ireland.* London: Pluto.

Fraser, N. 2003. Social justice in an age of identity politics: Redistribution, recognition and participation. In *Redistribution or recognition? A political-philosophical exchange*, ed. N. Fraser and A. Honneth. London: Verso.

Garland, D. 2001. *The culture of control: Crime and social order in contemporary society.* Oxford: Oxford University Press.

Geertz, C. 1983. *Local knowledge: Further essays in interpretive anthropology.* New York: Basic Books.

Giddens, A. 1984. *The constitution of society.* Cambridge: Polity.

Girling, E., I. Loader, and R. Sparks. 2000. *Crime and social change in Middle England: Questions of order in an English town.* London: Routledge.

Goldstein, H. 1990. *Problem-oriented policing.* London: McGraw-Hill.

Harcourt, B. 2001. *Illusion of order: The false promise of broken windows policing.* Cambridge, MA: Harvard University Press.

Hirschman, A. 1970. *Exit, voice and loyalty: Responses to decline in firms, organisations and states.* Cambridge, MA: Harvard University Press.

Home Office. 2004. *Building communities, beating crime: A better police service for the 21st century* (cm 6360). London: Home Office.

Honneth, A. 2003. Redistribution as recognition. In *Redistribution or recognition? A political-philosophical exchange,* ed. N. Fraser and A. Honneth. London: Verso.

Hope, T., S. Karstedt, and S. Farrall. 2001. *The relationship between calls and crimes.* London: Home Office.

Innes, M. 2004a. Reinventing tradition: Reassurance, neighbourhood security and policing. *Criminal Justice* 4 (2): 151-71.

———. 2004b. Signal crimes and signal disorders: Notes on deviance as communicative action. *British Journal of Sociology* 55 (3): 335-55.

Innes, M., S. Hayden, T. Lowe, H. MacKenzie, C. Roberts, and L. Twyman. 2004. *Signal crimes and reassurance policing.* Vol. 1, *Concepts and analysis.* Guildford, UK: University of Surrey.

Johnston, L. 2003. From "pluralisation" to "the extended police family": Discourses on the governance of community policing in Britain. *International Journal of the Sociology of Law* 31:185-204.

Karstedt, S. 2006. Democracy, values, and violence: Paradoxes, tensions, and comparative advantages of liberal inclusion. *Annals of the American Academy of Political and Social Science* 605:50-81.

Keane, J. 2004. *Democracy and violence.* Cambridge: Cambridge University Press.

Kelling, G., and C. Coles. 1996. *Fixing broken windows: Restoring order and reducing crime in our communities.* New York: Free Press.

Kempa, M., R. Carrier, J. Wood, and C. Shearing. 1999. Reflections on the evolving concept of "private policing." *European Journal on Criminal Policy and Research* 7:197-223.

Kinsey, R., J. Lea, and J. Young. 1986. *Losing the fight against crime.* Oxford: Basil Blackwell.

Lee, J. 1981. Some structural aspects of police deviance in relation to minority groups. In *Organizational police deviance,* ed. C. Shearing. Toronto, Canada: Butterworths.

Levy, J. 2000. *The multiculturalism of fear.* Oxford: Oxford University Press.

Loader, I. 2000. Plural policing and democratic governance. *Social and Legal Studies* 9 (3): 323-45.

———. 2006. Playing with fire? Democracy and the emotions of crime and punishment. In *Emotions, crime and justice,* ed. S. Karstedt, I. Loader, and H. Strang. Oxford: Hart.

Loader, I., and A. Mulcahy 2003. *Policing and the condition of England: Memory, politics and culture.* Oxford: Oxford University Press.

Loader, I., and N. Walker. 2006. Necessary virtues: The legitimate place of the state in the production of security. In *Democracy, society and the governance of security,* ed. J. Wood and B. Dupont. Cambridge: Cambridge University Press.

Marenin, O. 1982. Parking tickets and class repression: The concept of policing in critical theories of criminal justice. *Contemporary Crises* 6:241-66.

Margalit, A. 1996. *The decent society.* Cambridge, MA: Harvard University Press.

Margalit, A., and J. Raz. 1994. National self-determination. In *Ethics in the public domain,* ed. J. Raz. Oxford: Oxford University Press.

Markell, P. 2003. *Bound by recognition.* Princeton, NJ: Princeton University Press.

Miller, D. 1995. *On nationality.* Oxford: Oxford University Press.

Neumann, F. 1957. Anxiety and politics. In *The democratic and authoritarian state: Essays in political and legal theory,* ed. H. Marcuse. New York: Free Press.

Oakley, R., M. Dziedzic, and E. Goldberg, eds. 2002. *Policing the new world disorder: Peace operations and public security.* Honolulu, HI: University Press of the Pacific.

Parenti, C. 1999. *Lockdown America.* London: Verso.

Patten, C. 1999. *A new beginning: The future of policing in Northern Ireland*. Belfast, UK: Independent Commission.

Pettit, P. 2001. *A theory of freedom: From the psychology to the politics of agency*. Cambridge: Polity.

Povey, K. 2001. *Open all hours*. London: Her Majesty's Inspectorate of Constabulary.

Pratt, J. 2006. The power and limits of populism: An illustration from recent penal developments in New Zealand. In *Emotions, crime and justice*, ed. S. Karstedt, I. Loader, and H. Strang. Oxford: Hart.

Pratt, J., D. Brown, M. Brown, S. Hallsworth, and W. Morrison, eds. 2005. *The new punitiveness: Trends, theories, perspectives*. Cullompton, UK: Willan.

Rorty, R. 2004. Post-democracy. *London Review of Books*, April 1, pp. 10-11.

Sennett, R. 2003. *Respect in a world of inequality*. New York: Norton.

Skogan, W. 1990. *Disorder and decline: Crime and the spiral of decay in American neighborhoods*. New York: Free Press.

Sparks, J. R., and A. E. Bottoms. 1995. Legitimacy and order in prisons. *British Journal of Sociology* 46 (1): 45-62.

Tamir, Y. 1997. The land of the fearful and the free. *Constellations* 3 (3): 296-314.

Taylor, C. 1995. *Philosophical arguments*. Cambridge, MA: Harvard University Press.

———. 2000. Democratic exclusion (and its remedies?). In *Citizenship, diversity and pluralism: Canadian and comparative perspectives*, ed. A. Cairns, J. Courtney, P. MacKinnon, H. Michelmann, and D. Smith. Montreal, Canada: McGill-Queen's University Press.

Tully, J. 2000. Struggles of recognition and distribution. *Constellations* 7 (4): 469-82.

Tyler, T. 1990. *Why people obey the law*. New Haven, CT: Yale University Press.

Walden, K. 1982. *Visions of order: The Canadian Mounties in symbol and myth*. Toronto, Canada: Butterworths.

Walker, N. 2000. *Policing in a changing constitutional order*. London: Sweet and Maxwell.

———. 2002. Policing and the supranational. *Policing and Society* 12 (4): 307-22.

Wilson, Jeremy M. 2006. Law and order in an emerging democracy: Lessons from the reconstruction of Kosovo's police and justice systems. *Annals of the American Academy of Political and Social Science* 605:152-77.

Wilson, J. Q., and G. Kelling. 1982. Broken windows. *Atlantic Monthly*, March, pp. 29-38.

Zimring F. E., and D. T. Johnson. 2006. Public opinion and the governance of punishment in democratic political systems. *Annals of the American Academy of Political and Social Science* 605:266-80.

Policing Uncertainty: Countering Terror through Community Intelligence and Democratic Policing

By
MARTIN INNES

This article explores how counterterrorism policing strategies and practices in the United Kingdom have changed in the face of recent terrorist attacks. It considers the evident limitations of these developments and how a local, democratic style of neighborhood policing could be used to manufacture the community intelligence "feed" that offers the best probability of preventing and deterring future forms of such violence. These substantive concerns are set against a theoretical backdrop attending to how policing can respond to risks where the contours of the threat are uncertain. The analysis is informed by interviews with U.K. police officers involved in intelligence and counterterrorism work conducted during the early part of 2005.

Keywords: counterterrorism; democratic policing; neighborhood policing; signal crimes; community intelligence; uncertainty

Terrorist violence is a form of communicative action. Designed to impact upon public perceptions by inducing fear in pursuit of some political objective, violence is dramaturgically enacted as a solution to a sociopolitical power imbalance (Karstedt 2003). It is thus ultimately an attempt at social control, where a less powerful actor seeks to exert influence over the norms, values, and/or conduct of another more powerful grouping (Black 2004).

Martin Innes is a senior lecturer in sociology at the University of Surrey. He is author of the books Investigating Murder (Clarendon Press, 2003) and Understanding Social Control (Open University Press, 2003), as well as articles in the British Journal of Sociology and the British Journal of Criminology. He is currently the editor of the journal Policing and Society. His current research focuses upon public reactions to crime in urban environments and police intelligence processes.

NOTE: I would like to thank Colin Roberts and Sarah Maltby, who conducted parts of the original research upon which this article draws. Thanks also to David Tucker, who managed the original project and also provided detailed commentary upon an earlier draft of this article, and to Susanne Karstedt and Gary LaFree. The research upon which this article draws was sponsored by the Association of Chief Police Officers for England and Wales.

DOI: 10.1177/0002716206287118

Terrorists can seek to act upon political processes and public perceptions in two subtly different modes. The first is where violence is directed toward a symbol of the social and cultural order to which the perpetrator is opposed. In these *symbolic crimes*, exemplified by the 9/11 attack on the Pentagon as a building that is both a connotative and denotative signifier of U.S. military power. The salience of the act is derived from the drama of violence performed against an iconic representation of some facet of a cultural or social order. The second mode is where the impact of the incident is contingent to a greater degree upon the logic illuminated by the *signal crime* concept (Innes 2004). Terrorist attacks that signal risk and threat tend to be located in routine public settings where mass civilian casualties are likely to occur. They exert political and perceptual influence by signaling the risks and threats that can be manufactured in everyday life situations by a determined minority and in so doing, induce changes in how citizens think, feel, or act in relation to their security. Recent examples of where this signaling logic has been enacted through terrorist attacks are the Bali nightclub bombings and the bombings on the public transport systems in Madrid and London. Some instances of terrorist violence, such as the 9/11 attack on the World Trade Center, embody both a symbolic and a signaling logic. For the most part though, the accent tends toward one or the other of these two communicative modes.

In the wake of the 7/7 bombings on London's transport networks, there is a real concern across the police and security sector about their capacity to calibrate the contours of the threat al-Qaeda poses.

Differentiating between the symbolic and signal modes by which terrorist violence acts upon political processes and public perceptions provides insight into the subtly different ways that locally situated terrorisms can affect a democratic social order (Laqueur 2001). But for both modes, the potency and power of violence depends upon inducing a sense of uncertainty about security in the public mind and political process. Terrorism seeks to manufacture uncertainty to induce a reaction that destabilizes a social order to render it more precarious in some manner. That it sometimes achieves this is perhaps evidenced by the aftermath of the Madrid train bombings where commentators have suggested that the al-Qaeda sponsored attack altered the outcome of the subsequent democratic elections.[1]

It has long been the case that democratic institutional orders and the civil society institutions to which they relate have demonstrated a reasonably high degree of resilience to terrorism, and broadly this remains so. Nevertheless, there is growing concern about the extent to which terrorist violence can impact negatively upon democratic order and the routines of civil society (Blair 2005). As terrorism induced uncertainty intermingles with and amplifies a wider "ambient insecurity" emanating from more everyday experiences of crime and disorder under conditions of late modernity, a veneer of security becomes increasingly difficult to preserve (Garland 2001; Innes 2004). Terrorism not only directly affects political processes, as in Spain, but can also amplify social divisions based upon ethnicity and faith, keying into wider concerns about community cohesion. This is why the conceptual accent in this article is upon *counterterrorism* rather than *counterterrorist* work. The latter term restricts the issues to dealing with the protagonists, whereas the former captures how the response to terrorism in democratic states increasingly encompasses managing a range of potential harms.

With these issues as a backdrop, this article provides a case study of the United Kingdom police response to the changing contours of threat posed by al-Qaeda's jihadist terrorism. Of particular consequence to the analysis is the identification within the U.K. counterterrorism response of a second type of uncertainty to that outlined above. In the wake of the 7/7 bombings on London's transport networks, there is a real concern across the police and security sector about their capacity to calibrate the contours of the threat al-Qaeda poses. This connects to concerns about whether established methodologies for generating intelligence on possible terrorist organizations, of the type used in Ireland for example, are suitable to deal with the new risks posed by a morphing, fluid, and decentered al-Qaeda.[2]

I will propose that one possible solution to this uncertainty is to better integrate a system of local neighborhood policing (NP) into the counterterrorism apparatus. Based upon providing local communities with a degree of direct democratic influence over how they are policed, NP officers will be well positioned to build levels of interpersonal trust with members of Muslim and other minority communities upon which the communication of intelligence is often contingent. As such, NP processes, in addition to their everyday functions of policing volume crime and disorder, can be used for detecting the subtle indicators of suspicion that people may develop about activities connected to terrorism in their communities. To advocate better integrating NP into the counterterrorism effort is not to suggest that such maneuvers will be unproblematic. Rather more pragmatically, such moves may be more effective and ultimately less damaging to democratic traditions than extending covert policing methods and the sorts of reactionary legislative reform proposals that governments tend to issue in the wake of major terrorist incidents.

The article commences by outlining the key dimensions of counterterrorism work and how several factors have collectively encouraged Western policing agencies to reconfigure the ways in which they seek to understand and respond to the threats posed by al-Qaeda. Developing this analysis, there follows an empirically grounded exploration of some innovative police approaches that relate to counterterrorism activity. The focus then shifts to consider the limitations of the emergent police approach and how these may be overcome by adopting a highly localized form of democratic policing. Throughout, this article is set against a wider analytic theme of uncertainty. For while scholars have written much on how risk assessment and risk management practices are animating reform in the conduct of social control (Ericson and Haggerty 1997; Simon 1993), they have paid little attention to how social control is enacted in conditions of uncertainty resulting from incomplete or low information. Thus in focusing upon the contemporary configuration of counterterrorism policing in the United Kingdom, the discussion attends to the question of how social control agencies manage risks where the contours of the threat are opaque and uncertain.

Data and Method

The empirical data informing this article were collected between January and March 2005 as part of a research project examining the effectiveness of the U.K. police in collecting and handling "community intelligence" from minority groups[3] and young people in respect of several different issues including terrorism. Interviews were conducted with police officers from three police force areas purposively sampled to enable comparative analysis of how different organizations were dealing with similar intelligence issues. The Metropolitan Police Service (MPS) in London was selected because it is the largest police organization in the United Kingdom and has a national responsibility for counterterrorism. The second force located in the north of England was representative of the circumstances of many midsized U.K. police forces and had recent experience of dealing with significant public disorder between ethnic communities. The third police force area in the south of England was chosen to explore the issues being confronted by small forces in managing community intelligence.[4]

A total of twenty-six semistructured interviews were conducted with police officers and staff working with intelligence on counterterrorism issues at central and local levels.[5] This included the force intelligence directors responsible for managing the intelligence systems in northern and southern forces and officers with national responsibilities in the MPS. Officers who either were working with Special Branch or had done so recently were part of the sample in the three forces.[6] Of particular interest though for the concerns of this article was the inclusion of specialist officers from two units in the Metropolitan Police—the Muslim Contact Unit and the Strategic Contact Unit.[7] The officers in these recently established units focused upon working with particular community groups to manage their concerns. In addition, the head of the National Community Tension Team (NCTT) was interviewed. NCTT is a central policing unit working with all forces to monitor intercommunity and intracommunity tensions nationwide. As such, it has a key role in managing postincident responses to any major threats to public order, including terrorist incidents at home and overseas. Six interviews were also conducted with members of the public who had previously provided intelligence to police on activities of concern, capturing an often over-looked dimension in discussions of police intelligence.

The Social Organization of Counterterrorism

Counterterrorism work has prospective and retrospective aspects. The prospective "precrime" aspects are performed on an ongoing basis and are designed to prevent, deter, and disrupt the activities of those thought to be involved in activities related to terrorism.[8] Involving surveillance of and inter-ventions against people directly involved in groups supporting terrorist action, it also increasingly encompasses measures taken against the support infrastructures for such groups, particularly targeting their financial resources (McCulloch and Pickering 2005; Levi and Gilmore 2002). This is part of what Thacher (2005) dubbed "the offender search" strategy of counterterrorism.

The second dimension to counterterrorism work is more reactive "postcrime" activities and centers upon postincident response. This includes criminal investi-gations to identify the perpetrators of any attack and to locate any support infra-structure that can be targeted as part of future prevention and deterrence efforts. More recently, though, and particularly following the September 11, 2001, attacks, increasing interest has been directed to managing any wider impacts upon com-munities. As the attacks performed by al-Qaeda in Western countries have delib-erately sought to exploit innate tensions in what Karstedt (2006 [this volume]) terms the "liberal inclusionary project" of democracy, by using terrorist violence to create a fissure along the lines of religion. Police and security agencies have increasingly recognized a need to mitigate any perceptual harm that may result from terrorism in terms of exacerbating and enflaming interethnic and interfaith community tension. In the following quotation from a senior police officer, the ways in which these different aspects of counterterrorism coalesce are articulated:

> If something were to happen in the terrorist threat. . . . There would be a need for increased vigilance, . . . a need for increased policing all sorts of options around uncon-ventional ways of doing police work like the overt deployment of firearms and so on, which might cause fear. Our role would be to run the community side of that, making sure that we were into particular communities which might be targeted for backlash or whatever . . . and that's precisely what we did for post September 11th. (11)

In the second part of this quotation, the officer briefly touches upon some of the contingent and complex impacts of policing terrorist threats and how police responses can amplify levels of insecurity in vulnerable communities. An under-current in the interviews is that terrorist incidents can function as triggers for wider crime and public order problems that have to be dealt with by police.[9] Consequently, postincident response strategies in the United Kingdom now rou-tinely involve deploying police officers to undertake high-visibility "reassurance" patrols at strategic locations, mass media campaigns, and so forth as part of what Thacher (2005) labeled the "community protection" domain of counterterrorism.

TABLE 1
FOUR STRANDS OF COUNTERTERRORISM ACTIVITY

	Offender Search	Community Protection
Prospective	Identifying and surveillance of the activities of "high-risk" groups and their members; disrupting activities of potential threat groups; investigating and prosecuting acts preparatory to terrorism	Target hardening and creating a "harsh environment" for the conduct of terrorism; public resilience and preparedness
Retrospective	Investigating, arresting, and prosecuting suspects allegedly involved in committing an attack	Monitoring community tensions; public reassurance through "perceptual interventions"

Drawing these themes together produces four key strands of counterterrorism activity, as shown in Table 1.

Conceptualizing counterterrorism in this fashion enables one to map the division of labor in terms of how key agencies perform specific roles as part of the overall counterterrorism effort. In the United Kingdom, domestic counterterrorism activity has traditionally focused upon the Security Service (MI5), Special Branch police officers located in each of the fifty-six police forces and the Anti-Terrorist Branch of the MPS. Typically, the Security Service gathers clandestine and open source intelligence information, conducts threat assessments and intervenes to prevent and deter such terrorist threats as are located, and shares information with other agencies. The police, largely through their Special Branch officers and the Anti-Terrorist Branch, are responsible for pursuing counterterrorism investigations by collecting evidence for introduction into any legal proceedings (Masse 2003). While "firewalls" between these organizations inhibit exchanges of intelligence data, several interviewees confirmed that in recent years the working relationships between the Security Service and a number of specialist police units had become closer, not just as a result of counterterrorism issues, but also because of efforts to tackle organized and transnational crime (Innes and Sheptycki 2004). Overall, though, domestic policing agencies have been more involved in community protection functions.

As intimated previously, a particular concern for retrospective community protection work is trying to prevent the possibility of a terrorist incident functioning as a "flashpoint" for wider public disorder. This encompasses domestic incidents but also trying to understand the local impact of geopolitical events:

When the original invasion of Afghanistan was going on, we were holding weekly meetings with community leaders within [town name] to see what the impact was of what was going on elsewhere . . . recognising the political implications of what was going on. . . . Because obviously a lot of people are from the area of Pakistan which borders Afghanistan and there's going to be family ties and there's going to be concerns . . . and whether they had any concerns within their own communities or indeed, because [town name], the one thing about Muslim communities, they interact with each other, Muslim communities around the country and you may not have a problem in [town name] but there are family members living in Slough. (23)

The concern on this occasion was that the military actions being undertaken in Afghanistan would trigger problems in the United Kingdom. As this quotation illuminates, current concerns with national security are more complex than simply preventing and deterring terrorist attacks. Countering terrorism also encompasses trying to predict and manage how incidents overseas may function as signal events to communities residing in Western countries increasing domestic community tensions.

[C]ollecting and using intelligence does seem to be part of the "dirty work" of democracy.

Counterterrorist work performed by both high- and low-policing agencies encompasses several interconnected strands, ranging from attempts at preventing and disrupting potential assailants to minimizing the repercussions and harm should such efforts be unsuccessful.[10] There is, though, set against the backdrop of the September 11 attacks and the bombings in London and Madrid, an increasingly widely articulated suggestion that given the new risks and threats faced, the role of local policing in counterterrorism activity needs to be enhanced (cf. Kelling 2004, 3).

In sum, the reasons this view has been strongly espoused are threefold:

- uncertainty about the contours of the threat, in terms of the individuals willing to perform terrorist violence and the locations where they and their support groups are to be found;
- appreciation of the need to manage public fears through reassurance-oriented perceptual interventions to mitigate the overall social, economic, and political harms of terrorism; and
- concern that terrorist incidents can enflame community tensions, causing other crimes, increasing public disorder, and producing longer-term detrimental impacts upon the cohesion of particular communities.

Community Intelligence

A significant intelligence deficit in terms of defining and understanding the threat posed by affiliates of al-Qaeda residing in Western countries is a motive for enhancing the role of police agencies, particularly around the prospective offender search functions of counterterrorism. This is exemplified by the recent bombings in London on 7/7, where intelligence was undeveloped on the individuals involved. Moreover, they came from Leeds, a city in the north of England not renowned for radicalism or community tension. In several other cases currently going through the English courts, individuals from very different parts of the country are subject to prosecution for acts preparatory to terrorism. Collectively, these cases suggest a worrying picture for the authorities and public. It is widely recognized that traditional intelligence methods have achieved only limited penetration of many Muslim communities, and yet these cases involve individuals and areas that one might not expect or predict to be involved in terrorist activities. This raises questions about whether the architecture of the extant intelligence system is suited for responding to the emerging situation.

All agencies across the policing and security sector make use of intelligence, although they define, understand, and use it in a variety of ways according to their organizational imperatives and concerns. Due to its widespread abuse, the concept of intelligence has frequently acquired pejorative connotations, associated in the public mind with clandestine and secretive political policing activities (Innes and Sheptycki 2004). Nevertheless, collecting and using intelligence does seem to be part of the "dirty work" of democracy. It is enmeshed in how democratic institutions employ increasingly specialized and technical covert modes of social control to preserve an appearance of social order (Marx 1988) and for countering the threats posed by groups such as al-Qaeda that seek to subvert democratic processes. Stripped of any normative associations and imputations though, intelligence is simply a mode of information. For organizations, it is information that has been processed to provide foresight—a predictive capacity about how to act at some point in the future to achieve particular objectives given certain conditions.

Treverton (2005) contended that, compared to policing agencies, intelligence used by national security agencies tends to be relatively undefined. He attributed this to the fact that security agencies are typically working to build a generalized picture of risks and threats, whereas police are focused upon constructing individual legal cases. According to Wark (2005), during the 1990s the orientation of national security agencies shifted, due largely to an "open source intelligence revolution." Driven by significant developments in information and communication technologies, most notably the Internet, national security agencies invested in and focused upon "signals intelligence" (Sigint) processing technologies to better locate open source intelligence at the expense of conducting more basic and fundamental "human intelligence" (Humint) work (Eddy 2005).

Police too during the 1990s altered the configuration of their intelligence usage. Under the auspices of intelligence-led policing, police agencies were encouraged to improve their efficiency and effectiveness by proactively identifying problems and targeting the individuals and crimes responsible for causing most harm. This was particularly pronounced in the United Kingdom, where the National Intelligence Model (NIM) was introduced to provide a national framework for how police agencies acquire and process intelligence data (National Criminal Intelligence Service 2000). Based upon differentiating between three levels of intelligence (local/regional/national and international), in principle if not always in practice, the NIM was intended to connect information flows and exchange between "high"- and "low"-policing agencies (John and Maguire 2004).

The implementation of the NIM processes is an explicit manifestation of a broader trend that Ericson and Shearing (1986) dubbed "the scientification" of police work and Manning (2003) its "rationalization." As Maguire (2000) noted, the rationalization of the intelligence function induces a shift toward a more proactive mode of working based upon the principles of risk management. However, a number of criticisms can be made of NIM, its use of intelligence, and the biases it introduces into police practice (Sheptycki 2004), three of which are especially pertinent to this article.

In his study of police intelligence, Gill (2000) noted a systemic bias resulting from how the provenance of intelligence is established that induces a focusing of efforts upon particular recurring individuals and problems. In part, this stems from the problems experienced in managing the volumes of intelligence data produced but also from difficulties associated with searching across existing data to locate new and emerging risks (Innes, Fielding, and Cope 2005). The implication is that while current intelligence systems and processes are likely to be fairly effective in identifying threats that are connected to people or places where intelligence is previously available, they may be less effective in locating new or emerging threats—a problem directly relevant to current counterterrorism concerns in the United Kingdom.

Interrelated with the above is a more general feeling that while the NIM has improved police handling of crime intelligence, it has induced an overreliance upon information resulting from "professional" police informants at the expense of other kinds of community intelligence (Innes 1999). Community intelligence is different in a number of ways when compared with more traditional kinds of crime and criminal intelligence (Innes, Fielding, and Cope 2005). It tends to be open source, rather than acquired from covert human sources, and is often provided by ordinary members of the public, rather than those who have some connection to criminal activity—the quality that, according to the dictates of police culture, provides criminal or crime intelligence with unique purchase (Innes 1999). Whereas criminal intelligence tends to target particular individuals, and crime intelligence particular incident types, community intelligence covers a range of issues, frequently being used by police to build a picture of the contextual risks that a particular community group feels concerned about. Community intelligence applied to counterterrorism is precisely the type of data that might help police to circumvent the intelligence gaps and blind spots that seemingly inhere in their established methods.

One important application of community intelligence to counterterrorism policing, as several police interviewees candidly admitted, was to facilitate a better understanding of the makeup of different communities—in terms of the social networks to which individuals and groups belong and the intracommunity tensions that may exist between them. As one of the police officers interviewed, himself a practicing Muslim, described it,

> There is no such thing as THE Muslim community. There is a hugely complex set of people making up different sub-sections of a community who have different divisions, rivalries and factions. (04)

Subtle intricacies and nuances of this sort are not the kind of things that police have been especially well tuned to in the past but are of significant consequence in prospectively and retrospectively countering terrorist threats both domestically and internationally.

This sense that the policing environment had become more complex was apparent also in the comments of members of different Muslim communities spoken to in the course of the research. For example, one man said,

> The problem is that there's a huge range of different communities within a community . . . just because everybody's brown in that area doesn't make them part of that same community. . . . There are now three Mosques in [town name] and those three Mosques obviously mean that the groups that go to each of those Mosques follow something slightly different. So you've effectively got three community groups within the culture of Muslims immediately in one particular area. I mean clearly if I think back to [town name] 20 years ago I would have been able to walk down the street and I would know everybody that was there . . . however. If I look at it now, if I walk from one end of my street right to the other, I may bump into, you know, 15 or 20 people from my community, in inverted commas, and yet I might not know a single one of them. (25)

Two important implications for counterterrorism policing can be disaggregated from such social trajectories. First, as peoples' conceptions of belonging become more tightly defined (Williams 2000), and they no longer feel that who they are is sufficiently represented by broader classifications of identity, the potential for intergroup tensions is increased. The more groups there are, the greater the potential for their norms or values to come into conflict with those of other groups. Community intelligence is one way in which police can obtain some understanding of any tensions that might be exacerbated following a terrorist incident. Second, as more social groups represent increasingly distinctive social identities, so there are more groups who can be potential victims and/or perpetrators. Consequently, as the number of identity groups increases, so the number of contacts that the police maintain needs to be increased in an effort to monitor the activities of any people who might be a risk or at risk. But of course, the police have a finite amount of resources to undertake such work, and cultivating and developing effective human intelligence sources is notoriously difficult (Dunnighan and Norris 1999). Thus, building a network of community intelligence contacts provides a comparatively effective way of maintaining surveillance over groups and communities that are especially hard for the police to penetrate either overtly or covertly.

At least in part, then, calls to increase the role of community intelligence in U.K. counterterrorism reflect worries that aspects of the current intelligence systems, developed particularly through years of dealing with the situation in Ireland, may not be as effective in dealing with al-Qaeda.[11] The reasons for this can be traced back to differing organization and methods. The Irish Republican Army (IRA) and other Irish groups were based upon fairly traditional hierarchical organizational structures. Consequently, if a human intelligence source could penetrate the organization at a particular level, or an existing member be persuaded to inform on colleagues, then intelligence on a range of other members and their activities could be collected fairly readily. This mode of social organization does not apply to the current arrangements of al-Qaeda, however, which is based upon largely autonomous, disparate cells and groups that are not connected by any formal command and control structures. This means that successful penetration of one cell or group may not yield much intelligence on others. Furthermore, in terms of methods, IRA cells often provided warnings about imminent attacks, whereas al-Qaeda operatives have not done so and indeed do not expect to be alive after launching their attack. It is this shift in the methodology of violence alongside changes in organizational structure and the difficulty of establishing knowledge about them that has served to induce such a sense of uncertainty among those charged with countering terrorist threats. And while a reduction in this uncertainty may occur over time as the relevant agencies become more accustomed to the nature of the threat, the diagnosis presented herein suggests that reconfiguring the intelligence architecture would increase this likelihood.

Strategic Engagement as Soft Power

Reflecting these problems with intelligence and the increasing complexities surrounding notions of collective identity, some units within the U.K. police service have sought to respond to such issues creatively. Specialist community engagement units have been established by police to develop and manage relationships with what are termed "strategic contacts." Strategic contacts are where police seek to deliberately establish relationships with community leaders and opinion formers from groups perceived as strategically important in understanding the policing environment. From the police point of view, the purpose of such contacts is twofold. Primarily, it is anticipated that they can be used to develop a "community intelligence feed" about the activities of individuals and groups in these communities of interest to the police (this intelligence is not restricted to terrorism but rather covers all aspects of policing). Additionally, police specialists recognize that such relationships also provide a communication channel into these communities to counteract rumors or other information. The nature of this second function was described by the head of the MPS Strategic Contact Unit:

> What we try to do is to link with strategic partners within those faith communities and try to keep them in the loop so to speak, in respect of telling them what is actually happening as far as we know, rather than any rumours. (03)

Strategic engagement with various vulnerable communities by the police as part of their counterterrorism work is a direct response to the range of problems and issues outlined previously. Unlike more traditional forms of police intelligence work, strategic contacts are undertaken overtly. Officers engaged in developing them do not mask their police status from the people with whom they are interacting. As such, success depends upon officers' ability to build interpersonal trust between themselves and particular key individuals. For the community representatives, these strategic contacts offer a chance to bring their concerns to the police and to hopefully influence the style of policing received by what are, after all, often comparatively vulnerable communities.

In all of the three police force areas studied, building strategic contacts was performed by a small number of officers. That this work is largely restricted in this way says something about how it is perceived within the environs of the police organization. But to a degree, it also reflects more pragmatic considerations. On aggregate, citizens are increasingly disinclined to trust institutions (LaFree 1998), but they may trust particular individual representatives of those institutions. Consequently, propagating personal relationships between individual police officers and community representatives is potentially a comparatively effective way of building trust with groups who are often antipathetical to police.

The processes used to generate strategic community intelligence are based upon different principles than those typically used in the manufacture of criminal intelligence, which is structured by ideas of covertness and the "need to know" principle (Sheptycki 2004). Human criminal intelligence sources are seen as resources of the police organization as a whole to be managed via an intelligence system rather than being dependent upon any personal relationship with an individual police handler. Indeed, processes of criminal intelligence are now systematized in such a way as to explicitly discourage personal relations being formed between handlers and sources (Innes 1999). This contrasts with how strategic community intelligence contacts are developing, where they are overtly conducted and personal relationships constitute the working capital of how trust is built for community intelligence to be passed to the police. One way to understand this emergent approach is as the importation of some of the principles of community policing into the national security arena. The police are effectively seeking to achieve their objectives by operationalizing a form of "soft power."[12]

The concept of soft power was coined by Joseph Nye (2004) to describe processes of geopolitical influence that shape the world system and relations between nation states therein. For Nye, "hard power" derives from coercive interventions where the capacity to invoke physical force underpins the action performed. In contrast, soft power works through processes of persuasion, negotiation, and agenda setting, providing a far more subtle mode of influence. This notion of soft power seems to be analogous to how police in the United Kingdom are seeking to use their strategic engagement contacts.

In the following account, a member of the MPS Strategic Contact Unit describes an occasion where the unit used soft power by drawing upon intelligence about escalating community tensions to try to persuade particular groups not to respond to the provocations of radical Islamist agitators:

> Last year as well there was some issues which we picked up from the Sikh and Hindu communities that they were unhappy with a particular Islamic group called [xxxx] and they'd actually put some stuff on a website which was deemed to be anti-religion. . . . But what was going to happen was that these communities were so incensed that they were going to mount a counter demonstration in Trafalgar Square against this particular group who were going to set up a stall there . . . we had a meeting, and we said these are what the issues are, this is the work we are doing in terms of intelligence on this particular group, we would appreciate it if you would actually go back to your communities and say the police are dealing with this effectively and any counter demonstration would cause more difficulties. And effectively we reduced the policing demand for that event. (01)

This exemplifies the negotiated and persuasive qualities of soft power. It starts also to give a sense of the subtleties and intricacies of the police work involved.

The Limitations of Strategic Engagement

Following the attacks in London in July 2005, police and national intelligence agencies publicly stated that there was no developed intelligence about the activities of the two terrorist cells. That this situation transpired is potentially suggestive of some of the weaknesses of the strategic engagement approach more broadly.

By identifying individual members of particular communities as leaders and/or opinion formers, police are seeking to establish contact with people who are most likely to be able to help them to accomplish their objectives. In so doing, however, it is of vital importance to be able to connect with the right people. Given some of the complex issues about collective identity and group formation discussed previously, it is difficult to know who really represents a community's views. Similarly, there must be a concern about whether community leaders are really in touch with those most at risk of alienation and radicalization.

The officers interviewed who were working to foster strategic contacts themselves voiced concerns about the limitations of this approach:

> So although we have this ongoing relationship this strategic attitude and these strategic contacts . . . what we miss out on is that sort of common view, i.e., from the common Muslim, the common gay person, the common black person. I don't think we necessarily get their voice coming through in strategic relations. And I think that needs to be sieved a bit. Whenever we go to people and say "What is the community's view?" I think we end up with a one track view. (02)

In part, such concerns are symptomatic of the ways in which this style of community engagement work has rapidly evolved in the context of modern policing organizations. But it also illuminates a more fundamental weakness that is directly analogous to Granovetter's (1982) conceptualization of the "strength of weak ties." Police strategic engagements seek to instigate "strong ties" to key individuals located within particular communities. But what Granovetter's work demonstrates is that, especially in situations where information is diffusely located, an extensive social network of weak ties has greater utility than a more restricted network of strong ties. Applied to issues of counterterrorism, where the key pieces of intelligence may well be diffusely located among different community members, it would seem that police strategic engagements need to be supplemented with a far more extensive network of community contacts. This could be accomplished by greatly expanding the capacity of the "high"-policing agencies and their established covert methods for developing intelligence sources or, alternatively, better integrating "low"-policing agencies into the conduct of counterterrorism activities. In the United Kingdom, under the auspices of the Neighbourhood Policing (NP) program, a suitable vehicle for this is currently being rolled out in the form of a democratically oriented, highly localized policing system.

NP and Local Democracy

Under the U.K. government's current reform program, it is intended that by 2008 all neighborhoods in England and Wales will have their own dedicated policing teams. NP officers are to be assigned to specific neighborhoods and tasked to engage with individuals and groups therein to generate community intelligence on the key collective problems affecting local security. Once a profile of local problems is assembled, then all local people are given an opportunity to vote on their priorities for police action at specially convened police and community meetings of the sort popularized through the Chicago Alternative Policing Strategy (Skogan and Hartnett 1997). It then becomes the responsibility of the neighborhood officers to address these problems. In effect, this process amounts to constructing a knowledge base about the drivers of insecurity in the neighborhoods where officers are working and providing the opportunity for local people to democratically influence how they are policed.

The integration of rudimentary democratic mechanisms to provide for local community influence over policing is a marked departure in terms of the traditions of police governance in the United Kingdom. Unlike the County Sheriff system in the United States, in the United Kingdom the dictum of "constabulary independence" has meant that the conduct of policing has, at least nominally, been deliberately sequestered from any notion of direct political influence (Reiner 1992). Citizen governance of local policing has been restricted to membership of Police Authorities, although in practice they have been dominated by local councilors and magistrates rather than "ordinary" people. The Police Authorities are one component of a tripartite governance structure, with power shared between the local Chief Constable and Home Secretary. There is widespread recognition, though, that there is an accretion of power to the role of central government under this tripartite structure. Counterposed to this overarching trend, NP processes move mechanisms of accountability far closer to the public, providing greater ownership and control in terms of how individual communities are policed. Indeed, one way of understanding such moves is as supplementing the representative democracy provided by police authorities, with a form of direct, proximate democratic influence practiced at neighborhood level police-community forums.

Any benefits in improving public trust and confidence resulting from such processes are likely to be particularly important where relations with police have been historically difficult, which would include many Muslim communities in the United Kingdom. Minority ethnic communities have consistently voiced concern that they are simultaneously and consistently over policed as suspects and under-policed as victims, as a consequence of which trust and confidence has been low (Bowling 1999). But these same communities are now of most importance in terms of countering the domesticated jihadist threat. Because under NP processes, police are tasked to become more responsive to community defined problems, they are more likely to persuade community members of the benefits of assisting police and, unlike high-policing agencies, can provide something explicit in return to vulnerable communities by managing their more routine security concerns.

The architecture of the NP system is designed to generate and collect community intelligence on a community's self-defined crime and disorder problems (Innes 2005). It is a process that can be harnessed to establish the presence of any suspicions about potential terrorist activities. The importance of developing this local network is that indicators of suspicion for terrorist activities are often subtle and may not be known to any one individual but rather shared between several individuals in a community. Individuals may have snippets of information that on their own provide only a mild suggestion of a risk but when brought together collectively provide a more substantial picture. It is this capacity to deal with a diffusion of information that a network of weak community ties developed through NP provides.

In his analysis of the U.S. federal system, Thacher (2005) suggested that integrating local policing agencies in homeland security efforts has negatively affected the delivery of normal policing services. He maintains that as local agencies have become involved in surveillance of Muslim communities, so trust has been corroded. NP is similarly vulnerable, and the potential tensions between roles that local officers perform on an ongoing daily basis and the more exceptional tasks of countering terrorism need to be acknowledged. However, the fundamental problem remains that at the current time, state authorities do not have a textured and high-resolution understanding of the evolving terrorist threat. There is, therefore, a fundamental need to find a way to improve the intelligence feed. The particular strength of the NP approach is that it can perform such a function as part of working to address more routine neighborhood security concerns.

The significance of grounding such an intelligence network in a NP system, and why it may prove more effective over the longer term than simply expanding the number of Special Branch and Security Service officers engaged in this work, is that NP aims to build trust. By being responsive to community defined problems and because they are on long-term assignments in particular communities, NP officers are well placed to foster and develop the trust that is required for people to provide information to them. NP processes thereby offer a significant complement to existing intelligence channels. The community intelligence accessed may not generate the hard leads of the sort provided by other more traditional covert methods. But it may overcome the problem of the diffusion of information by developing indicators of suspicion about individuals, groups, and locations that the police should examine more closely. What local policing potentially provides is an ongoing sensitization to the normal state of a community and thus may detect early signs that risks have increased in some manner.

Examining the current counterterrorism situation . . . illuminates traces of the more generalizable features of how policing responds and tries to reconfigure itself when it has only an opaque image of a problem to counter.

The trust negotiated by NP may only be thin, but having individual local officers delivering services tailored to address community defined problems means this can be sustained across a broad-based community network over the longer term, and it should thus be sufficient for maintaining the social relationships that underpin the provision of intelligence.[13] It is, however, important to outline the contingencies present in any such process. During the interviews with the strategic contact officers, they voiced their frustrations about how government policies and pronouncements made by senior politicians often rendered their work on the ground interacting with Muslim communities far more difficult. These political interventions often made individuals feel particularly vulnerable and under suspicion and, thus, disinclined to work with police. As a consequence, the strategic-contact officers were continually negotiating a path of trying to build greater trust and stop what they had previously built from being undermined by events in the political realm. Similar processes are likely to create tensions in terms of the capacity of NP processes to generate community intelligence. But because NP is primarily focused upon addressing neighborhood security concerns, it should demonstrate greater resilience when confronted with such pressures.

Conclusion

Violent terrorist acts throughout Europe and beyond committed by supporters of the al-Qaeda ideology have signaled the risks to security that can be manufactured by small groups acting in difficult-to-predict ways and, in so doing, have symbolized a profound opposition to the values of liberal-democratic order. In the wake of the 9/11 attacks in the United States, probing questions were raised about the extant intelligence apparatus and the suitability of its structures and practices for countering the new threats posed by al-Qaeda (National Commission on Terrorist Attacks upon the United States 2003). Similar debates have been taking place in Europe, where, in the aftermath of attacks in London, Madrid, and elsewhere, police and security services are concerned about whether they have sufficient intelligence and the right systems to detect and prevent any future threats. Driven by the fact that al-Qaeda has evolved in a way that has made it hard to define its essence and capacity, uncertainty abounds as to what the precise threat being faced is and how it may be properly calibrated.

Given the long history of difficult relations between many minority communities and the police, it is probable that only a comparatively thin form of trust can be cultivated by police.

That the issue of uncertainty is illuminated to such a degree by examining current responses to terrorist violence exposes a particular quality of the policing of risk. For as Ericson and Haggerty (1997) among others have identified, contemporary policing is embedded within institutionalized risk communication systems. But what has been neglected in such debates is the presence and role of uncertainty. That is, how do policing agencies respond when the contours of a risk are only vaguely known? All risk and threat assessment methodologies seek to divine a degree of pattern and order in future events on the basis of past occurrences, but any such probabilistic calculations are contingent upon the knowledge base that can be compiled. Consequently, they are likely to be wrong some of the time—either predicting false positives or false negatives. Examining the current counterterrorism situation and concerns about the quantity and quality of intelligence that state authorities have available thereby illuminates traces of the more generalizable features of how policing responds and tries to reconfigure itself when it has only an opaque image of a problem to counter. Under such conditions, it seems that a tension arises between investing in and expanding extant practices and systems and more radical reconfiguration.

At the time of writing, one proposed response is to expand the resources available to the Security Service and Special Branch so that they can extend their existing covert and undercover methods. A second response, not incompatible with the first, is legislative reform, introducing new laws intended to make it easier for suspects to be apprehended or prosecuted in some manner. But in assessing their respective potentials to reduce the terrorist threat, we should take seriously Lustgarten's (2003) contention that it is often through the political reactions that they trigger that terrorist acts work upon the legitimacy of the institutional orders of democratic states. Extending covert policing practices, where comparatively little public accountability or oversight is available, and rendering the law more assertive run contrary to some of the key values of liberal democracy. Both of these measures require a degree of democratic freedom to be suspended by citizens in an effort to manufacture enhanced security.

In contrast to such responses, I have argued for connecting the conduct of "high" and "low" policing, accompanied by a rethinking of the nature and functions of intelligence. The particular advantages of NP are that it provides local communities with a degree of collective influence over how they are policed and that in acting to address locally defined problems, neighborhood officers are well placed to generate trust and collect community intelligence. This connecting of trust and intelligence is important in that in traditional covert intelligence methodologies, the significance of trust could be glossed over on the basis that an informant exchanged their information for a financial or nonfinancial incentive. The rather different overt intelligence methodology being developed by NP renders generating and sustaining social trust far more critical. Given the long history of difficult relations between many minority communities and the police, it is probable that only a comparatively thin form of trust can be cultivated by police. Thin trust is always fragile, and in the particular context of counterterrorist work, tensions can easily develop between national security imperatives and local demands that have to be sensitively managed. Despite any such equivocations, on balance, it is an approach that, when compared with the alternatives, is more coherent with the key values of the liberal democratic tradition. This is notable given that the violence enacted by those affiliating to al-Qaeda is intended to destabilize the legitimacy of and ultimately undermine democratic processes. If this diagnosis is correct, then it would seem that democratic principles mediated through the institution of policing may provide a mechanism to effectively counter those who would seek to use violence to disrupt and destabilize democratic order.

Notes

1. See, for example, Keith Richbury, "Madrid Attacks May Have Targeted Election," *Washington Post*, October 17, 2004; and Isambard Williamson, "Election Blow to Bush's War on Terror," *Daily Telegraph*, March 15, 2004.

2. On the organization of al-Qaeda, see Manhattan Institute (2005, 9) and Burke (2003).

3. This includes minority ethnic groups, faith communities, and gay groups.

4. Reflecting the sensitivity of some of the data, these two forces have been made anonymous. In this article, respondents are identified by a unique number. For obvious security reasons, data on some issues have been edited.

5. Ten interviews were from the Metropolitan Police Service (MPS), six from the southern force, and nine from the northern.

6. Special Branch was originally formed in the 1880s to deal with Irish terrorism and subsequently acquired a wider remit. Today all the main police forces in the United Kingdom have a Special Branch office with responsibilities for a variety of surveillance and clandestine policing functions, including aspects of counterterrorist activity.

7. The Muslim Contact Unit specializes in dealing with individuals from this faith community, whereas the Strategic Contact Unit has a wider remit dealing with a diverse array of community groups.

8. The concepts of "precrime" and "postcrime" are Zedner's (2005).

9. For example, following the bombings in London in July 2005, there was a 600 percent increase in the numbers of race hate and faith hate crimes reported to police ("Scapegoats: Huge Rise in Race Attacks across the UK," *The Independent*, August 4, 2005).

10. Brodeur (1983) distinguished between "high" and "low" policing, where the former is concerned with political and national security issues and the latter with more routine everyday policing matters.

11. For a summary of the situation in Northern Ireland, see Ellison and Smyth (2000).

12. On the concept of soft power as applied to community policing, see Innes (2005).

13. On "thin" trust, see Williams (1988).

References

Black, Donald. 2004. Terrorism as social control. In *Terrorism and counter-terrorism: Criminological perspectives*, ed. Mathieu Deflem. Greenwich, CT: JAI.

Blair, Ian. 2005. What kind of police service do we want? The Richard Dimbleby Lecture, London, November 16, 2005.

Bowling, Ben. 1999. *Violent racism: Victimization, policing and social control*. Oxford: Clarendon.

Brodeur, Jean-Paul. 1983. High policing and low policing. *Social Problems* 30:507-20.

Burke, Jason. 2003. *Al-Qaeda: Casting a shadow of terror*. London: I.B. Tauris.

Dunnighan, Clive, and Clive Norris. 1999. The detective, the snout and the Audit Commission: The real costs in using informants. *Howard Journal* 38:67-86.

Eddy, R. P. 2005. In the end all terrorism is local. *TimesOnline*. http://www.timesonline.co.uk/article/0,,1072-1684947,00.html (accessed August 16, 2005).

Ellison, Graham, and B. Smyth. 2000. *The crowned harp: Policing Northern Ireland*. London: Pluto.

Ericson, Richard, and Kevin Haggerty. 1997. *Policing the risk society*. Oxford: Oxford University Press.

Ericson, Richard, and Clifford Shearing. 1986. The scientification of police work. In *The knowledge society: The growing impact of scientific knowledge on social relations*, ed. G. Bohme and N. Stehr, 129-59. Dordrecht, the Netherlands: D. Riedel

Garland, David. 2001. *The culture of control*. Oxford: Oxford University Press.

Gill, Peter. 2000. *Rounding up the usual suspects: Developments in contemporary law enforcement intelligence*. Aldershot, UK: Ashgate.

Granovetter, Mark. 1982. The strength of weak ties: A network theory revisited. *Sociological Theory* 1:201-33.

Innes, Martin. 1999. "Professionalizing" the police informant: The British experience. *Policing and Society* 9 (4): 357-83.

———. 2004. Signal crimes and signal disorders: Notes on deviance as communicative action. *British Journal of Sociology* 55 (3): 335-55.

———. 2005. Why soft policing is hard: On the curious development of Reassurance Policing, how it became Neighbourhood Policing and what this signals about the politics of police reform. *Journal of Community and Applied Social Psychology* 15:1-14.

Innes, Martin, Nigel Fielding, and Nina Cope. 2005. The appliance of science: The logic and practice of crime intelligence analysis. *British Journal of Criminology* 45:39-57.

Innes, Martin, and James Sheptycki. 2004. From detection to disruption: Some consequences of intelligence-led crime control in the UK. *International Criminal Justice Review* 14:1-14.

John, Tim, and Mike Maguire. 2004. *The National Intelligence Model: Key lessons from early research*. Home Office Online Report 30/04. www.homeoffice.gov.uk/rds/pdfs04/rdsolr3004.pdf (accessed November 18, 2005).

Karstedt, Susanne. 2003. Terrorism and "new wars." In *11 September 2001: War, terror and judgement*, ed. B. Gokai and R. J. B. Walker, 139-54. London: Frank Cass.

———. 2006. Democracy, Values and violence. *Annals of the American Academy of Political and Social Science* 605:50-81.

Kelling, George. 2004. Introduction: Do police matter? In *Hard won lessons: How police fight terrorism in the United Kingdom*. New York: Manhattan Institute.

LaFree, Gary. 1998. *Losing legitimacy: Street crime and the decline of social institutions in America*. Boulder, CO: Westview.

Laqueur, Walter. 2001. *A history of terrorism*. New York: Transaction.

Levi, Mike, and B. Gilmore. 2002. Terrorist finance, money laundering and the rise and rise of mutual evaluation: A new paradigm for crime control? *European Journal of Law Reform* 4 (2): 337-64.

Lustgarten, Lawrence. 2003. National security and political policing: Some thoughts on values, ends and laws. In *Democracy, law and security: Internal security services in Europe*, ed. Jean-Paul Brodeur. Aldershot, UK: Ashgate.

Maguire, Mike. 2000. Policing by risks and targets: Some consequences of intelligence led crime control. *Policing and Society* 9 (1): 315-36.

Manhattan Institute. 2005. *Hard won lessons: Policing terrorism in the United States*. New York: Manhattan Institute.

Manning, Peter. 2003. *Policing contingencies*. Chicago: University of Chicago Press.

Marx, Gary. 1988. *Undercover: Police surveillance in America*. Berkeley: University of California Press.

Masse, Todd. 2003. *Domestic intelligence in the United Kingdom: Applicability of the MI-5 model to the United States*. Washington, DC: Library of Congress.

McCulloch, Jude, and Sharon Pickering. 2005. Suppressing the financing of terrorism: Proliferating state crime, eroding censure and extending neo-colonialism. *British Journal of Criminology* 45 (4): 470-86.

National Commission on Terrorist Attacks upon the United States. 2003. *The 9/11 Commission report: Authorized edition*. New York: Norton.

National Criminal Intelligence Service. 2000. *The National Intelligence Model*. London: National Criminal Intelligence Service

Nye, Joseph. 2004. *Soft power: The means to success in world politics*. New York: Public Affairs.

Reiner, Robert. 1992. *The politics of the police*. 2nd ed. Hemel Hempstead, UK: Harvester Wheatsheaf.

Sheptycki, James. 2004. *Review of the influence of strategic intelligence on organised crime policy and practice*. Home Office Crime and Policing Group Special Interest Series Paper no. 14. London: Home Office.

Simon, Jonathan. 1993. *Poor discipline*. Chicago: University of Chicago Press.

Skogan, Wesley, and Katherine Hartnett. 1997. *Community policing, Chicago style*. New York: Oxford University Press.

Thacher, David. 2005. The local role in homeland security. *Law and Society Review* 39 (5): 635-76.

Treverton, Geoffrey. 2005. Terrorism, intelligence and law enforcement: Learning the right lessons. In *Twenty-first century intelligence*, ed. Wesley Wark. Abingdon, Oxfordshire, UK: Frank Cass.

Wark, Wesley. 2005. Learning to live with intelligence. In *Twenty-first century intelligence*, ed. Wesley Wark. Abingdon, Oxfordshire, UK: Frank Cass.

Williams, B. 1988. Formal structures and social reality. In *Trust: Making and breaking cooperative relations*, ed. Diego Gambetta. Oxford: Basil Blackwell.

Williams, Robin. 2000. *Making identity matter*. York, UK: Sociology Press.

Zedner, Lucia. 2005. Security and justice. Keynote address to the British Society of Criminology Conference, Leeds, UK, July 12, 2005.

Civil Democracy, Perceived Risk, and Insecurity in Brazil: An Extension of the Systemic Social Control Model

By
CORINNE DAVIS
RODRIGUES

This article examines the possible relationship between democracy and perceptions of risk and safety in the Brazilian city of Belo Horizonte. The author combines the argument that violence and insecurity in Brazil are consequences of the lack of civil democracy with insights from systemic social control theorists, who argue that perceptions of risk depend on the interaction of social control on private, parochial, and public levels. While social bonds at the private and parochial level did not affect perceptions of safety, public-level bonds, such as support for democratic government and legitimacy of neighborhood police, had positive effects on perceptions of security. However, contrary to the author's hypotheses, support for authoritarianism and generalized distrust of the police also decreased perceptions of risk in the case of robbery.

Keywords: perceived risk; Brazil; democracy; social control; disjunctive democracy

During the 1980s and 1990s, much of Latin America underwent a process of transition to democracy, following, in many cases, decades of military or authoritarian rule. While initial expectations about the impact of this new wave of democratization on economic development and social change were optimistic, many of the newly redemocratized countries in Latin America

Corinne Davis Rodrigues is a PRODOC/CAPES Post-Doctoral Fellow in the Sociology and Politics Doctoral Program and an associate researcher at the Center for Studies in Criminality and Public Safety (CRISP) at the Federal University of Minas Gerais, Brazil. Her current research focuses on intraurban differences in criminal victimization risk and social control in Brazil. She has a forthcoming article (jointly with Enrique Arias) on drug traffickers and perceptions of safety in Brazilian favelas in Latin American Politics and Society.

NOTE: This research is based on data from the Belo Horizonte Metropolitan Region Survey Project, directed by Neuma Aguiar, who kindly authorized its use. The author would like to thank Mark Stafford, Enrique Desmond Arias, and especially editors Susanne Karstedt and Gary LaFree for their valuable comments on earlier drafts of this article. In addition, the author thanks Valeria Oliveira, Daniel Brooke, Rodrigo Fernandes, and Braulio da Silva for help in preparing the data used here.

DOI: 10.1177/0002716206287144

currently face growing social problems. One of the most pressing of these is the rise of violent crime throughout the region. Since the mid-1980s, levels of violent crime in Latin America have increased substantially, making it one of the most violent regions in the world. Homicide rates in Latin America in the 1990s averaged 22.9 per 100,000 inhabitants, more than double the world average of 10.7 (Beato 2001). Along with the rise in violent crime, fear of crime has also increased.

In this article, I consider the possibility that both the recent increase in crime and fear of victimization in Brazil may be a consequence of democratization.

Brazil, in particular, exemplifies this trend. In 1986, Brazil held general elections for the first time in more than twenty years. Since that time, Brazil's democracy has been consolidated with three subsequent presidential elections and numerous general elections at the state and municipal level. At the same time, Brazil experienced a rise in crime rates, especially violent crime, concentrated mostly in urban areas. This rapid acceleration of crime in major urban centers such as Rio de Janeiro, São Paulo, and Belo Horizonte has been accompanied by an increased interest in crime, both from the general population and elected officials. While some authors argue that there is little or no relationship between rising crime rates and fear of crime, most Brazilian academics agree that fear of crime in Brazil is associated with the rise in crime (Adorno 1998; Cardia 2002; Caldeira 2000).

In this article, I consider the possibility that both the recent increase in crime and fear of victimization in Brazil may be a consequence of democratization. The specific process of democratization in Brazil has resulted in a "disjunction" between the successful consolidation of political rights and electoral processes and a continued lack of civil democracy and democratic rule of law (Caldeira and Holston 1999; Caldeira 2000; O'Donnell 1999). The current trends in violence, human rights abuses, and fear in Brazil are considered by some researchers to be a consequence of this disjunction (Caldeira and Holston 1999; Caldeira 2000; O'Donnell 1999; Ahnen 2003). Building on these ideas, I examine how measures of disjunction are related to perceptions of victimization risk and fear of crime in one major Brazilian city.

While many researchers have discussed the impact of disjunctive democracy on citizenship, violence, or human rights abuses generally (Caldeira and Holston 1999; Caldeira 2000; O'Donnell 1999; Ahnen 2003), a few studies also focus on perceived risk and fear of crime in the Brazilian context (see, for example, Villarreal and Silva 2004; Caldeira 2000; Cardia 2002). Most of these studies use qualitative data and do not link their discussions of disjunctive democracy with other models that predict perceived victimization risk and fear of crime (see Villarreal and Silva [2004] for a notable exception). In this article, I use the systemic social control model to help explain victimization risk and fear of crime. In this model, different levels of social control (private, parochial, and public) interact to create communities where residents perceive less fear and risk of victimization (Hunter 1985; Bursik and Grasmick 1993, 1995). I argue that the public level of social control, usually focused only on the police (Hunter 1985; Bursik and Grasmick 1993), should be extended to include the concept of disjunctive democracy.

In this article, then, I link theoretical arguments about disjunctive democracy and systemic social control and explore their relationship to fear of crime and victimization risk. Specifically, I extend the concept of the public level of social control to include measures of civil democracy, such as civic participation, general distrust of the police, and support for democratic governance. I argue that including these measures that take into account the Brazilian context of disjunctive democracy provides a more valid test of the systemic social control model.

Fear of Crime, Perceived Risk of Victimization, and Informal Social Control

Most individual-level measures of perceived risk and fear of crime are conceptualized under the "vulnerability" perspective. Under this perspective, individual characteristics that indicate greater physical or social vulnerability will correlate positively with fear of crime and perceived risk. Typically, these indicators of vulnerability have included sociodemographic characteristics and prior victimization. In general, the literature has shown that women and the elderly are more fearful and perceive more risk due to greater physical vulnerability (Warr 1984; Skogan & Maxfield 1981; Stafford and Galle 1984) and that minorities and individuals of low socioeconomic status perceive greater victimization risk and fear due to social vulnerability (Skogan and Maxfield 1981; Lee 1981). However, other studies have shown that these demographic characteristics may have different interaction effects when other factors, such as neighborhood characteristics, are taken into account (Baumer 1985; Rountree 1998). Also within this perspective, prior victimization is expected to correlate positively with fear and perceived risk, indicating greater vulnerability for future victimization. However, evidence supporting this latter hypothesis is mixed (Garofalo 1979; Skogan 1987; Baumer 1985; McGarrell, Giacomazzi, and Thurman 1997).

Beyond individual-level covariates of perceived victimization risk and fear of crime, extant research has also emphasized the impact of community-level covariates (Skogan 1990; Taylor 1997). Research in this area, following the ecological tradition in criminology, examines the impact of structural and social characteristics of places, most specifically neighborhoods, on individual perceptions of victimization risk and fear of crime. This research has identified a number of covariates of perceived risk and fear of crime that can be roughly grouped into two related categories: covariates that focus on neighborhood crime and disorder and covariates that focus on indicators of neighborhood social control (Skogan 1990; Taylor 1997; Rountree and Land 1996; Rountree 1998; Kanan and Pruitt 2002).

Within the first category, some researchers have shown that fear of crime and perceived risk is related to neighborhood crime rates (Skogan and Maxfield 1981) and that crime-specific fear may be related to specific crime rates (Rountree 1998). However, others have argued that perceived risk and fear is related more closely to other community factors, especially social and physical disorder (Skogan 1990; Taylor 1997, 2002; Rountree and Land 1996). Neighborhood disintegration and neglect produce signs of physical and social disorder, or incivilities, such as graffiti, panhandling, or public drug use. Supporters of the "incivilities hypothesis" argue that more than actual crime rates, these signs of disorder operate as risk indicators and correlate with greater fear of crime and perceptions of higher risk (Skogan 1990; Kelling and Coles 1996; Taylor 1997).

The other category of community-level covariates examines the impact of neighborhood social control on fear of crime and perceived risk. Within the social disorganization perspective, the better the social organization of a community, the higher its capacity for social control. Social organization broadly refers to the strength of social bonds within a neighborhood, such as relations among neighbors, friendship, and kinship ties, as well as the existence and participation in institutions and organizations such as churches, schools, and voluntary associations (Shaw and McKay 1969; Hunter 1985; Bursik 1988; Bursik and Grasmick 1993; Taylor 1997; Kubrin and Weitzer 2003). The type of social bonds present in a community can vary, producing different types of informal social control. Residents in communities with higher levels of social control will perceive less victimization risk and fear of crime.

Bursik and Grasmick (1993), building on work by Hunter (1985), emphasized how mechanisms of informal social control act on three social bond levels: public, parochial, and private. Within the private level of social bonds are friendship and kinship ties in the neighborhood (Hunter 1985; Bursik and Grasmick 1993). The parochial level of social bonds refers to links among neighbors, such as the exchange of favors, as well as participation in local voluntary organizations. Public-level social bonds are residents' ties outside the community, especially with public agencies such as the police and government (Hunter 1985; Bursik and Grasmick 1993). In Bursik and Grasmick's systemic social control model, social bonds on all three levels are the key to successful informal social control.

Most of the research examining the impact of social control on perceived risk and fear of crime has focused on the effect of private- and parochial-level social bonds, using measures of social integration (Skogan and Maxfield 1981) or social cohesion (Baumer 1985; Rountree and Land 1996; Villarreal and Silva 2004) to measure bonds at the community level (usually joining both friendship and neighbor ties). Support for the fear- and risk-reducing effect of these measures is mixed. In some studies, social bonds among neighbors decrease levels of fear and perceived risk (Skogan and Maxfield 1981; Baumer 1985; Rountree and Land

1996; Gibson et al. 2002). In others, social bonds have had the opposite effect, increasing fear through vicarious victimization (Covington and Taylor 1991; Villarreal and Silva 2004). Still others have found that social bonds have no effect on fear or perceived risk (Kanan and Pruitt 2002).

Missing from most of this literature is an examination of the effect of all the levels and dimensions of the systemic model on perceived risk and fear of crime. Most of the literature excludes measures of participation in local organizations as part of the parochial level. Bursik and Grasmick's (1993) systemic model emphasizes the role of participation in local organizations as an important component of parochial control, as well as a principal means through which public control operates. Unlike measures of social integration or social cohesion, however, the effect of community participation on fear of crime has been indirect through its impact on social control (Gibson et al. 2002; Taylor, Gottfredson, and Brower 1984).

The lack of civil democracy has hampered the ability of the state to secure civil rights and institute a democratic rule of law, creating what [can be referred to] as disjunctive democracy.

Focus on the public-level social bonds and/or social control is an even more neglected component of studies that examine fear of crime and perceived risk from a social control perspective. Most studies that do include the public level of social control examine the effect of neighborhood policing and demonstrate that certain types of policing (especially community policing) and positive perceptions of the police reduce levels of fear of crime and perceived risk (Xu, Fielder, and Flaming 2005; Kelling 1988; Skogan 1990; Velez 2001; Reiseg and Parks 2004). Research that focuses on other dimensions of public level control is also limited, but generally supportive of the systemic model. Carr (2003), in his study of the Beltway neighborhood in Chicago, showed how residents use links to outside resources such as the police and politicians (what he referred to as "new parochialism") to control crime in an area where private and "traditional" parochial controls are weak. Bursik and Grasmick (1995) argued that neighborhood networks with municipal agencies responsible for the delivery of other city services related to general quality of life (sanitation, street repair, and physical maintenance of public facilities) are important for shaping the physical ambiance of the neighborhood. Weak connections to these agencies can lead to the physical and social deterioration of the neighborhood, increasing the signs of disorder and incivilities and subsequently increasing fear of crime and perceived risk of victimization (Wilson and Kelling 1982).

The Public Sphere of Social Control and Democracy

Hunter (1985, 232) described the social bonds of the public level of social control as relationships of "citizen to citizen . . . embedded in a pattern of civility or mutually acknowledged rights among equals." In addition to relationships between citizens, the public bond also includes the individual's relationship to the state, defined in terms of rights and duties. While Hunter focused on the public social control exercised by the police, his definition of the public level of social control permits the inclusion of measures that examine the social bonds of this level in broader terms. Rather than just perceptions of actions of the state in the community context (such as policing), more general perceptions of the individual's relationship to the state should be considered.

In the Latin American context, this discussion of rights and duties in the public level of social control is especially relevant. Many authors argue that in Latin America, the process of democratization has created a limited form of democracy—a political rather than civil democracy (O'Donnell 1993; Diamond 1995; Caldeira and Holston 1999; Ahnen 2003). That is, political rights necessary for meaningful, free, and fair elections have been consolidated, but other rights, such as equal access to justice or freedom from abuses of power by the state, have not. Highlighting the distinction between political and civil rights of democracy, Diamond (1996) distinguished between electoral democracies (those that hold free and fair elections but do not guarantee civil liberties) and liberal democracies (those that in addition to the electoral process also have institutionalized the respect of civil liberties for all citizens). For the past two decades, most Latin American democracies have been classified as electoral as opposed to liberal democracies (Ahnen 2003).

O'Donnell (1999) and others (e.g., Caldeira and Holston 1999; Ahnen 2003) argue that it is this lack of consolidation of civil democracy that has led to the increase in violence and human rights abuses in Latin American countries since redemocratization, especially in Brazil, but also in Argentina (Tadesco 2002). The lack of civil democracy has hampered the ability of the state to secure civil rights and institute a democratic rule of law, creating what Caldeira and Holston (1999) refer to as disjunctive democracy. Within the systemic model of social control, disjunctive democracy has serious implications for the proper functioning of the public level of social control.

In a disjunctive democracy, while citizens participate in free elections and associations, civil democracy is limited in three key ways. First, limited civil citizenship affects participation in the public sphere, whether it is use of public space or civic engagement (Caldeira and Holston 1999; O'Donnell 1993). In both the Latin American and other contexts, levels of civic participation have been linked to government performance, particularly in terms of effective social policy and reduced corruption (Averitzer 1997) as well as to increased confidence in state institutions (Putnam 2000) and the maintenance of democracy (Paxton 2002).

Second, citizens in a disjunctive democracy have unequal access to the judicial system. As Caldeira and Holston (1999, 709) argue, the financial costs and complexity of the judicial system in Brazil makes it extremely class biased, with "the poor suffering criminal sanctions from which the rich are generally immune, while the rich enjoy access to private law (civil and commercial) from which the poor are systematically excluded." This process discredits the judicial system as a viable means of obtaining justice. In terms of the systemic model of social control, belief in equal access to and treatment by the state is crucial for the mantainance of the state's legitimate monopoly of force that is the basis of public social control. As Hunter (1985, 234) stated, "The calculus of legitimacy is questioned to the degree that this monopoly by the state is seen by some as capricious, selective, inequitable, or ineffective. . . . It is in this sense that inequality in the provision of citizenship rights creates the conditions for eroding a sense of individual duty to the public collective."

I expect that individuals with higher levels of civic participation, general trust in the police, and preference for democratic governance will also experience lower levels of perceived risk and insecurity.

Finally, and most important, the judicial system is incapable of successfully regulating the practices of citizens or the state, in particular agencies such as the police. This leads to a further discrediting of the judicial system and legitimates violence, on both private and public levels, as a response to increasing violent crime, stimulating a "culture of fear" (Caldeira and Holston 1999). This, in turn, can further undermine civil democracy, as citizens call for more violent practices both from the state and private agencies to combat this violence (Caldeira and Holston 1999; Caldeira 2000).

O'Donnell (1993) also points to this inability of the state to successfully regulate social relations as a consequence of the lack of civil democracy. The violence witnessed in Latin America with redemocratization is an expression of this inability of regulation by the state. O'Donnell (1993) further argues that in Latin American democracies the law, rather than being universalistic, varies in its reach and effectiveness. In some areas, (what O'Donnell [1993] refers to as blue areas), law is both fully present and effective. In other areas, (green areas), the law is present but not effective. In still other areas (brown areas), the law is neither present nor effective (O'Donnell 1993). Brazil, then, according to O'Donnell, is "dominated by brown"—"a state whose components of democratic legality, and hence publicness and citizenship, fade away at the frontiers of various regions and class and ethnic relations" (O'Donnell 1993, 13). Echoing the argument of Caldeira and Holston (1999), this lack of democratic legality leads to increases in violence, police abuses, vigilantism, and fear (O'Donnell 1993). In some cases, like in the poor areas of Rio de Janeiro, violent vigilante practices, especially those by drug traffickers, have been shown to actually increase residents' perceptions of neighborhood safety (Arias and Rodrigues forthcoming). However, these perceptions of safety depend on ever-changing relations between residents and drug traffickers, providing limited predictability for residents of their actual risk of violence.

Vigilante violence by nonstate actors further erodes the public order of social control. The public order is "ultimately structured by the state's claim to a legitimate monopoly of the use of coercion, force, and violence. . . . To the degree that coercion or violence are used by institutions of the private and especially the parochial order, they undermine the social control of the rational legal public order" (Hunter 1985, 234). Thus, the lack of democratic rule of law in disjunctive democracy, delegitimizes the state, undermines the public order of social control, and as Caldeira and Holston (1999) argue, can undermine the legitimacy of political democracy as well.

In the Latin American and specifically the Brazilian case, conditions of disjunctive democracy create new threats to the public order of social control. It is no longer adequate to focus only on direct links of residents to public agencies that interact with the community (such as local police). To understand the impact of the public order of social control on perceived risk and fear, it is necessary to focus as well on more general measures of distrust of the police and judicial system and even democratic governance itself.

This study seeks to extend the work of Bursik and Grasmisk, Bursik, Taylor, and others by focusing on the impact of different levels of social bonds on individual's perceived risk and safety in their neighborhoods. In addition to the traditional measures of social bonds for each of the three levels (i.e., friendship ties, neighbor relations, and perceptions of local police), I examine the impact of civic participation, more generalized trust in the police, and democratic governance as important elements of the public level of social control in a disjunctive democracy. Following the systemic model, I present two hypotheses. First, traditional social bonds at all three levels (private, parochial, and public) will decrease the perceptions of victimization risk and increase perceptions of security, independent of individual characteristics and neighborhood conditions such as social disorder and violent crime. Second, I expect that individuals with higher levels of civic participation, general trust in the police, and preference for democratic governance will also experience lower levels of perceived risk and insecurity.

Data and Method

To tests the two hypotheses above, data from the 2002 Survey of the Metropolitan Region of Belo Horizonte (Pesquisa da Região Metropolitana de Belo Horizonte, hereafter referred to as the 2002 BH Area Survey) were used. The 2002 BH Area Survey provides unique data to test the impact of an extended model of systemic social control on perceived risk in the Brazilian context. First, it is one of few random samples of Brazilian data with measures of perceived risk.[1] Second, the survey has a number of questions pertaining to social bonds at the private and parochial level. Third and most important, the survey contains a series of questions measuring varied types of local and civil participation as well as confidence in the police and democratic government.

The 2002 BH Area Survey is a multistage stratified cluster sample of individuals in the metropolitan region of Belo Horizonte, the capital city of the state of Minas Gerais, Brazil. Belo Horizonte is the third largest city in Brazil with a population of approximately 2.2 million people. It is located in the southeast region of the country, approximately 316 miles northeast of São Paulo and 201 miles north of Rio de Janeiro. According to the 2000 Census, 50.46 percent of the population of Belo Horizonte are white, 42.86 percent are mulatto, 6.26 percent are black, with minimal percentages of people of Asian descent and indigenous—0.12 percent and 0.07 percent, respectively. The city's economy is composed mainly of service and government-related jobs with a moderate (18 percent) percentage of industrial jobs, due to large auto manufacturing and mining operations in nearby municipalities.

The survey includes respondents from the capital city, Belo Horizonte, as well as from each of the thirty-two surrounding municipalities, resulting in a representative sample of both the city of Belo Horizonte and the metropolitan region. A total of 1,029 respondents completed the survey, 599 residents of Belo Horizonte and 430 residents in other municipalities of the metropolitan region.[2] Due to the lack of geo-referenced crime data on the other municipalities in the Belo Horizonte Metropolitan Region, this study uses only data on residents in the city of Belo Horizonte, for a total sample size of 599 individuals.

Dependent variables

Most previous fear of crime studies use a single measure of fear of crime—perceived nighttime safety in the neighborhood (Skogan and Maxfield 1981; Baumer 1985). However, recent research (Ferraro and LaGrange 1987; Rountree and Land 1996) has argued that the fear of crime concept is multidimensional, incorporating psychological and emotive components (feeling afraid or worry about crime) as well as cognitive assessments (perceptions of victimization risk). Other criticisms of the use of the nighttime safety measure of fear of crime are that it does not measure the frequency of fear or its severity within a specific time frame (Farrall and Gadd 2004). To capture the multidimensionality of perceived risk, three different measures were used here. While all three are considered cognitive assessments of risk, rather than emotive assessments of fear (Ferraro and LaGrange 1987; Farrall and Gadd 2004), the inclusion of both the traditional safety measure (perception of nighttime safety) and crime-specific perceived risk provides a better measure of risk than a single measure (Kanan and Pruitt 2002; Rountree 1998).

I recoded the dependent variables as binary for the logistic regression analysis. Table 1 contains the descriptive statistics for all the variables in the analysis. Perceived risk of criminal victimization is operationalized by two dummy variables: respondents' perceived risk of being robbed and respondents' perceived risk of being assaulted in their neighborhoods. The original survey questions used a 5-point scale to indicate risk (*very great, great, medium, little,* and *very little*). I collapsed both of the dependent variables so that (1) denotes individuals who indicated their risk as great or very great and (0) denotes individuals who indicated their risk as medium, little, or very little.

Perceived insecurity is operationalized as whether the respondent feels unsafe walking in his or her neighborhood at night, constructed by collapsing the original 4-point scale of the survey question into a dummy variable (where 1 = unsafe and very unsafe; and 0 = safe and very safe).

Independent variables

The independent variables in the model are divided into three categories: social bond variables, contextual variables of perceived social disorder and crime rates in the neighborhood, and individual sociodemographic variables. The last two groups serve as controls in the model to better determine the impact of the systemic social control variables on perceived victimization risk and insecurity.

Social bond variables

Following the systemic model, I created variables to capture social bonds at each of the three levels: private, parochial, and public. Following Hunter (1985), I operationalize private level bonds with a dummy variable measuring the presence of friends in the neighborhood (original survey question: "Do you have friends in your neighborhood or in the area near your home?").

To capture bonds at the parochial level, I include measures of neighbor relations and participation in local associations. Neighbor relations are measured using a standardized index representing neighborliness generated from a factor analysis of three survey questions: the frequency that individuals exchanged favors with neighbors, how much the respondent considered his or her neighbors to be helpful, and how much the respondent trusted his or her neighbors.[3]

The 2002 BH Area Survey includes three measures that can be considered participation in local organizations: participation in community organizations, participation in four different types of religious organizations (political groups, youth groups, couples groups, and any other type of religious group) and participation in informal discussions with neighbors about neighborhood problems. Due to the low number of respondents that indicated participation in each one of these specific groups, I created a single measure of participation in local organizations using a dummy variable indicating if the respondent participated in any of the organizations or meetings detailed above (1 = yes, 0 = no).

According to the systemic model, public social bonds measure links of residents to public agencies. I measured public social bonds by two variables, indicating links with the city and the police. The first variable is a dummy variable based on participation in neighborhood meetings with city representatives (1 = participation, 0 = no participation). I measured links with the police using a standardized index

TABLE 1
DESCRIPTIVE STATISTICS

	Category	Value	N	Min.	Max.
Dependent variables					
Perceived risk of	Yes	40.4%	598	0	1
robbery in neighborhood	No	59.6%			
Perceived risk of	Yes	14.6%	596	0	1
assault in neighborhood	No	85.4%			
Perceived nighttime	Yes	80.4%	591	0	1
insecurity in neighborhood	No	19.6%			
Systemic social control variables					
Private-level social bonds					
Friends in neighborhood	Yes	85.6%	599	0	1
	No	14.4%			
Parochial-level social bonds					
Neighborliness	(Mean)	50	582	37.4	60.1
	(SD)	5			
Participation in local	Yes	31.4%	598	0	1
associations	No	69.6%			
Public-level social bonds					
Participation in meetings	Yes	7.5%	598	0	1
with city officials	No	92.5%			
Perceived legitimacy of police	(Mean)	50	462	29.8	64.8
in neighborhood	(SD)	5			
Civic participation	Yes	23.3%	599	0	1
	No	76.7%			
General distrust of the police	(Mean)	50	564	37	56
	(SD)	5			
Preference for democracy	Yes	83.7%	574	0	1
	No	16.3%			
Preference for authoritarianism	(Mean)	50	560	42.06	61.44
	(SD)	5			
Control variables					
Demographic characteristics					
Sex (ref: female)	Female	51.6%	599	0	1
	Male	48.4%			
Age (in years)	(Mean)	41.5	599	18	89
	(SD)	17.13			
Nonwhite	Nonwhite	62.7%	597	0	1
	White	37.3%			
Socioeconomic status	(Mean)	50	597	33.95	99
	(SD)	10			
Neighborhood contextual variables					
Perceived social disorder	(Mean)	50	572	39.81	56.11
	(SD)	5			

(Continued)

TABLE 1 (continued)

	Category	Value	N	Min.	Max.
Violent crime rates per one	(Mean)	14.01	599	0.62	198.63
thousand inhabitants	(SD)	23.84			
Natural log of crime rates	(Mean)	2.16	599	−0.47	5.29
per one thousand inhabitants	(SD)	0.92			

indicating legitimacy of police acting in the neighborhood. This index was created through the factor analysis of two questions: level of confidence in the police in the neighborhood and perceptions of effectiveness of the police in solving problems in the neighborhood.[4]

Following the proposed extended model of systemic social control, I include four additional measures in the public level. The first is a measure of civic participation of residents, indicating further links outside the neighborhood. The 2002 BH Area Survey has very detailed information about civic participation, asking about participation in seventeen different types of organizations. However, because a small number of respondents indicated participation in each of these organizations, I measure civic participation here with a dummy variable indicating a respondent's participation in any of the following activities: a political party, any organization related to human rights (rights of women, children, the elderly, minorities—such as blacks or homosexuals or the disabled), any organization related to social rights (health, environment, education, or cultural issues), or any occupational organization (unions and professional or student associations), where 1 = participation and 0 = no participation.

The second additional measure on the public level attempts to capture residents' perceptions of equity and fairness in the justice system. To measure this concept, I use an index of distrust of the police, created from a factor analysis of two survey questions measuring perceptions of the number of corrupt police officers in the city and perceptions of the amount of police discrimination against rich or poor people.[5] The third measure, preference for democracy, is based on a survey question asking respondents whether political democracy is a good way to govern the country (1 = very good and good, 0 = bad and very bad). Finally, preference for authoritarianism is a standardized index derived from factor analysis of two questions pertaining to preference for type of government: a strong leader or a military regime.[6]

Control variables

Sociodemographic variables

The model contains the following sociodemographic variables: sex, age, race, and socioeconomic status. Sex is a dummy variable with males as the reference category.

Age is measured in years. Determination of race in Brazil (both self-declared and attributed) is based almost exclusively on skin color and the distinction between mulatto and black is not clear and can change depending on social context. For this reason, I use a binary variable distinguishing only between white and nonwhite, a standard categorization used by others when examining race in Brazil (Silva 1988; 1 = nonwhite [mulatto, black, and indigenous]; 0 = white [white and Asian]). Socio-economic status is a 100-point index created by standardizing the results of factor analysis of years of education and the natural log of family income.[7]

Perceived social disorder and neighborhood crime

Two contextual measures of neighborhood conditions were included in the model: perceived social disorder and neighborhood violent crime rates. Perceived social disorder was measured using a standardized index constructed from factor analysis of three survey questions regarding presence of street children, drug dealing, and gangs in the neighborhood.[8] While measures of prior victimization were not possible using these data, rates of violent crime[9] by census tract were attributed to the individuals in each census tract. These rates were calculated per one thousand inhabitants using the total number of violent crimes occurring in each census tract based on geo-referenced police incidence data and population estimates for each census tract based on the 2000 national census. Due to the skewed nature of these data, the natural log of the crime rates was used in the model.

Results

Table 2 presents the coefficients for the three logistic regressions: perceived risk of robbery, perceived risk of assault, and perceived nighttime insecurity in the neighborhood, with the odds ratios in parentheses.

The results show limited support for the extended systemic social control model. Contrary to my expectations, none of the variables measuring the private- or parochial-level social bonds had significant effects on perceived risk or insecurity. While this evidence is contrary to the systemic social control model of social disorganization theory, it is consistent with some prior research (Kanan and Pruitt 2002).

The public-level measures were more successful in predicting perceived risk than the private or parochial levels. Looking first at the traditional measures of the public level (meetings with city officials and legitimacy of neighborhood police), only legitimacy of local police had a significant effect on perceived risk. As perceptions of legitimacy of neighborhood police increased, perceived risk of robbery and insecurity declined. Each unit increase in the index of perceptions of legitimacy of neighborhood police decreased perceived robbery risk by 9.3 percent and perceived insecurity by 7.6 percent. This result is consistent with the systemic model and other findings on the importance of perceptions of the police on perceived risk (Xu, Fielder, and Flaming 2005; Kelling 1988; Skogan 1990; Velez 2001; Reiseg and Parks 2004).

TABLE 2
LOGISTIC REGRESSION COEFFICIENTS AND ODDS RATIOS FOR PERCEIVED
RISK AND PERCEIVED INSECURITY IN THE NEIGHBORHOOD

	Perceived Risk of Robbery	Perceived Risk of Assault	Perceived Nighttime Insecurity
Systemic social control			
Private-level social bonds			
Friends in neighborhood	−.269 (−25.6%)	−.428 (−24.8%)	.461 (58.5%)
Parochial-level social bonds			
Neighborliness	.003 (0.3%)	−.018 (−1.8%)	−.032 (−3.1%)
Participation in local associations	−.092 (−8.8%)	.022 (2.2%)	−.141 (−13.1%)
Public-level social bonds			
Participation in meetings with city officials	−.222 (−19.9%)	−.233 (−20.8%)	−.925 (−61.4%)
Perceived legitimacy of police in neighborhood	−.097 (−9.3%)°°°	−.009 (−.01%)	−.079 (−7.6%)°°
Civic participation	.438 (55%)	1.182 (226.2%)°°	.855 (135%)
General distrust of the police	−.055 (−5.3%)°	.072 (7.4%)	−.062 (−6%)
Preference for democracy	.020 (2%)	.309 (36.2%)	−1.078 (−66%)°
Preference for authoritarianism	−.054 (−5.2%)°	.056 (5.8%)	.047 (4.8%)
Control variables			
Demographic characteristics			
Sex (ref: male)	−.120 (−17.3%)	.308 (36.1%)	1.015 (175.8%)°°°
Age (in years)	−.014 (−1.4%)	−.010 (−1%)	−.011 (−1.1%)
Nonwhite	−.268 (−23.5)	.089 (9.3%)	−.025 (−2.4%)
Socioeconomic status	−.023 (−2.3%)	−.028 (−6.7%)	.065 (6.7%)°°
Neighborhood characteristics			
Perceived social disorder	.136 (14.5%)°°°	.184 (20.2%)°°°	.076 (7.9%)°°
Violent crime rates per one thousand (natural log)	.012 (1.2%)	.389 (47.5%)°	−.087 (−8.4%)

NOTE: Odds ratios in parentheses.
°$p \le .05.$ °°$p \le .01.$ °°°$p \le .001.$

The variables of the extended model of systemic social control present some interesting results. First, civic participation had a significant effect only in the case of perceived risk of assault, although opposite of that expected. Respondents who participated in civic organizations had a considerably *higher* perceived assault risk (226.2 percent). While this result contradicts the systemic model, it is possible that such participation increases information regarding victimization, resulting in greater perceptions of fear (Skogan 1986).

Generalized distrust in the police only had significant effects for perceived robbery risk. Surprisingly, general distrust in the police *decreased* perceived robbery risk by 5.3 percent. While this is contrary to the extended systemic model, it is supportive of the argument by Caldeira (2000) and Ahnen (2003) that systematic violation of civil rights by the police are perceived as necessary to decrease crime and hence insecurity.

Contrary to my hypotheses, greater preference for authoritarianism was associated with *decreased* perceptions of robbery risk. Each unit of increase in the preference for authoritarianism index decreased perceived robbery risk by 5.2 percent. However, as predicted, stronger preferences for democracy decreased perceptions of insecurity. Those with a preference for democracy had 66 percent less perceived insecurity than those who did not prefer democracy as a form of government.

The lack of significance for the private- and parochial-level social bonds lends support to the argument . . . that community-level bonds alone are not sufficient for determining neighborhood safety.

The control variables in the model confirm the incivilities hypothesis but showed weak support for the vulnerability hypothesis. By far the strongest predictor of perceived risk, perceived disorder had a significant positive effect in all of the models, although slightly less so in the case of perceived insecurity. This is congruent with other studies that found differences in the predictors for perceived risk and fear of crime (Rountree 1998). These results corroborate existing research that disorder is a strong correlate of perceived risk and safety (Skogan 1990; Kelling and Coles 1996; Taylor 1997). However, the results here differ from previous results for Belo Horizonte (Villarreal and Silva 2004), where social disorder did not have an effect on perceived risk. In that study, social disorder was measured using less serious norm violations (arguments or parties late at night and neighbors listening to loud music) than those used here (street children, gangs, and drug dealing). Thus, the impact of social disorder on perceptions of risk and safety in the Brazilian context may depend on the type of social disorder being measured. This is especially plausible because in the poor neighborhoods of urban Brazil, moderate levels of physical and social disorder (especially trash and noise) are the norm, due to lack of basic infrastructure and extremely dense housing conditions. Thus, it is reasonable to expect that only more serious measures of social disorder (e.g., drug dealing, prostitution, and vagrancy) will have significant effects on perceived risk.

Neighborhood violent crime rates had a positive effect on perceived risk, although only in the case of perceived risk of assault. Whereas some prior studies have found that previous victimization has a significant effect on perceived risk (Garofalo 1979), other research has demonstrated that the effect of crime rates on perceived risk may be crime specific (Rountree 1998). While the measure of violent crime rates used in these models included robbery, its effect was only significant on the perception of risk of assault. Thus, it could be that violent crime rates (which here included both homicide and assault) had an impact only on assault, given that these crimes account for the majority of the crimes comprising the violent crime rate.

The results of the sociodemographic variables for each model presented little support for the vulnerability hypothesis. That is, in these models, the sociodemographic variables were only significant for perceptions of insecurity and not for perceived crime-specific risks. Furthermore, only gender and socioeconomic status had significant effects. In the case of gender, women had much greater perceived insecurity than men (175.8 percent), a result congruent with the existing literature (Warr 1984; Skogan and Maxfield 1981; Stafford and Galle 1984). However, in the case of socioeconomic status, the effect was opposite that normally expected under the vulnerability hypothesis. That is, the rich perceived less safety (more insecurity) than the poor. Each unit of increase in socioeconomic status increased perceived insecurity by 6.7 percent. While there was no effect of socioeconomic status on perceived robbery risk here, prior analyses of objective robbery victimization risk show that in Belo Horizonte, the rich are more likely to be victimized (see Beato et al. 2004; Villarreal and Silva 2004). The effect of socioeconomic status shown here, then, would be congruent with the vulnerability hypothesis. That is, the results for perceived insecurity may capture feelings of increased vulnerability of this group.

Discussion and Conclusions

The results above provide mixed support for the extended systemic social control model proposed here. The measures of social bonds at the private and parochial level did not have an impact on perceived risk or safety. While in contrast to most of the social disorganization literature, these results are congruent with some ethnographic studies in the United States (Patillo 1998; Venkatesh 2000) and other previous results for perceived risk (Kanan and Pruitt 2002). These results showed that increased social cohesion does not always increase social control or diminish perceived risk. Patillo (1998) argued, for instance, that neighborhood social ties may include criminals and thus limit the willingness of residents to act against them, thus diminishing social control. Evidence about the relationship between drug dealers and residents in poor urban areas, or *favelas*, in Rio de Janeiro, also supports this idea (Leeds 1996; Alvito 2001; Arias and Rodrigues forthcoming). In other research done in Belo Horizonte, social cohesion in fact *increased* perceived risk, by possibly expanding the level of information about victimization in the neighborhood (Villarreal and Silva 2004).

In addition, the measures used here for social bonds contain general normative elements (trust in neighbors and perceptions of helpfulness of neighbors) rather than just measures of frequency, type of contact, and reciprocity typically used to measure social cohesion (Villarreal and Silva 2004; Sampson, Raudenbush, and Earls 1997). It could be that these normative measures are less important for perceived risk and safety than measures of level of contact among neighbors.

[W]hile support for civil democracy may increase general perceptions of safety, it is the support of institutions that violate civil rights (authoritarian governments and corrupt and discriminatory police) that impact on perceptions of crime-specific victimization risk.

The lack of significance for the private- and parochial-level social bonds lends support to the argument of Hunter and others (Hunter 1985; Bursik and Grasmick 1993) that community-level bonds alone are not sufficient for determining neighborhood safety. In urban Brazil, most violence, especially homicide, is concentrated in poor neighborhoods (Beato et al. 2004). These neighborhoods also have a tradition of high levels of internal social cohesion. Most of these neighborhoods were first settled through organized occupation of unused land by immigrants from rural areas who helped each other in constructing their houses (Leeds and Leeds 1972; Perlman 1976). In addition, strategies for economic survival in these areas depend on mutual support and exchange among neighbors (Leeds and Leeds 1972; Pearlman 1976; Zaluar 1985). However, these poor areas have fewer public-level social bonds. Policing in these areas is irregular and usually violent (Caldeira 2000; Caldeira and Holston 1999). These areas have access to fewer city services, including even basic infrastructure, such as sanitation, electricity, and trash collection. For these reasons, in Brazil, perhaps even more so than in disadvantaged neighborhoods in other countries, parochial-level social bonds are not sufficient to decrease perceptions of risk of victimization.

This idea is somewhat supported by the results for the public level of social bonds. Looking at the traditional measures of public-level social bonds (meetings with city officials and perceptions of legitimacy of neighborhood police), perceptions of legitimacy of neighborhood police were an important predictor of perceived robbery risk and perceived insecurity. Perceptions of legitimacy of neighborhood police, as expected, were related to decreased perceptions of risk of robbery and decreased perceptions of insecurity. These results are consistent with the systemic model and other research that highlights the role of perceptions of the police in community crime control (Xu, Fielder, and Flaming 2005; Kelling 1988; Skogan 1990; Velez 2001; Reiseg and Parks 2004). However, it is important to note that perceptions of legitimacy did not affect the perceived risk of assault. It could very well be that the police are rarely seen in areas with high rates of violent crime, affecting possible perceptions of their actions, legitimate or not.

Looking at the extended model measures of public-level bonds, the results provide some interesting evidence about the consequences of disjunctive democracy. First, civic participation had a significant effect only for perceived risk of assault. However, contrary to disjunctive democracy arguments, civic participation *increased* perceptions of risk. This is also contrary to literature that argues that civic participation enforces social control (Putnam 2000; Bursik and Grasmick 1995). The positive effect of civic participation on risk has two possible explanations. First, given the lack of temporal order among the questions of perceived risk and participation, it could be that perceptions of risk act as a catalyst for civic participation. It could also be that civic participation increases levels of information about violence in general, contributing to increased perceptions of risk and insecurity. Similar results were found for social cohesion in the Brazilian context (Villarreal and Silva 2004).

The results of general distrust of the police and preferences for democracy and authoritarianism demonstrate some of the contradictions present in a disjunctive democracy. Those who think that democracy is a good form of government feel safer. This result lends support to the claim by Caldeira and Holston and O'Donnell that fear, safety, and democracy in Latin America are linked. However, since no temporal order exists among these data, it could well be the opposite: those who feel safer endorse democracy. Thus, perceptions of safety may be a condition for supporting democratic government.

The relationship between civil democracy and perceptions of risk and safety become more complex when examining the impact of the last two extended public-level variables in the model. Contrary to the extended systemic model, preference for authoritarianism and general distrust of the police *decreased* perceptions of robbery risk. These results perhaps best demonstrate the disjunctive nature of democracy in Brazil. In Belo Horizonte, robbery is a frequent crime, with rates of 1,061.64 incidents per 100,000 for 2002 (the year of the survey) occurring in various areas of the city (for details on rates and geographic location of robbery incidences, see the "Atlas of Criminality of Belo Horizonte"; Centro de Estudos em Criminalidade e Segurança Pública [CRISP] 2003a). Thus, perceived risk of robbery could account for much of the insecurity experienced by residents in Belo Horizonte (see Caldeira [2000] for a similar argument for São Paulo).

Caldeira (2000) and others (Caldeira and Holston 1999; Ahnen 2003) have pointed out that these feelings of insecurity result in endorsements of get-tough policies against crime, including endorsements of the use of violence and other illegal or discriminatory practices by the police. Rather than perceive illegal police practices as a threat to democracy and democratic rule of law, these practices are seen as a justified and necessary response to protect the "good citizen" *(o cidadão de bem)* from criminals (Caldeira 2000; Caldeira and Holston 1999; Ahnen 2003; Huggins 2000). For the same reasons, many people speak with nostalgia about the military regime and its ability to maintain law and order (Caldeira 2000). Thus, while support for civil democracy may increase general perceptions of safety, it is the support of institutions that violate civil rights (authoritarian governments and corrupt and discriminatory police) that impact on perceptions of crime-specific victimization risk.

While the results presented here point toward the insignificance of private- and parochial-level bonds in diminishing perceptions of victimization risk and increasing safety in the face of social disorder, in this Brazilian city, the public-level bonds, especially perceptions of police and governmental preference, were important predictors of perceived victimization risk and safety. Although I could not fully test the propositions of the links between democracy, violence, distrust, and rule of law in the Brazilian context, these results demonstrate that models including measures of democracy and democratic values may be important for understanding citizen perceptions of victimization risk and insecurity. Further research is needed, both in Brazil and other Latin American countries, to confirm these results and to better understand the relationship between disjunctive democracy, social control, and perceived risk.

Notes

1. Other samples include recent victimization surveys such as the 2002 Belo Horizonte Victimization Study (Centro de Estudos em Criminalidade e Segurança Pública [CRISP] 2003b), the 1992 and 1996 International Crime Victimization Surveys (Alvazzi del Frate 1998; Zvekic and Alvazzi del Frate 1995), and the 2002 Instituto Latinoamericano das Nações Unidas para Prevenção do Delito e Tratamento do Delinquente (ILANUD) Victimization Survey (ILANUD 2002).

2. Detailed information on samples procedures of the 2002 Survey of the Metropolitan Region of Belo Horizonte (Pesquisa da Região Metropolitana de Belo Horizonte, or 2002 BH Area Survey) can be obtained from the author.

3. The Cronbach's alpha reliability score for these three variables was .5058. The factor analysis with varimax rotation resulted in one factor with eigenvalues greater than 1, containing 52 percent of all the variance. This factor was reverse-coded (as neighborliness rather than lack of neighborliness indicated in the original scales) and standardized using a one-hundred-point scale for ease of interpretation.

4. To correct for skewed distribution, the natural log of the original variables was used in the construction of the index. The Cronbach's alpha reliability score for these two logged variables was .6711. Factor analysis with varimax rotation yielded one factor, explaining 75.25 percent of the variance. This factor score was reverse-coded (to represent an index of police legitimacy) and standardized to a one-hundred-point scale to ease interpretation.

5. For both ordinal variables in the analysis to increase in the same direction (from more to less corrupt and more to less discrimination), the original dicrimination measure was transformed so that the value of no discrimination moved from the midpoint of the scale to the high point of the scale. The Cronbach's

alpha reliability score of these variables is .5159. Factor analysis with varimax rotation yielded one factor score, explaining 687.8 percent of the variance. This factor was reverse-coded and standardized on a one-hundred-point scale to ease interpretation (scale of police distrust).

6. The Cronbach's alpha reliability score for these two original variables is .5460. The factor analysis generated one factor after varimax rotation correlated at .829 for both variables and accounted for 68.79 percent of the variance.

7. Family income was used due to the fact that individual income had several missing cases (N = 242). The Cronbach's alpha reliability score for years of schooling and family income is low, only .2089; however, both the log of family income and years of schooling correlate highly on the resulting factor score (.816 for both variables), accounting for 51.36 percent of the total variance.

8. The Cronbach's alpha reliability score for these three variables (street children, drug dealing, and gangs) was .772. The factor analysis with varimax rotation resulted in one factor with eigenvalues greater than 1, containing 68.97 percent of all the variance. This factor was reverse-coded and standardized using a one-hundred-point scale for ease of interpretation.

9. Violent crime here refers to incidences of attempted and completed robbery and assault, homicide during a robbery, rape, and attempted rape.

References

Adorno, Sérgio. 1998. Violence, security and public perspectives in Brazil. Paper presented at 1998 Meeting of the Latin American Studies Association, Chicago, September.

Ahnen, Ron. 2003. Between tyranny of the majority and liberty: The persistence of human rights violations under democracy in Brazil. *Bulletin of Latin American Research* 22 (3): 319-39.

Alvazzi del Frate, Anna. 1998. *Victims of crime in the developing countries.* Publication no. 57. Rome: UNICRI.

Alvito, Marcos. 2001. *As cores de Acarí: uma favela carioca.* Rio de Janeiro, Brazil: Editora Fundação Getúlio Vargas.

Arias, Enrique Desmond, and Corinne Davis Rodrigues. Forthcoming. The myth of personal security: Dispute resolution, security, and identity in Rio de Janeiro's Favelas. *Latin American Politics and Society.*

Averitzer, Leonardo. 1997. Um desenho institucional para um novo associativismo. *Nova Lua* 39. São Paulo, Brazil: Cedec.

Baumer, Terry L. 1985. Testing a general model of fear of crime: Data from a national sample *Journal of Research in Crime and Delinquency* 22:239-55.

Beato, Claudio Chaves Filho. 2001. Crime e políticas sociais na América Latina. *Informativo CRISP* 1:1-9.

Beato, Claudio Chaves Filho, Betânia Totino Peixoto, and Mônica Viegas Andrade. 2004. Crime, Oportunidade e Vitimização. *Revista Brasileira de Ciências Sociais* 19 (55): 73-90.

Bursik, Robert J., Jr. 1988. Social disorganization and theories of crime and delinquency: Problems and prospects. *Criminology* 26:519-51.

Bursik, Robert J., Jr., and Harold G. Grasmick. 1993. *Neighborhoods and crime: The dimensions of effective community control.* New York: Lexington.

———. 1995. Neighborhood-based networks and the control of crime and delinquency. In *Crime and public policy: Putting theory to work,* ed. Hugh D. Barlow. Boulder, CO: Westview.

Caldeira, Teresa P. R. 2000. *City without walls: Crime, segregation and citizenship in São Paulo.* Berkeley: University of California Press.

Caldeira, Teresa P. R., and James Holston. 1999. Democracy and violence in Brazil. *Comparative Studies in Society and History* 41 (4): 691-729.

Cardia, Nancy. 2002. The impact of exposure to violence in São Paulo: Accepting violence or continuing horror? In *Citizens of fear: Urban violence in Latin America,* ed. Susana Rotker in collaboration with Katherine Goldman, 152-83. New Brunswick, NJ: Rutgers University Press.

Carr, Patrick J. 2003. The new parochialism: The implications of the beltway case for arguments concerning informal social control. *American Journal of Sociology* 108 (6): 1249-93.

Centro de Estudos em Criminalidade e Segurança Pública (CRISP). 2003a. *Atlas da Criminalidade em Belo Horizonte: Diagnósticos, Perspectivas e Sugestões de Programas de Controle.* Internal Document. Belo Horizonte, Brazil: CRISP.

————. 2003b. *Relatório Final de Pesquisa de Vitimização*. Internal Document. Belo Horizonte, Brazil: CRISP.

Covington, Jeanette, and Ralph B. Taylor. 1991. Fear of crime in urban residential neighborhoods: Implications of between- and within-neighborhood sources for current models. *Sociological Quarterly* 32 (2): 231-49.

Diamond, Larry J. 1995. Democracy in Latin America: Degrees, illusions and directions for consolidation. In *Beyond sovereignty: Collectively defending democracy in the Americas*, ed. Tom J. Farer. Baltimore: Johns Hopkins University Press.

————. 1996. Is the third wave over? *Journal of Democracy* 7 (3): 20-37.

Farrall, Stephen, and David Gadd. 2004. Evaluating crime fears: A research note on the pilot study to improve the measurement of the "fear of crime" as a performance indicator. *Evaluation* 10 (4): 493-502.

Ferraro, Kenneth F., and Randy LaGrange. 1987. The measurement of fear of crime. *Sociological Inquiry* 57:70-101.

Garofalo, James. 1979. Victimization and fear of crime *Journal of Research in Crime and Delinquency* 16:80-97.

Gibson, C., J. Zhao, N. Lovrich, and M. Gaffney. 2002. Social integration, individual perceptions of collective efficacy and fear of crime in three cities *Justice Quarterly* 19 (3): 537-64.

Huggins, Martha K. 2000. Urban violence and police privatization in Brazil: Blended invisibility. *Social Justice* 27 (2): 113-34.

Hunter, Albert J. 1985. Private, parochial and public orders: The problem of crime and incivility in urban communities. In *The challenge of social control: Citizenship and institution building in modern society*, ed. Gerald D. Suttles and Mayer N. Zald. Norwood, NJ: Ablex.

Instituto Latinoamericano das Nações Unidas para Prevenção do Delito e Tratamento do Delinquente (ILANUD). 2002. *Pesquisa de Vitimização 2002 e Avaliação do Plano de de Prevenção da Violência Urbana*. São Paulo, Brazil: ILANUD.

Kanan, James W., and Matthew V. Pruitt. 2002. Modeling fear of crime and perceived victimization risk: The (in)significance of neighborhood integration. *Sociological Inquiry* 72 (4): 527-48.

Kelling, George L. 1988. Police and communities: The quiet revolution. *Perspectives on Policing*, no. 1. Washington, DC: National Institute of Justice/Harvard University.

Kelling, George, and Catherine Coles. 1996. Fixing broken windows: Restoring order and reducing crime in our communities. New York: Free Press.

Kubrin, Charis E., and Ronald Weitzer. 2003. New directions in social disorganization theory. *Journal of Research in Crime and Delinquency* 40 (4): 374-402.

Lee, B. A. 1981. The urban unease revisited: Perceptions of local safety and neighborhood among metropolitan residents. *Social Science Quarterly* 62:611-29.

Leeds, Anthony, and Elizabeth Leeds. 1972. *Brazil in the 1960's: Favelas and polity, the continuity of the structure of social control*. Austin: Institute of Latin American Studies, University of Texas.

Leeds, Elizabeth. 1996. Cocaine and parallel polities in the Brazilian urban periphery: Constraints on local-level democratization. *Latin American Research Review* 31:47-83.

McGarrell, Edmund F., Andrew Giacomazzi, and Quint C. Thurman. 1997. Neighborhood disorder, integration and the fear of crime. *Justice Quarterly* 14:479-500.

O'Donnell, Guillermo. 1993. On the state, democratization, and some conceptual problems: A Latin American view with glances at some postcommunist countries. *The Kellogg Institute Working Paper Series*, no. 192 (April): 1-26.

————. 1999. Polyarchies and the (un)rule of law in Latin America: A partial conclusion. In *The (un)rule of law and the underprivileged in Latin America*, ed. Juan E. Mendez, Guillermo O'Donnell, and Paulo Sergio Pinheiro. South Bend, IN: Norte Dame University Press.

Pattillo, Mary. 1998. Sweet mothers and gangbangers: Managing crime in a middle-class black neighborhood. *Social Forces* 76:747-74.

Paxton, Pamela. 2002. Social capital and democracy: An interdependent relationship. *American Sociological Review* 67 (2): 254-77.

Perlman, Janice E. 1976. *The myth of marginality: Urban poverty and politics in Rio de Janeiro*. Berkeley: University of California Press.

Putnam, Robert. 2000. *Bowling alone: The collapse and revival of American community*. New York: Simon & Schuster.

Reiseg, Michael D., and Roger B. Parks. 2004. Can community policing help the truly disadvantaged? *Crime and Delinquency* 50 (2): 139-67.

Rountree, Pamela W. 1998. A reexamination of the crime-fear linkage. *Journal of Research in Crime and Delinquency* 35 (3): 341-72.

Rountree, Pamela W., and Kenneth Land. 1996. Perceived risk versus fear of crime: Empirical evidence of conceptually distinct reactions in survey data. *Social Forces* 74:1353-76.

Sampson, Robert J., Stephen W. Raudenbush, and Felton Earls. 1997. Neighborhoods and violent crime: A multilevel study of collective efficacy. *Science* 277:918-24.

Shaw, Clifford, and Henry D. McKay. 1969. *Juvenile delinquency in urban areas.* Rev. ed. Chicago: University of Chicago Press.

Silva, Nelson do Valle. 1988. Cor e processo de realização socio-econômica. In *Estrutura Social, Mobilidade e Raça*, ed. Carlos Hasenbalg and Nelson do Valle Silva. Rio de Janeiro, Brazil: IUPERJ.

Skogan, Wesley G. 1986. Fear of crime and neighborhood change. In *Communities and Crime*, ed. Albert J. Reiss and Micheal Tonry, 203-29. Chicago: University of Chicago Press.

———. 1987. The impact of victimization of fear. *Crime and Delinquency* 33:135-54.

———. 1990. *Disorder and decline*. New York: Free Press.

Skogan, Wesley G., and Michael G. Maxfield. 1981. *Coping with crime: Individual and neighborhood reactions*. Beverly Hills, CA: Sage.

Stafford, Mark C., and Omar R. Galle. 1984. Victimization rates, exposure to risk and fear of crime. *Criminology* 22:173-85.

Tadesco, Laura. 2002. La ñata contra el vidrio: Urban violence and democratic governability in Argentina. *Bulletin of Latin American Research* 19:527-45.

Taylor, Ralph B. 1997. Social order and disorder of streetblocks and neighborhoods: Ecology, microecology and the systemic model of social disorganization. *Journal of Research in Crime and Delinquency* 33:113-55.

———. 2002. Fear of crime, social ties and collective efficacy: Maybe masquerading measurement, maybe deja vu all over again. *Justice Quarterly* 19 (4): 773-92.

Taylor, Ralph B, Stephen D. Gottfredson, and Sidney Brower. 1984. Block crime and fear: Defensible space, local social ties, and territorial functioning. *Journal of Research in Crime and Delinquency* 21 (4): 303-31.

Velez, M. B. 2001. The role of public social control in urban neighborhoods. *Criminology* 39:837-64.

Venkatesh, Sudhir. 2000. *American project: The rise and fall of a modern ghetto*. Cambridge, MA: Harvard University Press.

Villarreal, Andres, and Braulio Figueiredo A Silva. 2004. Social cohesion, criminal victimization and perceived risk of crime in Brazilian neighborhoods. Paper presented at the annual meeting of the American Sociological Association, San Francisco.

Warr, Mark. 1984. Fear of victimization: Why are women and the elderly more afraid? *Social Science Quarterly* 65:681-702.

Wilson, James Q., and George L. Kelling. 1982. Broken windows. *Atlantic Monthly*, March, pp. 29-38.

Xu, Yili, Mora L. Fielder, and Karl H. Flaming. 2005. Discovering the impact of community policing: The broken windows thesis, collective efficacy, and citizens' judgment. *Journal of Research in Crime and Delinquency* 42 (2): 147-86.

Zaluar, Alba. 1985. *A maquina e a revolta: as organizacoes populares e o significado da pobreza*. Sao Paulo, Brazil: Editora Brasiliense.

Zvekic, U., and Anna Alvazzi del Frate. 1995. *Criminal victimisation in the developing world*. United Nations Publication no. 55. Rome: UNICRI.

Justice for All: Democracy and Criminal Justice

Public Opinion and the Governance of Punishment in Democratic Political Systems

By
FRANKLIN E. ZIMRING
and
DAVID T. JOHNSON

It is unlikely that hostile attitudes about criminals or beliefs that punishments for crime were too lenient were the major causes of the explosive increase in punishments in the United States after 1970. Public hostility toward criminals has been a consistent theme in this country for a long time, but it did not cause big increases in imprisonment before 1970 in the United States or large expansions of incarceration elsewhere. In this article, the authors argue that growth in the salience of crime as a citizen concern and increasing public distrust of government competence and legitimacy were two of a number of changes that transformed ever-present hostile attitudes into a dynamic force in American politics. Negative attitudes toward offenders are a necessary condition for anticrime crusades, but they are always present. It was the addition of fear and distrust into the law and politics of punishment setting that produced the perfect storm of punitive expansion.

Keywords: punishment; democracy; public attitudes; leniency; severity; salience; discretion; trust in government

The subject of this article is the structural arrangements that advanced democracies make to protect against the excessive punishment of criminals. What makes this perspective uncommon is its emphasis on the hardware of governance as well as the software, on how the power to punish is distributed in structures of government as well as on public attitudes toward

Franklin E. Zimring is the William Simon Professor of Law and director of the Criminal Justice Research Program at the University of California, Berkeley. His most recent books include The Contradictions of American Capital Punishment (Oxford University Press, 2003), An American Travesty (University of Chicago Press, 2004), and American Juvenile Justice (Oxford University Press, 2005).

David T. Johnson is associate professor of sociology at the University of Hawaii. He has published about crime and punishment in the United States, Japan, South Korea, China, and Italy; and he is the author of The Japanese Way of Justice: Prosecuting Crime in Japan (Oxford University Press, 2002), which received awards from the American Society of Criminology and the American Sociological Association.

DOI: 10.1177/0002716205285949

crime and government. We then focus on how changes in attitude toward government facilitate changes in the governance of criminal sentencing. The only governmental systems discussed in this article are democracies. Rather than consider the variations in punishment policy among a wider spectrum of governmental types, our focus is on the different ways that punishment policy is produced in democratic systems.

If our topical emphasis is novel, our rhetorical approach is not. We begin this analysis in the great academic tradition of double-barreled complaint. The first section laments the absence of serious discussion of the political science of punishment and then critiques those few scholars who have provided sustained attention to the politics of crime if not to its political science. The second section summarizes knowledge about public attitudes toward crime, criminal offenders, and punishment in a variety of advanced democracies. The third section proceeds in two installments. The first part posits a series of "leniency vectors" in society and government that help explain why so many democracies combine hostile public attitudes toward criminals and enthusiasm for greater punishment with stable levels of imprisonment far lower than their publics seem to prefer. The second part of this section describes a series of recent changes in crime-related matters in the United States that have pushed toward punitiveness. In particular, changes in the salience of crime and in the governance of punishment are important elements of the explanation for the distinctive expansion of punishment in the United States after 1970, but so is the increase of distrust in government itself.

Two Complaints about
the Politics of Punishment

The classic statement of the "two complaints" that provides the title for this section is the joke about the two problems with prison food. The first complaint is that the food is lousy. The second complaint is that they don't give you enough! In that tradition, the first problem we have with academic writing on the political science of punishment is that the topic is rarely addressed. Criminologists and sociologists rarely make the political dimension of crime policy a principal concern, and political scientists almost never do. Part of the problem may be the uncertain disciplinary jurisdiction of such issues: criminologists avoid dealing with political issues, while political scientists have traditionally avoided crime and punishment as scholarly concerns (but see Scheingold 1984, 1991, 1997, 1998). The location of the governance of punishment in a disciplinary no-man's-land may also have biased the nature of the coverage when criminologists do address the governance of punishment. The organization of punishment in the branches of government and the sociocultural context of crime are rarely compared with the political structure and context of other governmental powers or other social issues. What little discussion there is of crime policy and government is usually isolated from other areas of government activity.

Our second complaint is about the assumption in current writing that a hostile turn in citizen attitudes caused the punitive turn in policy. We will argue that, paradoxically, presuming that citizen hostility is the primary cause of punitive policy change may inhibit rigorous testing of the true relationship between attitudes and policies in the United States because observers do not take the trouble to measure citizen attitudes in representative, democratic crime policy environments where radical changes in punishment are uncommon. The operating assumption we wish to question is that changing public attitudes toward crime and criminals are a major explanation of changing punishment policies in the United States. The shift in attitudes imagined in this account is from neutral or lenient to negative and punitive, and the effect of the shift is said to be harsher punishment policy.

Many analysts have assumed that changes in American attitudes have caused the punitive turn. For example, in her exploration of the effects of popular psychology on criminal justice, social critic and lawyer Wendy Kaminer (1995) argued that

> popular solutions to the crime problem, such as "three time loser" laws, imposing life sentences on three time felons, reflect the same volatile mix of fear, fury, and wishful thinking about simple solutions to violent crime that drives demands for the death penalty. . . . Today, hope seems as out of date as beehive hairdos reaching improbably for the sky. The hopeful notion that prisons might rehabilitate people has long been dismissed as naïve, displaced by a belief in retributive justice and the demand that prisons serve as places of near permanent exile for the incorrigible among us. Some liberals still protest America's uniquely high incarceration rate, tirelessly pointing out that we imprison more people per capita than any other country in the world, except for Russia, but a majority of Americans favor building more prisons, despite their costs, and believe that sentencing practices are excessively lenient. (pp. 6, 179)

Similarly, the conservatives William Bennett, John DiIulio, and John Walters (1996) said that

> there is a growing, justified outrage at what is happening to modern American society. People are frustrated because government is failing to carry out its first and most basic responsibility: to provide for the security of its citizens in order to meet the promise of liberty and justice for all. . . . Government failure to restrain convicted violent or repeat criminals has done as much as any other policy failure of the last thirty years to bring about the loss of public trust and confidence in our political institutions. (pp. 15, 136)

Also on the Right, James Q. Wilson (1975, xvi) claimed that "public opinion was well ahead of political opinion in calling attention to the rising problem of crime [in the United States]," an assertion that was made just as the punitive turn began. Wilson later claimed that "public demands" were the key force pushing America's criminal justice policy in a more punitive direction, and he further contended that the "political openness of the American regime" to those demands best explains why crime declined in the United States while it was rising rapidly in England's "less responsive" political system (p. 1).

On the Left, Elliott Currie (1998) argued that the "revolutionary" growth in American prison populations—"a transformation unprecedented in our own his-

tory, or in that of any other industrial democracy" (p. 12)—occurred in part because three enabling "myths have become staples of the popular debate about
crime and punishment in recent years": the myth of leniency, according to which
Americans believe the main reason their country is so "frighteningly violent" is that
their criminal justice system is "shockingly lenient with criminals" (p. 38); the myth
of efficacy, which holds that "prison works" to control crime (p. 53); and the myth of
costlessness, which says that "prison pays" in dollar terms too (p. 67).

On some occasions, assumptions about shifts in public sentiment are parts of
nuanced and complicated treatments of the social construction of crime (Beckett
1997; Scheingold 1998; Garland 2001). More often, however, the assumption is a
simple bedtime story in which citizens who used to believe in understanding criminals and treating crime as a disease have turned so hostile that they now embrace
punishment as the only proper response to crime.

We do not doubt that American and British citizens fear violent crime and are
both punitive and hostile in their attitude toward persons who commit serious
offenses. However, this is far from showing that fear and hostility are sufficient
causes of escalations in punishment in democratic environments. One must ask,
what are the attitudes toward burglars and robbers in Stockholm, Sydney, and
Seoul? And what is the public reaction to widespread coverage of the rape and
murder of children in Ottawa and Brussels? In California, the horror following the
kidnapping, rape, and murder of twelve-year-old Polly Klaas precipitated the passing of the notorious "three strikes and you're out" penal legislation, yet equally hor-
rible crimes occurred in Ottawa and Brussels and seemed to provoke the same fear
and anger but without the massive restructuring of prison terms.

The point is that the way to determine whether public hostility and fear are sufficient conditions for repressive penal legislation in democracies is to sample public
attitudes in a wide variety of different countries with different political environments for penal lawmaking. If public hostility is not a precursor to repression in
many democratic political environments, then negative attitudes toward offenders
should not be regarded as a sufficient cause of punitive legislation or of other
aspects of a "culture of control." Furthermore, if we examine the features of democratic environments where negative attitudes toward offenders coexist with stable
and temperate punishment policies, then we can search those settings for features
of politics and government that ameliorate the punitive force of negative public
attitudes.

Public Attitudes:
In Search of the State of Nature

Little attention has been paid to what is normal in citizen attitudes regarding the
punishment content of government policy. Despite the regular occurrence of
"moral panics" throughout modern history, there is often an assumption that "the
war on crime" is a twentieth-century invention (Tonry 2004). We resist that

assumption and argue instead that one should think about hostility toward criminals as recurrent and normal behavior. Indeed, antipathy toward offenders seems to be the usual condition in modern human societies.

Thomas Hobbes believed that life in the state of nature, before governments and states existed, was "solitary, poor, nasty, brutish, and short" (Hobbes 1660/ 1985, 187). If the quality of life has generally improved in subsequent stages of political development, "nasty and brutish" acts still occur. People have always hated the perpetrators of such acts. Among other scoundrels, persons who rape children appear to be unpopular everywhere, and the same may be said for serial killers. These observations have two implications. First, the nature and intensity of attitudes toward offenders should be measured in a variety of social and political

---

Criminologists and sociologists rarely make the political dimension of crime policy a principal concern, and political scientists almost never do.

---

contexts. Second, if the data confirm our belief about what is ordinary in public opinion, then it is illogical to treat public antipathy to crime and criminals as the key cause of the late-modern turn to harshness that has occurred in places such as the United States, Britain, and the Netherlands. Repugnance toward serious offenders has been conspicuously common in human history, and that "state of nature" cannot explain the recent emergence of the large and widening divide in harshness between the United States and other democratic societies (Whitman 2003).

Although some of the data are thin, the available evidence does seem to suggest that there is substantial cross-national agreement in public opinion about crime, criminals, and punishment.

Crime. For instance, while the United States and Canada have markedly different per capita rates of crime and lethal violence, their citizens share remarkably similar perceptions of their respective crime problems. Studies have found that most Canadians believe the crime problem in their own country is "comparable to, or worse than, the crime problem in America" (Roberts and Stalans 1997, 27). When it comes to assessing the relative seriousness of criminal offenses, there is widespread agreement among people in countries as diverse as Canada, the United States, England, Holland, Denmark, Finland, Norway, Japan, and Kuwait, especially at the two extremes of the seriousness scale (Roberts and Stalans 1997,

63; Hamilton and Sanders 1992, 157). These perceptions of crime seriousness are not only shared cross-nationally, they remain relatively stable over time, and they can be explained by two main factors: the nature of the harm inflicted or threatened, and the offender's state of mind at the time of the offense (Roberts and Stalans 1997, 65).

Criminals. The available research also suggests two features of the state of nature of public opinion toward criminal offenders. First, public attitudes in some countries reflect the view that the typical offender is a "relentless predator" who does not just differ in degree from law-abiding folks but who falls into a distinct category of dangerous "other" (Roberts and Stalans 1997, 113). Second, members of the public frequently discount the causal relevance of external circumstances (such as provocation or socioeconomic stress), preferring instead to make "internal attributions" about what causes criminals to offend. One consequence is that publics tend to believe "once an offender, always an offender," a view that seems dissonant with orientations to rehabilitation (Roberts and Stalans 1997, 31).

Punishment. Finally, the state of nature of public opinion toward punishment reflects three core beliefs. First, "the public in all western countries share the view that the severity of penalties is not commensurate with the seriousness of the crimes for which they are imposed" (Roberts and Stalans 1997, 44). In Japan, too, the public thinks that criminal punishments are "too lenient" (Maeda 2003), and if decent data existed for other non-Western countries, we believe the same pattern would appear. Second, publics in many countries believe that crime is committed *because* punishments are insufficiently severe. Since excessive leniency is perceived to be a key cause of crime, "the vast majority of the public" in all countries express a desire for harsher punishments (Roberts and Stalans 1997, 207). This is the third and most notable feature of public opinion toward punishment in the state of nature. It should come as no surprise, but it does leave analysts with the task of explaining why only American prison populations have exploded if this brand of public hostility is a general phenomenon in democratic nations.

Though the evidence suggests that certain patterns of public opinion recur in a wide variety of cultures and contexts, this conclusion must be qualified in two ways. First, research on the attitudinal state of nature is both thick and thin: so abundant in some ways that it is hard to summarize, yet so lean in others that comparativists are "reduced to guesswork, weaving great swatches of narrative from little rags of data" (Friedman 1993, ix). Students of punishment and democracy need two types of data especially: cross-national measures of *public hostility* toward criminal offenders, and sensitive assessments of *the salience of crime*, both within political units over time and among political units cross-sectionally.

Our second qualification acknowledges that even though public hostility toward serious offenders seems "normal" in human societies, it probably varies in at least two ways. For one thing, the salience of resentment and antipathy seems to differ across time and space. Several factors may account for that variation, including crime rates (LaFree 2002), fear (Glassner 1999), perceptions of disorder (Skogan

1990), the motives of political leaders (Beckett 1997), opportunities to discuss crime and punishment issues (Hutton 2005), and inchoate anxieties about social change (Tyler and Boeckmann 1997). In addition, the state of nature changes over time as targets of hostility expand and contract in accordance with shifting views about what is repugnant. Over the past two decades, for example, "white-collar crimes have attained greater significance in the mind of the [American] populace" (Simpson 2002, 2), while over the past century or so, the most vilified drugs in the United States changed identity several times (Kleiman 1992).

More research is needed to determine whether the contours of similarity and variation in the attitudinal state of nature are as we argue (Zedner 1995). For now, the available evidence suggests that public attitudes about crime and punishment are not a sufficiently "moving part" to explain the vastly different levels of punishment that exist across time and space (Brown forthcoming).

Two Ways of Asking the Same Question

If citizen hostility is a chronic condition in advanced democracies, then the current policy environment in the United States (and to a much lesser extent in England) generates a mystery that can be expressed two ways. One way to phrase the question is to wonder why all democratic governments do not end up reflecting hostility toward criminal offenders with the sort of punitive generality that has been generated in the United States for the past three decades. If democracies reflect public will, and if publics hate and fear offenders, why aren't most advanced democracies engaged in permanent wars on crime? That is the question considered in the first part of this section. A second way to address the same puzzle is to ask what nonattitudinal features of recent American history might account for the singular U.S. escalation in punitive policy given that public hostility and fear of crime are not a sufficient condition. That is, what are the other contributing conditions that have made America different?

Why democracies maintain moderate crime policies

One reviewer of *Punishment and Democracy* (Zimring, Hawkins, and Kamin 2001) accused the elder of us and his associates of having asserted that democratic governments generate more punitive punishment policies than authoritarian states and then proceeded to dispute that proposition (Greenberg 2002, 246). The reviewer was wrong to impute to the authors of that book the notion that democracies are usually more punitive, but why *isn't* that true? If democracies reflect citizen preferences better than authoritarian regimes do, why aren't most democracies much tougher on street crime?

One reason democracies do not spend more energy and resources on punishing criminals is that crime is not an especially important issue in most advanced democratic systems. Theft is common in most countries but a minor threat to the populace, and life-threatening violence is uncommon (Zimring and Hawkins 1996).

Moreover, while citizens do not like criminal offenders, crime policy is not especially important to them in most circumstances (Scheingold 1984).

A second reason moderate crime policy gets implemented is that those places in government that set general crime policy are usually removed from review in elections and even from review by legislatures. They are located instead in parts of the executive and judicial branches of government that are distanced from direct or representative democratic accountability (Zimring, Hawkins, and Kamin 2001). If executive officers make correctional budgets, sentencing commissions make general penal policy, and individual sentencing decisions are made by judges, then we can say there exists the "professionalization of punishment." In professionalized systems, not only are punishment decisions removed from direct democratic control, but the criteria for making such decisions are regarded as involving principles that require professional judgment. Creating a set of purposes of punishment that require expertise to make sentencing decisions also creates a disconnect between citizen preferences and punishment outcomes.

The operating assumption we wish to question is that changing public attitudes toward crime and criminals is a major explanation of changing punishment policies in the United States.

One further method of reducing the connection between legislative determination of punishment for crime and actual punishment is the provision for individualized determination of punishments and the concomitant provision of discretion to legal actors making sentencing decisions to choose among a wide range of potential punishments at their discretion. A wide range of punishments to be selected at the discretion of legal actors might seem to be a neutral feature in a sentencing system, neither increasing nor decreasing severity, but we think that the effect of creating discretionary choices for sentencing usually operates in the direction of leniency, for two reasons. First, discretion removes the selection of a punishment from the legislative sphere and thus distances it from the punitive publics that legislators represent. Second, because the choice of punishment in a discretionary system is made after persons to be punished become known to decision makers, prisoners and their interests are transformed from abstractions into persons (Noonan 1976; Whitman 2003). Where discretionary powers are substantial, offenders and their

TABLE 1
MODERATING AND AGGRAVATING ELEMENTS IN
DEMOCRATIC PUNISHMENT SYSTEMS

Leniency Vectors	Severity Vectors
Software	
Low salience	High salience
Trust in government	Distrust in government
Norms of discretion	Fixed punishments
Hardware	
Delegation to nonresponsive branches of government	Referral to responsive branches of government
Individualization of punishment decisions	Offense-determined general rules of punishment
Professionalization and principles of punishment	Expressive and victim-centered purposes of punishment

advocates will be heard by judges before punishments are set. But why would voters tolerate these exercises of punishment power so far removed from direct democratic control? Mainly because citizens trust government to behave responsibly, and this trust encourages leniency by permitting structural arrangements (such as delegated discretion) that permit judges to individualize sentencing decisions.

Table 1 labels the influences we have described as "leniency vectors" in sentencing systems. The left-hand column lists some features that moderate the severity of punishment in democratic governments. Each leniency influence has a corresponding force called a "severity vector," an influence that, all things considered, will push in the direction of greater penal severity. Table 1 thus maps some of the influences that determine the intensity of penal sanctions. We omit a number of features, such as prosecutorial power, fiscal resources, race relations, and the political orientation of the government and the electorate, that ought to be considered in a comprehensive political science of punishment. We also note that some moderating and aggravating elements can be construed as "software" (the attitudes of citizen and governmental actors) or "hardware" (the structural arrangements that determine who holds power and how it is administered). For instance, because "norms of discretion" and "fixed punishments" imply cultural attitudes and assumptions about how decisions should be made (Friedman 1975), we treat them as software in Table 1. But of course, since norms and culture are also "external to and coercive on" individual decision makers (Durkheim 1895/1982), they could also be considered part of the punishment hardware.

The right-hand entries of Table 1, our list of "severity vectors," represent a short history of major changes in the government and social structure of the United States. Our approach to explaining the shift in U.S. penal policy is to review the development of features mentioned in Table 1, a task undertaken in the next section.

What produced the American changes?

We do not argue that the six entries in the right-hand column of Table 1 exhaust the important developments in U.S. criminal justice over the past three decades, but all of the severity vectors in the table have been prominent in recent history. To start with, fear of crime was not a major issue in the immediate postwar years in the United States, and most criminal justice observers would probably classify crime policy as a relatively unimportant question in the political life of the United States at all levels of government (Scheingold 1991; Roberts and Stalans 1997; Beckett 1997). There is universal agreement that by the late 1980s and early 1990s, crime and crime policy were of very high salience at every level of government (Garland 2001; Gest 2001; Windlesham 1998; Anderson 1995; Kaminer 1995). However, there is no consensus about why crime policy became so much more important in the United States than it had been before.

[O]ne should think about hostility toward criminals as recurrent and normal behavior. Indeed, antipathy toward offenders seems to be the usual condition in modern human societies.

One causal candidate is the increase in crime (LaFree 2002). Between 1964 and 1974, the homicide rate in the United States doubled to 10 per 100,000, and rates of most violent crimes increased as much or more (Zimring and Hawkins 1996). With the crime rise came an increase in media coverage of crime, increases in political concern with crime, and a proliferation of anticrime programs. After 1974, life-threatening violence fluctuated around the new peak rate, dropping from 10 homicides per 100,000 to 7 or 8 and then climbing back to the 1974 high rate in 1980 and close to that rate in 1991 and 1992. Some scholars see a natural relationship between high crime and the increased salience of the crime issue (LaFree 2002; Wilson 1997). Others believe that political manipulation of crime fears was a major cause of higher salience (Beckett 1997). Broader social settings of crime consciousness are also claimed as causes, including the crisis conditions of late modernity (Garland 2001), racism (Chambliss 1999), and fear (Glassner 1999). The higher salience of the crime issue generates stronger pressure for penal repression because the increase in salience does not change attitudes so much as it energizes people to act on a set of beliefs and preferences they may have long held but now regard as important.

The distribution of governmental power in American criminal justice also helps to explain the salience of criminal justice as an issue because more than 90 percent of punishment policy in the United States involves the state level of government (Zimring and Hawkins 1996). Since state government has limited powers except for schools, roads, and criminal justice, it has few domains of great power. This means that crime policy looms large on the horizon of state government because it has little with which to compete.

The current era will provide a key test of whether crime rates are a leading indicator of the salience of crime policy in political discourse. Between 1990 and 2000, crime rates in the United States dropped by almost 40 percent, and since then they have stayed close to the year 2000 lows. Thus, one question that must be followed is whether the salience of crime as a political issue will decline. For those who believe that public attitudes toward offenders might moderate with the crime declines, the most significant crime decline of the post–World War II era will provide a good test of that theory as well. Though the results to date are inconclusive, the five years after 2006 may be an important test of whether lower expectations of crime produce changing attitudes toward criminals and punishment (Zimring forthcoming).

A second major shift in rhetoric and opinion that was generated since the 1970s is a decline in trust in government. This occurred toward all levels of government but has had a number of criminal justice manifestations. The last thirty-five years of the twentieth century produced some epic provocations for distrust of government, including Vietnam and Watergate. While the rhetoric of distrust in criminal justice frequently has a right-wing flavor ("soft on crime," "revolving-door justice," and so on), the various crises of distrust have had broad participation across the political spectrum. In fact, the decline of the rehabilitative ideal in the United States and the assault on indeterminate sentencing in California united Left and Right, albeit temporarily, in an assault on the old order (Allen 1981; Zimring 1983). For one brief moment in history, prisoners and police chiefs were united by distrust of the existing system for governing punishments. How much that union owed to the larger environment of distrust and how that mistrust carried over to other elements of punishment determination are not yet known, but we believe that the seeds of "three strikes and you're out" in California may have been sown with the attack on indeterminacy in the 1970s (Zimring, Hawkins, and Kamin 2001).

Much of the punishment hardware that facilitates leniency depends on trust in government's expertise and benevolence. Citizens are restrained from acting on emotions and "throw away the key" sentiments when they believe that there are principles of punishment—legal proportionality, predictions of dangerousness, responsiveness to treatment—that require governmental expertise. As soon as the claim of expertise is discredited, people on the street (or their state representatives) are every bit as expert as judges, parole boards, or correctional administrators.

Discretion is an even more obvious derivative of trust in those who exercise it. Trust the judge and discretion makes sense. Distrust the judge and mandatory minimum penalties become a preferred method of ensuring that social enemies are punished. The irony is that the power of the state is expanded by those who dislike and distrust state power.

The thirty years after 1975 have witnessed several waves of change in the rules of punishment determination that were generated by distrust in government. Determinate sentencing removed parole power and put the legislature in charge of fixing terms of imprisonment. Mandatory punishment legislation became a staple of the federal and state drug war initiatives of the 1980s. "Three strikes" laws took the prediction of persistent dangerousness that had justified discretionary habitual criminal laws for a century (Morris 1950/1973) and made extended sentences mandatory. As parole and judicial discretion were cut back, the prosecutor's power and discretion have increased. As a result of these changes, criminal justice in early-twenty-first-century America has far fewer checks and balances than it did in earlier times.

---

*If democracies reflect public will,
and if publics hate and fear offenders,
why aren't most advanced democracies
engaged in permanent wars on crime?*

One reason so many changes have pushed in the same punitive direction is the deliberate design of political actors who desire to expand the scale of imprisonment. This type of deliberate engineering made the California version of three strikes generate ten times as many increased sentences as the identically labeled laws in all other jurisdictions combined (Zimring, Hawkins, and Kamin 2001, 17-22). Another example of "intelligent design" expanding punishment is the "truth in sentencing" laws of the 1990s, which expand the percentage of nominal sentences that must be served. This approach was pushed in jurisdictions with widely different sentencing systems, and the only unifying rationale was increasing the length of time served.

Appeals to fear make crime policy more salient. Distrust of government makes punishment policy more mechanically punitive. The close proximity of judges and prosecutors to the electorate and the concentration of criminal justice authority in state government create more sensitivity to political pressure (Bierie and Murphy 2005). In short, what sets the United States apart from other countries is both the greater political importance of crime and the larger structural vulnerability of criminal justice to the political process.

Conclusion

What has always distinguished the governance of punishment in the United States from other advanced democracies is a structural vulnerability to democratic pressures that arises out of federalism, the election of prosecutors and judges, and high levels of life-threatening violence. These enduring features have coexisted with hostility toward criminals and enthusiasm for punishment that seem typical of other advanced democracies. The combination of higher salience and distrust of government increased punishment directly and produced structural changes in sentencing that made punishments even harsher. In the immediate future, those who make crime policy in the United States are not going to do so on a clean slate. Current conditions and future policy decisions are complicated by the direct and indirect legacies of the prior high-salience era.

The path to reform in the United States will involve restoring faith in government and re-creating a role for professional expertise in the determination of punishments.

The path to reform in the United States will require restoring faith in government and re-creating a role for professional expertise in the determination of punishments (Gest 2001, 270). We hope for one other thing in the political science of punishment policy, and that is the involvement of political scientists. A few political scientists have made distinguished contributions to criminal justice scholarship (see, for example, Scheingold 1984, 1991, 1995, 1997, 1998; Scheingold, Olson, and Pershing 1994; Jacob 1984; Skogan 1990; Skogan and Hartnett 1999; Simon 1997, forthcoming; Eisenstein, Flemming, and Nardulli 1988; Flemming, Nardulli, and Eisenstein 1992; and Nardulli, Eisenstein, and Flemming 1988). The governance of punishment in democracies is an important and complicated topic, and scholars and reformers would both profit from a more developed political science of the subject.

References

Allen, Francis A. 1981. *The decline of the rehabilitative ideal: Penal policy and social purpose*. New Haven, CT: Yale University Press.

Anderson, David C. 1995. *Crime and the politics of hysteria: How the Willie Horton story changed American justice*. New York: Times Books.

Beckett, Katherine. 1997. *Making crime pay: Law and order in contemporary American politics*. New York: Oxford University Press.

Bennett, William J., John J. DiIulio, and John P. Walters. 1996. *Body count: Moral poverty . . . and how to win America's war against crime and drugs*. New York: Simon & Schuster.

Bierie, David, and Kathryn Murphy. 2005. The influence of press coverage on prosecutorial discretion: Examining homicide prosecutions, 1990-2000. *Criminal Law Bulletin* 41 (1): 60-74.

Brown, Elizabeth K. Forthcoming. The dog that did not bark: Punitive social views and the professional middle class. *Punishment & Society*.

Chambliss, William J. 1999. *Power, politics, and crime*. Boulder, CO: Westview.

Currie, Elliott. 1998. *Crime and punishment in America: Why the solutions to America's most stubborn social crisis have not worked . . . and what will*. New York: Metropolitan Books.

Durkheim, Emile. 1895/1982. *The rules of the sociological method and selected texts on sociology and its method*. Edited with an Introduction by Steven Lukes; translated by W. D. Halls. New York: Free Press.

Eisenstein, James, Roy B. Flemming, and Peter F. Nardulli. 1988. *The contours of justice: Communities and their courts*. Boston: Little, Brown.

Flemming, Roy B., Peter F. Nardulli, and James Eisenstein. 1992. *The craft of justice: Politics and work in court communities*. Philadelphia: University of Pennsylvania Press.

Friedman, Lawrence M. 1975. *The legal system: A social science perspective*. New York: Russell Sage Foundation.

———. 1993. *Crime and punishment in American history*. New York: Basic Books.

Garland, David. 2001. *The culture of control: Crime and social order in contemporary society*. Chicago: University of Chicago Press.

Gest, Ted. 2001. *Crime and politics: Big government's erratic campaign for law and order*. New York: Oxford University Press.

Glassner, Barry. 1999. *The culture of fear: Why Americans are afraid of the wrong things*. New York: Basic Books.

Greenberg, David. 2002. Striking out in democracy. *Punishment and Society* 4 (2): 237-52.

Hamilton, V. Lee, and Joseph Sanders. 1992. *Everyday justice: Responsibility and the individual in Japan and the United States*. New Haven, CT: Yale University Press.

Hobbes, Thomas. 1660/1985. *Leviathan*. New York: Penguin Group.

Hutton, Neil. 2005. Beyond populist punitiveness? *Punishment and Society* 7 (3): 243-58.

Jacob, Herbert. 1984. *The frustrations of policy: Responses to crime by American cities*. Boston: Little, Brown.

Kaminer, Wendy. 1995. *It's all the rage: Crime and culture*. Reading, MA: Addison-Wesley.

Kleiman, Mark A. R. 1992. *Against excess: Drug policy for results*. New York: Basic Books.

LaFree, Gary. 2002. Too much democracy or too much crime? Lessons from California's three-strikes law. *Law & Social Inquiry* 27 (4): 875-902.

Maeda, Masahide. 2003. *Nihon no Chian wa Saisei Dekiru ka* [Can Japan's social order be resurrected?]. Tokyo: Chikuma Shinsho.

Morris, Norval. 1950/1973. *The habitual criminal*. Westport, CT: Greenwood.

Nardulli, Peter F., James Eisenstein, and Roy B. Flemming. 1988. *The tenor of justice: Criminal courts and the guilty plea process*. Urbana: University of Illinois Press.

Noonan, John T., Jr. 1976. *Persons and masks of the law: Cardozo, Homes, Jefferson, and Wythe as makers of the masks*. Berkeley: University of California Press.

Roberts, Julian V., and Loretta J. Stalans. 1997. *Public opinion, crime, and criminal justice*. Boulder, CO: Westview.

Scheingold, Stuart A. 1984. *The politics of law and order: Street crime and public policy*. New York: Longman.

———. 1991. *The politics of street crime: Criminal process and cultural obsession*. Philadelphia: Temple University Press.

————. 1995. Politics, public policy and street crime. *Annals of the American Academy of Political and Social Science* 539:155-68.

————. 1997. Criminology and the politicization of crime and punishment. In *Politics, crime control and culture*, ed. Stuart A. Scheingold, xi-xxv. Aldershot, UK: Ashgate.

————. 1998. Constructing the new political criminology: Power, authority, and the post-liberal state. *Law & Social Inquiry* 23 (4): 857-96.

Scheingold, Stuart A., Toska Olson, and Jana Pershing. 1994. Sexual violence, victim advocacy, and Republican criminology: Washington State's Community Protection Act. *Law & Society Review* 28 (4): 729-63.

Simon, Jonathan. 1997. Governing through crime. In *The crime conundrum: Essays in justice*, ed. Lawrence M. Friedman and George Fisher, 171-89. Boulder, CO: Westview.

————. Forthcoming. *Governing through crime*. New York: Oxford University Press.

Simpson, Sally S. 2002. *Corporate crime, law, and social control*. Cambridge: Cambridge University Press.

Skogan, Wesley G. 1990. *Disorder and decline: Crime and the spiral of decay in American neighborhoods*. Berkeley: University of California Press.

Skogan, Wesley G., and Susan M. Hartnett. 1999. *Community policing, Chicago style*. New York: Oxford University Press.

Tonry, Michael. 2004. *Thinking about crime: Sense and sensibility in American penal culture*. New York: Oxford University Press.

Tyler, Tom, and Robert J. Boeckmann. 1997. Three strikes and you're out, but why? The psychology of public support for punishing rule breakers. *Law & Society Review* 31 (2): 237-65.

Whitman, James Q. 2003. *Harsh justice: Criminal punishment and the widening divide between America and Europe*. New York: Oxford University Press.

Wilson, James Q. 1975. *Thinking about crime*. New York: Basic Books.

————. 1997. Criminal justice in England and America. *The Public Interest*, winter, pp. 1-18.

Windlesham, Lord. 1998. *Politics, punishment, and populism*. New York: Oxford University Press.

Zedner, Lucia. 1995. In pursuit of the vernacular: Comparing law and order discourse in Britain and Germany. *Social and Legal Studies* 4:517-34.

Zimring, Franklin E. 1983. Sentencing reform in the states: Lessons from the 1970s. In *Reform and punishment: Essays in criminal sentencing*, ed. Michael Tonry and Franklin Zimring. Chicago: University of Chicago Press.

————. Forthcoming. *The great American crime decline*. New York: Oxford University Press.

Zimring, Franklin E., and Gordon Hawkins. 1996. Toward a principled basis for federal criminal legislation. *Annals of the American Academy of Political and Social Science* 543:15-26.

————. 1997. *Crime is not the problem: Lethal violence in America*. New York: Oxford University Press.

Zimring, Franklin E., Gordon Hawkins, and Sam Kamin. 2001. *Punishment and democracy: Three strikes and you're out in California*. New York: Oxford University Press.

Citizenship, Democracy, and the Civic Reintegration of Criminal Offenders

CHRISTOPHER UGGEN,
JEFF MANZA,
and
MELISSA THOMPSON

Convicted felons face both legal and informal barriers to becoming productive citizens at work, responsible citizens in family life, and active citizens in their communities. As criminal punishment has increased in the United States, collateral sanctions such as voting restrictions have taken on new meaning. The authors place such restrictions in comparative context and consider their effects on civil liberties, democratic institutions, and civic life more generally. Based on demographic life tables, the authors estimate that approximately 4 million former prisoners and 11.7 million former felons live and work among us every day. The authors describe historical changes in these groups; their effects on social institutions; and the extent to which they constitute a caste, class, or status group within American society. The authors conclude by discussing how reintegrative criminal justice practices might strengthen democracy while preserving, and perhaps enhancing, public safety.

Keywords: crime; punishment; voting; democracy; reintegration

Recent increases in U.S. correctional populations have stirred both academic and public interest in the emergence and growth of "America's criminal class" (Cose 2000, 48; Pettit and Western 2004; Sutton 2004). Yet in spite of rising awareness of criminal justice expansion, we lack precise information about the number of convicted felons and former felons in society. Furthermore, few attempts have been made to theorize how former felons fit into, and reshape, American democracy. To what extent do former felons share similar life chances? Does a criminal conviction represent a temporary or a permanent blot on their records? How does the growth of the felon and ex-felon population spill over to affect other individuals, families, and groups? In particular, how does the social production of felons and ex-felons ripple outward to affect social and political institutions?

[T]he civil penalties imposed with a criminal conviction effectively deny felons the full rights of citizenship. This denial, in turn, makes performing the duties of citizenship difficult.

We address these questions in this article. We begin by presenting a new analysis of the size and scope of the felon and ex-felon population and some of the characteristics of its members. Applying demographic methods to criminal justice data, we develop estimates of the size and social distribution of the ex-felon population. We chart the growth of this group over time, showing not only the increase in prisoners, but also the even greater growth in the ex-prisoner population, and the much larger ex-felon population that also includes former probationers and jail inmates. In the second part, we summarize and synthesize research on the impact of felony convictions across three social spheres: work, family, and civic life. This information provides the foundation for the third part of the article, where we apply what we know about the felon population to consider how they should be analyzed in terms of the political and stratification system. Finally, we

Christopher Uggen is a professor and chair of sociology at the University of Minnesota. He studies crime, law, and deviance, especially how former prisoners manage to put their lives back together. With Jeff Manza, he has written a book (Oxford, 2006) and a series of articles on felon disenfranchisement and American democracy. Other interests include crime and drug use, discrimination and inequality, and sexual harassment.

Jeff Manza is a professor of sociology and associate director of the Institute for Policy Research at Northwestern University. His work is in the area of social stratification and political sociology. In addition to his work on felon disenfranchisement, he has worked on the social sources of voting behavior and, most recently, on how and when public opinion influences welfare state policy making. He is the coauthor of Social Cleavages and Political Change *(Oxford, 1999) and the coeditor of* Navigating Public Opinion *(Oxford, 2002).*

Melissa Thompson is an assistant professor of sociology at Portland State University. Her research interests include crime, gender, mental illness, and illegal drug use. Her current research focuses on analyzing how gender affects transitions into and out of substance abuse and criminal careers; this research particularly emphasizes life course transitions, mental illness, and the effect of various socioeconomic conditions on gender differences in crime, illicit substance use, and desistance.

make use of these analytical tools to consider their implications for crime and reintegration. To the extent that felons belong to a distinct class or status group, the problems of desistance from crime and reintegration into civil society can be interpreted as problems of mobility—moving felons from a stigmatized status as outsiders to full democratic participation as stakeholders.

[A] "felon class" of more than 16 million felons and ex-felons [represents] 7.5 percent of the adult population, 22.3 percent of the black adult population, and an astounding 33.4 percent of the black adult male population.

The citizenship status and social position of felons raise important questions about the meaning and practice of democracy. The barriers to full polity membership faced by convicted felons are substantial and wide ranging, although they are usually ignored in public debates. A dizzying array of informal barriers also impedes the performance of citizenship duties, in particular those related to employment, education, and reestablishing family and community ties. As we will see, the civil penalties imposed with a criminal conviction effectively deny felons the full *rights* of citizenship. This denial, in turn, makes performing the *duties* of citizenship difficult.

Scope and Composition

It is important to clarify at the outset why we focus on felons. "Felony" is a generic term, historically used to distinguish certain "high crimes" or "grave offenses" such as homicide from less serious offenses known as misdemeanors. In the contemporary United States, felonies are considered crimes punishable by incarceration of more than one year in prison, whereas misdemeanors are crimes punishable by jail sentences, fines, or both. Not all felons go to prison, however, and many serve time in jail or on probation in their communities.

Misdemeanants as well as felons experience wide-ranging criminal penalties and disruptions in their lives. Nevertheless, the line between a felony and misdemeanor is significant because convicted felons face far more substantial and frequently permanent consequences. They typically confront legal restrictions on employment, access to public social benefits and public housing, and eligibility for educational benefits. Depending on their state of residence, they may also lose parental rights, the right to vote, the right to serve on juries, and the right to hold public office. In many states, their criminal history is public record, readily searchable for anyone who wants to know.

Determining the size and characteristics of the total felon population—including current felons in prison, those on probation and parole, and those who have completed their entire sentences—is a difficult task. To be sure, it is relatively easy to obtain data on people currently under criminal justice supervision; the U.S. Department of Justice has long provided detailed information on current correctional populations. Yet as we discuss in more detail below, many of the civil disabilities imposed on felons represent permanent rather than temporary suspensions of their rights. To estimate the size of the entire group, we need information about *former* felons who are no longer under supervision. Although some recent work has estimated the number of former prisoners in the population (Bonczar 2003; Pettit and Western 2004), no one has yet attempted to estimate the scope of the much larger population of former felons. In addition to ex-prisoners and parolees, the ex-felon population also contains ex-probationers and ex–jail inmates. After outlining our methodology, we present our estimates of ex-prisoner and ex-felon populations and describe historical changes in these groups.

Method

Our estimates of the number of ex-prisoners in the United States are based on the number exiting prisons each year (including those conditionally released to parole) since 1948. In addition to these former prisoners, our estimates of ex-felons include those felons leaving probation supervision and jails each year. Using demographic life tables, we compute the number of these former felons lost to recidivism and mortality annually. Based on national studies of probationer and parolee recidivism, we assume that most ex-prisoners will ultimately return to prison and that a smaller percentage of ex-probationers and jail inmates will cycle back through the justice system. We further assume a much higher mortality rate among felons relative to the nonfelon population. Both groups are removed from the ex-felon pool—the recidivists because they would already be counted among the "current" felon population, and the deaths because they are permanently removed from the population. Each existing release cohort is thus successively reduced each year and joined by a new cohort of releasees, allowing us to compute the number of ex-felons no longer under supervision in each year. Details for this technique are discussed in the appendix.

Population data and previous estimates

Based on his classic analysis of Philadelphia men born in 1945, Marvin Wolfgang (1983) estimated that nearly 50 percent of urban males would experience at least one arrest by age thirty. For more recent cohorts, that percentage would almost

FIGURE 1
CORRECTIONAL POPULATIONS IN THE UNITED STATES, 1980-2004

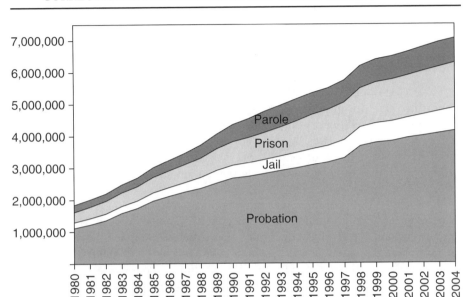

certainly be higher. Arrest, conviction, and incarceration are becoming increasingly common life events, particularly for young men of color (Pettit and Western 2004). Indeed, all categories of correctional populations—prisoners, parolees, jail inmates, and probationers—have grown at astounding rates since the 1970s. As shown in Figure 1, a total of 7.0 million people were under some form of correctional supervision in 2004, relative to 1.8 million as recently as 1980. Prisons and jails in the United States now house more than 2.2 million inmates, representing an overall incarceration rate of 726 per 100,000 population (U.S. Department of Justice 2005). By comparison, approximately 210,000 were imprisoned in 1974, or 149 per 100,000 adult U.S. residents. The number of probationers and parolees has grown rapidly as well. In 1980, there were only 1.1 million probationers and 220,000 parolees, compared to more than 4.1 million probationers and 765,000 parolees in 2004. In short, more incarcerated and nonincarcerated felons are serving sentences today than at any other time in U.S. history.

These increases are unprecedented. Yet their impact is further magnified because the felon population is not drawn at random from the entire U.S. population. With regard to incarceration, young African American men are dramatically overrepresented relative to other groups. In fact, African American males born from 1965 to 1969 are currently more likely to have prison records (22 percent) than either military records (17 percent) or bachelor's degrees (13 percent)

(Pettit and Western 2004). The Bureau of Justice Statistics further estimates that about 32 percent of African American men and 17 percent of Latino men born in 2001 will go to prison during their lifetimes, compared to less than 6 percent of white men (Bonczar 2003).

The prison population

To develop our estimates, we begin with the relatively restrictive focus of previous work on imprisonment in a state or federal penitentiary. We know that there are currently 2.3 million prisoners and parolees under supervision. As columns 1 and 2 of Table 1 show, this figure is almost eight times the 1968 figure. Today, about 1 percent of the adult population, 2 percent of the adult male population, and 6.6 percent of the black adult male population are in prison or conditionally released from prison on parole.

How many former prisoners are in the population? Our life tables produce estimates of an additional 4 million ex-prisoners in the population by 2004. Combining the current and the ex-prisoner figures, more than 6 million U.S. citizens have served time in a penitentiary, as shown in columns 5 and 6 of Table 1. This group represents about 2.9 percent of the adult population, 5.5 percent of the adult male population, and 17 percent of the black adult male population. As illustrated in Figure 2, the ex-prisoner population was stable at approximately 1 million persons from the 1950s to the late 1970s. Following the incarceration increases since the mid-1970s, however, this group has cumulated very rapidly, reaching 2 million by 1994 and 3 million by 2000. Figure 3 expresses these changes in rates rather than raw numbers, showing how prisoners and former prisoners have increased as a percentage of the U.S. adult population since the mid-1980s.

These estimates for former prisoners are comparable to those provided by other researchers applying different demographic techniques. For example, Bonczar (2003) estimated that in 2001, 2.7 percent of adults, 4.9 percent of adult males, and 16.6 percent of African American adult males had been to prison. Pettit and Western (2004) noted that black men born between 1945 and 1949 had a 10.6 percent chance of imprisonment, relative to a 20.5 percent chance for black men born between 1965 and 1969. These figures are generally congruent with our overall estimate that 17 percent of black men had experienced imprisonment by 2004. This consistency with earlier research provides an important check on our approach, as we next apply it to develop estimates of the much broader class of convicted felons.

The total felon population

Although imprisonment is an important marker of serious punishment, convicted felons who do not serve time in prison are also members of a stigmatized criminal class. In thirty-one states, for example, convicted felons serving probation sentences lose the right to vote (Manza and Uggen 2006). Though others have estimated the risk of imprisonment and the size of the ex-prisoner population, we

TABLE 1
ESTIMATED U.S. CURRENT AND EX-PRISONERS BY YEAR AND RACE

Year	Current Prison/Parole		Ex-Prison/Parole		Total Prison/Parole	
	(1) Total	(2) Black	(3) Total	(4) Black	(5) Total	(6) Black
1968	298,711	110,122	1,031,279	320,118	1,329,990	430,240
Percentage adult population	0.25	0.95	0.86	2.77	1.11	3.72
Percentage adult male population	0.49	1.87	1.66	5.37	2.15	7.24
1978	485,123	198,190	1,020,182	307,651	1,505,305	505,841
Percentage adult population	0.31	1.21	0.64	1.88	0.95	3.10
Percentage adult male population	0.60	2.37	1.24	3.60	1.83	5.97
1988	1,035,196	492,819	1,487,730	492,977	2,522,926	985,796
Percentage adult population	0.57	2.42	0.82	2.42	1.39	4.84
Percentage adult male population	1.10	4.69	1.56	4.58	2.66	9.27
1998	2,004,060	1,001,819	2,790,155	1,096,014	4,794,215	2,097,833
Percentage adult population	1.00	4.22	1.39	4.62	2.38	8.85
Percentage adult male population	1.90	8.07	2.62	8.66	4.52	16.73
2000	2,107,419	928,645	3,200,076	1,306,559	5,307,495	2,235,204
Percentage adult population	1.02	3.77	1.55	5.30	2.58	9.07
Percentage adult male population	1.95	7.14	2.92	9.87	4.87	17.01
2004	2,318,218	981,798	4,007,829	1,613,937	6,326,047	2,595,735
Percentage adult population	1.07	3.85	1.86	6.33	2.93	10.18
Percentage adult male population	2.03	6.56	3.45	10.52	5.49	17.08

NOTE: Assumes three-year recidivism rate of 41.4 percent for prisoners and parolees (65.9 percent lifetime). Includes prison and parole only.

FIGURE 2
U.S. PRISONERS AND ESTIMATED EX-PRISONERS, 1948-2004

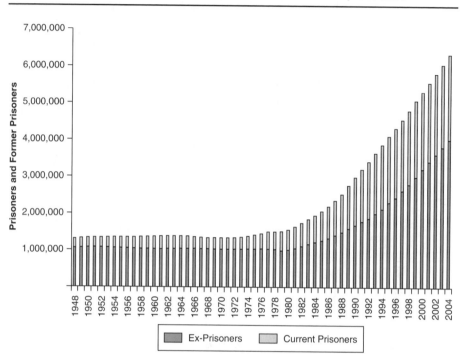

are unaware of any estimates of the ex-felon population, which includes felons sentenced to probation and jail. We adopt this more inclusive view of the total felon class in Table 2.

As shown in column 1 of Table 2, more than 4.4 million felons are currently serving time in prison or jail, or supervised in the community on parole or probation.[1] This represents about 2 percent of the adult population, 3.6 percent of adult males, 6.3 percent of black adults, and about 10.1 percent of black adult males. Columns 3 and 4 show our estimates of the ex-felon population: about 11.7 million overall, representing 5.4 percent of adults, 9.2 percent of adult males, and almost one-fourth of all black adult males. When combined with the current felon group, this produces a "felon class" of more than 16 million felons and ex-felons, representing 7.5 percent of the adult population, 23.3 percent of the black adult population, and an astounding 33.4 percent of the black adult male population. These figures are shown in columns 5 and 6 of Table 2.

The number of ex-felons cumulates more rapidly than the number of ex-prisoners because of the lower recidivism rate of probationers relative to prisoners. As

FIGURE 3
U.S. PRISONERS AND ESTIMATED EX-PRISONERS AS PERCENTAGE
OF ADULT POPULATION BY RACE, 1948-2004

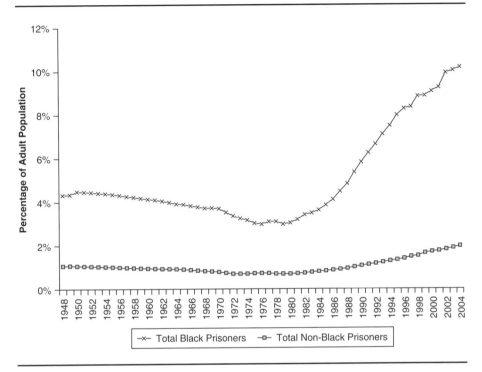

Figures 4 and 5 show, the ex-felon population has risen steadily since the late 1960s, when data on nonincarcerated correctional populations began to be more consistently reported. As might be expected, women account for a minority of the population of former felons: more than 82 percent of all current and ex-felons are male.

We realize that these estimates are large in magnitude. Despite our precautions to avoid double counting and our conservative assumptions about mortality and recidivism, it is possible that they may overstate the size of the ex-felon population. On the other hand, our estimates seem far more reasonable when considered alongside *current* correctional populations. The population of current prisoners and felons is based on very-high-quality data by social science standards—we have an accurate census of the total number under supervision at a given time, and good information about their distribution by race and sex. How do the former prisoner and felon numbers stack up against the current numbers? We estimate the ex-prisoner population at 1.7 times the size of the current prisoner population and the ex-felon

TABLE 2
ESTIMATED U.S. CURRENT AND EX-FELONS BY YEAR AND RACE

Year	Current Felons		Ex-Felons		Total Felons	
	(1) Total	(2) Black	(3) Total	(4) Black	(5) Total	(6) Black
1968	659,462	201,963	3,039,950	750,757	3,699,413	952,720
Percentage adult population	0.55	1.75	2.53	6.49	3.08	8.24
Percentage adult male population	1.03	3.30	4.46	11.55	5.49	14.85
1978	922,282	321,556	3,814,600	908,474	4,736,882	1,230,031
Percentage adult population	0.58	1.97	2.41	5.56	2.99	7.53
Percentage adult male population	1.08	3.68	4.20	9.74	5.28	13.42
1988	1,947,177	791,417	5,520,836	1,448,953	7,468,013	2,240,369
Percentage adult population	1.07	3.88	3.03	7.11	4.10	10.99
Percentage adult male population	1.96	7.20	5.27	12.38	7.24	19.59
1998	3,654,388	1,561,462	8,598,894	2,677,426	12,253,282	4,238,887
Percentage adult population	1.82	6.58	4.27	11.29	6.09	17.87
Percentage adult male population	3.25	11.96	7.38	19.54	10.63	31.51
2000	4,166,091	1,625,044	9,324,621	3,092,869	13,490,711	4,717,914
Percentage adult population	2.02	6.60	4.53	12.55	6.55	19.15
Percentage adult male population	3.58	11.74	7.79	21.61	11.37	31.51
2004	4,409,826	1,606,639	11,704,462	3,890,130	16,114,288	5,496,770
Percentage adult population	2.04	6.30	5.43	15.25	7.47	21.55
Percentage adult male population	3.59	10.11	9.18	23.29	12.77	33.40

NOTE: Assumes three-year recidivism rate of 41.4 percent for all prisoners and parolees (65.5 percent lifetime) and 36 percent for probationers (57.3 percent lifetime). Includes prison, parole, felony probation, and convicted felony jail populations.

population at 2.7 times the current felon population. In light of the average age at release, the large number who never recidivate, and the similarity of our ex-prisoner estimates to those of other researchers (Bonczar and Beck 1997; Pettit and Western 2004), we believe that these ratios are reasonable and lend our estimates some degree of face validity.

FIGURE 4
U.S. FELONS AND ESTIMATED EX-FELONS, 1968-2004

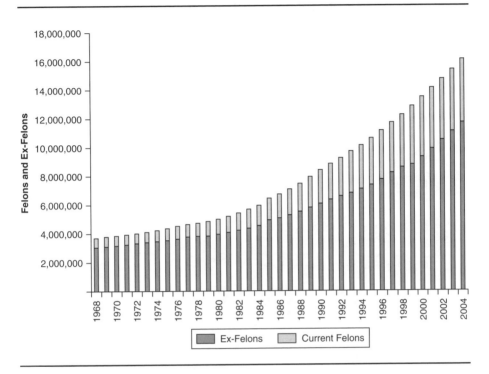

Social characteristics of felons

Having counted the current felon population and estimated the ex-felon population, we now summarize what we know about these groups. The U.S. Department of Justice regularly conducts large, nationally representative surveys of state prison inmates and occasional surveys of probationers and parolees. As shown in Table 3, men and racial minorities are vastly overrepresented in the criminal justice system relative to the general population. By the late 1990s (the most recent year of data collection), 94 percent of all prison inmates, 90 percent of parolees, and 79 percent of probationers were males. Today, only one-third of all prison inmates are non-Hispanic whites, while approximately half are non-Hispanic blacks. The parole population mirrors the prison population, whereas whites comprise a greater share of the probation population. Although the race distribution has not changed dramatically since 1974, imprisonment clearly affects a much greater proportion of black than white Americans. African Americans make up almost half of the prison and parole populations and almost one-third of the felony probation population, as compared with 12 percent of the general population and 13 percent of the male population aged twenty-five to thirty-four.

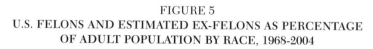

FIGURE 5
U.S. FELONS AND ESTIMATED EX-FELONS AS PERCENTAGE
OF ADULT POPULATION BY RACE, 1968-2004

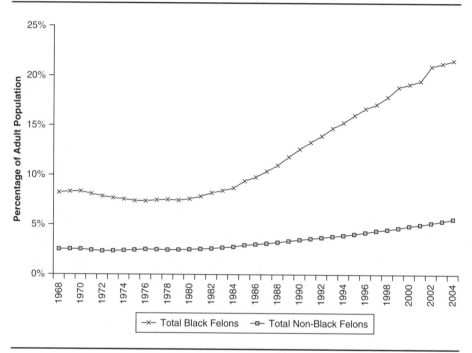

Sociological models of inequality suggest
three major conceptual schemes
for understanding the place of felons
in American politics and society: castes,
classes, *and* status groups.

While the rate and absolute number of incarcerated persons has changed dramatically, so too have the conviction offenses. Drug crimes, which had accounted for about 10 percent of the prison population in 1974, increased to more than 26 percent by 1997. The mean age of prison entry has also risen steadily since the

TABLE 3
CHARACTERISTICS OF PRISON INMATES
PRIOR TO INCARCERATION, 1974-1997

	Prison Inmates			Parole, 1999	Felony Probation, 1995	U.S. Men Aged Twenty-Five to Thirty-Four, 1997
	1974	1986	1997			
Sex (percentage male)	96.7	95.6	93.7	90.1	79.1	100
Race						
Percentage black, non-Hispanic	49	45	47	47.3	31	12.8
Percentage white, non-Hispanic	39	40	33	35.4	55	68.9
Percentage Hispanic	10	13	17	16.1	11	13.2
Percentage other	2	3	3	1.2	3	5.0
Conviction offense						
Percentage violent offense	52.5	64.2	46.4	24.4	19.5	
Percentage property offense	33.3	22.9	14.0	30.8	36.6	
Percentage drug offense	10.4	8.8	26.9	35.3	30.7	
Percentage public order offense	1.9	3.3	8.9	9.0	12.1	
Percentage other offense	2.0	0.9	3.7	0.5	1.0	
Age at admission to prison	26.5	27.6	32.5			
	(9.3)	(8.7)	(10.4)			
Current age	29.6	30.6	34.8	34.0	31.9	29.7
	(10.0)	(9.0)	(10.0)			

(continued)

TABLE 3 (continued)

	Prison Inmates			Parole, 1999	Felony Probation, 1995	U.S. Men Aged Twenty-Five to Thirty-Four, 1997
	1974	1986	1997			
Education						
Years of education	9.9	10.9	10.7			
Percentage with high school diploma/GED	21.1	31.9	30.6	49.2	54.4	87.3
Employment						
Percentage full-time employed	61.6	57.3	56.0			77.0
Percentage part-time/occasional employed	7.3	11.6	12.5			12.1
Percentage looking for employment	12.5	18.0	13.7			3.9
Percentage not employed and not looking for work	18.5	13.0	17.8			7.0
Family status						
Percentage never married	47.9	53.7	55.9		50.8	40.4
Percentage married	23.7	20.3	17.7		26.8	53.0
Percentage with children	60.2	60.4	56.0			
Number of children	1.7	2.3	2.5			
	(2.0)	(1.7)	(1.9)			

SOURCE: *Survey of Inmates in State and Federal Correctional Facilities, 1974-1997* (U.S. Department of Justice 2000b); *Trends in State Parole 1990-1999* (U.S. Department of Justice 2001b); *Characteristics of Adults on Probation, 1995* (U.S. Department of Justice 1997); *Statistical Abstract of the United States* (U.S. Census Bureau 1998). Adapted from Manza and Uggen (2006).
NOTE: Standard deviations for continuous variables are in parentheses.

1970s, with prisoners now averaging more than thirty years of age at the time of admission. Yet prison inmates remain socioeconomically disadvantaged relative to other U.S. men aged twenty-five to thirty-four. They have very low levels of education: less than one-third have received a high school diploma or equivalency, compared to approximately half the parole and felony probation populations. Employment levels at the time of arrest have declined gradually since 1974, with a slim majority of prisoners (56 percent) holding a full-time job prior to their most recent arrest in the 1997 survey. By comparison, more than three-fourths of men of comparable age in the general population held full-time jobs and 87 percent had attained a high school degree.

With regard to family status, married prisoners declined from 24 percent of inmates in 1974 to 18 percent in 1997. The comparable figures for U.S. males in this age range were 80 percent in 1973 and 53 percent in 1997. Despite low marriage rates, most inmates are parents: 56 percent reported at least one child in the most recent survey. Although these trends in marriage and nonmarital births mirror larger societal shifts, the characteristics of the inmate population have remained relatively stable over the past twenty-five years. Prison and jail inmates lag furthest behind their contemporaries in the general population. Probationers and parolees are somewhat better off socioeconomically than prisoners, though they are less likely to be married than males aged twenty-five to thirty-four.

The major political parties need not attend to the concerns of more than 5 million citizens—mostly poor people and people of color—who are currently locked out of the democratic process.

Compared to the nonincarcerated population, prisoners have long been undereducated, underemployed, relatively poor, and disproportionately non-white. What has changed, however, are the absolute numbers as well as the proportion of Americans under correctional supervision. Since it is much easier to survey confined inmates than released offenders, we know less about felons after they have been released from supervision. Moreover, most state and national studies of released prisoners are based upon record searches for official recidivism rather than representative surveys about their work, family, and civic life. Qualitative research on desistance from crime provides some evidence on the social position of ex-felons after their release from correctional supervision. Although most criminal offenders eventually desist from crime as they age, few go on to become successful by conventional standards in work, family, or community life (Irwin 1987; Laub and Sampson 2003).

Individual and Aggregate Consequences

Why do former felons have such difficulties becoming stakeholding citizens? One reason is the formal and informal collateral consequences attending to felony convictions. Collateral sanctions operate as an interconnected system of disadvantage that amplifies disparities in economic and social well-being (Wheelock 2005; Wheelock and Uggen 2005). As suggested above, former felons must fulfill the *duties* of citizenship, but their conviction status effectively denies their *rights* to participate in social life. Table 4 lists examples of formal postincarceration penalties imposed on felons, including those affecting housing, jury service, education, employment, and family life. States differ greatly in the extent to which they apply such consequences. As Jeremy Travis (2002) has pointed out, these "collateral sanctions" are much less visible than the penitentiary, though their consequences to felons may be equally profound. The research literature has only begun to explore the independent contribution of each sanction to the problem of reintegration, although scholarly volumes on "invisible punishment" and "civil penalties" have recently appeared (Mauer and Chesney-Lind 2002; Mele and Miller 2005; Uggen 2005).

We next consider the impact of felony convictions for individuals and for U.S. society as a whole, across three interrelated domains: (1) civic, including political participation and electoral outcomes; (2) socioeconomic, including labor market opportunities and occupational attainment; and (3) familial, including intergenerational transmission of crime and class and aggregate demand for social services.

Civic consequences

British sociologist T. H. Marshall's (1950) concept of citizenship vividly illustrates how felons are set apart from others in democratic societies. Marshall viewed citizenship as "a status bestowed on those who are full members of a community. All who possess the status are equal with respect to the rights and duties to which the status is endowed" (p. 84). If citizenship implies "full membership," what happens when felons lose the rights to perform the duties of citizenship, such as voting and serving on juries? More than thirty years ago, the National Advisory Commission on Criminal Justice Standards and Goals (1973) singled out such political sanctions in its *Report on Corrections*:

> Limitations on political rights and those involving courts, such as the right to sue and the use of an ex-offender's record as grounds for impeaching his testimony, are the most onerous restrictions. They involve in essence a statement by the government that offenders and

TABLE 4
RIGHTS AND OPPORTUNITIES POTENTIALLY
AFFECTED BY A FELONY CONVICTION

Domain	Examples	States
Employment	Right to employment; public employment; licensure in specific occupations	Twenty-nine states permit employers to consider arrests that never led to conviction.
Financial aid	Eligibility for student grants and loans	Fifty states restrict for those convicted of drug-related offenses.
Firearm ownership	Right to possess firearms	Forty-three states have firearms, pistol, or handgun restrictions
Immigration status	Residence in United States	Resident aliens may be deported in all states.
Jury service	Right to serve as a member of a jury	Forty-seven states restrict right to serve on jury.
Marital dissolution	Allow criminal conviction as grounds for divorce	Twenty-nine states consider criminal conviction as grounds for marital dissolution.
Parental rights	Termination of parental rights; restrictions on becoming an adoptive or foster parent	Forty-eight states allow for termination of parental rights for some offenses. Fifteen states bar felons from becoming adoptive or foster parents.
Privacy	Registration and community notification for sex offenders	Fifty states mandate criminal registration of sex offenders
Public assistance	Receipt of food stamps and Temporary Assistance for Needy Families	Seventeen states permanently deny benefits for those convicted of drug felonies.
Public housing	Right to reside in public housing	Forty-seven states permit individualized determinations; three states have broad bans.
Public office	Right to hold public office	Forty states restrict the right to hold public office.
Voting	Right to vote	Forty-eight states deny the right to current prisoners.

SOURCE: Buckler and Travis (2003); Chin (2002); Grant et al. (1970); Kalt (2003); Mauer and Chesney-Lind (2002); Office of the Pardon Attorney (2000); Olivares, Burton, and Cullen (1997); Samuels and Mukamal (2004); Steinacker (2003).

former offenders, as a class, are worth less than other men. This lessening of status on the outside reinforces the debasement so common in the institutional setting and hardens the resentment offenders commonly feel toward society in general. (p. 47)

In addition to the individual impact of such restrictions, felon disenfranchisement can affect political elections by reshaping the electorate. Because felons are drawn disproportionately from the ranks of racial minorities and the poor, disenfranchisement laws tend to take votes from Democratic candidates (Uggen and Manza 2002). Although estimated turnout among felons is well below that of nonfelons, our National Election Study analysis strongly suggests that felon disenfranchisement played a decisive role in the 2000 U.S. presidential election and in several U.S. Senate elections since 1978 (Manza and Uggen 2006). A less visible but perhaps equally important political impact may be in the subtle shifting of the terms of political debate. The major political parties need not attend to the concerns of more than five million citizens—mostly poor people and people of color—who are currently locked out of the democratic process.

Socioeconomic consequences

Arrest, conviction, and incarceration impose immediate wage penalties and alter long-term earnings trajectories by restricting access to career jobs (Freeman 1992; Pager 2003; Western 2002). These findings are not surprising in view of what we know about employer preferences and state laws regulating employment of felons and access to felony records. A number of occupations are closed to some or most categories of ex-felons—for example, jobs requiring contact with children, certain health service occupations, and security services (Dietrich 2002; May 1995). In California, some 261 ineligible job titles span diverse fields and activities; in New York, ineligible occupations include barber shop owner, boxer/wrestler, commercial feed distributor, and emergency medical technician; in Florida, the list includes acupuncturist, speech-language pathologist, and cosmetologist (Samuels and Mukamal 2004).

Another important employment disadvantage for felons is the widespread availability of criminal history information (including, in some cases, arrest records). A 1999 survey found that twenty-three states had some form of public access or freedom of information statutes that permitted access to job applicants' criminal histories (U.S. Department of Justice 1999). In these states, it is relatively easy for employers to conduct criminal background checks of prospective employees. One recent survey of employers in Atlanta, Boston, Detroit, and Los Angeles found that 32 percent always checked, and 17 percent sometimes checked, the criminal histories of prospective employees (Holzer, Raphael, and Stoll 2004, 213). Such employer checks have been justified, in part, by the legal theory of negligent hiring, in which employers may be held liable for an employee's criminal or tortuous acts while on the job (Bushway 2004).

Concerns about the socioeconomic reintegration of large numbers of felons and ex-felons into the labor force are increasingly attracting policy attention. For example, some states are debating whether to seal conviction records of some misdemeanants and nonviolent felons to enhance the employability of these groups (Lueck 2000). Even if such efforts were to become law, however, they would not affect millions of additional felons and ex-felons in these and other states. Background checks, job restrictions, and other socioeconomic consequences of felony convictions clearly suppress employability and economic attainment. These deficits, in turn, likely hinder former felons from participating as full members of their communities.

Family consequences

Taking care of one's children is a key responsibility of citizenship. The socio-economic and civic consequences of punishment are thus intimately tied to family life and the position of felons and ex-felons within their families. As detailed above, most prison inmates are unmarried fathers, though the number of mothers in prison has risen steadily in recent years. The two family issues receiving the greatest scholarly attention have been the intergenerational transmission of crime and class (Rowe and Farrington 1997) and the effects of criminal punishment on family formation and marriage markets (Lichter et al. 1992; Wilson 1987). A father's criminal conviction is closely correlated with his children's criminality (Rowe and Farrington 1997). Hagan and Palloni (1990, 266) emphasized "reproductive processes" by which incarcerated parents and crime control agents socialize children toward crime. Consistent with these ideas, a national study of prison inmates found the highest rates of parental incarceration among violent recidivists, lower rates among nonviolent recidivists, and the lowest rates among first-time prisoners (Uggen, Wakefield, and Western 2005).

As the felon population has risen, so too has the population of children whose parents have been convicted of felonies. The U.S. Department of Justice (2000a) has estimated that the number of minor children with a parent in state or federal prison rose from 1 million to 1.5 million between 1991 and 1999 alone. Overall, about 2 percent of all children and more than 7 percent of African American children *currently* have an incarcerated parent. A far greater number have parents who are ex-prisoners, ex-felons, and felons currently serving sentences outside of prison.

Theorizing the Social Position of Felons and Ex-Felons

Sociological models of inequality suggest three major conceptual schemes for understanding the place of felons in American politics and society: *castes*, *classes*, and *status groups*. At the most extreme, felons might be viewed as a distinct caste, or caste-like group. In one sense, they are marked for life by a criminal conviction that excludes them from labor markets, educational opportunities, family rights, and, in many states, the right to vote. In class models, they might constitute a distinct "criminal class" or a central part of a larger excluded group, such as a "lumpenproletariat," "underclass," or the disenfranchised poor. Here, their economic disadvantages are highlighted over other characteristics. Finally, felons may be viewed as a distinctive status group, sharing similar life chances determined by a specific social estimation of honor or dishonor. We discuss how each of these concepts may be used to understand the citizenship status and social position of felons.

Felons as caste

Caste systems of inequality are based on extreme social closure, in which group boundaries are rigidly enforced across wide-ranging social domains that span generations. According to Beteille (1996), a caste is a named group characterized by "endogamy, hereditary membership and a specific style of life which some-times includes the pursuit by tradition of a particular occupation and is usually associated with a more or less distinct ritual status...based on concepts of purity and pollution." Caste relations are most clearly developed in (Hindu) India, where the concept famously originated.[2]

The caste concept has been used to characterize U.S. race relations, beginning with the early work of Warner (1936), Dollard (1937/1988), and Gunnar Myrdal (1944) and more recently in the writings of historian George Fredrickson (1981) on South Africa and the U.S. South. Evidence for the "caste school of race relations" includes residential and occupational segregation by race (the latter especially in the U.S. South prior to the 1960s), extremely low rates of intermarriage, and min-imal group contact. Oliver Cox (1948) and other critics have challenged such arguments on grounds that the U.S. post–Civil War system of race relations never assumed the same degree of coherence as the caste system in India, and thus the analogy does not quite hold. Nevertheless, prior to the destruction of Jim Crow, the caste concept highlighted key enduring features of racial inequality (Klinkner and Smith 1999). Caste-like models have also been applied to the upper class (Baltzell 1964; Domhoff 2002).

In tracing the origins of felon disenfranchisement, Pettus (2005) made the important point that unlike the period before 1965—when numerous ballot restrictions were progressively eliminated—felon disenfranchisement is today the *only* real ballot restriction imposed on American citizens. In this sense, it is the defining feature of a modern caste of noncitizens with regard to enfranchise-ment. A contemporary application of the caste concept to felons and ex-felons would rest on two points. First, it suggests social exclusion from a wide range of institutional settings, including schools, workplaces, and polling places. As we have seen, felons and ex-felons are denied full participation in each of these are-nas to varying degrees. Second, as with classical untouchables in India, felons and ex-felons are excluded not merely on the basis of some social characteristic but as a result of an indelible felony conviction that cannot be removed for life. As we discuss below, caste-like relations perhaps best apply to sex offenders, whose addresses, photographs, and personal and criminal histories are widely dissemi-nated through permanent registries in many states.

Felons as class

The concept of the *lumpenproletariat*, introduced by Marx in part V of *The Eighteenth Brumaire* to derisively characterize the supporters of Louis Bonaparte,[3] might help place convicted felons in the class structure. But the lumpenproletariat is a loose characterization of all societal dropouts, without much analytical rigor. More recently, however, two notable efforts have been made to theorize the class position of the "disenfranchised" poor. The first are the various attempts, especially among European social scientists, to characterize the poor as an "out" group, excluded from economic opportunities available to other actors. The growing numbers of unemployed citizens without immediate employment prospects in capitalist countries poses a clear problem for conventional class analysis, which assigns people based on current class location (van Parijs 1989). Wacquant's (2001) view of the "meshing" of ghetto and prison is largely consistent with such an excluded class model of felons and ex-felons.

The second innovation, developed in the United States in the 1980s, is the "underclass" concept (Wilson 1987). The underclass concept addresses the hyperdisadvantage faced by residents of low-income neighborhoods with limited access to jobs, good educations, and other avenues for upward mobility. In particular, poor urban males face very high rates of incarceration and shuttle between poverty on the streets and prison. As a number of analysts have suggested, however, the underclass model draws only loosely upon related social trends and lumps together such diverse individuals that it has only limited analytical utility (see, e.g., Jencks 1992, chap. 5; Gans 1994; Gilbert 1999; Whelan 1996). Further problems arise out of any effort to use it to characterize felons and ex-felons, who have clear disadvantages not shared by other members of an underclass.

While some significant scholarship has employed a class language to characterize the intergenerational transmission of crime (Hagan and Palloni 1990), the application of a straightforward class model to characterize felons is clearly problematic. Felons do not share a common relationship to the economic system simply by virtue of a felony conviction. Those felons with some social or cultural resources are in a better position to rejoin the community of citizens than other felons. Furthermore, because of the importance of noneconomic aspects of felon status in shaping economic opportunities, class concepts provide only a limited view of felons' place in the stratification order.

Felons as status group

In his incomparable *Economy and Society*, Max Weber (1922/1978) proposed a typology of the distribution of power and inequality within a community, distinguishing classes (rooted in property ownership), different types of status groups (stretching from those based on honor to those rooted in group identities such as ethnicity), and castes. As distinct from classes, status groups are determined on the basis of "a specific, positive or negative, social estimation of honor" (p. 932). Honor can arise from many sources, including occupation, membership in a particular group, or unique individual actions that are accorded prestige. Group boundaries are maintained through processes of social closure in which outsiders are precluded from membership (cf. Parkin 1979; Manza 1992). Caste segregation is the extreme form of such closure; "the normal form in which ethnic communities that believe in blood relationship and exclude exogamous marriage and social intercourse usually interact with one another" (Weber 1922/1978, 932).

The Weberian schema provides a useful foundation for puzzling through the social position of felons in contemporary democracies. To be sure, Weber's (1922/1978) literal definition of caste and class would not provide viable characterizations of the felon population. Felons are not bound by blood relationships or endogamous marriages and, thus, could not literally be a caste. They may be (mostly) unified in their lack of property and may share similar life chances, but the former is too broad to identify a distinctive felon class, and the latter arises primarily out of the negative status honor that attaches to a felony conviction (rather than lack of property ownership, which is true for all lower-class individuals and households).

Weber's (1922/1978) conception of status group, however, may be more applicable to felons. Weber defined status groups through either "positive" or "negative" processes: for example, he argued that "the road to legal privilege, positive or negative, is easily traveled as soon as a certain stratification of the social order has in fact been 'lived in' and has achieved stability by virtue of a stable distribution of economic power" (p. 933). In the case of felons and ex-felons, the stigmas attached to their legal standing produce a unique status dishonor that, as we have seen, impacts their standing as citizens, their political participation, and their community involvement.

Contingencies by offense and state

All three categorical schemes (caste, class, and status group) are useful in understanding the individual and aggregate consequences of the growing population of felons and ex-felons. Indeed, insights from each are necessary to understand the full range of disabilities imposed on felons and their social consequences. A felony is a broad categorization, encompassing everything from marijuana possession to homicide. Sex offenders represent the most stigmatized group—and the one to which a caste model most readily applies. Since the advent of federal legislation in the 1990s, (1994's "Wetterling Act," later amended as "Megan's Law"), convicted sex offenders have been required to register their whereabouts and states have been required to establish community notification procedures (U.S. Department of Justice, FBI 2005). All but two states (Oregon and South Dakota) currently maintain a searchable Internet site for public use, providing varying levels of detail— everything from MapPoint maps of the offenders' neighborhoods, to the names and addresses of their employers, to lurid descriptions of their offenses.

Apart from their treatment of sex offenders, however, there are other important differences in stigmatization across the fifty states. Thus, a state-contingent interpretation may provide the most robust way of thinking about the citizenship status of felons and ex-felons. Consider, at one extreme, a state such as Florida. In that state, information about past felony convictions is easily accessible on a free public Internet site, and felons are disenfranchised for life unless they receive formal restoration of their civil rights (Florida Department of Corrections 2005). The former felon's full address is listed, along with a color photograph and detailed information about offense history and release dates. Here, in the name of public safety, a felony conviction may provide an indelible lifetime stain, and in that sense felons can plausibly be characterized in caste-like terms.

At the other extreme, even currently incarcerated prisoners may vote in states such as Maine and Vermont, and these states list cities rather than street addresses on their sex offender registries. We would argue that in such a context, a felony conviction does not produce social exclusion consistent with either caste segregation or class (in the underclass or excluded class models). While the conceptual categorization of felons is an important question for theory, it also raises the practical issue posed by John Braithwaite (1989): does a model of permanent stigmatization or one of reintegration best ensure public safety? Moreover, which policies are best suited for the remaking of citizens and the community involvement and political participation that citizenship implies?

Civic Reintegration

Much of the research literature has focused on socioeconomic (Laub and Sampson 2003; Uggen 2000) and family reintegration (Laub, Nagin, and Sampson 1998) of felons, rather than civic reintegration and citizenship (Uggen, Manza, and Behrens 2004). Yet crime itself is explicitly defined in relation to the state and its citizens. Felons and ex-felons face disadvantages arising out of incomplete citizenship and the temporary or permanent suspension of their rights and privileges. It therefore makes sense to ask whether political participation and community involvement, as well as work and family factors, are central to successful reintegration.

To date, there is little empirical research on civic reintegration and none that would establish a definitive causal relationship between civic participation and desistance from crime. Nevertheless, some evidence suggests a strong negative association between political participation and recidivism. Analyzing a community sample of young adults, Uggen and Manza (2004) compared the subsequent arrest rates of voters and nonvoters in the 1996 presidential election. Approximately 16 percent of the nonvoters were arrested between 1997 and 2000, relative to about 5 percent of the voters. Similarly, approximately 12 percent of the nonvoters were incarcerated between 1997 and 2000, relative to less than 5 percent of the voters. A study of a 1990 Minnesota prison release cohort yielded similar results among convicted felons. Participation in the previous biennial election significantly reduced the likelihood of recidivism, net of age, gender, race, and offense characteristics (Uggen and Schaefer 2005). Of course, such work barely scratches the surface of the impact of collateral consequences. Far more research is needed on collateral sanctions and recidivism, such as community notification of sex offenders and restrictions on public aid, housing, employment, and educational opportunities (Mauer and Chesney-Lind 2002; Mele and Miller 2005).

Discussion

We have estimated the size of the American criminal class and considered its implications for citizenship and democracy. If we use current or former imprisonment as the criterion for class membership, we estimate its size at approximately 6.3 million in 2004. By our estimates, about 5.5 percent of adult males and 17 percent of black adult males have once served or are currently serving time in a state or federal prison. If we adopt a more inclusive definition of the criminal class, including all convicted of felonies regardless of imprisonment, these numbers increase to more than 16 million persons, representing almost 13 percent of the adult male population and approximately one-third of the black adult male population.

As rising waves of men and women leave criminal justice supervision each year, the time has come for a reasoned reassessment of those sanctions that strip them of their rights as citizens.

Any group of this size can have profound and far-reaching implications for democracy. Because they are disproportionately drawn from extremely disadvantaged groups, however, the felon population exerts particularly strong effects on labor markets, family dissolution, and partisan politics. Perhaps the most important lesson from this analysis builds on an emerging consensus in life course criminology. Long-term studies of serious criminal offenders suggest that virtually all will desist from crime at some point (Laub and Sampson 2003). This tells us that while the march to desistance is difficult and halting, it is also inexorable. The importance of this simple social fact cannot be overstated. If putatively "hardened" criminals can indeed become decent citizens, policies that impose a caste-like stigma upon them may erode democratic institutions.

The data presented here show that literally millions of former felons are successfully living and working among us every day. Many of them pay taxes; raise their children and grandchildren; and, in states where they are permitted to do so, participate in democratic elections. As rising waves of men and women leave criminal justice supervision each year, the time has come for a reasoned reassessment of those sanctions that strip them of their rights as citizens. The problem of recidivism and desistance from crime is thus recast as a problem of reintegration and restoration of full citizenship rights.

To best fulfill the duties of responsible citizenship in a democratic society, former felons require the basic rights and capacities enjoyed by other citizens in good standing.

Appendix
Methodology for Computing Ex-Felon and Ex-Prisoner Estimates

Because these numbers are important, we need to explain carefully how we derive them. Our data sources included a wide range of reports and data generated by the U.S. Department of Justice (DOJ) on correctional populations. The most important of these are the annual *Sourcebook of Criminal Justice Statistics* (DOJ 1973-2004) and *Correctional Populations in the United States* (DOJ 1989-1997) series, *Probation and Parole in the United States* (DOJ 2001a), and *Prison and Jail Inmates at Midyear* (DOJ 2005). For early years, we also referenced *National Prisoner Statistics* (U.S. Bureau of Prisons 1948-1971) and *Race of Prisoners Admitted to State and Federal Institutions, 1926-1986* (DOJ 1991). We determined the median age of released prisoners based on annual data from the National Corrections Reporting Program. We then compiled demographic life tables for the period 1948 to 2004 to determine the number of released felons lost to recidivism (and therefore already included in our annual head counts) and to mortality each year. This allows us to compute the number of ex-felons no longer under correctional supervision.

We made a number of simplifying assumptions in obtaining these estimates. First, the recidivism rate we use to decrease the releasee population each year is based upon the Bureau of Justice Statistics *Recidivism of Prisoners Released in 1983* (DOJ 1989) study and *Recidivism of Felons on Probation 1986-1989* (DOJ 1992). For prisoners and parolees, we use a reincarceration rate of 18.6 percent at one year, 32.8 percent at two years, 41.4 percent at three years. Although rearrest rates appear to have increased since 1983, the overall reconviction and reincarceration rates used for this study are much more stable (Langan and Levin 2002). For probationers and jail inmates, the corresponding three-year failure rate is 36 percent. To extend the analysis to subsequent years, we calculated a trend line using the ratio of increases provided by Hoffman and Stone-Meierhoefer (1980) on federal prisoners. By year ten, we estimate a 59.4 percent recidivism rate among released prisoners and parolees, which increases to 65.9 percent by year fifty-seven (the longest observation period in this analysis). Because these estimates are higher than most long-term recidivism studies, they are likely to yield conservative estimates of the ex-felon population. Our three-year probation and jail recidivism rate is 36 percent; by year fifty-seven, the recidivism rate is 57.3 percent.

We begin by applying these recidivism rates to all felon populations, then relax this assumption in subanalyses. We calculate mortality based on the expected deaths for black males at the median age of release for each year, multiplied by a factor of 1.46 to reflect the higher death rates observed among releasees in the Bureau of Justice Statistics' *Recidivism of Prisoners Released in 1983* study.

Our second simplifying assumption concerns our start date for calculating ex-felons. We begin following these groups in 1948 primarily for data reasons; 1948 is the earliest year for which data are available on releases from supervision. As a result, when we cumulate the number of remaining (nonrecidivist, nondeceased) ex-felons, our estimates are for individuals released 1948 or later. This may slightly underestimate the number of ex-felons in earlier years, but it should have little effect on more recent years, since less than 2 percent of 1948 releases remain in the ex-felon population by 2004. To account for this problem in our earlier estimates, we add to our calculated ex-felon population an estimate of ex-felons released in the years 1925 through 1947. This is done by taking all prison releases in these years, reducing for death and recidivism, and adding the number remaining to each year's total.

The third assumption made by this estimation technique concerns the sex and race of released felons. Historical data reporting the race and sex of prisoners are typically available but difficult to obtain for other correctional populations. Prior to the mid-1970s, we used race and sex data for prison to estimate the race and sex distributions in the jail, probation, and parole populations. This estimation entailed starting with the earliest year for which we have race and sex information for the specific correctional population (e.g., parole) and altering this number based on the percent change in the prison population with that same characteristic. As a result, our estimate of the sex and race of the ex-felon population assumes stability in the ratio of African American probationers and parolees to African American prisoners over time.

In our estimates of the ex-prison and ex-felon populations, we make two alterations to our original methodology to account for the higher rate of recidivism among male and among black offenders. We first recalculate ex-prisoner estimates using the higher three-year rate of 45.3 percent for African American prisoners, as reported by the 1983 recidivism study. By applying the trend line used for the total population estimates to this higher three-year rate, we estimate a lifetime (fifty-seventh year) recidivism rate of 72.2 percent for African American ex-prisoners. Using the same logic, we calculate a 62.7 percent lifetime recidivism rate for African American probationers. The resulting population totals are then more conservative estimates of the African American ex-felon population.

A second alteration to our original estimates is used to calculate the impact of the felon population by gender (presented in Tables 1 and 2). Because women have a significantly lower recidivism rate than men, we again recalculated our estimates, using the three-year reincarceration rate of 33.0 percent for women provided by the 1983 Bureau of Justice Statistics recidivism study. Again, we apply this percentage to our trend line and apply a lifetime rate of 52.6 percent for female prisoners and (when used together with the African American estimates) a lifetime recidivism rate of 57.5 percent for African American female prisoners. For probation populations, these rates are 45.7 and 50.0 percent, respectively. Once the female rates are calculated, we simply subtract the total female population from the total felon population to obtain estimates for males. Similarly, we subtract the African American female population from the total African American population to obtain estimated African American male populations.

Notes

1. This number is smaller than the total correctional population shown in Figure 1 because misdemeanants serving jail or probation sentences are counted among persons under correctional supervision but not counted among the total *felon* population.

2. Recent anthropological and historical work on the Indian caste system has challenged the view that caste relations were a defining feature of Indian society prior to the British colonization (see, e.g., Fuller 1996).

3. In Marx's (1963) vivid descriptions, the *lumpenproletariat* is the "refuse of all classes," composed of "ruined and adventurous offshoots of the bourgeoisie, vagabonds, discharged soldiers, discharged jailbirds . . . pickpockets, brothel keepers, rag-pickers, beggars, etc."

References

Baltzell, E. Digby. 1964. *The Protestant establishment*. New York: Random House.

Beteille, Andre. 1996. *Caste, class, and power: Changing patterns of stratification in a Tanjore village*. 2nd ed. New York: Oxford University Press.

Bonczar, Thomas P. 2003. *Prevalence of imprisonment in the U.S. population, 1974-2001*. Bureau of Justice Statistics Special Report. Washington, DC: Government Printing Office.

Bonczar, Thomas P., and Allen J. Beck. 1997. *Lifetime likelihood of going to state or federal prison*. Bureau of Justice Statistics Bulletin, NCJ 160092. Washington, DC: U.S. Department of Justice.

Braithwaite, John. 1989. *Crime, shame, and reintegration*. Cambridge: Cambridge University Press.

Buckler, Kevin G., and Lawrence F. Travis III. 2003. Reanalyzing the prevalence and social context of collateral consequence statutes. *Journal of Criminal Justice* 31:435-53.

Bushway, Shawn D. 2004. Labor market effects of permitting employer access to criminal history records. *Journal of Contemporary Crime and Justice* 20:276-91.

Chin, Gabriel J. 2002. Race, the war on drugs, and the collateral consequences of criminal conviction. *Journal of Gender, Race, and Justice* 6:253-75.

Cose, Ellis. 2000. The prison paradox. *Newsweek*, November 13.

Cox, Oliver C. 1948. *Caste, class, and race*. New York: Doubleday.

Dietrich, Sharon M. 2002. Criminal records and employment: Ex-offenders' thwarted attempts to earn a living for their families. In *Every door closed: Barriers facing parents with criminal records*, 13-26. Washington, DC/Philadelphia: Center for Law and Social Policy/Community Legal Services, Inc. http://www.soros.org/initiatives/justice/articles_publications/publications/every_door_closed_20020101/ Every%20Door%20Closed.pdf.

Dollard, John. 1937/1988. *Caste and class in a Southern town*. Madison: Unversity of Wisconsin Press.

Domhoff, G. William. 2002. *Who rules America? Power and politics*. New York: McGraw-Hill.

Florida Department of Corrections. 2005. Inmate release information search. http://www.dc.state.fl.us/inmateinfo/inmateinfomenu.asp (accessed September 3, 2005).

Fredrickson, George M. 1981. White supremacy: A comparative study in American and South African history. New York: Oxford University Press.

Freeman, Richard. 1992. Crime and the employment of disadvantaged youth. In *Urban labor markets and job opportunity*, ed. George Peterson and Wayne Vroman, 171-92. Washington, DC: Urban Institute.

Fuller, C. J. 1996. Introduction: Caste today. In *Caste today*, ed. C. J. Fuller, 1-31. New York: Oxford University Press.

Gans, Herbert. 1994. Positive functions of the undeserving poor: Uses of the *underclass* in America. *Politics and Society* 22:269-83.

Gilbert, Neil. 1999. The size and influence of the *underclass*: An exaggerated view. *Society* 37:43-45.

Grant, Walter Matthews, John LeCournu, John Andrews Pickens, Dean Hill Rivkin, and C. Roger Vinson. 1970. The collateral consequences of a criminal conviction. *Vanderbilt Law Review* 23:929-1241.

Hagan, John, and Alberto Palloni. 1990. The social reproduction of a criminal class in working-class London, circa 1950-1980. *American Journal of Sociology* 96:265-99.

Hoffman, Peter B., and Barbara Stone-Meierhoefer. 1980. Reporting recidivism rates: The criterion and follow-up issues. *Journal of Criminal Justice* 8:53-60.

Holzer, Harry J., Steven Raphael, and Michael A. Stoll. 2004. Will employers hire former offenders? Employer preferences, background checks, and their determinants. In *Imprisoning America, the social effects of mass incarceration,* ed. Mary Pattillo, David Weiman, and Bruce Western, 205-46. New York: Russell Sage Foundation.

Irwin, John. 1987. *The felon.* 2nd. ed. Berkeley: University of California Press.

Jencks, Christopher. 1992. *Rethinking social policy.* Cambridge, MA: Harvard University Press.

Kalt, Brian C. 2003. The exclusion of felons from jury service. *American University Law Review* 53:65–189.

Klinkner, Philip, and Rogers Smith. 1999. *The unsteady march.* Chicago: University of Chicago Press.

Langan, Patrick A., and David J. Levin. 2002. *Recidivism of prisoners released in 1994.* Bureau of Justice Statistics Special Report. Washington, DC: Government Printing Office.

Laub, John H., Daniel S. Nagin, and Robert J. Sampson. 1998. Trajectories of change in criminal offending: Good marriages and the desistance process. *American Sociological Review* 63:225-38.

Laub, John H., and Robert J. Sampson. 2003. *Shared beginnings, divergent lives: Delinquent boys to age 70.* Cambridge, MA: Harvard University Press.

Lichter, Daniel T., Diane K. McLaughlin, George Kephart, and David J. Landry, 1992. Race and the retreat from marriage: A shortage of marriageable men. *American Sociological Review* 57:781-99.

Lueck, Thomas J. 2000. Plan to seal some criminal records debated. *New York Times*, October 20.

Manza, Jeff. 1992. Classes, status groups, and social closure: A critique of neo-Weberian social theory. *Current Perspectives in Social Theory* 12:275-302.

Manza, Jeff, and Christopher Uggen. 2006. *Locked out: Felon disenfranchisement and American democracy.* New York: Oxford University Press.

Marshall, T. H. 1950. *Citizenship and social class.* Cambridge: Cambridge University Press.

Marx, Karl. 1963. *The eighteenth brumaire of Louis Bonaparte.* New York: International Publishers.

Mauer, Marc, and Meda Chesney-Lind, eds. 2002. *Invisible punishment: The collateral consequences of mass imprisonment.* New York: New Press.

May, Bruce E. 1995. The character component of occupational licensing laws: A continuing barrier to the ex-felon's employment opportunities. *North Dakota Law Review* 71:187-210.

Mele, Christopher, and Teresa A. Miller, eds. 2005. *Civil penalties, social consequences.* New York: Routledge.

Myrdal, Gunnar. 1944. *An American dilemma: The Negro problem and modern democracy.* New York: Harper & Brothers.

National Advisory Commission on Criminal Justice Standards and Goals. 1973. *Report on corrections.* Washington, DC: Government Printing Office.

Office of the Pardon Attorney. 2000. *Federal statutes imposing collateral consequences upon conviction.* Washington, DC: U.S. Department of Justice.

Olivares, Kathleen M., Velmer S. Burton Jr., and Francis T. Cullen. 1997. The collateral consequences of a felony conviction: A national study of state legal codes ten years later. *Federal Probation* 60:10–17.

Pager, Devah. 2003. The mark of a criminal record. *American Journal of Sociology* 108:937-75.

Parkin, Frank. 1979. *Marxism and class theory: A bourgeois critique*. New York: Columbia University Press.

Pettit, Becky, and Bruce Western. 2004. Mass imprisonment and the life course: Race and class inequality in U.S. incarceration. *American Sociological Review* 69:151-69.

Pettus, Katherine. 2005. *Felony disenfranchisement in America: Historical origins, institutional racism, and modern consequences*. New York: LFB Scholarly Publishing.

Rowe, David C., and David P. Farrington. 1997. The familial transmission of criminal convictions. *Criminology* 35:177-201.

Samuels, Paul, and Debbie Mukamal. 2004. *After prison: Roadblocks to reentry. A report on state legal barriers facing people with criminal records*. New York: Legal Action Center.

Steinacker, Andrea. 2003. The prisoner's campaign: Felony disenfranchisement laws and the right to hold public office. *Brigham Young University Law Review* 2003 (2): 801-28.

Sutton, John R. 2004. The political economy of imprisonment in affluent Western democracies, 1960-1990. *American Sociological Review* 69:170-89.

Travis, Jeremy. 2002. Invisible punishment: An instrument of social exclusion. In *Invisible punishment: The collateral consequences of mass imprisonment*, ed. Marc Mauer and Meda Chesney-Lind, 15-36. New York: New Press.

Uggen, Christopher. 2000. Work as a turning point in the life course of criminals: A duration model of age, employment, and recidivism. *American Sociological Review* 65:529-46.

———. 2005. Editorial comment on collateral consequences of criminal sanctions. *Journal of Contemporary Criminal Justice* 21:1.

Uggen, Christopher, and Jeff Manza. 2002. Democratic contraction? Political consequences of felon disenfranchisement in the United States. *American Sociological Review* 67:777-803.

———. 2004. Voting and subsequent crime and arrest: Evidence from a community sample. *Columbia Human Rights Law Review* 36:193-215.

Uggen, Christopher, Jeff Manza, and Angela Behrens. 2004. Less than the average citizen: Stigma, role transition, and the civic reintegration of convicted felons. In *After crime and punishment: Pathways to offender reintegration*, ed. Shadd Maruna and Russ Immarigeon, 258-90. Cullompton, Devon, UK: Willan.

Uggen, Christopher, and Shelly Schaefer. 2005. Voting and the civic reintegration of former prisoners. Manuscript, Department of Sociology, University of Minnesota, Twin Cites.

Uggen, Christopher, Sara Wakefield, and Bruce Western. 2005. Work and family perspectives on reentry. In *Prisoner reentry and crime in America*, ed. Jeremy Travis and Christy Visher, 209-43. New York: Cambridge University Press.

U.S. Bureau of Prisons. 1948-1971. *National prisoner statistics*. Washington, DC: Government Printing Office.

U.S. Census Bureau. 1998. *Statistical abstract of the United States*. Washington, DC: Government Printing Office.

U.S. Department of Justice. 1973-2004. *Sourcebook of criminal justice statistics*. Washington, DC: Government Printing Office.

———. 1989. *Recidivism of prisoners released in 1983*. Washington, DC: Government Printing Office.

———. 1989-1997. *Correctional populations in the United States*. Washington, DC: Government Printing Office.

———. 1991. *Race of prisoners admitted to state and federal institutions, 1926-1986*. Washington, DC: Government Printing Office.

———. 1992. *Recidivism of felons on probation, 1986-1989*. Washington, DC: Government Printing Office.

———. 1994-2004. *Prisoners in 2003*. Washington, DC: Government Printing Office.

———. 1997. *Characteristics of adults on probation, 1995*. Washington, DC: Government Printing Office.

———. 1999. *Compendium of state privacy and security legislation: 1999*. Washington DC: Government Printing Office..

———. 2000a. *Incarcerated parents and their children*. Bureau of Justice Statistics Special Report. Washington, DC: Government Printing Office.

———. 2000b. *Survey of inmates of state correctional facilities series, 1974-1997*. [MRDF]. Washington, DC: U.S. Department of Commerce, Bureau of the Census/Ann Arbor, MI: Inter-University Consortium for Political Science Research [producer/distributor].

———. 2001a. Probation and parole in the United States, 2000. Press Release. Washington, DC: Government Printing Office.

———. 2001b. *Trends in state parole 1990-2000.* Washington, DC. Government Printing Office.

———. 2005. *Prison and jail inmates at midyear 2004.* Washington, DC: Government Printing Office.

U.S. Department of Justice, Federal Bureau of Investigation. 2005. Investigative programs—Crimes against Children: State sex offender Web sites. http://www.fbi.gov/hq/cid/cac/states.htm (accessed September 3, 2005).

van Parijs, Philippe. 1989. A revolution in class theory. In *The debate on classes*, ed. Erik Olin Wright, 213-41. London: Verso.

Wacquant, Loic. 2001. Deadly symbiosis: When prison and ghetto meet and mesh. *Punishment and Society* 3:95-134.

Warner, W. Lloyd. 1936. American caste and class. *American Journal of Sociology* 42:234-37.

Weber, Max. 1922/1978. *Economy and society.* Berkeley: University of California Press.

Western, Bruce. 2002. The impact of incarceration on wage mobility and inequality. *American Sociological Review* 67:526-46.

Wheelock, Darren. 2005. Collateral consequences and racial inequality: Felon status exclusions as a system of disadvantage. *Journal of Contemporary Criminal Justice* 21:82-90.

Wheelock, Darren, and Christopher Uggen. 2005. Race, poverty and punishment: The impact of criminal sanctions on racial, ethnic, and socioeconomic inequality. Paper presented at the National Poverty Center at the University of Michigan, Ann Arbor, September 15-16.

Whelan, Christopher. 1996. Marginalization, deprivation, and fatalism in the Republic of Ireland: Class and *underclass* perspectives. *European Sociological Review* 12:33-51.

Wilson, William J. 1987. The truly disadvantaged: The inner city, the underclass, and public policy. Chicago: University of Chicago Press.

Wolfgang, Marvin E. 1983. Delinquency in two birth cohorts. In *Prospective studies of crime and delinquency*, ed. K. Teilmann Van Duesen and S. A. Mednick, 7-16. Boston: Kluwer-Nijhoff.

Democracy and Criminal Justice in Cross-National Perspective: From Crime Control to Due Process

By
HUNG-EN SUNG

In this article, the author argues that the transformation of justice administration in democratizing countries is a transition from a crime control to a due process orientation. In authoritarian states, criminal justice systems rely on a larger law enforcement–punishment apparatus for order maintenance and produce higher rates of arrest, prosecution, conviction, and incarceration. By contrast, in liberal democracies, justice is sought as the defense of civil liberties through the due process of law, which leads to a heavier investment in the judiciary and a higher rate of case attrition in the criminal justice process. The analysis of United Nations data refutes the hypothesis of larger police and prison workforce in authoritarian countries and larger judicial staff in liberal democracies. Instead, democracy increases both the personnel strength of the courts and that of the police and the prisons. The proposed relationship between democracy and increased criminal case attrition receives very strong support.

Keywords: democracy; democratization; criminal justice; comparative analysis

The loosely connected bureaucratic structures of police, courts, and prisons are commonly referred to as the criminal justice system. This organization of justice administration grew out of the same historical period that also produced the modern nation-state (Newman and Bouloukos 1996). As different forms of government impose different sets of demands and constraints on their legal institutions, the global trend of democratization carries the promise of creating transparent and accountable criminal justice systems worldwide. Nevertheless, while many countries have succeeded in bringing down

Hung-En Sung, Ph.D., is a research associate at the National Center on Addiction and Substance Abuse at Columbia University. He received his doctorate in criminal justice from the State University of New York at Albany. He has published on drug abuse and treatment and comparative analysis of corruption. He has also authored several studies on the impact of democratic governance on crime and justice. Among his recent publications is The Fragmentation of Policing in American Cities *(Praeger, 2002).*

DOI: 10.1177/0002716206287546

authoritarian regimes and replacing them with freely elected governments, only some of them have successfully developed criminal justice institutions and practices consonant with the democratic ideals of equality, openness, and fairness (Prillaman 2000; Solomon and Foglesong 2000; Ungar 2002).

The subordination of justice to the executive authority defines the outlook of a nondemocratic legal system.

Unfortunately, regular cycles of elections are not by themselves a sufficient determinant of a mature democracy. An authoritarian society can become a "disjunctive democracy" (see Rodrigues 2006 [this volume]) by holding recurring competitive elections without becoming a liberal democracy. Liberal democracy, also known as constitutional liberalism, is a form of representative democracy where the power of elected officials is moderated by functioning constitutional institutions that protect the rights and freedoms of individuals and minorities and constrain the extent to which the will of the majority can be exercised (Zakaria 2003). Socially, it is characterized by tolerance and pluralism. Disjunctive democracies differ from liberal democracies in that they still suffer serious defects in interethnic relations, discrimination against minorities and disadvantaged groups, an unrestrained executive power, and/or a subdued press. The juxtaposition of the steady expansion of electoral democracies over the past two decades, and the stagnation in levels of civil liberties in many countries, demonstrates a disturbing gap between the two standards (Zakaria 2003; Freedom House 2005). Only in a liberal democracy can the strength of the state and the rule of law be effectively embedded and harmonized in the daily operations of the criminal justice system (Allen 1996).

How governments react to crime and administer justice reflects the nature of the political regime. Justice systems in authoritarian regimes are known for their arbitrariness, secrecy, and brutality (Smykla 1989; McElligott 1994; Shelley 1994; Trevaskes 2004). In contrast, criminal justice is democratically administered by increasing popular access to justice and counterbalancing the exercise of state authority with the promotion of civic participation in the criminal justice process and the accountability of justice officials to the law rather than to the government (Zalman 2000; Bayley 2005). Although all societies have about the same basic types of criminal justice agencies (e.g., police, prosecutors, courts, and prisons), systems of criminal justice differ significantly in their organization, operational outcomes, and mission goals. The major difference lies in the political soil in which each system is planted: the patterns of power distribution and the shared beliefs about government determine the character of criminal justice processing.

This study seeks to overcome the traditional indifference among social scientists toward cross-national analysis of the relationship between the modality of political regime and criminal justice. I first formulate a theory of criminal justice development to account for the diversity and multiplicity of criminal justice organizations and operations observed in countries with different levels of democratic consolidation. Hypotheses are then evaluated with a pooled series of nations between 1997 and 2002 on crime and justice data collected by the United Nations.

The Analytical Framework

Crime control model versus due process model

The administration of criminal justice is a fundamental task of government in every sovereign state. Most criminal justice research focuses on one component of the system (e.g., police, courts, corrections) and proposes interpretations and predictions limited to that component. But to appreciate the impact of democracy on criminal justice, the administration of justice must be seen as an integral part of the political reality, and the interdependence among individual criminal justice branches in some shared mission must also be explained. To begin with, the institutionalized pattern of criminal justice is formally founded on both substantive criminal law and procedural criminal law and materializes in the system's organizational structure and operational output (Reichel 2002). The organizational structure refers to the differential allocation of human and material resources across different components of the system, and the operational outcomes include the aggregate levels of law application, such as arrest, prosecution, conviction, and incarceration. Criminal justice can be fruitfully analyzed as behavior because as a changing aspect of society it varies quantitatively in time and space (Black 1976); that is, both the relative size and the operational outcomes of criminal justice systems change from one country to another and from one historical epoch to another.

Based on Packer's (1968) analysis of the two competing models of justice administration, I propose that the democratization process is characterized and facilitated by a simultaneous transition of the criminal justice system from crime control–oriented structure and operations to due process–oriented organization and functions. In Packer's original thesis, the *crime control model* emphasizes individual responsibility and is designed to protect the rights of law-abiding citizens by stressing efficient apprehension and punishment of criminals, whereas the *due process model* stresses human rights and is devised to protect the rights of the accused by presenting formidable impediments to moving them past each step in the legal process. According to Packer, the two models are opposite ends of the spectrum and represent simplifications of reality that in practice coexist to varying degrees and with different blends. Despite the inherent strain between the two models, Packer acknowledged a gradual progression from the crime control model to the due process model in American history. It is a progression always contested and never finalized. In this article, I assume that this experience is universal to all democratizing countries.

Crime control–oriented criminal justice. Authoritarian regimes give priority to social control over dispute resolution as the main mission of justice administration (Tate and Haynie 1993; Shelley 1994). Social control in this context implies the unilateral suppression of disturbances, which is best carried out in Packer's (1968) crime control paradigm with its affirmative emphasis, stressing at every turn the legitimacy and supremacy of state power over the claims of the accused. The subordination of justice to the executive authority defines the outlook of a nondemocratic legal system. As the most visible agents of the state, authoritarian police forces display unrestrained power and emphasize deterrence through extensive regulation of citizens and symbolic demonstrations of force rather than prevention through amelioration and persuasion. So indistinguishable are the character of government and police action that dictatorial regimes are often labeled "police states" (Bayley 1985). Likewise, prosecutors in these societies are widely perceived as an organ of state coercion and, despite their influence, the target of public mistrust (Smith 1992). Judges play the role of administrative bureaucrats and meticulously apply the laws of the ruler. In general, authoritarian regimes are also known for punitive sanctions; they are more likely to retain the death penalty and to show higher rates of imprisonment than democratic governments (Neapolitan 2001; Ruddell and Urbina 2004).

I hypothesize that the organization and operation of criminal justice administration vary according to the attained level of democratization.

The values and practices found in authoritarian societies fit all the basic traits of Packer's (1968) crime control model of justice administration, which is organized around the suppression of criminal behavior. The entire system is designed to deter crime as well as to identify and to contain lawbreakers at maximum efficiency. Efficiency, according to Packer, is "the system's capacity to apprehend, try, convict, and dispose of a high proportion of criminal offenders whose offenses become known" (p. 158). The center of gravity for the criminal justice process lies in the initial administrative fact-finding stages supervised by the police, prosecutors, or investigative judges. At the same time, the subsequent stages of adjudication are relatively unimportant and often truncated. Speed and finality are achieved by granting law enforcement agencies superior manpower and legal permission to screen suspects and to determine factual guilt with a minimum level of disruption. The efficiency of the legal process under this model is enhanced by the assumption of guilt and evidenced by a continual flow of cases to officials who handle the cases in a uniform and routine manner. Finality, the attainment of the last stage of criminal processing, is also guaranteed by minimizing the number of dismissed cases during adjudication and prosecution, which ensures that lawbreakers pay for their harmful acts.

Due process–oriented criminal justice. A due process–oriented criminal justice system emerges in liberal democracies. These countries not only presume the vertical accountability of government officials to the citizenry through the electoral process or indirectly via civic organizations or the news media, but also require horizontal accountability in which legally empowered and factually willing state agencies routinely monitor other branches of the government and effectively punish acts of abuse or neglect by state officials (Diamond 1996; O'Donnell 1999). A commitment to professionalism and respect for expertise provide the foundation for an increased insulation of criminal justice operations from political interferences and populist demands. Because the due process framework is essentially a negative model, asserting limits on the scope of state power, its validating authority is judicial and demands an appeal to supralegislative law, the law of the constitution. With extensive provisions for individual rights in place, liberal democracies are characterized by legal restrictions against unreasonable searches and seizures, respect for habeas corpus, the right to legal counsel, and prohibition of illegal detention, torture, and cruel punishment. A liberal political culture encourages individual freedom by restraining the intrusion of the state into citizens' lives; this is achieved by insisting on a formal adjudicative fact-finding process, often at the cost of increasing inefficiency and a high rate of case attrition in the criminal justice process.

Precisely because of its aversion to subjecting the individual to the coercive power of the state, the criminal justice process in due process systems is submitted to judicial controls that prevent it from indiscriminately repressing suspected offenders. The adoption of the doctrine of legal guilt as opposed to factual guilt requires that an individual be declared guilty only when the factual determination of evidence has been made under a strict set of formal procedures, including jurisdiction, venue, statutes of limitations, double jeopardy, and evidentiary hearings. Each stage of the process is *judicialized* to enhance the capacity of the accused to challenge the operation of the process, and all defendants are allowed to take advantage of the opportunities thus created. All these activities require the existence of an impartial, well-trained, and resourceful tribunal.

Based on Packer's (1968) argument above, I hypothesize that the organization and operation of criminal justice administration vary according to the attained level

FIGURE 1
LEVELS OF DEMOCRATIZATION AND THE CHANGING ORIENTATION
OF CRIMINAL JUSTICE OPERATIONS

Authoritarianism	Consolidated Liberal Democracy
Crime Control Orientation	*Due Process Orientation*
Personnel structure	**Personnel structure**
Large police force	Small police force
Large prosecutorial staff	Small prosecutorial staff
Small judicial body	Large judicial body
Large prison system	Small prison system
Operational output	**Operational output**
High arrest rates	Low arrest rates
High prosecution rates	Low prosecution rates
High conviction rates	Low conviction rates
High incarceration rates	Low incarceration rates

of democratization. In authoritarian societies, an extensive police-prosecutorial machine linked to a large prison system constitutes the backbone of criminal justice; this criminal justice system typically produces high rates of arrest, prosecution, conviction, and incarceration. In the same way, the criminal justice system in liberal democracies is structurally distinguished by a well-staffed judicial body and operationally characterized by low rates of arrest, prosecution, conviction, and incarceration. Variability in criminal justice administration exists for each stage of democratization, but on average the emphasis on the protection of individual liberties over the maintenance of social stability would be stronger for more mature democracies. Figure 1 summarizes this proposition.

The proposed hypothesis deals with ideal types, and one may always find exceptions to these ideal types. Indeed, the United States in the twenty-first century may represent in part just such an exception. Historically, freedom and respect for human rights have long been the core values of American political culture. But over the years, the series of wars on crime, drugs, and terror has led the country to rely on massive incarceration, to maintain the death penalty, and to adopt degrading practices (e.g., holding someone in secret and without trial, applying torture on terrorist suspects, etc.) condemned in other Western democracies as cruel and illegal treatment of human beings. No discussion of democracy and justice can avoid confronting the test posed by the United States, and no analysis can be deemed satisfactory without a careful scrutiny of the American criminal justice system in relation to other democratic systems. I will address this issue in the light of empirical evidence at the end of this article.

This analytical scheme should not be used to imply that inquisitorial legal systems found in civil law countries are inherently less fair and more oppressive than adversarial systems within the common law tradition. However tempting it may be to equate the two conceptual models with major legal traditions, Packer (1968) never suggested that his theoretical types were useful for distinguishing between legal traditions. Although the inquisitorial approach has an historical tie to the safeguard of the interests of imperial regimes (Bayley 1975; Damaska 1986; Thome 1998), civil law systems in advanced democracies have developed powerful protections against abuses from state authorities such as robust constitutional review mechanisms (Murphy 1991; Kessler 2005); and the adversarial framework based on common law is known to generate its own share of unfairness (e.g., abuse of plea bargaining, unequal access to expert testimony and scientific evidence) (Havard 1992; Meintjies-Van der Walt 2001; Ma 2002). Vis-à-vis the observation that the adoption of adversarial elements (e.g., jury trials and victims' rights to initiate private prosecution of an offender) has often accompanied the democratization of countries with a civil law tradition (see O'Reilly 1997; Liu and Situ 1999; Diehm 2001; Nemityna 2001), the central assumption of this study remains that broader political institutions and culture determine the nature of national criminal justice policies and outputs (DiIulio 1997; Karstedt 2001; Ruddell 2005). Criminal justice practices, however "liberal," may reinforce the democratic development already in motion but cannot bring about its initiation or completion on their own (Bayley 2005).

Method

Data and sample

The hypothesis is examined with data from the United Nations Surveys on Crime Trends and the Operations of Criminal Justice Systems (UNS), which gather information on the incidence of reported crime and the operations of criminal justice systems. Crime statistics from the earlier versions of the UNS have been criticized for their low reliability (Kalish 1988), but previous methodological weaknesses have been appreciably corrected (Neapolitan 1997). UNS crime statistics are currently based on data garnered by national police organizations, which renders their reliability comparable to that of information directly collected from police organizations, such as the Interpol crime statistics (Neumayer 2005). With regard to operational statistics of national criminal justice systems, UNS have simply been the only source of information that provides comparable data for a fairly large number of countries. UN researchers now employ several methods to control the quality of UNS, such as the use of standard definitions for all survey categories to reduce semantic discrepancies and automatic accuracy checks after detection of unusual fluctuations in reported yearly statistics or inconsistent numbers across different criminal justice stages (Howard, Newman, and Pridemore 2000). Despite its great potential to enrich comparative criminal justice research, UNS statistics remain underutilized (Newman and Howard 1999; Howard, Newman, and Pridemore 2000; Maguire and Schulte-Murray 2001).

Yet despite continuing data quality control efforts, UNS remain vulnerable to methodological shortcomings inherent in the use of convenience samples and to disparities in tallying across countries (Lewis 1999).[1] Like any cross-national databases, the UNS are limited by the fact that published crime and justice statistics are susceptible to political manipulations because they affect the country's image and may be used to assess its social stability by foreign organizations with important political or economic ramifications (Newman and Howard 1999). Because it was impossible to determine how these potential distortions are differentially distributed across countries, I treated them as random measurement errors in this study. Moreover, the legal definitions of criminal events and the organizational classification of criminal justice components vary across countries. Although the number of countries that have adapted their own crime and criminal justice statistical definitions and procedures to the standard UNS categories has been steadily increasing over the years (Newman and Howard 1999), cautious interpretation of findings is still advised.

Statistics for the 1997 to 2002 period were examined. Four hundred thirty-five country-year units with valid responses to at least one of the eight criminal justice items analyzed in this study were selected (see Appendix A).[2]

Variables

The eight dependent variables are shown in Table 1. Four variables measure the structural strength of individual criminal justice components, including police, prosecutors, courts, and prisons. Each of these indicators was operationalized as the number of staff personnel per one hundred thousand inhabitants. The remaining four dependent variables measure the operational output of the same agencies; these are police contact, prosecution, conviction, and incarceration rates. The police contact rate, used as the proxy for police arrest rate, is a ratio expressed as a percentage calculated by dividing the number of suspects or arrestees brought into initial formal contact with the police by the total number of crimes reported in police statistics. The rates of prosecution and conviction are ratios expressed as percentages calculated by dividing the number of people receiving a specific formal legal action (i.e., prosecution or conviction) in a specific year by the number of all individuals formally sanctioned at the prior processing point (i.e., arrest or prosecution) during the same year. These ratios of aggregate data only measure an overall probability of proceeding from one stage to the next. The incarceration rate differs from these aggregate ratios, as it is based on cumulative incidence, rather than the period incidence, of imprisonment as the numerator. In other words, the incarceration rate comprises all persons who were in prisons in a given year, and not just those receiving a new prison sentence in that particular year, in the numerator, while the denominator consists of the number of offenders convicted in courts in the specific year. Therefore, incarceration rates can exceed 100 percent. High incarceration rates thus reflect both high incarceration rates of those convicted *and* long prison sentences imposed on incarcerated offenders, indicating in sum a more punitive approach.

TABLE 1
DESCRIPTION OF VARIABLES

Variable Name	Description	M (SD)	N (%)	N Cases
Dependent variables				
Police personnel rate	Number of police personnel per 100,000 population	301.66 (154.27)	—	285
Prosecutorial personnel rate	Number of prosecutorial personnel per 100,000 population	12.75 (4.37)	—	226
Judicial personnel rate	Number of judges or magistrates per 100,000 population	12.89 (13.24)	—	252
Prison personnel rate	Staff in adult prisons per 100,000 population	53.80 (35.77)	—	302
Police contact rate	Suspects and arrestees brought into initial formal contact with the police as percentage of total crimes recorded	55.63 (39.46)	—	246
Prosecution rate	Persons prosecuted as percentage of persons brought into contact with the police	78.76 (39.85)	—	171
Conviction rate	Persons convicted in criminal courts as percentage of persons prosecuted	65.97 (36.37)	—	193
Incarceration rate	Persons incarcerated as percentage of persons convicted	60.49 (79.56)	—	231
Independent variable				
Democracy	Combined average ratings of civil liberties and political rights (1 = nondemocratic; 7 = most democratic)	5.24 (1.74)	—	435
Control variables				
Total population	Total country population (in millions)	36.45 (120.28)	—	435
GDP per capita	GDP per capita in 1990 U.S. dollars (in thousands)	9.40 (10.61)	—	427
Total crime rate	Total of crimes recorded in police statistics per 100,000 population	3,319.01 (3,376.99)	—	350
Civil law system	Criminal justice system based on civil law tradition (1 = civil law system; 0 = other legal traditions)	—	245 (56.3)	435

I dropped ten country-year units from the analysis that reported many more convictions than prosecutions.[3] Both sets of outcome measures closely reflected the structural and operational dimension of the hypothesis.

Freedom status as rated by Freedom House (FH) provided the indicator of democratic development. FH scores are not only one of the most widely used political indicators in comparative research but also highly correlated with other democracy measures including the Polity Index (Vanhanen 2000; Bowman, Lehoucq, and Mahoney 2005). FH combined average freedom scores cover both political rights and civil liberties ratings and indicate the strength of democracy in a country. To measure strength of political rights, FH includes the extent to which elections in the country are fair, free, and open as well as the extent to which elected governments are accountable and transparent between elections (Piano and Puddington 2004). Countries holding formal elections may receive low scores on political rights if autocratic bodies such as the military, a king, or a religious council retain significant power over the elected officials. Civil liberties ratings assess the existence of constitutional guarantees of basic human rights and the degree to which they are protected in practice. Countries that receive the highest rating come closest to the ideals of freedom of expression, assembly, association, and religion. They are distinguished by a vigorous system of rule of law, enjoy free economic activity, and tend to strive for equality of opportunity. Together, the two FH freedom categories mirror the political openness and constitutionalism that characterize a consolidated liberal democracy. In FH's original scoring system, the combined average ratings rank countries on a scale from 1 to 7, with 1 representing the *most free* and 7 the *least free*. Given the way the hypothesis was set up, it made sense in this analysis to invert the freedom scores so that 1 represents the *least democratic* and 7 the *most democratic* countries. Scores are listed in Appendix A.

Three variables that have been repeatedly found to predict criminal justice behaviors in cross-national studies were incorporated in multivariate tests as control variables: population size, gross domestic product per capita, and overall crime rate (e.g., Neapolitan 2001; Ruddell and Urbina 2004; Sung 2006). The UNS total crime rate measures the number of offenses recorded by the police per one hundred thousand inhabitants and includes rape, assault, homicide, robbery, theft, burglary, fraud, drug offenses, and embezzlement. Additionally, because differences in criminal justice processing are likely to result from variations in legal proceedings, the confounding effect of the inquisitorial, adversarial, Islamic, or socialist nature of the justice system should be removed. Therefore, I included in the regression analysis a civil law tradition dummy control variable from Mukherjee and Reichel (1999), which contrasts the inquisitorial system with all others, including adversarial, Islamic, and socialist systems.[4] Year dummy variables (1997-2000) were also added in the multivariate models to remove time-specific effects.

Statistical methods

Pearson correlation coefficients were computed to measure the bivariate associations between the dependent variables and the other variables. Combining six cross sections (1997-2002) of countries to form a set of panel data increased the degrees of freedom at the costs of serious heteroscedasticity and serial correlation of error terms. The violation of the assumptions of constant variance and independence of errors threatened the reliability of the estimation of the confidence intervals and hypothesis testing using the traditional ordinary least squares (OLS) regression. Therefore, multiple regression with robust standard errors computed from the asymptotic covariance matrix was used for multivariate testing; it generated point estimates of the regression coefficients that were exactly the same as in regular OLS regression, but with much more conservative standard errors and t-tests (STATA Corporation 2001; Huber 2003; Kézdi 2004).

Authoritarian countries allocated lower manpower to operate their penitentiaries, whereas more democratic countries devoted more human resources to their prisons, as they did to their police forces.

The inclusion of year-specific dummies in multivariate analysis means that this study essentially focused on cross-country variation and did not investigate the democracy–criminal justice relationship across time, which would require a lengthier and more balanced cross-sectional time series. Given that the hypothesis explicitly stated the direction of the predicted relationships, I used one-tailed significance tests.

Results

Levels of democratization and the personnel structure of the criminal justice system

According to the arguments developed above, I expect the rates of police, prosecutorial, and prison personnel to be inversely related to the strength of democracy scale and the rate of judicial personnel to be positively associated with the strength of democracy scale. Table 2 shows that at the bivariate level, democracy was indeed inversely related to the staffing of the prosecutorial offices and the courts but failed to demonstrate the hypothesized inverse relationship with police and prison personnel. There was no relationship between democracy and the size of police personnel; that is, the size is essentially independent of the democracy

TABLE 2
PEARSON CORRELATION COEFFICIENTS BETWEEN DEMOCRACY
AND CRIMINAL JUSTICE PERSONNEL

	Democracy
Police personnel rate	.04
Prosecutorial personnel rate	−.12°
Judicial personnel rate	.18°°
Correctional personnel rate	.17°°

$°p < .05.$ $°°p < .01.$

rating. As predicted, democracy was negatively correlated with the rate of prosecutorial personnel and positively associated with the rate of judges and magistrates in the population. Contrary to my hypothesis, I found a positive, significant relationship between democracy and the size of the correctional staff in prisons.

A higher rate of case retention in [more authoritarian] countries proved that the opportunities for challenging the incriminating accusations were minimized at virtually every stage of the criminal justice process.

Table 3 presents the results of the multivariate analysis. When the effects of the control variables were held constant, only the impact of democracy on the judicial body was statistically significant and in the predicted direction. The remaining three regression models yielded either nonsignificant findings or significant results but in the direction opposite to the hypothesis. The first unexpected outcome was the positive and significant relationship between democracy and police personnel; on average, for every 1-point increase in the FH combined democracy scale, the police force increased by 26.3 per 100,000 inhabitants. According to Table 3, the hypothesized negative association between democracy and prosecutorial staff failed to reach the conventional significance threshold, indicating that the statistically significant bivariate relationship was largely spurious and most likely dependent on the legal tradition in which the criminal justice system operated.

TABLE 3
REGRESSION ANALYSIS OF CRIMINAL JUSTICE PERSONNEL

	Police Personnel Rate		Prosecutorial Personnel Rate		Judicial Personnel Rate		Correctional Personnel Rate	
	b	Robust SE	b	Robust SE	b	Robust SE	b	Robust SE
Intercept	459.47***	43.45	7.97***	1.79	12.04***	2.29	42.30***	6.68
Independent variable								
Democracy	26.28*	11.91	-0.17	0.33	1.33*	0.68	2.27*	1.36
Control variables								
Total population	-0.23***	0.05	0.01***	0.00	0.01	0.01	-0.02	0.01
GDP per capita	-1.10	1.21	-0.17***	0.05	-0.15**	0.05	0.07	0.21
Total crime rate	-0.01***	0.00	-0.00	0.00	0.00	0.00	0.00*	0.00
Civil law system (dummy)	-31.36	26.18	4.99***	1.31	6.87***	1.61	17.71***	3.44
Year 1997 (dummy)	-14.17	30.21	-0.71	1.66	0.43	2.26	2.04	4.63
Year 1998 (dummy)	-31.40	26.18	-1.33	1.31	-1.42	1.82	4.53	5.54
Year 1999 (dummy)	12.55	30.18	0.03	1.80	-0.46	1.95	5.07	5.58
Year 2000 (dummy)	12.55	30.18	0.04	1.35	-0.48	1.60	-1.78	4.60
N	257		196		213		252	
R^2	.115***		.169***		.159***		.207***	

*$p < .05$. **$p < .01$. ***$p < .001$.

TABLE 4
PEARSON CORRELATION COEFFICIENTS BETWEEN DEMOCRACY
AND CRIMINAL JUSTICE PROCESSING

	Democracy
Police contact rate	$-.36$°°°
Prosecution rate	$-.07$
Conviction rate	$-.18$°°
Incarceration rate	$-.37$°°°

°°$p < .01$. °°°$p < .001$.

   Consistent with predictions was the finding that the more democratic a country, the better its judicial body was staffed. A 1-point increase in the democracy
scale was connected to a judicial manpower increase of 1.3 judges per 100,000
inhabitants. The unanticipated positive relationship between democracy and correctional personnel withstood the multivariate test. Authoritarian countries allocated lower manpower to operate their penitentiaries, whereas more democratic
countries devoted more human resources to their prisons, as they did to their
police forces. An average increase of 2.3 correctional employees per 100,000
inhabitants was observed for each 1-point improvement in democracy.
   Judged by the obtained multiple correlation coefficients (R^2s) that oscillated
between .12 and .21, the explanatory power of the regression models was moderate at best, which is a reminder of the complex nature of criminal justice staffing.
But the specific relationship between democracy and criminal justice staffing
proved to be different from hypothesized. More democratic countries not only had
a larger number of judges manning their courts as predicted but had also larger
police forces and correctional staff. Rather than disproportionately strengthening
their courts, more democratic countries seem to have invested heavily in most of
the individual criminal justice components comprising the system.

*Levels of democratization and the operational output
of the criminal justice system*

   Very powerful support was found for the argument that the rate of case attrition in the criminal justice process is lower in more authoritarian countries and
higher in more democratic countries. Bivariate statistics are displayed in Table 4
and show negative correlations between democratic development and the rates
of police contact, prosecution, conviction, and incarceration as predicted. Only
the correlation coefficient for the prosecution rate did not attain the minimum
significance level, whereas the remaining three coefficients were both statistically
and substantively significant.
   Regression results in Table 5 show that, all else being equal, the three significant negative relationships between the degree of democratization and the rates

TABLE 5
REGRESSION ANALYSIS OF CRIMINAL JUSTICE PROCESSING

	Police Contact Rate		Prosecution Rate		Conviction Rate		Incarceration Rate	
	b	Robust SE	b	Robust SE	b	Robust SE	b	Robust SE
Intercept	60.30***	9.50	48.43**	14.92	36.04*	13.56	89.28**	32.58
Independent variable								
Democracy	-3.15*	1.60	-2.72	2.63	-9.21***	2.01	-8.65*	3.89
Control variables								
Total population	0.09***	0.01	0.03**	0.03	-0.03*	0.01	-0.00	0.06
GDP per capita	-0.90***	0.22	-0.53	0.37	-0.49	0.36	-1.29*	0.58
Total crime rate	-0.00*	0.00	0.01**	0.00	0.00***	0.00	-0.00	0.00
Civil law system (dummy)	-11.52*	5.04	8.65	8.27	10.78	8.29	-37.41*	17.71
Year 1997 (dummy)	-2.65	6.50	10.64	8.93	-1.98	7.29	-15.59	11.70
Year 1998 (dummy)	5.11	7.98	-2.07	8.36	0.96	7.96	-5.04	13.48
Year 1999 (dummy)	1.13	7.05	-3.70	8.45	1.44	7.84	-3.08	14.12
Year 2000 (dummy)	8.38	7.88	3.11	11.03	1.59	8.42	1.00	18.49
N	241		165		175		211	
R^2	.260***		.077***		.149***		.228***	

$p < .05.$ $**p < .01.$ $***p < .001.$

of operational output detected in the bivariate analysis remained significant in the multivariate models. Police were less likely to initiate formal contacts with suspects in more democratic countries (a 3-percentage-point decrease for each 1-point improvement in FH's democracy scale). Courts were much less likely to convict prosecuted defendants in more democratic countries regardless of the legal system (a 9-percentage-point decrease for each 1-point increase in FH's democracy scale). Judges in democratic societies were also less likely to sentence convicted criminals to incarceration or to impose long prison sentences on them (a 9-percentage-point decrease for every 1-point increase in FH's democracy scale). The influence of democracy on prosecution rate remained statistically nonsignificant.

The probability of bringing a criminal suspect into the legal system and securing a conviction and incarceration sentence was much higher in more authoritarian societies. A higher rate of case retention in these countries proved that the opportunities for challenging the incriminating accusations were minimized at virtually every stage of the criminal justice process. The result is a highly "efficient" social control machine in which each successive stage was likely to pass the case along to the next processing stage. In comparison, lower rates of arrest, conviction, and incarceration revealed that the administration of criminal justice in democratic countries, with their better-staffed agencies, appeared more devoted to the screening out of legally innocent suspects.

Discussion

In the study presented in this article, I performed a systemic comparison of how countries with different levels of democratization deployed their human resources at different stages of the criminal justice process and processed criminal cases. Of the eight examined criminal justice indicators, four (i.e., judicial personnel rate, police contact rate, conviction rate, and incarceration rate) demonstrated statistically significant variations that were consistent with the hypothesis, two personnel categories (i.e., rates of police staff and correctional personnel) showed statistically significant relationships that contradicted the hypothesis, and both prosecutorial variables proved consistently unrelated to the level of democracy. While the personnel indicators provided only partial support to the proposition of structural differences, the operational indicators strongly corroborated the argument of higher criminal case attrition among democratic countries.

The hypothesis predicted a large law enforcement–prison complex and a high rate of case retention in the criminal process in more authoritarian societies. Results were mixed. The size of both the police and prison staff turned out to be significantly larger in more democratic countries. One plausible explanation for the smaller size of authoritarian police forces is that the domestic surveillance of political figures and the suppression of opposition groups are usually conducted not by the regular police but by the state security or by secret police organizations (Hills 1996; Waller 2004). Rather than expanding the regular police to enforce state security, authoritarian governments often create specialized units for political policing and devote the criminal police for the maintenance of law and order. On the other hand, liberal democracies might be under higher pressure from their citizenry to provide mundane, nonenforcement general assistance to the public through a larger police force (Bayley 1996). The unexpected large size of prison manpower in democratic societies could be at least partially accounted for by the rise of welfare spending with the concomitant ascension of the rehabilitation philosophy and humanitarian values in liberal democracies (Hornum 1988; Feeley and Rubin 1998; Sutton 2000). Despite the seemingly erratic swings in the approach to crime control in these societies (Rose 2000), quantitative research consistently demonstrates that the punitiveness of criminal sanctions against convicted offenders declined with greater political liberalization and welfare spending (Neapolitan 2001; Beckett and Western 2001), which typically led to an expansion in the range of correctional services offered to prison inmates (Faugeron and Le Boulaire 1988; Morris 1995; O'Brien 1995).

With the exception of the prosecution rate, criminal justice systems showed lower case attrition in the criminal process in more authoritarian settings. More criminal suspects were arrested, more prosecuted defendants were convicted, and more convicted criminals were incarcerated in less democratic countries or received longer prison sentences, or both. Although generally equipped with less manpower, criminal justice systems in more authoritarian countries were able to produce more arrestees, convictions, and inmates than democratic countries. This coordinated high efficiency among agencies should be taken as a hallmark of criminal justice processing in authoritarian countries. However, efficiency defined as the capacity to economically apply limited resources to accomplish statutory goals and to maximize the number of arrests and convictions does not necessarily make a criminal justice system effective or just. Rather, an excessive concern for efficiency in case processing will inevitably undermine the justice system's institutional integrity and its most basic mission: doing justice (Logan 1993).

The due process proposition argues that resourceful courts and low rates of criminal justice processing characterize the justice system in liberal democracies because in these societies justice is sought as the defense of civil liberties through the strengthening of the rule of law. UNS data strongly supported this hypothesis. In more democratic societies, the judiciary had more judges, convicted fewer prosecuted defendants, and employed more sanctions other than imprisonment and/or shorter prison sentences. It should be noted, however, that the increase in manpower was observed across various criminal justice components; there were more police officers, more judges, and more correctional personnel in these countries. This general growth of criminal justice manpower is likely to have resulted from the diversification of societal functions (e.g., crime prevention, punishment and rehabilitation of offenders, protection of human rights, etc.) expected from the administration of justice in liberal democracies (Burnham 1980). The multiplication of tasks and assignments that reflects the assortment of interests represented by the state, defense bars, civil liberties and victim rights groups, and others might lead to the observed personnel expansion. Also, the pursuit of these competing goals could turn the criminal justice process into an arena of intense contest with an ensuing erosion of its efficiency. Starting with a lower citizen arrest rate, each of the successive stages presented formidable impediments to processing the accused any further along in the system.

The type of political regime had no significant effects on the size of the prosecutorial staff and the rate of prosecution. Previous research reported that the prosecution role is found in almost all countries, but the methods used to fulfill the role differ considerably (Williams 1987; Fionda 1995; Di Federico 1998; Ma 2002). Also, there are important variations in the way criminal prosecution is managed; the prosecution of criminal suspects can be initiated by a public prosecutorial office (e.g., the United States), by a state procurator (e.g., France), or by the police (e.g., England and Wales) (Reichel 2002). However, the structural determinants of these cross-national disparities in prosecutorial practices are mostly unknown, as prosecution remains the least theoretically elaborated and empirically evaluated component of the criminal justice system in cross-national research. In this quantitative comparison of nations, three control variables (population size, income, and legal tradition) were associated with the rate of prosecutorial personnel and two (income and crime) with the rate of prosecution. The rejection of the hypothesis that the rates of prosecutorial personnel and prosecution would be lower in liberal democracies points to the need to explore, theoretically and empirically, other links between democratization and prosecution.

Correlational findings deal with averages, depict general trends, and can conceal important information about outliers. Readers familiar with the debate on the current American penal populism may raise questions about the standing of the United States in the scheme of classification proposed in this comparative analysis. Penal populism is a crime control approach geared toward the alleviation of public fear of crime and violence through an indiscriminate and disproportionate hostility toward all criminals (Forster 2001; Zimring, Hawkins, and Kamin 2001; du Plessis and Louw 2005). Rather than focusing on long-term solutions to crime and disorder, public pressure demands that elected officials focus on short-term fixes, such as harsh punishment of convicted criminals. Do the disproportionately large prison population and the use of the death penalty in the United States refute the hypothesis corroborated in this study, or do they make the United States an exception among advanced democracies (Zimring 2005)?

In the analyzed sample, the United States was classified as one of the most advanced liberal democracies (FH combined average rating = 7). However, while fourteen liberal democracies with a democracy rating of 7 averaged an incarceration rate of 15 percent (that is, the size of their prison populations was on average 15 percent of the number of offenders convicted in courts) between 1997 and 2002,[5] the average rate for the United States was 137 percent, ranking between those of Singapore (132 percent) and Malaysia (173 percent). This finding echoes with previous research that in many crime categories, convicted offenders in the United States were more likely to be sentenced to prison and to serve longer prison terms than offenders in other advanced democracies (Farrington, Langan, and Tonry 2004). Two conclusions can be drawn from this illustration and the general findings presented above. First, the inclusion of the United States in the sample did not significantly weaken the association between democracy and incarceration, which shows that the inverse relationship between democratic attainment and imprisonment rate was very strong. Second, public support for harsh criminal sanctions even in liberal democracies such as New Zealand, the United States, and the United Kingdom (Forster 2001; Tonry 2004; Pratt and Clark 2005; Zimring and Johnson 2006 [this volume]) should remind us that just as the progression of an authoritarian state toward democracy is neither automatic nor irreversible (Carothers 2002), so is the path of criminal justice development. Liberal democratic countries can reach a degree of rule of law, and then slip back to intrusive and punitive criminal justice practices common in more authoritarian states.

This study has documented a close connection between higher degrees of democratic achievement and the development of a resourceful criminal justice system characterized by a high rate of case attrition in the criminal justice process. That the deepening of democratization increases the size, and paradoxically decreases the efficiency, of the criminal justice system highlights the dramatic and interesting changes in the administration of justice that the rule of law can set in motion. The system loses some of its efficiency because different rights of the victims, offenders, and the public at large are taken seriously at different stages of the process. As such, evidence from past research indicates, the citizenry are likely to experience their criminal justice system as legitimate and responsive to their needs; people consent and cooperate with criminal justice authorities if they anticipate that the system will accord respect to and acknowledge the rights and concerns of individual citizens (Tyler 2003).

Support for democracy stems from a recognition of the legitimacy of the political process, while satisfaction with democratic governance arises from a calculation of its benefits, including gains in civil liberties (Moore 1997). Even though individual components of the justice system will not create democracy by themselves, their collective performance builds and maintains the sense of effectiveness and fairness on which loyalty to democratic institutions depends (Tyler 2003). The evolution from an authoritarian criminal justice system to a democratic one is cumulative but not inevitable, and the financial cost of creating and sustaining such a capable system would overwhelm many poor countries and take many years to develop fully. Thus, future research should incorporate discussions and measurement of economic performance and government spending to further identify the possibilities and constraints in the democratization of criminal justice administration.

Appendix A
List of Countries Included in the Sample
(N = 435 County-Year Units from 111 Countries)

Country	Number of Years[a]	Number of Justice Variables[b]	Average Democracy Rating[c]
Afghanistan	2	2	1.0
Albania	6	15	3.8
Andorra	1	8	7.0
Argentina	2	7	5.5
Armenia	3	3	3.8
Australia	6	8	7.0
Austria	2	3	7.0
Azerbaijan	6	29	2.8
Bahrain	1	3	1.5
Barbados	3	12	7.0
Belarus	6	36	2.0
Belgium	3	11	6.5
Belize	1	3	7.0
Bolivia	2	3	6.0
Botswana	3	3	6.0
Bulgaria	4	25	5.6
Canada	6	35	7.0
Chile	6	35	5.9
China	3	3	1.3
Colombia	4	25	4.1
Costa Rica	6	17	6.6
Cote d'Ivoire	1	1	3.0
Croatia	6	22	4.6
Cyprus	6	26	7.0
Czech Republic	6	45	6.5
Denmark	6	33	7.0
Dominica	1	5	7.0
Dominican Republic	4	13	5.3
Ecuador	2	2	5.0
Egypt	4	4	2.1
El Salvador	6	17	5.4
Estonia	4	24	6.5
Ethiopia	2	4	3.0
Fiji	1	5	4.5

(continued)

Appendix A (continued)

Country	Number of Years[a]	Number of Justice Variables[b]	Average Democracy Rating[c]
Finland	6	47	7.0
France	3	12	6.5
Georgia	4	25	6.3
Germany	6	34	6.5
Greece	4	9	6.0
Guatemala	3	7	4.5
Hong Kong	4	28	4.0
Hungary	6	33	6.5
Iceland	6	32	7.0
India	3	15	5.2
Ireland	4	19	7.0
Israel	1	8	6.0
Italy	6	32	6.4
Jamaica	3	6	5.8
Japan	6	39	6.3
Jordan	2	2	4.0
Kazakhstan	4	11	2.5
Korea, Republic of	6	35	6.0
Kuwait	2	5	3.5
Kyrgyz Republic	4	30	3.5
Latvia	6	44	6.4
Lesotho	1	5	4.0
Lithuania	6	39	6.5
Luxembourg	2	10	7.0
Macedonia FYR	4	25	4.5
Malaysia	3	19	3.0
Maldives	6	17	2.3
Malta	2	7	7.0
Mauritius	4	10	6.5
Mexico	5	19	5.3
Moldova	6	45	4.8
Morocco	2	5	3.3
Myanmar	2	15	1.0
Namibia	1	2	5.5
Nepal	2	7	4.5
Netherlands	6	34	7.0
New Zealand	6	25	7.0
Norway	4	16	7.0
Oman	5	8	2.2
Pakistan	3	5	3.0
Panama	6	10	6.0

(continued)

Appendix A (continued)

Country	Number of Years[a]	Number of Justice Variables[b]	Average Democracy Rating[c]
Papua New Guinea	3	21	5.3
Paraguay	3	3	4.5
Peru	3	9	5.2
Philippines	2	3	5.5
Poland	6	21	6.5
Portugal	6	42	7.0
Qatar	3	15	1.7
Romania	6	47	5.9
Russian Federation	3	16	4.0
Saudi Arabia	5	11	1.0
Senegal	1	3	4.0
Singapore	4	19	3.1
Slovak Republic	6	39	5.9
Slovenia	6	43	6.5
South Africa	6	16	6.5
Spain	4	20	6.5
Sri Lanka	4	8	4.4
Suriname	3	3	5.0
St. Kitts & Nevis	1	1	6.5
Swaziland	3	6	2.7
Sweden	6	31	7.0
Switzerland	6	17	7.0
Tajikistan	1	3	1.0
Tanzania	1	3	3.0
Thailand	4	21	5.3
Tonga	1	2	4.0
Turkey	5	19	3.5
Uganda	4	2	4.0
Ukraine	1	9	4.5
United Kingdom	5	30	6.5
United States	6	25	7.0
Uruguay	6	15	6.7
Venezuela	5	13	4.6
Yemen, Republic of	3	3	2.5
Zambia	3	18	3.5
Zimbabwe	4	20	2.9

a. Number of years the country has submitted valid criminal justice responses to the United Nations Surveys on Crime Trends and the Operations of Criminal Justice Systems (UNS) between 1997 and 2002.

b. Countries included in the study can have between 1 and 48 criminal justice outcome variables (8 variables, 6 years).

c. This is the average democracy score for the years for which outcome variables are available (1.0 = least democratic; 7.0 = most democratic).

Appendix B
Correlation Matrix

	1	2	3	4	5	6	7	8	9	10	11	12
Dependent variable												
1. Democracy												
Independent variables												
2. Police personnel	.04											
3. Prosecutorial personnel	-.12*	.16*										
4. Judicial personnel	.18**	.07	.21**									
5. Correctional personnel	.17*	.17**	.29***	.17**								
6. Police contact rate	-.34***	.01	-.10	-.05	-.35***							
7. Prosecution rate	-.03	-.01	.01	-.19*	-.15*	-.20**						
8. Conviction rate	-.23***	.07	.14*	-.14*	.04	-.03	-.39***					
9. Incarceration rate	-.37***	-.12	-.06	-.34***	-.33***	-.07	.10	-.12				
Control variables												
10. GDP per capital	.52***	-.13*	-.28	-.05	.13*	-.31***	.17*	-.15*	-.34***			
11. Population	-.13**	-.18**	.32	-.01	-.10	.22***	.11	-.09	.03	-.01		
12. Total crime rate	.56***	-.16**	-.14*	.10	.31***	-.35***	-.12	-.05	-.34***	.62	-.07	
13. Civil law system	.23***	.02	.24***	.31***	.20***	-.18**	-.15	.15*	-.18**	-.07	-.20***	.08

*p < .05. **p < .01. ***p < .001.

Notes

1. On average, industrialized countries responded to United Nations Surveys on Crime Trends and the Operations of Criminal Justice Systems (UNS) with greater consistency. Of the thirty-six countries that responded to at least one of the eight criminal justice items in all six of the yearly surveys, eight (22 percent) were low-income or lower-middle-income countries according to the latest World Bank classification (World Bank 2005) and twenty-eight (78 percent) were high-income or upper-middle-income countries. On the other hand, of the fourteen countries that replied to only one of the six yearly surveys, nine (64 percent) were low-income or lower-middle-income countries and five (36 percent) were high-income or upper-middle-income countries. Nevertheless, less industrialized countries still constituted the majority in the sample. Overall, 278 (64 percent) of the 435 country-year units in the sample were low-income or lower-middle-income countries, whereas the remaining 157 (36 percent) were upper-middle-income or high-income countries.

2. Not all participating countries provided full data for all questions contained in the survey instrument.

3. The ten country-year units dropped from the analysis were Cyprus (1998 and 1999), Guatemala (1998, 1999, and 2000), Moldova (2001 and 2002), and Zambia (1998, 1999, and 2000).

4. In this sample, all control variables were associated with levels of democratization at the bivariate level, affirming the need to control for them in the multivariate models. As shown in Appendix B, democracies had higher GDP, are smaller countries in terms of population, had higher overall crime rates, and had more often civil law systems.

5. These fourteen liberal democracies with valid incarceration data are Andorra, Australia, Canada, Cyprus, Denmark, Finland, Iceland, Luxembourg, the Netherlands, New Zealand, Portugal, Sweden, Switzerland, and the United States.

References

Allen, Francis A. 1996. *Habits of legality: Criminal justice and the rule of law*. New York: Oxford University Press.

Bayley, David H. 1975. The police and political development in Europe. In *The formation of national states in Western Europe*, ed. C. Tilly, 328-79. Priceton, NJ: Princeton University Press.

———. 1985. *Patterns of policing: A comparative international analysis*. New Brunswick, NJ: Rutgers University Press.

———. 1996. *Police for the future*. New York: Oxford University Press.

———. 2005. *Changing the guard: Developing democratic police abroad.* New York: Oxford University Press.

Beckett, Katherine, and Bruce Western. 2001. Governing social marginality: Welfare, incarceration, and the transformation of state policy. *Punishment & Society* 3:43-59.

Black, Donald. 1976. *The behavior of law*. New York: Academic Press.

Bowman, Kirk, Fabrice Lehoucq, and James Mahoney. 2005. Measuring political democracy: Case expertise, data adequacy, and Central America. *Comparative Political Studies* 38:939-70.

Burnham, Robert W. 1980. Criminal justice personnel and socio-economic development. *Police Studies* 3:3-9.

Carothers, Thomas. 2002. The end of the transition paradigm. *Journal of Democracy* 13:5-21.

Damaska, Mirjan R. 1986. *The faces of justice and state authority: A comparative approach to the legal process*. New Haven, CT: Yale University Press.

Diamond, Larry. 1996. Is the third wave over? *Journal of Democracy* 7:20-37.

Diehm 2001, James W. 2001. The introduction of jury trials and adversarial elements into the former Soviet Union and other inquisitorial countries. *Journal of Transnational Law & Polity* 11:1-38.

Di Federico, Giuseppe. 1998. Prosecutorial independence and the democratic requirement of accountability in Italy: Analysis of a deviant case in a comparative perspective. *British Journal of Criminology* 38:371-87.

DiIulio, John J., Jr. 1997. Are voters fools? Crime, public opinion, and representative democracy. *Corrections Management Quarterly* 1:1-5.

du Plessis, Anton, and Antoinette Louw. 2005. Crime and crime prevention in South Africa: 10 years after. *Canadian Journal of Criminology and Criminal Justice* 47:427-46.

Farrington, David P., Patrick A. Langan, and Michael Tonry, eds. 2004. *Cross-national studies in crime and justice.* NCJ 200988. Washington, DC: Office of Justice Programs.

Faugeron, Claude, and Jean-Michel Le Boulaire. 1988. *La Création du Service Social des Prisons et l'évolution de la Réforme Pénitentiaire en France de 1945 à 1958.* Guyancourt, France: Centre de Recherches Sociologiques sur le Droit et les Institutions Pénales.

Feeley, Malcom, and Edward L. Rubin. 1998. *Judicial policy making and the modern state: How the courts reformed America's prisons.* New York: Cambridge University Press.

Fionda, Julia. 1995. *Public prosecutors and discretion: A comparative study.* Oxford: Oxford University Press.

Forster, Peter. 2001. Law and society under a democratic dictatorship: Dr. Banda and Malawi. *Journal of Asian and African Studies* 36:275-93.

Freedom House. 2005. *Freedom in the world 2005: Civic power and electoral politics.* New York: Freedom House.

Havard, John D. J. 1992. Expert scientific evidence under the adversarial system: A travesty of justice? *Journal of the Forensic Science Society* 32:225-35.

Hills, Alice. 1996. Towards a critique of policing and national development in Africa. *Journal of Modern African Studies* 34:271-91.

Hornum, Finn. 1988. Corrections in two social welfare democracies: Denmark and Sweden. *Prison Journal* 68:63-82.

Howard, Gregory J., Graeme Newman, and William Alex Pridemore. 2000. Theory, method, and data in comparative criminology. In *Measurement and analysis of crime and justice; criminal justice 2000*, vol. 4, ed. D. Duffee, 139-211. Rockville, MD: National Institute of Justice.

Huber, Peter J. 2003. *Robust statistics.* New York: Wiley.

Kalish, Carol B. 1988. *International crime rates.* Rockville, MD: National Institute of Justice.

Karstedt, Suzanne. 2001. Durkheim, Tarde and beyond: The global travel of crime policies. *Criminal Justice* 2:111-23.

Kessler, Amalia D. 2005. Our inquisitorial tradition: Equity procedure, due process, and the search for an alternative to the adversarial. *Cornell Law Review* 90:1181-1275.

Kézdi, Gábor. 2004. Robust standard error estimation in fixed-effects panel models. *Hungarian Statistical Review* 9:95-116.

Lewis, Chris. 1999. Police records of crime. In *Global report on crime and justice*, ed. G. Newman, 43-64. New York: Oxford University Press.

Liu, Weizheng, and Yingyi Situ. 1999. Criminal courts in China transition: Inquisitorial procedure to adversarial procedure? *Crime & Justice International* 15:13-21.

Logan, C. H. 1993. Criminal justice performance measures for prisons. In *Performance measures for the criminal justice system*, ed. J. DiIulio Jr. et al., 19-59. Washington, DC: Bureau of Justice Statistics.

Ma, Yue. 2002. Prosecutorial discretion and plea bargaining in the United States, France, Germany, and Italy: A comparative perspective. *International Criminal Justice Review* 12:22-52.

Maguire, Edward R., and Rebecca Schulte-Murray. 2001. Issues and patterns in the comparative international study of police strength. *International Journal of Comparative Sociology* 42:75-100.

McElligott, Anthony. 1994. Authority, control, and class justice: The role of the Sondergerichte in the transition from Weimar Germany to the Third Reich. *Criminal Justice History: An International Annual* 15:209-33.

Meintjies-Van der Walt, Lirieka. 2001. *Expert evidence in the criminal justice process: A comparative approach.* Amsterdam: Rozenberg.

Moore, Mark H. 1997. Legitimizing criminal justice policies and practices. *FBI Law Enforcement Bulletin* 66:14-21.

Morris, Norval. 1995. The contemporary prison: 1965-present. In *The Oxford history of the prison: The practice of punishment in Western society*, ed. N. Morris and D. J. Rothman, 202-31. New York: Oxford University Press.

Mukherjee, Satyanshu, and Philip Reichel. 1999. Bringing to justice. In *Global report on crime and justice*, ed. G. Newman, 65-88. New York: Oxford University Press.

Murphy, Walter F. 1991. Civil law, common law, and constitutional democracy. *Louisiana Law Review* 52:92-126.

Neapolitan, Jerome L. 1997. *Cross-national crime: A research review and sourcebook*. Westport, CT: Greenwood.

———. 2001. Examination of cross-national variation in punitiveness. *International Journal of Offender Therapy and Comparative Criminology* 45:691-710.

Nemityna, Marina. 2001. Trial by jury: A Western or a peculiarly Russian model? *International Review of Penal Law* 72:365-70.

Neumayer, Eric. 2005. Inequality and violent crime: Evidence from robbery and violent theft. *Journal of Peace Research* 42:101-12.

Newman, Graeme, and Adam Bouloukos. 1996. What is a criminal justice system? A view from the *International Factbook of Criminal Justice Systems*. Paper presented at the annual meeting of the American Society of Criminology, Chicago, November.

Newman, Graeme, and Gregory J. Howard. 1999. Data sources and their use. In *Global report on crime and justice*, ed. Graeme Newman, 1-23. New York: Oxford University Press.

O'Brien, Patricia. 1995. The prison on the Continent: Europe, 1865-1965. In *The Oxford history of the prison: The practice of punishment in Western society*, ed. N. Morris and D. J. Rothman, 178-201. New York: Oxford University Press.

O'Donnell, Guillermo. 1999. Horizontal accountability in new democracies. In *The self-restraining state: Power and accountability in new democracies*, ed. A. Schedler, L. Diamond, and M. F. Plattner, 29-52. Boulder, CO: Lynne Rienner.

O'Reilly, Gregory W. 1997. Opening up Argentina's courts. *Judicature* 80:237-40.

Packer, Herbert. 1968. *Limits of the criminal sanctions*. Stanford, CA: Stanford University Press.

Piano, Aili, and Arch Puddington, eds. 2004. *Freedom in the World 2004: The annual survey of political rights and civil liberties*. Evanston, IL: Rowman & Littlefield.

Pratt, John, and Marie Clark. 2005. Penal populism in New Zealand. *Punishment & Society* 7:303-22.

Prillaman, William C. 2000. *The judiciary and democratic decay in Latin America: Declining confidence in the rule of law*. Westport, CT: Praeger.

Reichel, Philip L. 2002. *Comparative criminal justice systems: A topical approach*. 3rd ed. Upper Saddle River, NJ: Prentice Hall.

Rodrigues, Corinne Davis. 2006. Civil democracy, perceived risk, and insecurity in Brazil: An extension of the systemic social control model. *Annals of the American Academy of Political and Social Science* 605:242-63.

Rose, Nicholas. 2000. Government and control. *British Journal of Criminology* 40:321-39.

Ruddell, Rick. 2005. Social disruption, state priorities, and minority threat: A cross-national study of imprisonment. *Punishment & Society* 7:7-28.

Ruddell, Rick, and Martin G. Urbina. 2004. Minority threat and punishment: A cross-national analysis. *Justice Quarterly* 21:903-31.

Shelley, Louise. 1994. Sources of Soviet policing. *Police Studies* 17:49-65.

Smith, Gordon B. 1992. *Perestroika and the procuracy: The changing role of the prosecutor's office in the former USSR*. Washington, DC: Bureau of Justice Statistics.

Smykla, John Ortiz. 1989. Placing Uruguayan corrections in context, 1973-1984: A note on the visiting criminologist's role. *Journal of Criminal Justice* 17:25-37.

Solomon, Peter H., and Todd S. Foglesong. 2000. *Courts and transition in Russia: The challenge of judicial reform*. Boulder, CO: Westview.

STATA Corporation. 2001. How does XGTLS differ from regression clustered with robust standard errors? http://www.stata.com/support/faqs/stat/xtgls_rob.html.

Sung, Hung-En. 2006. Structural determinants of police effectiveness in market democracies. *Police Quarterly* 9:3-19.

Sutton, John R. 2000. Imprisonment and social classification in five common-law democracies, 1955-1985. *American Journal of Sociology* 106:350-86.

Tate, C. Neal, and Stacia L. Haynie. 1993. Authoritarianism and the functions of the courts: A time series analysis of the Philippine Supreme Court, 1961-1981. *Law & Society Review* 27:707-40.

Thome, Joseph R. 1998. Searching for democracy: The rule of law and the process of legal reform in Latin America. Paper presented at the Workshop Reforma Judicial, Motivaciones, Proyectos, Caminos Recorridos, Caminos por Recorrer, Instituto Internacional de Sociología Jurídica, Oñati, Gipuzkoa, Spain, April 6-7.

Tonry, Michael. 2004. *Thinking about crime: Sense and sensibility in American penal culture.* New York: Oxford University Press.

Trevaskes, Susan. 2004. Propaganda work in Chinese courts: Public trials and sentencing rallies as sites of expressive punishment and public education in the People's Republic of China. *Punishment & Society* 6:5-21.

Tyler, Tom R. 2003. Procedural justice, legitimacy, and the effective rule of law. In *Crime and justice: A review of research,* vol. 30, ed. M. Tonry, 283-357. Chicago: University of Chicago Press.

Ungar, Mark. 2002. *Elusive reform: Democracy and the rule of law in Latin America.* Boulder, CO: Lynne Rienner.

Vanhanen, Tatu. 2000. A new data set for measuring democracy. *Journal of Peace Research* 37:251-65.

Waller, J. Michael. 2004. Tropical Chekists: The secret police legacy in Nicaragua. *Demokratizatsiya* 12:427-49.

Williams, John Eryl Hall, ed. 1987. *Role of the prosecutor—Report of the International Criminal Justice Seminar held at the London School of Economics and Political Science.* Brookfield, VT: Gower.

World Bank. 2005. *World development report 2006: Equity and development.* Washington, DC: World Bank.

Zakaria, Fareed. 2003. *The future of democracy at home and abroad.* New York: Norton.

Zalman, Marvin. 2000. Criminal justice and the future of civil liberties. *Criminal Justice Review* 25:181-206.

Zimring, Franklin E. 2005. Capital punishment and hyper-incarceration: Does American exceptionalism have a future? Paper presented at the 14th World Congress of Criminology, Philadelphia, August 8.

Zimring, Franklin E., Gordon Hawkins, and Sam Kamin. 2001. *Punishment and democracy: Three strikes and you're out in California.* New York: Oxford University Press.

Zimring Franklin E., and David T. Johnson. 2006. Public opinion and the governance of punishment in democratic political systems. *Annals of the American Academy of Political and Social Science* 605:266-80.

QUICK READ SYNOPSIS

Democracy, Crime, and Justice

Special Editors: SUSANNE KARSTEDT
Keele University
and GARY LaFREE
University of Maryland

Volume 605, May 2006

Prepared by Herb Fayer, Jerry Lee Foundation
DOI: 10.1177/0002716206288394

To read the synopsis for this volume, please go to the American Academy of Political and Social Science (AAPSS) Web site: http://www.aapss.org/. Under the "Programs and News" menu, locate the "quick read synopsis" link for May 2006.